# I HAVE

## —A—

# DREAM

Dedication:
For Jill, who makes me happy.
And for my parents George and May –
love and thanks for putting up with me.

# I HAVE

## — A —

# DREAM

## INSPIRING WORDS AND THOUGHTS FROM HISTORY'S GREATEST LEADERS

TERRY BREVERTON

Quercus

# INTRODUCTION

*'Eloquence can be defined as the speech of one who knows what he is talking about and means what he says – it is thought on fire.'*

William Jennings Bryan *In His Image*
1922

**Throughout the centuries**, the greatest leaders and opinion-formers in all walks of life have had the ability to express themselves powerfully in speeches and orations to their followers and adherents. Aristotle's *Rhetoric* outlines the fundamentals of persuasive speaking: *ethos* (the credibility of the speaker), *pathos* (the emotions of the audience), and *logos* (the reasoning of the argument). The spoken word is far more effective than the written word when it is delivered with eloquence. In this book we will encounter famous generals averting mutinies by addressing stirring words to their troops, statesmen and men of religion urging the cause of peace or war, great lawyers arguing their cases, and many more. There are times in the passage of history – the American War of Independence and Civil War, the French Revolution, both World Wars – where orations miraculously flowered during terrible crises. We also see how dictators like Stalin and Hitler can use language to inflame their followers. Important speeches really illuminate the power of the spoken word throughout the ages, but many have been lost, as they were unrecorded. Those included in this book have been chosen for several reasons – some have made a massive impact on their audiences, others were made at a crossroads or a time of crisis in history, some are incredibly thought-provoking or emotional, and others are included just for their wonderful use of language. Great oratory should inspire and enlighten, and history shows us repeatedly that speeches can soothe or encourage a nation or a faction. Speeches can inspire a people to take up arms or to combat injustice. Speeches can impel us to make huge sacrifices or to throw off the shackles of prejudice or poverty. The power of the spoken word can make people rise up against racism, bigotry and oppression. However, as we see with Hitler and Goebbels, speeches can also act as the catalyst for terrible acts of hatred, torture, prejudice, violence, inhumanity and destruction.

Henry Hardwicke's *History of Oratory and Orators* (1896) tells us: *'Oratory is the parent of liberty. By the constitution of things it was ordained that eloquence should be the last stay and support of liberty, and that with her she is ever destined to live, to flourish, and to die. It is to the interest of tyrants to cripple and debilitate every species of eloquence. They have no other safety. It is then, the duty of free states to foster oratory. The importance of oratory is attested by the belief, according to the fables of Greece and Egypt, that the art of eloquence was of celestial origin, ascribed to the invention of a god, who, from the possession of this art, was supposed to be the messenger and interpreter of Olympus. It is also witnessed by the care with which the art was cultivated at a period of the remotest antiquity...*

Both oratory (the art of composing and delivering a speech in public) and rhetoric (the art of using language as a means of persuasion) are needed for a good speech. However, back in 1946, George Orwell warned us against the lies and 'weasel words' that increasingly fill political speeches these days. We all recognize the *'lessons must be learned'* mantra; the *'what counts are the issues'* drone; the *'let's get back to basics'* plea; clichés like *'the window of opportunity'*, *'the ticking of boxes'*, *'the pushing of envelopes'* (or whatever the current buzz-phrase is) abound. We now constantly see politicians refusing to answer questions except by asking other questions, always making their points in groups of three, and using sentences that meander through multiple unrelated clauses until they spiral down into meaninglessness. Unfortunately, the obfuscation and lack of coherent thought patterns all too common of modern speech-writers (many politicians are too illiterate to write speeches) has led to fewer heart-felt, emotive and factually correct political speeches in the 21st century. This is compounded by the rise of the 'sound bite', quickly prepared 24-hour rolling news and the growth of the Internet. Speeches and sermons used to last hours; they were often made on an extempore basis, but still developed with a clear logical flow. Today our attention spans are far, far shorter, as we piece together discrete bits of information from the TV or Internet-enabled mobile phones.

Despite all this, there is still room in a modern democratic society for eloquent speeches. Two of the greatest recent orators have been Presidents Reagan and Obama – very different men, from different parties, with differing intellects and educational achievements, but united by a belief in the progress of their democratic nation. Some speakers force you to listen to them by their sincerity and manner – they are believable. And if we believe in someone, we will follow their ideas and policies. Those of us involved in team sports know the difference between a 'good' captain's pre-game and half-time pep talks, and those of an uninspiring captain. They often make the difference between winning and losing. For the person making a well-constructed speech – whether it be a 'best man' making a wedding a joyous occasion, a preacher, a politician, a cultural icon, a lecturer or student, a lawyer, a military leader, a sports coach, a team leader, a 'captain of industry', a social reformer or activist – the correct choice of words, ideals and values can lift the spoken word into flights of eloquence. It can involve and change the audience. It can make a difference more profound than any other type of communication. The book is intended to be a demonstration of the power of great oratory. It is arranged chronologically, contextualizing excerpts from important speeches from around 170 men and women. I hope you enjoy reading it – it was a joy to research and write.

Terry Breverton

# MOSES

*c.*1250 – 1200 BCE

## The Ten Commandments

*c.*1250 – 1200 BCE

**Moses led his people** in the 'Exodus' out of captivity in Egypt, and in sight of the 'promised land' of Canaan he delivered the Ten Commandments after they had been revealed to him by God on Mount Sinai:

*Deuteronomy* 5.6: 'I am the Lord your God, who brought you out of the land of Egypt, out of the house of slavery; 5.7 You shall have no other gods before me. 5.8 You shall not make for yourself an idol, whether in the form of anything that is in heaven above, or that is on the earth beneath, or that is in the water under the earth. 5.9 You shall not bow down to them or worship them; for I the Lord your God am a jealous God, punishing children for the iniquity of parents, to the third and fourth generation of those who reject me, 5.10 But showing steadfast love to the thousandth generation of those who love me and keep my commandments. 5.11 You shall not make wrongful use of the name of the Lord your God, for the Lord will not acquit anyone who misuses his name. 5.12 Observe the Sabbath day and keep it holy, as the Lord your God commanded you. 5.13 For six days you shall labour and do all your work. 5.14 But the seventh day is a Sabbath to the Lord your God; you shall not do any work – you, or your son or your daughter, or your male or female slave, or your ox or your donkey, or any of your livestock, or the resident alien in your towns, so that your male and female slave may rest as well as you. 5.15 Remember that you were a slave in the land of Egypt, and the Lord your God brought you out from there with a mighty hand and an outstretched arm; therefore the Lord your God commanded you to keep the Sabbath day. 5.16 Honour your father and your mother, as the Lord your God commanded you, so that your days may be long and that it may go well with you in the land that the Lord your God is giving you. 5.17 You shall not kill. 5.18 Neither shall you commit adultery. 5.19 Neither shall you steal. 5.20 Neither shall you bear false witness against your neighbour. 5.21 Neither shall you covet your neighbour's wife. Neither shall you desire your neighbour's house, or field, or male or female slave, or ox, or donkey, or anything that belongs to your neighbour.'

# PERICLES
## c.495 – 429 BCE

## Funeral Oration, On those who Died in the War
### Winter 431 – 430 BCE

**Pericles was a statesman**, general and orator who presided over the 'Golden Age' of Athens, and the period 461–429 BCE is sometimes called 'the Age of Pericles'. Generally successful in war, he had fostered democracy and was responsible for many important public buildings such as the Parthenon on the Acropolis. Thucydides reported that this speech was delivered '*in the fairest suburb*' of Athens, as required by law, over the bodies of those who had fallen in the first year of the Peloponnesian War (431–404 BCE). The growth in the power of the Athenian empire had alarmed the oligarchy of Sparta and its allies, making war inevitable across Greece. Pericles's superb speech, after he had led the Athenian invasion of the city of Megara, a Spartan ally, demonstrates the Athenian pride in democracy, reminding both citizens and the bereaved that freedom is worth fighting for.

'...For we enjoy a form of government which does not copy the laws of our neighbouring states. We are ourselves rather a pattern to others than imitators of them. In name, from its not being administered for the benefit of the few, but of the many, it is called a democracy. With regard to its laws, all enjoy equality, as concerns their private differences. As regards social standing, advancement in public life falls to reputation for capacity, class considerations not being allowed to interfere with merit. Nor again does poverty bar the way – if a man is able to serve the state, he is not hindered by the obscurity of his condition...For while collectively they gave her their lives, individually they received that renown which never grows old, and the most distinguished tomb they could have. It is not that which they are laid in, but the glory which is left behind them, to be everlastingly recorded on every occasion for doing so, either by word or deed, that may from time to time present itself. For heroes have the whole earth for their tomb; and in lands far from their own, where the column with its epitaph declares it, there is enshrined in every breast a record unwritten with no tablet to preserve it, except that of the heart... Vying then with these men in your turn, and deeming happiness to consist in freedom, and freedom in valour, do not think lightly of the hazards of war...'

# PERICLES
### c.495 – 429 BCE

## *Third Oration – In Defence of Himself*
### late 430 BCE

**In 430 BCE, the Spartan army invaded** Attica, the region around Athens, but Pericles refused to fight their powerful army, instead leading a fleet to raid the Peloponnesian coastline. In that summer, plague devastated the crowded city of Athens, and Pericles was again forced to argue desperately against those who sought to make peace with Sparta. Pericles was deprived of his overall generalship by the city authorities, and Thucydides tells us: *'the public feeling against him did not subside until he had been fined. Not long afterwards, however, according to the way of the multitude, they again elected him general.'* His two legitimate sons died in the epidemic in 429 BCE, and, heartbroken and dismayed by public opposition, Pericles died soon after.

'...you cannot decline the burdens of empire and still expect to share its honours. You should remember also that what you are fighting against is not merely slavery as an exchange for independence, but also loss of empire and danger from the animosities incurred in its exercise...you must not be seduced by citizens like these or angry with me – who, if I voted for war, only did as you did yourselves...although besides what we counted for, the plague has come upon us – the only point indeed at which our calculation has been at fault. It is this, I know, that has had a large share in making me more unpopular than I should otherwise have been – quite undeservedly, unless you are also prepared to give me the credit of any success with which chance may present you...Remember, too, that if your country has the greatest name in all the world, it is because she never bent before disaster; because she has expended more life and effort in war than any other city, and has won for herself a power greater than any hitherto known, the memory of which will descend to the latest posterity. Even if now, in obedience to the general law of decay, we should ever be forced to yield, still it will be remembered that we held rule over more Hellenes than any other Hellenic state, that we sustained the greatest wars against their united or separate powers, and inhabited a city unrivalled by any other in resources or magnitude...'

# SOCRATES
## 469 – 399 BCE

### *In his own Defence*
### 399 BCE

**Socrates is possibly the greatest** teacher in the history of the Western world. In Athens, he constantly engaged in philosophical dialogues with his fellow citizens, focusing on discovering the truth of all things, and arguing that the *'unexamined life is not worth living'*. Athenian politicians saw Socrates as a threat, as he taught its young men to question everything, even Athenian authority. Thus Socrates was put on trial, and this *Apologia* is Plato's account of Socrates's defence against charges that he *'corrupted the young, refused to worship the gods, and created new deities'*. Instead of pleading for mercy, Socrates accepted the charges and attempted to persuade the jury with reason. He argued that it was his calling from the gods to seek knowledge, and that it was through his questions that he uncovered truth. Therefore, not to fulfil his calling would amount to blasphemy. Socrates begins by saying that he does not know if the men of Athens (his jury) have been persuaded by his accusers:

'How you, O Athenians, have been affected by my accusers, I cannot tell; but I know that they almost made me forget who I was, so persuasively did they speak. And yet they have hardly uttered a word of truth. But of the many falsehoods told by them, there was one which quite amazed me. I mean when they said that you should be upon your guard and not allow yourselves to be deceived by the force of my eloquence. To say this, when they were certain to be detected as soon as I opened my lips and proved myself to be anything but a great speaker, did indeed appear to me most shameless – unless by the force of eloquence they mean the force of truth – for if such is their meaning, I admit that I am eloquent. But in how different a way from theirs! Well, as I was saying, they have scarcely spoken the truth at all; but from me you shall hear the whole truth: not, however, delivered after their manner in a set oration duly ornamented with words and phrases. No, by heaven! but I shall use the words and arguments which occur to me at the moment; for I am confident in the justice of my cause (Or, I am certain that I am right in taking this course.) At my time of life I ought not to be appearing before you, O men of Athens, in the character of a juvenile orator – let no one expect it of me.

# SOCRATES
## 469 – 399 BCE

## *On being Declared Guilty*
### 399 BCE

**Socrates's accusers (three Athenian citizens)** were allotted three hours to present their case, after which the philosopher had three hours to defend himself. It is thought that there were about 500 judges in the court, and Socrates was found guilty by a majority of around 280 to 220 votes. Traditionally the prosecution and the defendant each proposed a penalty, between which the court would choose. For the prosecution, Miletus proposed the death sentence. Socrates could probably have avoided death by recommending exile, but he resumed his address and antagonized the court by pointing out that the vote was comparatively close. He proposed free meals for himself for life in the exclusive Prytaneum (the religious and political centre of the community). Socrates next considered imprisonment and banishment, before suggesting a small fine of 100 drachmae, as he had only meagre funds. Socrates's supporters immediately offered to increase the amount to 3,000 drachmae, but to the judges this was not an acceptable alternative, and it was decided that Socrates was to die by drinking hemlock. According to Xenophon, Socrates deliberately gave this defiant defence to the jury because '*he believed he would be better off dead*'.

'That I should not be grieved, O Athenians, at what has happened, namely, that you have condemned me, as well as many other circumstances concur in bringing to pass, and moreover this, that what has happened has not happened contrary to my expectations; but I much rather wonder at the number of votes on either side. For I did not expect that I should be condemned by so small a number, but by a large majority...The man then awards me the penalty of death. Well. But what shall I, on my part, O Athenians, award myself? Is it not clear that it will be such as I deserve? What then is that? Do I deserve to suffer or to pay a fine, for that I have purposely during my life not remained quiet, but, neglecting what most men seek after, – money-making, domestic concerns, military command, popular oratory, and moreover all the magistracies, conspiracies and cabals that are met with in the city, – thinking that I was in reality too upright a man to be safe if I took part in such things, I therefore did not apply myself to those pursuits...What treatment then do I deserve, seeing I am such a man? Some reward, O Athenians, if at least I am to be estimated according to my real deserts...'

# SOCRATES
## 469 – 399 BCE

## On being Condemned to Death
### 399 BCE

After being sentenced, Socrates concluded his speech, telling those who voted for the death sentence that his lack of time for preparation and his unwillingness to stoop to emotive appeals had influenced them. He assures those who voted for his acquittal that he was right to conduct his defence the way he did, and that death will be a blessing. It is an end to all worries, and therefore not to be feared, for his soul will meet Homer, Odysseus and other great men, with whom he can continue the practice of Socratic dialogue. He ends the *Apologia* saying that he does not blame those who accused and condemned him, and asks them to look after his three sons, ensuring that they put selflessness before selfish interests. Xenophon and Plato agree that Socrates had the opportunity to escape, as his followers would have been able to bribe the prison guards. Socrates chose to stay for several reasons. Flight would indicate a fear of death, which he believed no true philosopher has. His teachings would fare no better in another country, as he would continue questioning everything and undoubtedly incur further enmity. He also would also be breaking his 'social contract' having agreed to live under the laws of Athens.

'For the sake of no long space of time, O Athenians, you will incur the character and reproach at the hands of those who wish to defame the city, of having put that wise man, Socrates, to death. Those who wish to defame you, they will assert that I am wise, though I am not. If, then, you had waited for a short time, this would have happened of its own accord – for observe my age, that it is far advanced in life, and near death. But I say this not to you all, but to those only who have condemned me to die. And I say this too to the same persons. Perhaps you think, O Athenians, that I have been convicted through the want of arguments, by which I might have persuaded you, had I thought it right to do, saying anything so that I might escape punishment. Far otherwise: I have been convicted through want indeed, not of arguments, but want of audacity and impudence, and of the inclination to say such things to you as would have been most agreeable for you to hear, had I lamented and bewailed and done and said many other things unworthy of me, as I affirm, but such as you are accustomed to hear from others...'

# ISOCRATES
## 436 – 338 BCE

---

## Panegyricus – On the Union of Greece to Resist Persia
### 380 BCE

**The most influential rhetorician in Greece**, his teachings and style of speaking influenced Plato, Demosthenes and Cicero. Isocrates spent around ten years composing this call for Greece to unite under the spiritual and political leadership of Athens. Sparta (Lacedaemon) was the ruling power in Greece, but Artaxerxes II of Persia had overcome the Greeks in Asia, and the Aegean was overrun by pirates. Isocrates wished to rouse the Athenians to reassert their supremacy despite their military weakness. He recounted the services rendered by Athens to Hellas (Greece), dwelling upon the rivalry of Athens and Sparta during the Persian Wars. He defends Athenians against the charge of having behaved with cruelty towards the confederate states, and contrasts the past and present condition of the city, now that it is under the arbitrary rule of Sparta. In the second part of the speech he recommends that Athens and Sparta should now agree upon united action, especially when such a favourable opportunity presents itself. The Persians, he says, are weak, and preoccupied with problems, and the misery of the Hellenes has reached its height. Under the circumstances, even existing treaties should not prevent the Hellenes from declaring war against Persia. Isocrates was an influence upon Philip of Macedon (assassinated 336 BCE), and Philip's son Alexander crushed Greek opposition and then led Isocrates's proposed invasion of the Persian empire in 334 BCE.

'...For who, be he young or old, has a heart so unmoved that he will not wish to take his part in this expedition, an expedition led by Athenians and Lacedaemonians, mustering on behalf of the freedom of the allies, going forth at the bidding of all Hellas, and marching to the chastisement of the barbarians? What fame, and name, and glory must we deem that these men, who have been foremost in so great an enterprise, will enjoy while living, or dying, will leave behind them? For whereas they who fought against Alexander and took one city were deemed worthy of such praises, what eulogies must we expect will be won by the conquerors of all Asia? For surely everyone who has the gift of poetry or the power of speech will toil and study in the wish to leave behind him for all time a memorial at once of his own genius and of their valour?'

# DEMOSTHENES
## 384 – 322 BCE

*The Second Oration against Philip (the Second Philippic)*
### 344 BCE

**Philip of Macedon was constantly engaged** in intrigues against Athens. These manoeuvrings were the subjects of the four *Philippics* and other orations given by the Athenian statesman Demosthenes. A Philippic is the term now given to a tirade, a damning speech delivered against someone, and it dates from Demosthenes's orations that denounced Philip. Demosthenes travelled around Greek cities making speeches that encouraged them to throw off Macedon's influence. In response to complaints made by Macedonian-influenced Peloponnesian cities against Athens and Sparta, Demosthenes delivered this *Second Philippic*, a vehement attack on Philip and his supporters. The most serious accusation was that Philip violated the terms of the Peace of Philocrates of 346 BCE, concluded after Demosthenes, Aeschines and Philocratus travelled to the Macedonian capital of Pella in 347 BCE to negotiate a peace treaty.

'...First, then, Athenians, if there be a man who feels no apprehensions at the view of Philip's power, and the extent of his conquests, who imagines that these portend no danger to the state, or that his designs are not all aimed against you, I am amazed! and must entreat the attention of you all...to regard Philip as our real enemy; that if I appear to have looked forward with the more penetrating eye, you may join with me; if they who are thus secure and confident in this man, you may yield to their direction... you now behold Philip lavishing his gifts and promises on you. If you are wise, you will pray that he may never appear to have deceived and abused you. Various are the contrivances for the defence and security of cities; as battlements, and walls, and trenches, and every other kind of fortification; all which are the effects of labour, and attended with continual expense. But there is one common bulwark with which men of prudence are naturally provided, the guard and security of all people, particularly of free states, against the assaults of tyrants. What is this? Distrust. Of this be mindful: to this adhere: preserve this carefully, and no calamity can affect you. "What is it you seek?" said I. "Liberty? And do ye not perceive that nothing can be more adverse to this than the very titles of Philip? Every monarch, every tyrant is an enemy to liberty, and the opposer of laws. Will you not then be careful lest, while ye seek to be freed from war, you find yourselves his slaves?"...'

# DEMOSTHENES
## 384 – 322 BCE

---

*The Third Oration against Philip (the Third Philippic)*
### 341 BCE

**While Philip the II of Macedon** made bolder and bolder incursions into Greece, for years Demosthenes tried to rouse the Athenian people from their apathy. When Philip advanced on Thrace, the Athenians called an assembly to debate whether or not finally to heed Demosthenes's call to arms to preserve liberty and the Athenian way of life. Macedon and Athens were already de facto belligerent parties, as the Athenians were financing Diopeithes, who was launching attacks against cities allied with Macedon. Philip had violated the terms of the Peace of Philocrates, so Athens believed that it was only defending its legitimate rights. By delivering the *Third Philippic*, Demosthenes announced himself as the most influential politician in Athens, taking the offensive and destabilizing the pro-Macedonian faction of Aeschines. This speech is the signal for the Athenian uprising against Philip. Alarmed by Philip's military preparations, Demosthenes points out the danger of disunion among the Greek states, from their lack of patriotism, which he contrasts with the high and noble spirit of ancient times. The following year, Philip attacked the Propontine cities, fully justifying the warnings of Demosthenes. After this rousing speech, the assembly all cried out, '*To arms! To arms!*' Some of the concluding lines of his rousing speech are:

'I advise not this: I bid you send supplies to the troops in Chersonesus, and do what else they require; prepare yourselves and make every effort first, then summon, gather, instruct the rest of the Greeks. That is the duty of a state possessing a dignity such as yours. If you imagine that Chalcidians or Megarians will save Greece, while you run away from the contest, you imagine wrong. Well for any of those people, if they are safe themselves. This work belongs to you: this privilege your ancestors bequeathed to you, the prize of many perilous exertions. But if every one will sit seeking his pleasure, and studying to be idle himself, never will he find others to do his work, and more than this, I fear we shall be under the necessity of doing all that we like not at one time. Were proxies to be had, our inactivity would have found them long ago; but they are not. Such are the measures which I advise, which I propose: adopt them, and even yet, I believe, our prosperity may be re-established. If any man has better advice to offer, let him communicate it openly. Whatever you determine, I pray to all the gods for a happy result.'

# AESCHINES
## 389 – 314 BCE

---

*Against Crowning Demosthenes (Against Ctesiphon)*
### 330 BCE

**The main political opponent of Demosthenes**, and his rival for supremacy in Athens, Aeschines is generally ranked next to Demosthenes among all Greek orators. Another noted orator, Ctesiphon, had proposed that Athens should give a wreath of gold to Demosthenes in recognition of his public services. Aeschines, after the bill proposing it had come before the assembly, challenged it and gave notice of his intention to proceed against Ctesiphon for supporting an unconstitutional measure. One of Aeschines's reasons was that *'to record a bill describing Demosthenes as a public benefactor was to deposit a lying document among the public archives'*. After one of the most celebrated trials in history, Aeschines lost the case and went sent into banishment on Rhodes, dying in Samos.

'Our days have not fallen on the common chances of mortal life. We have been set to bequeath a story of marvels to posterity. Is not the King of Persia, he who cut through Athos, and bridged the Hellespont, he who demands earth and water from the Greeks, he who in his letters presumes to style himself lord of all men from the sunrise to the sunset, is he not struggling at this hour, no longer for authority over others, but for his own life? Do you not see the men who delivered the Delphian temple invested not only with that glory but with the leadership against Persia? While Thebes – Thebes, our neighbouring city – has been in one day swept from the face of Greece – justly it may be in so far as her general policy was erroneous, yet in consequence of a folly which was no accident, but the judgment of heaven. The unfortunate Lacedaemonians *[Spartans]*, though they did but touch this affair in its first phase by the occupation of the temple – they who once claimed the leadership of Greece – are now to be sent to Alexander in Asia to give hostages, to parade their disasters, and to hear their own and their country's doom from his lips, when they have been judged by the clemency of the master they provoked. Our city, the common asylum of the Greeks, from which, of old, embassies used to come from all Greece to obtain deliverance for their several cities at our hands, is now battling, no more for the leadership of Greece, but for the ground on which it stands. And these things have befallen us since Demosthenes took the direction of our policy...'

# DEMOSTHENES
## 384 – 322 BCE

*The Oration on the Crown*
### 330 BCE

**The advice Demosthenes had given** in his *Third Philippic* was followed. He was sent to Byzantium, where he renewed the alliance, and at the same time formed alliances with Abydos, Thracian princes, Rhodes, Chios, Cos, Chalcis, Corinth, Megara, Thebes and Persia. The Athenians voted Demosthenes a golden crown for distinguished services to the state, which was conferred on him in the theatre at the Great Dionysia (a festival to honour the god Dionysus) in March 340 BCE. Open war now broke out with Philip of Macedon. At the Dionysia of 338 Demosthenes was again crowned. However, late in the summer of 338, the decisive battle at Chaeronea resulted in the total defeat of Athens, Thebes and their allies by Philip of Macedon's army. Demosthenes had fought as a hoplite, a citizen-soldier, and was one of the fugitives from the battlefield. While Demosthenes was absent, the alliance between Athens and Philip was renewed and the independence of Athens guaranteed, but she lost some possessions. When Demosthenes returned to Athens, he proceeded to take all possible measures for the defence of the city, distrusting Philip's motives. Demosthenes was selected by the Assembly to deliver the funeral oration for those who fell at Chaeronea. Although the Macedonian party attacked him repeatedly in the law-courts, he was always acquitted.

In 337 Demosthenes was again Commissioner of Fortifications, as well as Controller of the Festival Fund – the most important office of state. Extremely efficient, he gave considerable sums from his private fortune for public purposes. In 336 Philip was assassinated, and was succeeded by Alexander, who destroyed Thebes. Alexander demanded from Athens the surrender of Demosthenes and other anti-Macedonian politicians and generals, and Athens promised to prosecute Demosthenes, but did not go ahead. Early in 336 Ctesiphon proposed, and the Council resolved, that Demosthenes should once more be crowned at the Dionysia. Before the proposal could be brought before the Assembly, Aeschines of the pro-Macedonian party indicted Ctesiphon for its alleged illegality. The trial did not take place until late in the summer of 330, and Demosthenes's answer to Aeschines's prosecution (see above) has been called '*the masterpiece of oratory*'. R.C. Jebb called it '*the most splendid and the most pathetic work of ancient eloquence*'. Henry Brougham Jr noted in his book *The Oration of Demosthenes upon the Crown* that: '*The attempt to translate the Greatest Oration of the Greatest of Orators into a language so different in its frame and idiom from that noble tongue in which it was pronounced, had long appeared so hopeless, that, after intentions repeatedly formed, the plan was for some years abandoned.'* The jury acquitted Ctesiphon. Aeschines, failing to obtain a fifth part of the votes, left Athens for exile on Rhodes. Below are the opening lines of Demosthenes's long masterpiece in defence of Ctesiphon:

'I begin, men of Athens, by praying to every god and goddess, that the same good will, which I have ever cherished toward the commonwealth and all of you, may be requited to me on the present trial. I pray likewise – and this specially concerns yourselves, your religion, and your honour – that the gods may put it in your minds, not to take counsel of my opponent touching the manner in which I am to be heard – that would indeed be cruel! – but of the laws and of your oath; wherein (besides the other obligations) it is prescribed that you shall hear both sides alike. This means, not only that you must pass no pre-condemnation, not only that you must extend your good will equally to both, but also that you must allow the parties to adopt such order and course of defence as they severally choose and prefer. Many advantages hath Æschines over me on this trial; and two especially, men of Athens. First, my risk in the contest is not the same. It is assuredly not the same for me to forfeit your regard, as for my adversary not to succeed in his indictment. To me – but I will say nothing untoward at the outset of my address. The prosecution, however, is play to him. My second disadvantage is, the natural disposition of mankind to take pleasure in hearing invective and accusation, and to be annoyed by those who praise themselves. To Aeschines is assigned the part which gives pleasure; that which is (I may fairly say) offensive to all, is left for me. And if, to escape from this, I make no mention of what I have done, I shall appear to be without defence against his charges, without proof of my claims to honour; whereas, if I proceed to give an account of my conduct and measures, I shall be forced to speak frequently of myself. I will endeavour then to do so with all becoming modesty; what I am driven to do by the necessity of the case, will be fairly chargeable to my opponent, who has instituted such a prosecution...'

# SCYTHIAN AMBASSADOR
## *fl.*329 BCE

*'Do not imagine that those whom thou conquerest can love thee'*
329 BCE

 **The historian Strabo** (*c.*63 BCE–24 CE) reported that the westward expansion of the Scythians ended in 339 BCE with defeat by Philip of Macedon. The Scythians were nomadic tribes who lived in the region extending from central Asia to the Danube, from southern Russia to the Balkans. Philip's son Alexander the Great was pushing Macedon's borders both northwards and westwards, and the Scythians sent ambassadors to Alexander to tell him not to cross the River Jaxartes (now the Syr Darya River). When the ambassadors waited on Alexander, they were disappointed to discover him less commanding in his person and personality than his great fame had led them to expect. Eventually the oldest of the ambassadors addressed Alexander as follows. Alexander ignored his warnings, and the Battle of Jaxartes ensued on a site not far from Tashkent, on the borders of Uzbekistan, Tajikistan, Kazakhstan and Kyrgyzstan. Alexander's victory, perhaps his most brilliant strategically, was the first recorded by Greeks or Macedonians over a mounted nomadic army.

'Had the gods given thee a body proportionable to thy ambition, the whole universe would have been too little for thee. With one hand thou wouldst touch the East, and with the other the West; and not satisfied with this, thou wouldst follow the sun, and know where he hides himself. Such as thou art, thou yet aspirest after what it will be impossible for thee to attain. Thou crossest over from Europe into Asia; and when thou shalt have subdued all the race of men, then thou wilt make war against rivers, forests and wild beasts. Dost thou not know, that tall trees are many years a growing, but may be torn up in an hour's time; that the lion serves sometimes as food for the smallest birds; that iron, though so hard, is consumed by rust; in a word, that there is nothing so strong, which may not be destroyed by the weakest thing?

What have we to do with thee? We never set foot in thy country. May not those who inhabit woods be allowed to live, without knowing who thou art, and whence thou comest? We will neither command over, nor submit to any man. And that thou mayest be sensible what kind of people the Scythians are, know that we received from heaven, as a rich present, a yoke of oxen, a ploughshare, a dart, a javelin, and a cup. These we make use of, both with our friends, and against our enemies. To our friends we give corn, which we procure by the labour of our oxen; with our friends we offer wine to the gods, in our cup; and with regard to our enemies, we combat them at a distance with our arrows, and near at hand with our javelins. It is with these that we formerly conquered the most warlike nations, subdued the most powerful kings, laid waste to all Asia, and opened ourselves a way into the heart of Egypt.

But thou, who boasteth thy coming to extirpate robbers, thou thyself art the greatest robber upon earth. Thou hast plundered all nations that thou hast overcome; thou hast possessed thyself of Libya, invaded Syria, Persia and Bactriana; thou art forming a design to march as far as India, and now thou comest hither to seize upon our herds of cattle. The great possessions thou hast, only make thee covet the more eagerly what thou hast not...Pass but the Jaxartes, and thou will behold the great extent of our plains. It will be in vain for thee to pursue the Scythians; and I defy thee ever to overtake them. Our poverty will be more active than thy army, laden with the spoils of so many nations; and, when thou shalt fancy us at a great distance, thou wilt see us rush suddenly on thy camp; for we pursue, and fly from our enemies with equal speed. I am informed that the Greeks speak jestingly of the Scythian solitudes and that they are even become a proverb; but we are fonder of our deserts, than of your great cities and fruitful plains. Let me observe to thee, that fortune is slippery; hold her fast therefore, for fear she should escape thee. Put a curb to thy felicity, if thou desirest to keep in possession of it. If thou art a god, thou oughtest to do good to mortals, and not deprive them of their possessions. If thou art a mere man, reflect always on what thou art. They whom thou shalt not molest will be thy true friends; the strongest friendships being contracted between equals; and they are esteemed equals who have not tried their strength against each other: but do not imagine that those whom thou conquerest can love thee, for there is no such thing as friendship between a master and his slave, and a forced peace is soon followed by a war...Consider, therefore, if thou will have us for friends, or enemies.'

# ALEXANDER THE GREAT, ALEXANDER III OF MACEDON
### 356 – 323 BCE

## To his Mutinous Troops
### 326 BCE

**In 336 BCE, Alexander's father** Philip was assassinated, and Alexander was proclaimed king, aged 20. He immediately executed rival claimants to the throne, put down the uprising in Thessaly, and headed north to Thrace to extinguish its attempt at independence. He secured Macedon's northern border but the Thebans and Athenians rose again, so he wiped out Thebes and forced Athens into submission, along with the rest of Greece. Alexander now invaded Asia Minor, defeating the Persians several times and then also taking Syria. He invaded Gaza and Egypt, then Mesopotamia (Iraq) taking Babylon and ravaging Persia again before conquering Afghanistan. Alexander fought constant battles through what is now Pakistan and India during the winter of 327/326 BCE. He narrowly defeated Porus in a savage engagement at the Battle of Hydaspes in 326, but then found himself face to face with the powerful Nanda and Gangaridai empires. Alexander's men were utterly exhausted – they had been campaigning for 11 years without returning home – and they mutinied on the Hyphasis River, refusing to march east. The Macedonians were exhausted but now were to face a combined army of 80,000 cavalry, 200,000 footmen, 8,000 chariots and 6,000 war elephants. They would have to cross, under attack, the River Ganges which was 4 miles (6.4 km) wide and hundreds of feet deep, to meet the Indian army on the other side. Alexander used all the talent for oration that he had developed while studying under Aristotle at Pella to infuse his men with the fire and determination they needed to continue, to fight and to win:

'O Macedonians and Grecian allies, seeing that you no longer follow me into dangerous enterprises with a resolution equal to that which formerly animated you, I have collected you together into the same spot, so that I may either persuade you to march forward with me, or may be persuaded by you to return. If indeed the labours which you have already undergone up to our present position seem to you worthy of disapprobation, and if you do not approve of my leading you into them, there can be no advantage in my speaking any further...I, for my part, think that to a brave man there is no end to labours except the labours themselves, provided they lead to glorious achievements. But if any one desires to hear what will be the end to our warfare itself; let him learn that the distance still remaining before we reach the River Ganges and the Eastern Sea is not great; and I inform you that the Hyrcanian Sea will be seen to be united with this, because the Great Sea encircles the whole earth. I will also demonstrate both to the Macedonians and to the Grecian allies, that the Indian Gulf is confluent with the Persian, and the Hyrcanian Sea with the Indian Gulf. From the Persian Gulf our expedition will sail round into Libya as far as the Pillars of Heracles. From the Pillars all the interior of Libya becomes ours, and so the whole of Asia will belong to us, and the limits of our empire, in that direction, will be those which God has made also the limits of the earth...For the land is yours, and you act as its viceroys. The greater part also of the money now comes to you; and when we have traversed the whole of Asia, then, by Zeus, not merely having satisfied your expectations, but having even exceeded the advantages which each man hopes to receive, those of you who wish to return home I will send back to their own land, or I will myself lead them back; while those who remain here, I will make objects of envy to those who go back.'

However, Alexander's words were met with dead silence from his men. He repeatedly asked his commanders' opinion, until Coenus, an old officer, spoke. Coenus told him that the officers would go forward with him regardless; they could do no less for all the riches and honour Alexander had showered upon them. But he was not speaking for the officers, but for the men. He pointed out how few were left of the Macedonians and Greeks who had set out for Asia with him '...*Sir, if there is one thing above all others a successful man should know, it is when to stop,*' he concluded. '*Assuredly for a commander like yourself, with an army like ours, there is nothing to fear from any enemy; but luck, remember, is an unpredictable thing, and against what it may bring no man has any defence.*' Alexander, amazed by the applause which greeted Coenus's words, dismissed his officers out of hand. After sulking in his tent for three days, Alexander eventually listened to this advice, and began to return home through Persia. Here he died three years later, never having returned to Macedon in the course of 13 years of undefeated warfare waged across three continents.

# HANNIBAL BARCA
## 247 – 183 or 182 BCE

*Encouraging his Soldiers to Cross the Alps*
218 BCE

**Saguntum was a province of New Carthage** (Cartagena) in Spain. Knowing that the Romans wished to take New Carthage and drive the Carthaginians out of Spain, Hannibal attacked Saguntum, so beginning the Second Punic War (218–201 BCE). As the Romans prepared to invade New Carthage, Hannibal took pre-emptive action, marching his army and 37 elephants over the Pyrenees, across the Rhône, over the Alps and into Italy. This speech was to encourage his men to undertake the most dangerous part of the expedition across the Alps. After this rousing appeal he advised his men to prepare themselves with food and rest for the arduous march ahead. The next day they advanced up the left bank of the Rhône towards the central districts of Gaul, not because this was the most direct route to the Alps but because Hannibal thought that there would be less likelihood of an advancing Roman army intercepting him, as he had no desire to engage in battle before he arrived in Italy.

'I am astonished to see how hearts that have been always dauntless have now suddenly become a prey to fear. Think of the many victorious campaigns you have gone through, and remember that you did not leave Spain before you had added to the Carthaginian Empire all the tribes in that country washed by two widely remote seas. The Roman people made a demand for all who had taken part in the siege of Saguntum to be given up to them, and you, to avenge the insult, have crossed the Ebro to wipe out the name of Rome and bring freedom to the world. When you commenced your march, from the setting to the rising sun, none of you thought it too much for you, but now when you see that by far the greater part of the way has been accomplished; the passes of the Pyrenees, which were held by most warlike tribes, surmounted; the Rhône, that mighty stream, crossed in the face of so many thousand Gauls, and the rush of its waters checked. Now that you are within sight of the Alps, on the other side of which lies Italy, you have become weary and are arresting your march in the very gates of the enemy. What do you imagine the Alps to be other than lofty mountains? Suppose them to be higher than the peaks of the Pyrenees, surely no region in the world can touch the sky or be impassable to man. Even the Alps are inhabited and cultivated, animals are bred and reared there, their gorges and ravines can be traversed by armies. Why, even the envoys whom you see here did not cross the Alps by flying through the air, nor were their ancestors native to the soil. They came into Italy as emigrants looking for a land to settle in, and they crossed the Alps often in immense bodies with their wives and children and all their belongings. What can be inaccessible or insuperable to the soldier who carries nothing with him but his weapons of war? What toils and perils you went through for eight months to effect the capture of Saguntum! And now that Rome, the capital of the world, is your goal, can you deem anything so difficult or so arduous that it should prevent you from reaching it? Many years ago the Gauls captured the place which Carthaginians despair of approaching; either you must confess yourselves inferior in courage and enterprise to a people whom you have conquered again and again, or else you must look forward to finishing your march on the ground between the Tiber and the walls of Rome.

Publius Cornelius Scipio tried unsuccessfully to check Hannibal's advances into Italy, and Hannibal won the battles of Ticinus, Trebia, Lake Trasimene and Cannæ in Italy in 218–216. He marched against Rome in 211. Scipio attacked New Carthage but was killed by the troops Hannibal had left there. For the next 16 years, Hannibal successfully waged war against every Roman legion sent to defeat him. However, the war became a stalemate, as Rome now used guerrilla tactics instead of meeting in pitched battle, and Carthage failed to supply Hannibal with any new troops or resources. Rome had lost half a million men in battle, when Scipio the Younger (Africanus) decided to attack Carthage. In 204 Scipio and an army of 25,000 men landed in Carthage. Hearing of the invasion, Hannibal headed back to North Africa in 203. On the plain of Zama in 202, Hannibal's soldiers were outflanked and defeated by the Roman legions. Hannibal then sent word to Carthage, '*We have lost not only a battle, but the war. Accept the terms of peace offered.*' He was exiled in about 195 BCE, and was forced to commit suicide rather than be given up to Rome.

# PUBLIUS CORNELIUS SCIPIO
### *d.*211 BCE

## *To his Army before the Battle of Ticinus*
### 218 BCE

**This speech was delivered** by the Roman consul and general on the eve of the Battle of Ticinus, fought by a tributary of the River Po near the present Vercelli in north Italy in 218. He was trying to halt Hannibal's advance into Italy, and in a sharp cavalry engagement was wounded, his death being *'warded off by the interposition of his son, then just arriving at the age of puberty'.* This son would later be called Scipio Africanus in recognition of his defeat of Hannibal's Carthaginians in North Africa. After this defeat, Scipio again lost at Trebia in December of the same year, but he continued to lead the Romans until he was killed in Spain in 211 BCE by Hasdrubal, the brother of Hannibal.

'...I would have you fight, not only with that spirit with which you are wont to encounter other enemies, but with a certain indignation and resentment, as if you saw your slaves suddenly taking up arms against you. We might have killed them when shut up in Eryx by hunger, the most dreadful of human tortures; we might have carried over our victorious fleet to Africa, and in a few days have destroyed Carthage without any opposition. We granted pardon to their prayers; we released them from the blockade; we made peace with them when conquered; and we afterward considered them under our protection when they were oppressed by the African war. In return for these benefits, they come under the conduct of a furious youth to attack our country. And I wish that the contest on your side was for glory, and not for safety; it is not about the possession of Sicily and Sardinia, concerning which the dispute was formerly, but for Italy that you must fight; nor is there another army behind, which if we should not conquer, can resist the enemy; nor are there other Alps, during the passage of which fresh forces may be procured: here, soldiers, we must make our stand, as if we fought before the walls of Rome. Let every one consider that he defends with his arms not only his own person, but his wife and young children: nor let him only entertain domestic cares and anxieties, but at the same time let him revolve in his mind that the senate and people of Rome now anxiously regard our efforts; and that according as our strength and valour shall be, such henceforward will be the fortune of that city and of the Roman empire.'

# HANNIBAL BARCA
## 247 – 183 or 182 BCE

*Address to his Soldiers before the Battle of Ticinus*
### 218 BCE

**Hannibal had gone to Spain** with his father Hamilcar in 238, aged nine, and swore eternal enmity to Rome for Carthage's defeat in the First Punic War. Realizing that the Romans wanted to take New Carthage (Cartagena), Hannibal had conquered Spain and Portugal by 219 BCE. This is the address on the eve of the Battle of Ticinus, his first battle in Italy after successfully crossing the Alps. The Romans expected Hannibal's force to be weakened, hungry and dispirited, and without supplies having lost most of them in the mountains and during fighting with hostile tribes. Hannibal made his speech as he rested his men, knowing that Scipio's legions were near. When he saw Publius Cornelius Scipio begin to draw up his infantry, Hannibal immediately ordered his cavalry to attack. The battle was so fast-moving that the javelin-throwers deployed by the Romans had no chance to fire even a single volley and simply milled around on the field, becoming a major cause of the Roman defeat. Hannibal did not press for absolute victory, probably because his exhausted forces were outnumbered by Roman infantry still in their nearby fort.

'If, soldiers, you shall by and by, in judging of your own fortune, preserve the same feelings which you experienced a little before in the example of the fate of others, we have already conquered. For neither was that merely a spectacle, but, as it were, a certain representation of your condition. And I know not whether fortune has not thrown around you still stronger chains and more urgent necessities than around your captives. On the right and left two seas enclose you, without your possessing even a single ship for escape. The river Po around you, the Po larger and more impetuous than the Rhône; the Alps behind, scarcely passed by you when fresh and vigorous, hem you in. Here, soldiers, where you will first meet the enemy, you must conquer or die; and the same fortune which has imposed the necessity of fighting holds out to you, if victorious, rewards than which men are not wont to desire greater, even from the immortal gods. If we were only about to recover by our valour Sicily and Sardinia, wrested from our fathers, the recompense would be sufficiently ample; but whatever, acquired and amassed by so many triumphs, the Romans possess, all, with its masters themselves, will become yours. To gain this rich reward, hasten, then, and seize your arms, with the favour of the gods...'

# PUBLIUS CORNELIUS SCIPIO AFRICANUS
## 235 – 183 BCE

*To his Mutinous Troops*
206 BCE

**Scipio fought in the defeat at Cannae** in 216 BCE, and as proconsul conquered Spain. Some 8,000 Roman troops had been garrisoned at Sucro in Spain to guard settlements against the Carthaginians north of the Ebro. Hearing that Scipio was seriously ill, and facing the possibility of not being paid, his soldiers mutinied. With this speech, Scipio courageously faced the mutineers. When the mutiny was put down, he only executed 30 ringleaders, which he said was like tearing out his own bowels. He went on to defeat Hannibal at the Battle of Zama in 202 BCE, an action which earned Scipio the nickname Africanus, *'the Roman Hannibal'*.

'I imagined that language would never fail me in which to address my army; not that I have ever accustomed myself to speaking rather than action, but because having been kept in a camp almost from my boyhood, I had become familiar with the dispositions of soldiers. But I am at a loss both for sentiments and expressions with which to address you, whom I know not even by what name I ought to call. Can I call you countrymen, who have revolted from your country? Or soldiers, who have rejected the command and authority of your general, and violated the solemn obligation of your oath? Can I call you enemies?...even in my own camp, so much was I deceived in my opinion, the report of my death was not only readily believed, but anxiously waited for. Not that I wish to implicate you all in this enormity; for, be assured, if I supposed that the whole of my army desired my death, I would here immediately expire before your eyes; nor could I take any pleasure in a life which was odious to my countrymen and my soldiers. But every multitude is in its nature like the ocean, which, though in itself incapable of motion, is excited by storms and winds. So, also, in yourselves there is calm and there are storms; but the cause and origin of your fury are entirely attributable to those who led you on; you have caught your madness by contagion. Nay, even this day you do not appear to me to be aware to what a pitch of frenzy you have proceeded; what a heinous crime you have dared to commit against myself, your country, your parents, your children; against the gods, the witnesses of your oath; against the auspices under which you serve; against the laws of war, the discipline of your ancestors, and the majesty of the highest authority...'

# MARCUS TULLIUS CICERO
## 3 January 106 – 7 December 43 BCE

## *The First Oration against Verres*
### 70 BCE

**One of Rome's greatest orators**, he was a philosopher, lawyer, statesman, political theorist and Roman constitutionalist. Cicero became one of the most formidable defence attorneys in the Republic and then was assigned to Sicily to oversee the vital grain supply to Rome. The governor of Sicily Caius Verres, was detested by the Sicilians and they asked Cicero to prosecute him, as Verres had been involved in various schemes to extort money from their island. Cicero had been careful during his rise to high office to avoid the powerful enmities that such a prosecution could create, but on this occasion agreed to take on this case. In his prosecution speeches in Rome, Cicero so brilliantly and sarcastically attacked the governor that Verres went into self-imposed exile before the trial was even finished. Of Cicero's remarkable orations, 57 have been preserved. Cicero begins by criticizing the ease with which the wealthy seem to avoid prosecution or evidence of guilt:

'That which was above all things to be desired, O judges, and which above all things was calculated to have the greatest influence towards allaying the unpopularity of your order, and putting an end to the discredit into which your judicial decisions have fallen, appears to have been thrown in your way, and given to you not by any human contrivance, but almost by the interposition of the gods, at a most important crisis of the republic. For an opinion has now become established, pernicious to us, and pernicious to the republic, which has been the common talk of every one, not only at Rome, but among foreign nations also, – that in the courts of law as they exist at present, no wealthy man, however guilty he may be, can possibly be convicted... I, O judges, have undertaken this cause as prosecutor with the greatest good wishes and expectation on the part of the Roman people, not in order to increase the unpopularity of the senate, but to relieve it from the discredit which I share with it. For I have brought before you a man, by acting justly in whose case you have an opportunity of retrieving the lost credit of your judicial proceedings, of regaining your credit with the Roman people, and of giving satisfaction to foreign nations; a man, the embezzler of the public funds, the petty tyrant of Asia and Pamphylia, the robber who deprived the city of its rights, the disgrace and ruin of the province of Sicily...'

# CATILINE (LUCIUS SERGIUS CATILINA)
## 108 – 62 BCE

*'I am well aware, soldiers, that words cannot inspire courage'*
62 BCE

**A candidate for consul**, his name is given to the Catiline conspiracy which attempted to overthrow the Roman Republic, in particular the over-powerful aristocrats in the Senate. Catiline was in the process of gathering an army when his fellow plotters were arrested in Rome by Cicero, who had them strangled without trial, despite protests from Catiline's ally Julius Caesar. Upon hearing of the death of Lentulus and the other plotters, most of his men deserted Cataline's ill-equipped army, reducing its size from about 10,000 to just 3,000. He tried to avoid a battle, but was forced to fight when Quintus Caecilius Metellus Celer in the north blocked his escape. Catiline saw that he was trapped in between mountains and the opposing legions, knew that his plans in Rome had failed, and that he had no hope of escape or reinforcements, so decided to engage Petreius's army straight away, near Pistoria. A victory would dishearten the other Republican legions which might join him to overthrow the corrupt regime. Catiline himself bravely fought as a soldier in the front lines of the battle. When the corpses were counted, all of Catiline's soldiers were found with frontal wounds, and his corpse was found far in advance of his own lines. Not one free citizen was left alive or captured. Catiline spurred on his troops, who followed him into almost certain death, with this rousing address:

'I am well aware, soldiers, that words cannot inspire courage; and that a spiritless army cannot be rendered active, or a timid army valiant, by the speech of its commander. Whatever courage is in the heart of a man, whether from nature or from habit, so much will be shown by him in the field; and on him whom neither glory nor danger can move, exhortation is bestowed in vain; for the terror in his breast stops his ears. I have called you together, however, to give you a few instructions, and to explain to you, at the same time, my reasons for the course which I have adopted. You all know, soldiers, how severe a penalty the inactivity and cowardice of Lentulus has brought upon himself and us; and how, while waiting for reinforcements from the city, I was unable to march into Gaul. In what situation our affairs now are, you all understand as well as myself. Two armies of the enemy, one on the side of Rome, and the other on that of Gaul, oppose our progress; while the want of grain, and of other necessaries, prevents us from remaining, however strongly we may desire to remain, in our present position. Whithersoever we would go, we must open a passage with our swords. I conjure you, therefore, to maintain a brave and resolute spirit; and to remember, when you advance to battle, that on your own right hands depend riches, honour, and glory, with the enjoyment of your liberty and of your country. If we conquer, all will be safe, we shall have provisions in abundance; and the colonies and corporate towns will open their gates to us. But if we lose the victory through want of courage, those same places will turn against us; for neither place nor friend will protect him whom his arms have not protected. Besides, soldiers, the same exigency does not press upon our adversaries, as presses upon us; we fight for our country, for our liberty, for our life; they contend for what but little concerns them, the power of a small party. Attack them, therefore, with so much the greater confidence, and call to mind your achievements of old.

We might, with the utmost ignominy, have passed the rest of our days in exile. Some of you, after losing your property, might have waited at Rome for assistance from others. But because such a life, to men of spirit, was disgusting and unendurable, you resolved upon your present course. If you wish to quit it, you must exert all your resolution for none but conquerors have exchanged war for peace. To hope for safety in flight, when you have turned away from the enemy the arms by which the body is defended, is indeed madness. In battle, those who are most afraid are always in most danger; but courage is equivalent to a rampart. When I contemplate you, soldiers, and when I consider your past exploits, a strong hope of victory animates me. Your spirit, your age, your valour, give me confidence; to say nothing of necessity, which makes even cowards brave. To prevent the numbers of the enemy from surrounding us, our confined situation is sufficient. But should Fortune be unjust to your valour, take care not to lose your lives unavenged; take care not to be taken and butchered like cattle, rather than, fighting like men, to leave to your enemies a bloody and mournful victory.'

# MARK ANTONY (MARCUS ANTONIUS)
## c.14 January 83 – 1 August 30 BCE

*Oration over the Dead Body of Cæsar*
### 44 BCE

**The eulogy was delivered** in the Roman forum by his kinsman Antony, who had allied with Julius Caesar in the Civil War, commanding his left wing at Pharsalia. Antony was a consul in 44 BCE, and publicly offered Caesar a diadem on 14 February. It was the symbol of a king, but Caesar refused it. Antony tried to warn Caesar that he was in danger on the Ides (15) of March, but was too late, and he fled from Rome dressed as a slave after Caesar was assassinated, fearing that all Caesar's supporters would also be killed. As consul, Antony was allowed back into Rome, and an amnesty was arranged for the assassins. At Caesar's funeral Antony was asked to give the eulogy, and unexpectedly accused the conspirators of murder. He dramatically pulled the toga from Caesar's body to show the crowd his stab wounds, pointing at each and naming the murderers. He then read Caesar's will, which left most of his property to the people of Rome, demonstrating that Caesar had no intention of forming a royal dynasty. Public opinion turned in Antony's favour, and that night the Roman populace attacked the assassins' houses, forcing them to flee for their lives. With Octavian (later to become Emperor Augustus) and Lepidus, Antony then formed the Second Triumvirate in 43, defeating Caesar's assassins Brutus and Cassius at the Battle of Philippi in 42. He followed Cleopatra to Asia in 41, and was defeated by Octavian in the Final War of the Roman Republic at Actium in 31 BCE. Antony fled to Egypt where he and Cleopatra committed suicide.

'...You yourselves have profited most by Cæsar's virtue; and you demand his praises not half-heartedly, as if he were no relation, but out of deep affection as one of your very own...by his bravery he overcame foreigners in war, but out of his humanity kept unharmed the seditious citizens, although many of them by their acts had often shown themselves unworthy of this favour. The same policy he followed again both in Africa and Spain, releasing all who had not before been captured and been made recipients of his mercy. To grant their lives invariably to such as frequently plotted against him he deemed folly, not humanity... For these and all his other acts of lawmaking and reconstruction, great in themselves, but likely to be deemed small in comparison with those others into which one cannot enter minutely, you loved him as a father and cherished him as a benefactor; you gloried him with such honours as you bestowed on no one else and desired him to be continual head of the city and of the whole domain. You did not dispute at all about titles, but applied them all to him as being still less than his merits, with the purpose that whatever was lacking in each one of them of what was considered a proper expression of the most complete honour and authority might be made up by what the rest contributed. Therefore, as regards the gods he was appointed high priest, as regards us consul, as regards the soldiers imperator, and as regards the enemy dictator. But why do I enumerate these details, when in one phrase you called him father of his country – not to mention the rest of his titles?

Yet this father, this high priest, this inviolable being, hero, god, is dead; alas! dead not by the violence of some disease, nor exhausted by old age, nor wounded abroad somewhere in some war, nor snatched away irresistibly by some supernatural force: but plotted against here within the walls – the man that safely led an army into Britain; ambushed in this city – the man who had increased its circuit; struck down in the senate-house – the man that had reared another such edifice at his own charge; unarmed, the brave warrior; defenceless, the promoter of peace: the judge beside the court of justice; the governor beside the seat of government; at the hands of the citizens – he whom none of the enemy had been able to kill even when he fell into the sea; at the hands of his comrades – he who had often taken pity on them. Where, Cæsar, was your humaneness, where your inviolability, where the laws? You enacted many laws to prevent anyone being killed by personal foes, yet see how mercilessly your friends killed you; and now slain you lie before us in that forum through which you, often crowned, led triumphal marches: wounded unto death you have been cast down upon that rostrum from which you often addressed the people. Woe for the blood-bespattered locks of grey. Alas for the rent robe, which you assumed, it seems, only to the end that you might be slain in it!'

# JESUS OF NAZARETH
### c.6 or 4 BCE – 30 or 33 CE

## *The Eight Beatitudes – the Sermon on the Mount*
### c.30 CE

**Jesus was born in or before** 4 BCE, because Herod died in 4 BCE. Alternatively, he was born on or after 6 CE, because Cyrenius became governor of Syria in 6 CE. The relevant verse is in *Luke: 2.2 'And this taxing was first made when Cyrenius was governor of Syria. 2.3 And all went to be taxed, every one into his own city. 2.4 And Joseph also went up from Galilee, out of the city of Nazareth, into Judaea, unto the city of David, which is called Bethlehem; (because he was of the house and lineage of David:) 2.5 To be taxed with Mary his espoused wife, being great with child.'* On the date of Christ's death, the Gospels disagree, but it seems to been in either 30 or 33 CE. Jesus Christ is the central figure of Christianity, which views him as the *Messiah* foretold in the *Old Testament*, and within which most denominations recognize him both as the Son of God and as God incarnate. Islam regards Jesus as a prophet and the Messiah, but Judaism rejects all these claims. Jesus Christ gave us the thoughtful Eight Beatitudes in the Sermon on the Mount. The *Gospel of Matthew* stresses that Jesus offers us a way of life that promises eternity in the Kingdom of Heaven through a life of humility, charity and brotherly love. Jesus presents the Beatitudes in a positive sense, as virtues in life which will ultimately lead to reward, love becoming the motivation for every true Christian. The Beatitudes promise each one of us salvation – not in this world, but in the next. While the Beatitudes of Jesus describe a way of life that promises salvation, they can also provide peace in the midst of our problems in this world:

Blessed are the poor in spirit, for theirs is the Kingdom of Heaven.

Blessed are they who mourn, for they shall be comforted.

Blessed are the meek, for they shall inherit the earth.

Blessed are they who hunger and thirst for righteousness, for they shall be satisfied.

Blessed are the merciful, for they shall obtain mercy.

Blessed are the pure of heart, for they shall see God.

Blessed are the peacemakers, for they shall be called children of God.

Blessed are they who are persecuted for the sake of righteousness, for theirs is the Kingdom of Heaven.

# PAUL THE APOSTLE, ST PAUL of TARSUS
### c.5 BCE – c.67 CE

---

## To an unknown God
### c.51 CE

**Paul's influence on Christian thinking** has probably been more significant than that of any other *New Testament* author. When this 'Apostle to the Gentiles' reached Athens, he saw an altar with an inscription TO AN UNKNOWN GOD, a god who existed but whose name was unknown to the Athenians. Invited to speak to the Athenian elite at the Areopagus, he gave the following speech, reminding them what they should know. Human shrines and statues could not possibly capture the majesty of the true Creator and that all move and think through his power. Men are the 'offspring' (*genos*), literally of the divine 'race' or 'class'. Probably Paul would have gestured towards the surrounding magnificent buildings, and portrayed the picture of a God who transcended them all in this sermon.

> *Acts of the Apostles*: 17.22 'And Paul stood in the midst of the Areopagus, and said, Ye men of Athens, in all things I perceive that ye are somewhat superstitious. 23 For as I passed along, and observed the objects of your worship, I found also an altar with this inscription, TO AN UNKNOWN GOD. What therefore ye worship in ignorance, this set I forth unto you. 24 The God that made the world and all things therein, he, being Lord of heaven and earth, dwelleth not in temples made with hands; 25 Neither is he served by men's hands, as though he needed anything, seeing he himself giveth to all life, and breath, and all things; 26 and he made of one every nation of men for to dwell on all the face of the earth, having determined their appointed seasons, and the bounds of their habitation; 27 that they should seek God, if haply they might feel after him, and find him, though he is not far from each one of us: 28 For in him we live, and move, and have our being; as certain even of your own poets have said, For we are also his offspring. 29 Being then the offspring of God, we ought not to think that the Godhead is like unto gold, or silver, or stone, graven by art and device of man. 30 The times of ignorance therefore God overlooked; but now he commandeth men that they should all everywhere repent: 31 Inasmuch as he hath appointed a day, in the which he will judge the world in righteousness by the man whom he hath ordained; whereof he hath given assurance unto all men, in that he hath raised him from the dead.'

# PAUL THE APOSTLE, ST PAUL of TARSUS

### c.5 BCE – c.67 CE

## 'Through a glass, darkly'
### c.54 CE

Here, 'charity' is a translation of the Latin *caritas*, and the original Greek *agape*, used to denote the highest and most self-transcending form of love, a self-sacrificing, all-embracing emotion. This sermon was probably written in Ephesus, Turkey, Paul's mother country. Paul was preaching in Corinth in 50–52 CE and 56–57 CE before he was held prisoner in Caesarea and then taken to Rome where he was executed. Her was not crucified, but beheaded as he was a Roman citizen. The major impetus in the spread of Christianity across Europe, his tomb may have been confirmed at the Basilica of St Paul outside the Walls (San Paolo fuori le Mura) in Rome. In 2009 Pope Benedict announced that the insertion of a probe into Paul's sarcophagus had revealed bits of incense and purple and blue linen as well as small bone fragments. The bone was radiocarbon-dated to the first or second century CE.

> I *Corinthians*: 13 'Though I speak with the tongues of men and of angels, and have not charity, I am become as sounding brass or a tinkling cymbal. And though I have the gift of prophecy, and understand all mysteries, and all knowledge; and though I have all faith, so that I could remove mountains, and have not charity, I am nothing. And though I bestow all my goods to feed the poor, and though I give my body to be burned, and have not charity, it profits me nothing. Charity suffers long, and is kind; charity envies not; charity vaunts not itself, is not puffed up, doth not behave itself unseemly, seeks not her own, is not easily provoked, thinks no evil; rejoices not in iniquity, but rejoices in the truth; bears all things, believes all things, hopes all things, endures all things. Charity never fails; but whether there be prophecies, they shall fail; whether there be tongues, they shall cease; whether there be knowledge, it shall vanish away. For we know in part, and we prophesy in part. But when that which is perfect is come, then that which is in part shall be done away. When I was a child, I spoke as a child, I understood as a child, I thought as a child; but when I became a man, I put away childish things. For now we see through a glass, darkly; but then face to face: now I know in part; but then shall I know even as also I am known. And now abides faith, hope, charity, these three; but the greatest of these is charity.'

# BOUDICA (BOADICEA, BUDDUG)
## d.60 or 61 CE

*'On this spot we must either conquer, or die with glory'*
60 or 61 CE

**Queen Boudica ruled the Iceni tribe** of East Anglia alongside her husband King Prasutagus, who made Emperor Nero co-heir with his daughters to keep his kingdom and household free from attack. On the king's death, the Roman governor of Britain Suetonius Paulinus plundered Iceni lands, whipping Boudica and raping her daughters. This provoked the Iceni, Trinobantes and other tribes to rebel, and they captured Colchester, London and St Albans. Suetonius assembled an army of 10,000 regulars and auxiliaries. Boudica and her daughters paraded in her chariot in front of all her tribes before the final battle, exhorting them to be brave. Roman accounts vary as to whether she died on the battlefield or took poison shortly after. Nero had been close to withdrawing his legions from Britain, and replaced Suetonius with a more conciliatory governor. Women were regarded as equals in Celtic law, as is demonstrated in her speech to her warriors.

'This is not the first time that the Britons have been led to battle by a woman. But now she did not come to boast the pride of a long line of ancestry, nor even to recover her kingdom and the plundered wealth of her family. She took the field, like the meanest among them, to assert the cause of public liberty, and to seek revenge for her body seamed with ignominious stripes, and her two daughters infamously ravished. From the pride and arrogance of the Romans nothing is sacred; all are subject to violation; the old endure the scourge, and the virgins are deflowered. But the vindictive gods are now at hand. A Roman legion dared to face the warlike Britons: with their lives they paid for their rashness; those who survived the carnage of that day, lie poorly hid behind their entrenchment, meditating nothing but how to save themselves by an ignominious flight. From the din of preparation, and the shouts of the British army, the Romans, even now, shrink back with terror. What will be their case when the assault begins? Look round, and view your numbers. Behold the proud display of warlike spirits, and consider the motives for which we draw the avenging sword. On this spot we must either conquer, or die with glory. There is no alternative. Though a woman, my resolution is fixed: the men, if they please, may survive with infamy, and live in bondage.'

# CALGACUS
*fl.* 50 – 90 CE

## 'They make a solitude and call it peace'
83 or 84 CE

 **This is the origin of the phrase:** *'they make a desert and call it peace'.* Tacitus records a battle at Mons Graupius in northern Scotland, where a confederacy of Scottish tribes were led against Agricola by the chieftain Calgacus, said to be *'among the many leaders, one superior to the rest in valour and in birth.'* There are no records of Calgacus's death or capture in the defeat. This is part of his speech to his army:

'Whenever I consider the origin of this war and the necessities of our position, I have a sure confidence that this day, and this union of yours, will be the beginning of freedom to the whole of Britain. To all of us slavery is a thing unknown; there are no lands beyond us, and even the sea is not safe, menaced as we are by a Roman fleet. And thus in war and battle, in which the brave find glory, even the coward will find safety. Former contests, in which, with varying fortune, the Romans were resisted, still left in us a last hope of succour, inasmuch as being the most renowned nation of Britain, dwelling in the very heart of the country, and out of sight of the shores of the conquered, we could keep even our eyes unpolluted by the contagion of slavery. To us who dwell on the uttermost confines of the earth and of freedom, this remote sanctuary of Britain's glory has up to this time been a defence. Now, however, the furthest limits of Britain are thrown open, and the unknown always passes for the marvellous. But there are no tribes beyond us, nothing indeed but waves and rocks, and the yet more terrible Romans, from whose oppression escape is vainly sought by obedience and submission. Robbers of the world, having by their universal plunder exhausted the land, they rifle the deep. If the enemy be rich, they are rapacious; if he be poor, they lust for dominion; neither the east nor the west has been able to satisfy them. Alone among men they covet with equal eagerness poverty and riches. To robbery, slaughter, plunder, they give the lying name of empire; they make a solitude and call it peace.

...Since then you cannot hope for quarter, take courage, I beseech you, whether it be safety or renown that you hold most precious. Under a woman's leadership the Brigantes were able to burn a colony, to storm a camp, and had not success ended in supineness, might have thrown off the yoke. Let us, then, a fresh and unconquered people, never likely to abuse our freedom, show forthwith at the very first onset what heroes Caledonia has in reserve. Do you suppose that the Romans will be as brave in war as they are licentious in peace? To our strifes and discords they owe their fame, and they turn the errors of an enemy to the renown of their own army, an army which, composed as it is of every variety of nations, is held together by success and will be broken up by disaster. These Gauls and Germans, and, I blush to say, these numerous Britons, who, though they lend their lives to support a stranger's rule, have been its enemies longer than its subjects, you cannot imagine to be bound by fidelity and affection. Fear and terror there certainly are, feeble bonds of attachment; remove them, and those who have ceased to fear will begin to hate. All the incentives to victory are on our side. The Romans have no wives to kindle their courage; no parents to taunt them with flight; many have either no country or one far away. Few in number, dismayed by their ignorance, looking around upon a sky, a sea, and forests which are all unfamiliar to them; hemmed in, as it were, and enmeshed, the gods have delivered them into our hands. Be not frightened by idle display, by the glitter of gold and of silver, which can neither protect nor wound. In the very ranks of the enemy we shall find our own forces. Britons will acknowledge their own cause; Gauls will remember past freedom; the other Germans will abandon them, as but lately did the Usipii. Behind them there is nothing to dread. The forts are ungarrisoned; the colonies in the hands of aged men; what with disloyal subjects and oppressive rulers, the towns are ill-affected and rife with discord. On the one side you have a general and an army; on the other, tribute, the mines, and all the other penalties of an enslaved people. Whether you endure these for ever, or instantly avenge them, this field is to decide. Think, therefore, as you advance to battle, at once of your ancestors and of your posterity.'

# GNAEUS JULIUS AGRICOLA
## 13 June 40 – 23 August 93 CE

*'Death with honour is preferable to life with ignominy'*
83 or 84 CE

**Agricola was a military tribune** in Britain from
58–62 CE, then served in Asia until 68 CE when he supported
Vespasian in the civil war in Rome known as 'the Year of the Four
Emperors'. Vespasian became emperor after Nero (committed
suicide), Galba (murdered) and Otho (suicide). As governor of
Britannia from 77 CE, Agricola was responsible for most of the
conquest of Britain, finally pacifying Wales before moving in
force into Scotland. The speech to his troops was delivered on
the eve of the battle of Mons Graupius in northern Scotland,
facing Calgacus and the Caledonian confederation of tribes.
Agricola's son-in-law Tacitus recorded that, '*While Agricola was yet speaking, the ardour
of the soldiers declared itself; and as soon as he had finished, they burst forth into cheerful
acclamations, and instantly flew to arms. Thus eager and impetuous, he formed them so
that the centre was occupied by the auxiliary infantry, in number 8,000 and 3,000 horse
were spread in the wings.*' Agricola used his auxiliaries in the front line, keeping the
legions in reserve, and relied on close-quarters fighting to render the Caledonians'
slashing, unpointed swords ineffective. The Caledonians were routed, but two-thirds
of their army managed to escape and hide in what Tacitus called the '*trackless wilds*'.
Tacitus writes:

> 'They received his *[Calgacus's]* speech with enthusiasm, and as is usual
> among barbarians, with songs, shouts and discordant cries. And now
> was seen the assembling of troops and the gleam of arms, as the boldest
> warriors stepped to the front. As the line was forming, Agricola, who,
> though his troops were in high spirits and could scarcely be kept within
> the entrenchments, still thought it right to encourage them, spoke as
> follows – It is now the eighth year, my fellow soldiers, in which, under
> the high auspices of the Roman empire, by your valour and perseverance
> you have been conquering Britain. In so many expeditions, in so many
> battles, whether you have been required to exert your courage against
> the enemy, or your patient labours against the very nature of the country,
> neither have I ever been dissatisfied with my soldiers, nor you with
> your general. In this mutual confidence, we have proceeded beyond the
> limits of former commanders and former armies; and are now become

acquainted with the extremity of the island, not by uncertain rumour, but by actual possession with our arms and encampments. Britain is discovered and subdued. How often, on a march, when embarrassed with mountains, bogs, and rivers, have I heard the bravest among you exclaim, "When shall we descry the enemy? When shall we be led to the field of battle?" At length they are unharboured from their retreats; your wishes and your valour have now free scope, and every circumstance is equally propitious to the victor, and ruinous to the vanquished. For, the greater our glory in having marched over vast tracts of land, penetrated forests, and crossed arms of the sea, while advancing towards the foe, the greater will be our danger and difficulty if we should attempt a retreat. We are inferior to our enemies in knowledge of the country, and less able to command supplies of provision; but we have arms in our hands, and in these we have everything. For myself, it has long been my principle, that a retiring general or army is never safe. Not only, then, are we to reflect that death with honour is preferable to life with ignominy, but to remember that security and glory are seated in the same place. Even to fall in this most extreme verge of earth and of nature can not be thought an inglorious fate.

If unknown nations or untried troops were drawn up against you, I would exhort you from the example of other armies. At present, recollect your own honours, question your own eyes. These are they who, the last year, attacking by surprise a single legion in the obscurity of the night, were put to flight by a shout – the greatest fugitives of all the Britons, and, therefore, the longest survivors. As in penetrating woods and thickets the fiercest animals boldly rush on the hunters, while the weak and timorous fly at their very noise; so the bravest of the Britons have long since fallen. The remaining number consists solely of the cowardly and spiritless, whom you see at length within your reach, not because they have stood their ground, but because they are overtaken. Torpid with fear, their bodies are fixed and chained down in yonder field, which to you will speedily be the scene of a glorious and memorable victory. Here bring your toils and services to a conclusion; close a struggle of fifty years with one great day; and convince your countrymen, that to the army ought not to be imputed either the protraction of the war or the causes of rebellion.'

# THE VENERABLE BEDE
## c.672 – 26 May 735 CE

*The Torments of Hell*
c.720 CE

**This Anglo-Saxon monk** is best known as the author of the *Ecclesiastical History of the English People*, and he left a considerable collection of sermons, many of them allegorical. He is known as 'the Father of English History'. Bede was sent to a monastery aged seven, and from adulthood spent his life writing about the scriptures. Bede's reputation spread not only across England but throughout Western Europe and to Rome. He refused all attempts to advance him or bestow honours on him, and gave instruction to hundreds of monks in St Peter's monastery at Jarrow in Northumbria. Bede also wrote on music and astronomical chronology, calculating the Creation to have occurred in 3952 BCE. Absolutely orthodox in his writings, he vehemently opposed the older Celtic Christian church for its lack of allegiance to Rome. In 1899 Bede was made a Doctor of the Church by Pope Leo XIII, the only native of Britain to be granted this appellation.

'The Sunday is a chosen day, in which the angels rejoice. We must ask who was the first to request that souls might (on Sunday) have rest in hell; and the answer is that Paul the Apostle and Michael the Archangel besought the Lord when they came back from hell; for it was the Lord's will that Paul should see the punishments of that place. He beheld trees all on fire, and sinners tormented on those trees; and some were hung by the feet, some by the hands, some by the hair, some by the neck, some by the tongue, and some by the arm. And again, he saw a furnace of fire burning with seven flames, and many were punished in it; and there were seven plagues round about this furnace; the first, snow; the second, ice; the third, fire; the fourth, blood; the fifth, serpents; the sixth, lightning; the seventh, stench; and in that furnace itself were the souls of the sinners who repented not in this life. There they are tormented, and every one receiveth according to his works; some weep, some howl, some groan; some burn and desire to have rest, but find it not, because souls can never die. Truly we ought to fear that place in which is everlasting dolour *[sadness]*, in which is groaning, in which is sadness without joy, in which are abundance of tears on account of the tortures of souls; in which a fiery wheel is turned a thousand times a day by an evil angel, and at each turn a thousand souls are burnt upon it. After this he beheld a horrible river, in which were many diabolic beasts, like fishes in the midst of the sea, which devour the souls of sinners; and over that river there is a bridge, across which righteous souls pass without dread, while the souls of sinners suffer each one according to its merits.

There Paul beheld many souls of sinners plunged, some to the knees, some to the loins, some to the mouth, some to the eyebrows; and every day and eternally they are tormented. And Paul wept, and asked who they were that were therein plunged to the knees. And the angel said, "These are detractors and evil speakers; and those up to the loins are fornicators and adulterers, who returned not to repentance; and those to the mouth are they who went to Church, but they heard not the word of God; and those to the eyebrows are they who rejoiced in the wickedness of their neighbour." And after this, he saw between heaven and earth the soul of a sinner, howling betwixt seven devils, that had on that day departed from the body. And the angels cried out against it and said, "Woe to thee, wretched soul! What hast thou done upon earth? Thou hast despised the commandments of God, and hast done no good works; and therefore thou shalt be cast into outer darkness, where shall be weeping and gnashing of teeth." And after this, in one moment, angels carried a soul from its body to heaven; and Paul heard the voice of a thousand angels rejoicing over it, and saying, O most happy and blessed soul! Rejoice to-day, because thou hast done the will of God. And they set it in the presence of God...And the angel said, "Whoso keepeth the Sunday shall have his part with the angels of God." And Paul demanded of the angel, how many kinds of punishment there were in hell. And the angel said, there are a hundred and forty-four thousand, and if there were a hundred eloquent men, each having four iron tongues, that spoke from the beginning of the world, they could not reckon up the torments of hell. But let us, beloved brethren, hearing of these so great torments, be converted to our Lord that we may be able to reign with the angels.'

# WILLIAM THE CONQUEROR, KING WILLIAM I OF ENGLAND
## c.1028 – 9 September 1087

*'If you will not contend for glory, you must fight for life'*
14 October 1066

**At dawn of day**, the invading Norman army of 'William the Bastard' was drawn out in battle array at Hastings, facing King Harold's Saxon army. William stood on a small eminence in front of his army and shouted to his men that there was no escape if they lost the battle. He then privately told his officers that by nightfall he would either be the dead duke of Normandy or the living king of England.

'It is not only to acquire a kingdom that I brought you hither, O gallant Normans, the first of men, the most renowned for victory over thrice your numbers, far over the deep sea. No! for, while your devotion to my cause deserves my warmest gratitude, it is to punish the English for the murders and misdeeds committed by them. Did they not slay in cold blood the young prince Alfred, the brother of their deceased king? Did they not, by treason, rise and massacre the Danes throughout the breadth of the land, even at public festivals to which they invited their victims; and does not the blood of your ancestors cry for vengeance from the ground? There, before you, stand the malefactors awaiting their sentence; such crimes deserve death; and it is for you to execute it at the point of the sword. By victory, O Normans! You will obtain vengeance, fortune, spoil; yea, spoil beyond your hopes: by defeat certain death; for no bravery nor conduct of mine can save you from that ignominious fate; there are no ships, and nothing is left but to assure yourselves of the protection of Heaven, and in that to confide and conquer. If I become king of England, you will be the owners of the land. Before you is the son of that Godwin, who was charged with the murder of my unhappy cousin. You only can avenge me. Oh, remember the glorious actions of our ancestors, the conquest of Sicily, your own exploits against Henry of France, and his greatest allies; and then think of all the treasures which this country will afford you. You are in a hostile country, unknown to you, and must make it yours; for before you is the sword, the vast ocean behind, and no place of retreat; so that, if you will not contend for glory, you must fight for life.'

# ST ANSELM of CANTERBURY
## c.1032 or 1033 – 21 April 1109

### *The Sea of Life*
#### c.1090

**The profoundest theologian of his day** was born in Piedmont in Italy, travelling to England in 1093 and becoming archbishop of Canterbury. Anselm was banished by William Rufus over conflict between royal and ecclesiastical prerogative, returned during the reign of Henry I, but was exiled again. His translator, Neale, calls him the last of the great fathers except for St Bernard, and adds that *'he probably possessed the greatest genius of all except St Augustine'*. This sermon is an example of the medieval practice of interpreting all Christian scripture as metaphor and parable. Described as the founder of scholasticism, Anselm used ontological argument (using intuition and reason alone) to prove the existence of God, and is regarded as the first scholastic philosopher of Christian theology.

'...You love God; you walk upon the sea; the swellings of this world are under your feet. You love the world; it swallows you up; its wish is to devour, not to bear up, its lovers. But when your heart fluctuates with the desire of sin, call on the divinity of Christ, that you may conquer that desire. You think that the wind is then contrary when the adversity of this world rises against you, and not also when its prosperity fawns upon you. For when wars, when tumults, when famine, when pestilence comes, when any private calamity happens even to individual men, then the wind is thought adverse, and then it is held right to call upon God; but when the world smiles with temporal felicity, then, forsooth, the wind is not contrary. Do not, by such tokens as these, judge of the tranquillity of the time; but judge of it by your own temptations. See if you are tranquil within yourself; see if no internal tempest is overwhelming you. It is a proof of great virtue to struggle with happiness, so that it shall not seduce, corrupt, subvert. Learn to trample on this world; remember to trust in Christ. And if your foot be moved, – if you totter, – if there be some temptations that you cannot overcome, – if you begin to sink, cry out to Jesus, Lord, save me. In Peter, therefore, the common condition of all of us is to be considered; so that, if the wind of temptation endeavours to upset us in any matter, or its billows to swallow us up, we may cry to Christ. He shall stretch forth his hand, and preserve us from the deep...'

# ST BERNARD OF CLAIRVAUX
## 1090 – 20 August 1153

### Why another Crusade?
#### 31 March 1145

 **The builder of the Cistercian monastic order,** Bernard was abbot of Clairvaux from 1115. He refused offers of preferment, but was influential in church politics across Europe. Known as the 'Doctor of the Church', Bernard was secretary of the Council of Troyes in 1128, where he traced the outlines of the Rule of the Knights Templar, which soon became the ideal of Christian nobility and the defenders of the Holy Land. Following the Christian defeat on Christmas Eve 1144 at the Siege of Edessa, north of Jerusalem, Pope Eugenius III commissioned Bernard to preach the Second Crusade (1146–49), granting indulgences to those who took up the cross. The pope feared that Jerusalem and other crusader states were also threatened by the Seljuk Turks. There was at first no enthusiasm for the crusade as there had been in 1095. Thus Bernard focused in his speech upon crusaders gaining absolution for sin and attaining grace. On 31 March, with King Louis VII of France present, Bernard preached to an enormous crowd in a field at Vézelay. When he finished, the crowd rushed to enlist en masse, and the organizers supposedly ran out of cloth to make crosses for the volunteers to 'take the cross'. Unlike the First Crusade, the new venture attracted the support of royalty as well as of nobles and the common people. Bernard wrote to the pope: '*Cities and castles are now empty. There is not left one man to seven women, and everywhere there are widows to still living husbands.*' Bernard preached throughout Germany, France and Italy, and miracles were reported that would ensure the success of the Second Crusade. However, it was a fiasco, caused by poor discipline and misconduct, and the last years of Bernard's life were saddened because responsibility for the failure was thrown upon him. Edessa was never recovered from the forces of Islam. It is interesting to read how the language of religious intolerance has not been softened, and we must remember that in Islamic history, Christianity has always been perceived as an aggressive religion.

'You can not but know that we live in a period of chastisement and ruin; the enemy of mankind has caused the breath of corruption to fly over all regions; we behold nothing but unpunished wickedness. The laws of men or the laws of religion have no longer sufficient power to check depravity of manners and the triumph of the wicked. The demon of heresy has taken possession of the chair of truth, and God has sent forth His malediction upon His sanctuary. Oh, ye who listen to me, hasten then to appease the anger of Heaven, but no longer implore His goodness by vain complaints; clothe not yourselves in sackcloth, but cover yourselves with your impenetrable bucklers; the din of arms, the dangers, the labours, the fatigues of war are the penances that God now imposes upon you. Hasten then to expiate your sins by victories over the infidels, and let the deliverance of holy places be the reward of your repentance. If it were announced to you that the enemy had invaded your cities, your castles, your lands; had ravished your wives and your daughters, and profaned your temples – which among you would not fly to arms? Well, then, all these calamities, and calamities still greater, have fallen upon your brethren, upon the family of Jesus Christ, which is yours. Why do you hesitate to repair so many evils – to revenge so many outrages? Will you allow the infidels to contemplate in peace the ravages they have committed on Christian people? Remember that their triumph will be a subject for grief to all ages and an eternal opprobrium upon the generation that has endured it. Yes, the living God has charged me to announce to you that He will punish them who shall not have defended Him against His enemies.

Fly then to arms; let a holy rage animate you in the fight, and let the Christian world resound with these words of the prophet, "Cursed be he who does not stain his sword with blood!" If the Lord calls you to the defence of His heritage think not that His hand has lost its power. Could He not send twelve legions of angels or breathe one word and all His enemies would crumble away into dust? But God has considered the sons of men, to open for them the road to His mercy. His goodness has caused to dawn for you a day of safety by calling on you to avenge His glory and His name. Christian warriors, He who gave His life for you, today demands yours in return. These are combats worthy of you, combats in which it is glorious to conquer and advantageous to die. Illustrious knights, generous defenders of the Cross, remember the example of your fathers who conquered Jerusalem, and whose names are inscribed in Heaven; abandon then the things that perish, to gather unfading palms, and conquer a Kingdom which has no end.'

# ST FRANCIS OF ASSISI (GIOVANNI FRANCESCO DI BERNARDONE)
## 1181/82 – 3 October 1226

### *For the Birds*
#### c.1211

**The sermon is taken from the** 13th-century *Fioretti di San Francesco d'Assisi (Little Flowers of Francis of Assisi)*, a collection of legends about the saint. It is believed St Francis preached from on top of a large stone that still rests inside the church of San Francesco in Bevagna, and the roadside shrine of Pian d'Arca a short distance north of the village of Cantalupo di Bevagna commemorates *'the Miracle of the Birds'*. Living in poverty, he founded the Franciscan Order of Friars Minor, and is the patron saint of Italy, the environment and animals. He believed commoners should be able to pray to God in their own language, and he wrote often in the dialect of Umbria, instead of in Latin. We can date the sermon to around 1211 because on Palm Sunday that year Francis received Clara of Assisi and established with her the Order of Poor Ladies, later called Poor Clares. Francis, Clara and his followers were walking through the Spoleto Valley near his birthplace of Bevagna, when Francis spotted a great number of birds of all varieties. His speech shows how Francis's love extended to all the animals, birds and plants in creation, and how the variety of life inspired and moved him.

'Brother birds', he said to them then, 'you ought to praise and love your Creator very much. He has given you feathers for clothing, wings for flying, and all that is needful for you. He has made you the noblest of his creatures; he permits you to live in the pure air; you have neither to sow nor to reap, and yet he takes care of you, watches over you and guides you.' Then the birds began to arch their necks, to spread out their wings, to open their beaks, to look at him, as if to thank him, while he went up and down in their midst stroking them with the border of his tunic, sending them away at last with his blessing. In this same evangelizing tour, passing through Alviano, he spoke a few exhortations to the people, but the swallows so filled the air with their chirping that he could not make himself heard. 'It is my turn to speak', he said to them; 'little sister swallows, hearken to the word of God; keep silent and be very quiet until I have finished.'

# ST ALBERTUS MAGNUS (ALBERT OF COLOGNE)
### c.1205 – 15 November 1280

## *The Meaning of Crucifixion*
### c.1250

**The Dominican friar and bishop** taught St Thomas Aquinas, and was a leading orator. In 1260 he was made bishop of Regensburg, but after three years resigned the bishopric and returned to work in the ranks of the clergy, teaching at Cologne. More of a philosopher than a theologian, he strongly argued for the peaceful coexistence of science and religion, writing: '*Natural science does not consist in ratifying what others have said, but in seeking the causes of phenomena.*' A renowned scholar with encyclopedic knowledge of all sciences, Albertus became the most well-read author of his era. Most modern knowledge of Aristotle was preserved and presented by Albertus, and the following sermon shows the power of his belief.

 '...It was surrounded by the thick wreath of thorns even to the tender brain. Whence in the Prophet, – the people hath surrounded me with the thorns of sin. And why was this, save that thine own head might not suffer – thine own conscience might not be wounded? His eyes grew dark in death; and those lights, which give light to the world, were for a time extinguished. And when they were clouded, there was darkness over all the earth, and with them the two great lights of the firmament were moved, to the end that thine eyes might be turned away, lest they should behold vanity; or, if they chance to behold it, might for his sake condemn it. Those ears, which in heaven unceasingly hear "Holy, Holy, Holy," vouchsafed on earth to be filled with: "Thou hast a devil, – Crucify him, Crucify him!" to the intent that thine ears might not be deaf to the cry of the poor, nor, open to idle tales, should readily receive the poison of detraction or of adulation. That fair face of him that was fairer than the children of men, yea, than thousands of angels, was bedaubed with spitting, afflicted with blows, given up to mockery, to the end that thy face might be enlightened, and, being enlightened, might be strengthened, so that it might be said of thee, "His countenance is no more changed." That mouth, which teaches angels and instructs men "which spoke and it was done," was fed with gall and vinegar, that thy mouth might speak the truth, and might be opened to the praise of the Lord; and it was silent, lest thou should lightly lend thy tongue to the expression of anger.'

# JOHN WYCLIFFE
### c.1328 – 31 December 1384

*'And thus speaketh holy writ and no man can disprove it'*
*c.1370*

**This theologian and dissenter** was the first to translate the Bible from Latin into English in 1382, and his followers, the Lollards, preached anti-clerical reforms looking instead to the Scriptures for their religious authority. Wycliffe has been called *'the Morning Star of the Reformation'*, and his preaching and his oratory made him popular with the masses and despised by the higher orders of the clergy.

'*Nisi granum frumenti* – JOHN xii:24 – In this short Gospel be doubts, both of conscience and of other. First philosophers doubt, whether [the] seed loseth his form when it is made a new thing, as the Gospel speaketh here; and some men think nay, for since the same quantity or quality or virtue that was first in seed, liveth after in the fruit, as a child is often like to his father or to his mother, or else to his old father, after that the virtue lasteth, – and since all these be accidents, that may not dwell without subject, – it seemeth that the same body is first seed and after fruit, and thus it may oft change from seed to fruit and again. Here many cleped [called] philosophers glaver [talk] diversely; but in this matter God's law speaketh thus, as did old clerks, that the substance of a body is before that it be seed, and now fruit and now seed, and now quick and now dead. And thus many forms must be together in one thing, and especially when the parts of that thing be meddled together; and thus the substance of a body is now of one kind and now of another. And so both these accidents, quality and quantity, must dwell in the same substance, all if it be changed in kinds, and thus this same thing that is now a wheat corn shall be dead and turn to grass, and after to many corns. But variance in words in this matter falleth to clerks, and showing of equivocation, the which is more ready in Latin; but it is enough to us to put, that the same substance is now quick and now dead, and now seed and now fruit; and so that substance that is now a wheat corn must needs die before that it is made grass, and since be made an whole ear. And thus speaketh holy writ and no man can disprove it. Error of friars in this matter is not here to rehearse, for it is enough to tell how they err in belief.'

# JOHN BALL
## c.1338 – 15 July 1381

*'When Adam delved and Eve span...' (Cast off the Yoke of Bondage)*
12 June 1381

**A radical Lollard priest**, Ball sermonized using the doctrines of John Wycliffe, travelling across the country as a 'hedge priest' without an established parish. His insistence on social equality meant that he was thrown into prison three times and excommunicated. It was forbidden to hear him preach, but nevertheless his popularity grew. There was widespread discontent over capped wages and poll taxes after the Black Death, and Ball was in prison at Maidstone Castle, Kent when the Peasants' Revolt began, being released by the rebels on 7 June. Insurgents from Essex assembled at Mile End, London, while Ball preached to the Kentish rebels at Blackheath in an open-air sermon. He argued that it was unfair that gentlemen did no work and lived off the peasants' slavery, whereas all men were originally created equal in The Bible. The rebels dispersed on 15 June, after their leader Wat Tyler had been killed, and after receiving false promises from King Richard II. Ball and another leader, Jack Straw, were taken prisoner and hung, drawn and quartered in the presence of Richard II, Ball's head being displayed on London Bridge.

'When Adam delved [dug] and Eve span [spun], Who was then the gentleman? From the beginning all men by nature were created alike, and our bondage or servitude came in by the unjust oppression of naughty men. For if God would have had any bondsmen from the beginning, he would have appointed who would have had any bond and who free. And therefore I exhort you to consider that now the time is come, appointed to us by God, in which ye may, if ye will, cast off the yoke of bondage, and recover liberty. I counsel you therefore well to bethink yourselves, and to take good hearts unto you, that after the manner of a good husband that tilleth his ground, and riddeth out thereof such evil weeds as choke and destroy the good corn, you may destroy first the great lords of the realm, and after, the judges and lawyers, and questmongers, and all other who have undertaken to be against the commons. For so shall you procure peace and surety to yourselves in time to come; and by dispatching out of the way the great men, there shall be an equality in liberty, and no difference in degrees of nobility; but a like dignity and equal authority in all things brought in among you.'

# MARTIN LUTHER
## 10 November 1483 – 18 February 1546

*'I neither can nor will retract anything'*
19 April 1520

**Luther became an Augustinian monk** at Erfurt, Germany in 1505 and published, at Wittenberg in 1517, his *Ninety-Five Theses* against indulgences. Indulgences were sold by the church as a method of freeing the purchaser from God's punishment of sin. Luther refused to retract this heresy despite a letter from Pope Leo X in 1520, and the Holy Roman Emperor summoned him to a general assembly, the Diet of Worms, in 1521. Luther obtained a safe conduct from the Elector of Saxony for the meeting before agreeing to attend. Luther taught that salvation is received by faith in Jesus, and that the Bible is the only source of divinely revealed knowledge, not the Roman Church. On the second day at Worms, Luther answered his accusers *'I am bound by the Scriptures I have quoted and my conscience is captive to the Word of God. I cannot and will not recant anything, since it is neither safe nor right to go against conscience. May God help me. Amen.'*

Over the next five days, private conferences were held to determine Luther's fate. The emperor presented the final draft of the Diet of Worms on 25 May 1521, declaring Luther an outlaw, banning his literature, and requiring his arrest: *'We want him to be apprehended and punished as a notorious heretic.'* It also made it a crime for anyone in Germany to give Luther food or shelter. It permitted anyone to kill Luther without legal consequence. Luther's disappearance during his return trip was planned, as the Elector of Saxony had him intercepted on his way home by masked horsemen and escorted to the security of Wartburg Castle. Excommunicated, Luther managed to return to Wittenberg, and set in motion the Protestant movement across Europe. His refusal at the Diet of Worms to bow to the demands of the pope and emperor led to a permanent schism in the Christian church.

'Most Serene Emperor, and you illustrious princes and gracious lords: –
I this day appear before you in all humility, according to your command,
and I implore your majesty and your august highnesses, by the mercies
of God, to listen with favour to the defence of a cause which I am well
assured is just and right. I ask pardon, if by reason of my ignorance, I am
wanting in the manners that befit a court; for I have not been brought
up in king's palaces, but in the seclusion of a cloister. Two questions
were yesterday put to me by his imperial majesty; the first, whether I

was the author of the books whose titles were read; the second, whether I wished to revoke or defend the doctrine I have taught. I answered the first, and I adhere to that answer. As to the second, I have composed writings on very different subjects. In some I have discussed Faith and Good Works, in a spirit at once so pure, clear, and Christian, that even my adversaries themselves, far from finding anything to censure, confess that these writings are profitable, and deserve to be perused by devout persons. The pope's bull, violent as it is, acknowledges this. What, then, should I be doing if I were now to retract these writings? Wretched man! I alone, of all men living, should be abandoning truths approved by the unanimous voice of friends and enemies, and opposing doctrines that the whole world glories in confessing! I have composed, secondly, certain works against popery, wherein I have attacked such as by false doctrines, irregular lives, and scandalous examples, afflict the Christian world, and ruin the bodies and souls of men. And is not this confirmed by the grief of all who fear God?

...In speaking thus, I do not suppose that such noble princes have need of my poor judgement; but I wish to acquit myself of a duty that Germany has a right to expect from her children. And so commending myself to your august majesty, and your most serene highnesses, I beseech you in all humility, not to permit the hatred of my enemies to rain upon me an indignation I have not deserved. Since your most serene majesty and your high mightinesses require of me a simple, clear and direct answer, I will give one, and it is this: I can not submit my faith either to the pope or to the council, because it is as clear as noonday that they have fallen into error and even into glaring inconsistency with themselves. If, then, I am not convinced by proof from Holy Scripture, or by cogent reasons, if I am not satisfied by the very text I have cited, and if my judgement is not in this way brought into subjection to God's word, I neither can nor will retract anything; for it can not be right for a Christian to speak against his country. I stand here and can say no more. God help me. Amen.'

# JOHN CALVIN (JEAN CAUVIN)
## 10 July 1509 – 27 May 1564

*Enduring Persecution for Christ*
*c.1540s*

**This is probably the most famous sermon** of the Frenchman who has been called the greatest of Protestant commentators and theologians. He is said to have inspired the Puritan exodus from the Catholic Church, often preaching every day for weeks in succession. He argued that *'True preaching must not be dead, but living and effective. No parade of rhetoric, but the Spirit of God must resound in the voice in order to operate with power.'* For advocating church reform Calvin was forced to flee from Paris, and he was in Basle in Switzerland in 1534. In 1536, his greatest work, the *Institutes of the Christian Religion* was published. In 1540, he was a pastor at Strasbourg, and in 1541 went to Geneva, where he became practically the ruler of the city. Calvin exercised his religious beliefs passionately, expounding the doctrine of predestination and the absolute sovereignty of God in the salvation of the soul from eternal damnation. Calvin was directly responsible for the burning at the stake of the remarkable scientist and theologian Michael Servetus. His preachings and writings are still followed by Presbyterian and Reformed churches around the world.

'...If He permits tyrants to slay us, it is not because our life is not dear to Him, and held in a hundred times greater honour than it deserves. Such being the case, having declared by the mouth of David (*Psalm* cxvi., 13), that the death of the saints is precious in His sight, He says also by the mouth of Isaiah (xxvi., 21), that the earth will discover the blood which seems to be concealed. Let the enemies of the gospel, then, be as prodigal as they will of the blood of martyrs, they shall have to render a fearful account of it even to its last drop. In the present day, they indulge in proud derision while consigning believers to the flames; and after having bathed in their blood, they are intoxicated by it to such a degree as to count all the murders which they commit mere festive sport. But if we have patience to wait, God will show in the end that it is not in vain He has taxed our life at so high a value. Meanwhile, let it not offend us that it seems to confirm the gospel, which in worth surpasses heaven and earth...'

# QUEEN ELIZABETH I OF ENGLAND
## 7 September 1533 – 24 March 1603

---

### *'I have the heart of a king, and of a king of England, too'*
#### 19 August 1588

**Philip II of Spain had decided** to put an end to privateering attacks on his ships by English sea captains by conquering and subduing England and restoring Catholic rule there. He assembled a huge fleet of warships known as the Spanish Armada and in 1588 sailed into the English Channel, intending to rendezvous with his armies in the Low Countries and ferry the troops over in order to invade England. Elizabeth's troops were awaiting the imminent invasion of the Spanish Armada at Tilbury Fort, ready for deployment where the Spanish landed. This is the speech with which Elizabeth roused her troops for the forthcoming battle. In the event, the Armada was intercepted and harried by English warships, attacked with fireships and finally forced to take flight. The invading armies never set foot on ship.

'My loving people, we have been persuaded by some, that are careful of our safety, to take heed how we commit ourselves to armed multitudes, for fear of treachery; but I assure you, I do not desire to live to distrust my faithful and loving people. Let tyrants fear; I have always so behaved myself that, under God, I have placed my chief strength and safeguard in the loyal hearts and good will of my subjects. And therefore I am come amongst you at this time, not as for my recreation or sport, but being resolved, in the midst and heat of the battle, to live or die amongst you all; to lay down, for my God, and for my kingdom, and for my people, my honour and my blood, even the dust. I know I have but the body of a weak and feeble woman; but I have the heart of a king, and of a king of England, too; and think foul scorn that Parma or Spain, or any prince of Europe, should dare to invade the borders of my realms: to which, rather than any dishonour should grow by me, I myself will take up arms; I myself will be your general, judge, and rewarder of every one of your virtues in the field. I know already, by your forwardness, that you have deserved rewards and crowns; and we do assure you, on the word of a prince, they shall be duly paid you. In the mean my lieutenant general *[the Earl of Leicester]* shall be in my stead, than whom never prince commanded a more noble and worthy subject; not doubting by your obedience to my general, by your concord in the camp, and by your valour in the field, we shall shortly have a famous victory over the enemies of my God, of my kingdom, and of my people.'

# QUEEN ELIZABETH I OF ENGLAND
## 7 September 1533 – 24 March 1603

*'My heart was never set on any worldly goods'*
30 November 1601

**In 1601, the queen had ruled for** 43 years and was over 68 years old. Earlier that year, her favourite, the young earl of Essex, had rebelled against her but he had been apprehended and executed. The following year, an observer reported that *'Her delight is to sit in the dark, and sometimes with shedding tears to bewail Essex'*. She was deeply unhappy when she summoned Parliament to meet her for a speech expected to address recent financial problems. However, the 'Virgin Queen' surprised the House by revealing that it would be her final Parliament. The following account is by the diarist, Hayward Townsend, who was among the 141 members of the Commons, including the Speaker, kneeling before Elizabeth in the Presence Chamber. Elizabeth alluded to the love and respect she had for the country, her position, and the members themselves. Also known as *'the Farewell Speech'*, it marks the end of her reign, considered the most successful and glorious in British history. Her 'golden words' were reprinted time and time again up to the 18th century, whenever England was in danger, as *'The Golden Speech of Queen Elizabeth'*. The term was first used in a version of the speech printed near the end of the Puritan interregnum with a headline beginning, *'This speech ought to be set in letters of gold'*. Within 16 months Elizabeth was dead.

'Mr Speaker, We have heard your declaration and perceive your care of our estate. I do assure you there is no prince that loves his subjects better, or whose love can countervail our love. There is no jewel, be it of never so rich a price, which I set before this jewel: I mean your love. For I do esteem it more than any treasure or riches; for that we know how to prize, but love and thanks I count invaluable. And, though God hath raised me high, yet this I count the glory of my Crown, that I have reigned with your loves. This makes me that I do not so much rejoice that God hath made me to be a Queen, as to be a Queen over so thankful a people. Therefore I have cause to wish nothing more than to content the subject and that is a duty which I owe. Neither do I desire to live longer days than I may see your prosperity and that is my only desire. And as I am that person still yet, under God, hath delivered you and so I trust by the almighty power of God that I shall be his instrument to preserve you from every peril, dishonour, shame, tyranny and oppression, partly by means of your intended helps which we take very acceptably because it manifests the largeness of your good loves and loyalties unto your sovereign. Of myself I must say this: I never was any greedy, scraping grasper, nor a strait fast-holding Prince, nor yet a waster. My heart was never set on any worldly goods. What you bestow on me, I will not hoard it up, but receive it to bestow on you again...

I know the title of a King is a glorious title, but assure yourself that the shining glory of princely authority hath not so dazzled the eyes of our understanding, but that we well know and remember that we also are to yield an account of our actions before the great judge. To be a king and wear a crown is a thing more glorious to them that see it than it is pleasant to them that bear it. For myself I was never so much enticed with the glorious name of a King or royal authority of a Queen as delighted that God hath made me his instrument to maintain his truth and glory and to defend his kingdom as I said from peril, dishonour, tyranny and oppression. There will never Queen sit in my seat with more zeal to my country, care to my subjects and that will sooner with willingness venture her life for your good and safety than myself. For it is my desire to live nor reign no longer than my life and reign shall be for your good. And though you have had, and may have, many princes more mighty and wise sitting in this seat, yet you never had nor shall have, any that will be more careful and loving. For I, oh Lord, what am I, whom practices and perils past should not fear? Or what can I do? That I should speak for any glory, God forbid. And I pray to you Mr Comptroller, Mr Secretary and you of my Council, that before these gentlemen *[assembled MPs]* go into their countries, you bring them all to kiss my hand.'

# SIR WALTER RALEIGH
## c.1552 – 29 October 1618

*'I thank my God heartily that He hath brought me
into the light to die'*
29 October 1618

**A courtier, statesman, chemist, poet**, historian, soldier, explorer, colonist and privateer, his last speech was delivered in the Old Palace Yard at Westminster. In it Raleigh defended himself against various false charges. When Raleigh's head lay on the block awaiting the axe, someone remarked that it ought to be turned to the east. Raleigh responded *'What matter how the head lie, if the heart be right?'* He had urged his executioner *'Let us dispatch. At this hour my ague comes upon me. I would not have my enemies think I quaked from fear.'* After he was allowed to see the axe that would behead him, he said *'This is a sharp Medicine, but it is a Physician for all diseases and miseries'*. Raleigh had been involved in Ireland and Virginia before serving against the Spanish Armada, exploring the River Orinoco in 1594 and commanding a squadron in the defeat of the Spanish fleet at Cadiz in 1596. A favourite of Elizabeth I, he fell out of favour with the Catholic James I on his accession. Raleigh was falsely accused of taking part in the 'Main Plot' of Protestants to remove James from the throne. Raleigh eloquently defended himself, thereby escaping the death penalty, but was still convicted of treason and sent to the Tower in 1603. Here he wrote his *History of the World* and other books. Although legally a 'dead man', he conceived his son Carew during his 13 years imprisoned in the Tower of London. Raleigh was eventually allowed out of prison to lead a second expedition to Guiana in 1616, searching the country and down the Orinoco River again for *El Dorado*. An unauthorized attack on the Spanish during this expedition, in the course of which his son Walter was killed, and for which Raleigh was not responsible, led to a show trial on his return. The previous charges of treason were renewed and his sentence reinstated on the insistence of the Spanish ambassador. Raleigh was beheaded to appease the king and the pro-Spanish faction in court. Raleigh's head was embalmed and his wife Margaret carried it with her for the remaining 29 years of her life. She wrote: *'The Lords have given me his dead body, though they have denied me his life. God hold me in my wits!'*

'I thank my God heartily that He hath brought me into the light to die, and not suffered me to die in the dark prison of the Tower, where I have suffered a great deal of adversity and a long sickness; and I thank God that my fever hath not taken me at this time, as I prayed God it might not...But this I say: For a man to call God to witness to a falsehood at any time is a grievous sin! And what shall we hope for at the Day of Judgement? But to call God to witness to a falsehood at the time of death is far more grievous and impious, and there is no hope for such a one. And what should I expect that am now going to render an account of my faith? I do, therefore, call the Lord to witness, as I hope to be saved, and as I hope to be seen in his kingdom (which will be within this quarter of an hour), that I never had any commission from the King of France, nor any treaty with the French agent, nor with any from the French King; neither knew I that there was an agent, or what he was, till I met him in my gallery at my lodging unlocked for. If I speak not truth, O Lord, let me never come into thy glory...

But in this I speak now, what have I to do with kings? I have nothing to do with them, neither do I fear them; I have now to do with God; therefore, as I hope to be saved at the last day, I never spoke dishonourably, disloyally, nor dishonestly of the King, neither to this Frenchman, nor to any other; neither had I ever, in all my life, a thought of ill against his Majesty; therefore I cannot but think it strange that this Frenchman, being so base, so mean a fellow, should be so far credited; and so much for this point. I have dealt truly, and I hope I shall be believed...And now I entreat you all to join with me in prayer, that the great God of Heaven, whom I have grievously offended, being a man full of all vanity, and having lived a sinful life, in all sinful callings, having been a soldier, a captain, a sea captain, and a courtier, which are all places of wickedness and vice; that God, I say, would forgive me, cast away my sins from me, and receive me into everlasting life. So I take my leave of you all, making my peace with God.'

# SIR JOHN ELIOT
### 11 April 1592 – 27 November 1632

*'The exchequer...is empty...the jewels pawned'*
3 June 1628

**A major English constitutional document**, the *Petition of Right* sets out specific liberties of the subject that any king would be prohibited from infringing. It was drawn up by Sir John Eliot, John Selden, Sir Edward Coke and John Pym to restore rights dating from the time of *Magna Carta*. The petition called upon the Charles I to acknowledge that he could not levy taxes without Parliament's consent, impose martial law on civilians, imprison them without due process, or quarter troops in their homes. On 27 May 1628 it was approved by both houses of Parliament, but King Charles tried to avoid assenting to it on 2 June. Eliot's speech in Parliament on 3 June infuriated Charles, but on 7 June he approved the Petition (although he had no intention of abiding by it). Nine months later Charles dissolved Parliament, determining to rule without its aid or interference. Just two days after that, the king committed Sir John Eliot and other members of Parliament to the Tower of London for words spoken during the sitting of Parliament. In his breach of privilege, and violation of the Petition of Right, Charles was assisted by specially chosen law courts. Eliot, as *'the greatest offender and ringleader'*, was sentenced to pay a punitive fine of £2000, and he died in the Tower of London, being refused release. Quarrels between any parliaments that Charles was forced to convene and the monarch emphasized the gulf between the court and the representatives of the nation. In November 1640 the Long Parliament consisted of 399 MPs who were opposed to the king, with only 94 supporting him. The English Civil War began upon 22 August 1642, and Charles I was eventually executed in 1649.

'Mr Speaker – We sit here as the great Council of the King, and in that capacity, it is our duty to take into consideration the state and affairs of the kingdom, and when there is occasion, to give a true representation of them by way of counsel and advice, with what we conceive necessary or expedient to be done...Our want of true devotion to heaven – our insincerity and doubling in religion – our want of councils – our precipitate actions – the insufficiency or unfaithfulness of our generals abroad – the ignorance or corruption of our ministers at home – the impoverishing of the sovereign – the oppression and depression of the subject – the exhausting of our treasures – the waste of our provisions

– consumption of our ships – destruction of our men – these make the advantage to our enemies, not the reputation of their arms; and if in these there be not reformation, we need no foes abroad; Time itself will ruin us…For the next, the insufficiency and unfaithfulness of our generals (that great disorder abroad), what shall I say? I wish there were not cause to mention it; and, but for the apprehension of the danger that is to come, if the like choice hereafter be not prevented, I could willingly be silent. But my duty to my sovereign, my service to this House, and the safety and honour of my country, are above all respects; and what so nearly trenches to the prejudice of these, must not, shall not be forborne…

The exchequer, you know, is empty, and the reputation thereof gone; the ancient lands are sold; the jewels pawned; the plate engaged; the debts still great; almost all charges, both ordinary and extraordinary, borne up by projects! What poverty can be greater? What necessity so great? What perfect English heart is not almost dissolved into sorrow for this truth?…For the oppression of the subject, which, as I remember, is the next particular I proposed, it needs no demonstration. The whole kingdom is a proof; and for the exhausting of our treasures, that very oppression speaks it. What waste of our provisions, what consumption of our ships, what destruction of our men there hath been; witness that expedition to Algiers – witness that with Mansfeldt – witness that to Cadiz – witness the next – witness that to Rhé – witness the last (I pray God we may never have more such witnesses) – witness, likewise, the Palatinate – witness Denmark – witness the Turks – witness the Dunkirkers – WITNESS ALL! What losses we have sustained! How we are impaired in munitions, in ships, in men! It is beyond contradiction that we were never so much weakened, nor ever had less hope how to be restored…These are the things, sir, I shall desire to have taken into consideration; that as we are the great council of the kingdom, and have the apprehension of these dangers, we may truly represent them unto the King; which I conceive we are bound to do by a triple obligation – of duty to God, of duty to his Majesty, and of duty to our country.'

# JOHN PYM
## 1584 – 8 December 1643

### *The Cry of all England*
#### 11 January 1642

**A leader of the Parliamentary cause** against Charles I, Pym had helped to draft the *Grand Remonstrance* of October 1641, a list of grievances against the king's rule. On 3 January 1642, Charles I named Pym and four other MPs as being guilty of High Treason, and went to the House of Commons to arrest them. The MPs had fled to the city, and the king left, saying '*I see all the birds are flown*'. Pym and the others returned to Parliament, and, on the day afterwards, Pym made this radical speech to the Lords and Commons, arguing that the House of Commons was prepared to act independently of the House of Lords, and that the Commons was now effectively Parliament. Parliament now no longer felt safe from the king, or the Lords, and formed its own army. Pym became leader of the Parliamentary party and the Civil War began six months later.

'...We are united in the public trust, which is derived from the commonwealth, in the common duty and obligation whereby God doth bind us to the discharge of that trust; – and the Commons' desire to impart to your lordships whatsoever information or intelligence, whatsoever encouragement or assistance, they have received from those several counties which they represent; that so likewise we may be united in the same intentions and endeavours of improving all to the service of his majesty, and the common good of the kingdom...My lords, in these four petitions you may hear the voice, or rather the cry, of all England; and you cannot wonder if the urgency, the extremity of the condition wherein we are, do produce some earnestness and vehemence of expression more than ordinary. The agony, terror, and perplexity in which the kingdom labours, are universal; all parts are affected with them; and therefore in these you may observe the groans and miserable complaints of all...Lastly, I come to the evil influences which have caused this distemper; and I shall content myself with mentioning those which are most important. 1. I shall remember the evil counsels about the king, whereof we have often complained. Diseases of the brain are most dangerous, because from thence sense and motion are derived to the whole body. The malignity of evil counsels will quickly be infused into all parts of the state. None can doubt but we have exceedingly laboured under most dangerous and mischievous counsels...And I appeal to your lordships' own consciences, whether the giving and receiving of evil counsel hath not been almost the only way to favour and advancement. 2. Divers honest and approved counsellors have been put from their planes, others so discountenanced, as that the way of favour hath been shut against them, and that of danger and destruction only open to them. 3. The great power that an interested and factious party hath in the parliament, by the continuance of the votes of the bishops and popish lords in your lordships' house; and the taking in of others, both out of the House of Commons, and otherwise, to increase their strength. 4. The fomenting and cherishing of a malignant party throughout the whole kingdom. 5. The manifold jealousies betwixt the king, his parliament, and good subjects; whereby his protection and favour hath, in a great measure, been withheld from them; and their inclination and resolution to serve and assist him, hath been very much hindered and interrupted.

...I am now come to a conclusion. I have nothing to propound to your lordships by way of request or desire from the House of Commons. I doubt not but your judgments will tell you what is to be done. Your consciences, your honours, your interests, will call upon you for the doing of it. The Commons will be glad to have your concurrence and help in saving of the kingdom; but, if they fail of it, it shall not discourage them in doing their duty. And whether the kingdom be lost or saved (I hope, through God's blessing, it will be saved!), they shall be sorry that the story of this present parliament should tell posterity that, in so great a danger and extremity, the House of Commons should be enforced to save the kingdom alone, and that the peers should have no part in the honour of the preservation of it, having so great an interest in the good success of·those endeavours in respect of their great estates and high degrees of nobility. My lords, consider what the present necessities and dangers of the commonwealth require, what the Commons have reason to expect, to what endeavours and counsels the concurrent desires of all the people do invite you! So that, applying yourselves to the preservation of the king and kingdom, I may be bold to assure you – in the name of all the Commons of England, that you shall be bravely seconded!'

# OLIVER CROMWELL
## 25 April 1599 – 3 September 1658

*'Is there a single virtue now remaining amongst you?*
*Is there one vice you do not possess?'*
20 April 1653

**In the 1630s Cromwell had a religious** revelation that convinced him that he would be guided to carry out God's purpose. An MP in 1642 when the Civil War broke out between Parliament and Charles I, he drilled a superb force of cavalry known as Ironsides. After securing a string of victories, he was the prime mover in the execution of the king in 1649, and he then defeated Prince Charles in the Second Civil War. Cromwell had helped to transform Britain into a republican Commonwealth, but was displeased when he learned that Parliament intended staying in session although it had agreed to dissolve. On 20 April he attended a sitting of Parliament and listened to one or two speeches, then stood up and harangued the members of the House of Commons. Troops cleared the chamber and took away the Speaker's mace, the symbol of Parliamentary power. A month later, Cromwell set up a short-lived Parliament of Congregationalists, before becoming Lord Protector.

'It is high time for me to put an end to your sitting in this place, which you have dishonoured by your contempt of all virtue, and defiled by your practice of every vice; ye are a factious crew, and enemies to all good government; ye are a pack of mercenary wretches, and would like Esau sell your country for a mess of pottage, and like Judas betray your God for a few pieces of money. Is there a single virtue now remaining amongst you? Is there one vice you do not possess? Ye have no more religion than my horse; gold is your God; which of you have not bartered your conscience for bribes? Is there a man amongst you that has the least care for the good of the Commonwealth? Ye sordid prostitutes, have you not defiled this sacred place, and turned the Lord's temple into a den of thieves, by your immoral principles and wicked practices? Ye are grown intolerably odious to the whole nation; you who were deputed here by the people to get grievances redressed, are yourselves gone! So! Take away that shining bauble there, and lock up the doors. In the name of God, go!'

# OLIVER CROMWELL
## 25 April 1599 – 3 September 1658

### 'Let God be judge between you and me!'
#### 4 February 1658

**In 1654, Lord Protector Cromwell** summoned the First Protectorate Parliament, but there was distrust between his generals and civilian politicians. Angry debates aimed at strengthening Parliament's powers at the expense of Cromwell's, and criticism of his leadership by republican MPs, prompted Cromwell to dissolve this Parliament at the earliest possible opportunity, in January 1655. In 1656, his major-generals desperately needed money for their armies, so Cromwell called an election for the Second Protectorate Parliament. MPs expected to be summoned to Whitehall to receive Cromwell's assent to their offer to make him king of England. However, a petition by army officers against the restoration of the monarchy was taken to Parliament on 8 May 1657. Cromwell instructed the Speaker to inform Parliament that he had no wish to become king, and on 26 June he was reaffirmed as Lord Protector. In 1658 he became furious because pay to the army in Scotland and Ireland remained in arrears, and only 15 days after his second Parliament had reassembled, he addressed both Houses. He spoke of his refusal of the kingship, and of the threat of invasion. At the conclusion of his scornful speech, he masterfully dismissed an amazed Parliament. Disillusioned, Cromwell now withdrew from public life, and died just seven months later of malarial fever. Buried in Westminster Cathedral, his body was dug up after the Restoration.

'It hath been not only your endeavour to pervert the army while you have been sitting, and to draw them to state the question about a "Commonwealth", but some of you have been listing of persons, by commission of Charles Stuart, to join with any insurrection that may be made. And what is like to come upon this, the enemy being ready to invade us, but ever-present blood and confusion? And if this be so, I do assign it to this cause: Your not assenting to what you did invite me to by your Petition and Advice, as that which might prove the settlement of the nation. And if this be the end of your sitting, and this be your carriage, I think it high time that an end be put to your sitting. And I do dissolve this Parliament! And let God be judge between you and me!'

# JACQUES-BÉNIGNE BOSSUET
## 27 September 1627 – 12 April 1704

*'Here is a man that led us through all hazards'*
early 1687

**The funeral orations of Bossuet,** a French bishop and theologian, are his most celebrated works, and he is often acknowledged to have been the first great master of such speeches. H. Morse Stephens wrote: 'Bossuet, in the simple grandeur of his language, stands alone among the orators of the golden age of French pulpit eloquence.' A courtier and politician, Bossuet became tutor to the Dauphin in 1670, and bishop of Meaux in 1681. This is his eulogy to 'the Great Condé'. Condé was Louis de Bourbon, Duc d'Enghien (1621–1686), who gained fame in the Thirty Years War as one of its greatest generals. Louis de Bourbon became prince of Condé on his father's death, and was known as le Grand Condé for his military prowess.

'Such as he had been in all combats – serene, self-possessed, and occupied without anxiety, only with what was necessary to sustain them – such also he was in that last conflict. Death appeared to him no more frightful, pale, and languishing, than amid the fires of battle and in the prospect of victory. While sobbings were heard all around him, he continued, as if another than himself were their object, to give his orders; and if he forbade them weeping, it was not because it was a distress to him, but simply a hindrance. At that time he extended his cares to the least of his domestics. With a liberality worthy of his birth and of their services, he loaded them with gifts, and honoured them still more with mementos of his regard. What was then taking place in that soul? What new light dawned upon him? What sudden ray pierced the cloud, and instantly dissipated, not only all the darkness of sense, but the very shadows, and, if I dare to say it, the sacred obscurities of faith? What then became of those splendid titles by which our pride is flattered? On the very verge of glory, and in the dawning of a light so beautiful, how rapidly vanish the phantoms of the world! How dim appears the splendour of the most glorious victory! How profoundly we despise the glory of the world, and how deeply regret that our eyes were ever dazzled by its radiance! Come, ye people, come now – or, rather, ye princes and lords, ye judges of the earth, and ye who open to man the portals of heaven; and more than all others, ye princes and princesses, nobles descended from a long line of kings, lights of France, but today in gloom, and covered with your grief as with a cloud – come and see how little remains of a birth so august, a grandeur so high, a glory so dazzling! Look around on all sides, and see all that magnificence and devotion can do to honour so great a hero: titles and inscriptions, vain signs of that which is no more; shadows which weep around a tomb, fragile images of a grief which time sweeps away with everything else; columns which appear as if they would bear to heaven the magnificent evidence of our emptiness – nothing, indeed, is wanting in all these honours but he to whom they are rendered! Weep, then, over these feeble remains of human life; weep over that mournful immortality we give to heroes.

But draw near, especially ye who run, with such ardour, the career of glory – intrepid and warrior spirits! Who was more worthy to command you, and in whom did ye find command more honourable? Mourn, then, that great captain, and weeping, say: "Here is a man that led us through all hazards, under whom were formed so many renowned captains, raised by his example, to the highest honours of war; his shadow might yet gain battles; and lo! in his silence his very name animates us, and at the same time warns us, that to find, at death, some rest from our toils, and not arrive unprepared at our eternal dwelling, we must, with an earthly king, yet serve the King of Heaven." Serve, then, that immortal and ever-merciful King, who will value a sigh, or a cup of cold water, given in His name, more than all others will value the shedding of your blood. And begin to reckon the time of your useful services from the day on which you gave yourselves to so beneficent a Master. Will not ye, too, come – ye whom he honoured by making you his friends? To whatever extent you enjoyed this confidence, come all of you, and surround this tomb. Mingle your prayers with your tears; and while admiring, in so great a prince, a friendship so excellent, an intercourse so sweet, preserve the remembrance of a hero whose goodness equalled his courage. Thus may he ever prove your cherished instructor; thus may you profit by his virtues and may his death, which you deplore, serve you at once for consolation and example.'

# JEAN BAPTISTE MASSILLON
## 24 June 1663 – 28 September 1742

### *Of a Malignant Tongue*
#### *c.1718*

**During his lifetime**, the French clergyman Massillon preached thousands of times, and wrote extensively about the art of preaching. He was compared to the great Bossuet and praised for his eloquence by Voltaire. From 1699 Massillon was the Advent preacher at the court of Versailles, where he gave sermons before King Louis XIV, and was appointed court chaplain. Louis XIV had the most magnificent court in the world, and planned for his own funeral to be equally spectacular. He instructed Massillon that upon his death he was to lie in state in a golden coffin at Notre Dame cathedral in Paris and that at his funeral service the entire cathedral was to be completely dark, lit dimly by only one candle positioned above the coffin. Thus all would be awed by the late king's presence, even in death. Massillon did exactly what the king had told him. Thousands waited in silence as they peered at the exquisite casket. As he began his funeral oration, Massillon slowly reached down, snuffed out the candle, and proclaimed in his opening sentence: '*Only God is great*', a rebuff to the late king's pretensions and to all those who called him *Louis XIV the Great*. In 1718 he preached a series of ten Lenten sermons, known as the *Petit Carême*, before King Louis XV, which became the most highly regarded model of pulpit eloquence of the 18th century. Throughout France and beyond, Massillon's oratorical skills had established him as the greatest preacher of his age. This sermon displays his remarkable command of language.

'The tongue, says the Apostle James, is a devouring fire, a world of iniquity, an unruly evil, full of deadly poison. And behold what I would have applied to the tongue of the evil-speaker, had I undertaken to give you a just and natural idea of all the enormity of this vice: I would have said that the tongue of the slanderer is a devouring fire which tarnishes whatever it touches; which exercises its fury on the good grain, equally as on the chaff; on the profane, as on the sacred; which, wherever it passes, leaves only desolation and ruin; digs even into the bowels of the earth, and fixes itself on things the most hidden; turns into vile ashes what only a moment before had appeared to us so precious and brilliant; acts with more violence and danger than ever in the time when it was apparently smothered up and almost extinct; which blackens what it can not consume, and sometimes sparkles and delights before it destroys. I would have told you that evil-speaking is an assemblage of iniquity; a secret pride, which discovers to us the mote in our brother's eye, but hides the beam which is in our own; a mean envy, which, hurt at the talents of prosperity of others, makes them the subject of its censures, and studies to dim the splendour of whatever outshines itself; a disguised hatred, which sheds, in its speeches, the hidden venom of the heart; an unworthy duplicity, which praises to the face and tears to pieces behind the back; a shameful levity, which has no command over itself or its words, and often sacrifices both fortune and comfort to the imprudence of an amusing conversation; a deliberate barbarity, which goes to pierce your absent brother; a scandal, where you become a subject of shame and sin to those who listen to you; an injustice, where you ravish from your brother what is dearest to him. I should have said that slander is a restless evil, which disturbs society, spreads dissension through cities and countries, disunites the strictest friendships; is the source of hatred and revenge; fills, wherever it enters, with disturbances and confusion; and everywhere is an enemy to peace, comfort, and Christian good-breeding. Lastly, I should have added that it is an evil full of deadly poison; whatever flows from it is infected, and poisons whatever it approaches; that even its praises are empoisoned, its applauses malicious, its silence criminal; its gestures, motions, and looks have all their venom, and spread it each in their way...

But, after all, you do not feel yourselves guilty, you say, of all these vile motives; and that it is merely through indiscretion and levity of speech, if it sometimes happens that you defame your brethren. But is it by that you can suppose yourself more innocent? Levity and indiscretion; that vice so unworthy of the gravity of a Christian, so distant from the seriousness and solidity of faith, and so often condemned in the Gospel – can it justify another vice? What matters it to the brother whom you stab whether it be done through indiscretion or malice? Does an arrow, unwittingly drawn, make a less dangerous or slighter wound than if sent on purpose? Is the deadly blow which you give to your brother slighter because it was lanced through imprudence and levity? And what signifies the innocence of the intention when the action is a crime?...'

# ANDREW HAMILTON
## c.1676 – 4 August 1741

*'The loss of liberty, to a generous mind, is worse than death'*
4 August 1735

**The 80-year-old Philadelphia lawyer** defended newspaper publisher and printer John Zenger, who had been imprisoned on a charge of seditious libel, after the *New York Weekly Journal* had attacked the government. At the New York trial, he defended Zenger 'pro bono' in the face of immense legal and governmental opposition. Hamilton argued that what was at stake was not Zenger's cause but that of American liberty. The trial established no new law with respect to seditious libel, but massively demonstrated the public's opposition to such prosecutions, and press freedom blossomed. A half-century after the Zenger trial, as members of the First Congress debated the proposed Bill of Rights, one of the Constitution's principal drafters, Gouverneur Morris, wrote of the Zenger case: *'The trial of Zenger in 1735 was the germ of American freedom, the morning star of that liberty which subsequently revolutionised America.'* Hamilton's summation to the jury still stands as an eloquent defence not just of a German-born printer, but of a free press:

'It is natural, it is a privilege, I will go farther, it is a right, which all free men claim, that they are entitled to complain when they are hurt. They have a right publicly to remonstrate against the abuses of power in the strongest terms, to put their neighbours upon their guard against the craft or open violence of men in authority, and to assert with courage the sense they have of the blessings of liberty, the value they put upon it, and their resolution at all hazards to preserve it as one of the greatest blessings heaven can bestow...The loss of liberty, to a generous mind, is worse than death. And yet we know that there have been those in all ages who for the sake of preferment, or some imaginary honour, have freely lent a helping hand to oppress, nay to destroy, their country... This is what every man who values freedom ought to consider. He should act by judgment and not by affection or self-interest; for where those prevail, no ties of either country or kindred are regarded; as upon the other hand, the man who loves his country prefers its liberty to all other considerations, well knowing that without liberty life is a misery... Power may justly be compared to a great river. While kept within its due bounds it is both beautiful and useful. But when it overflows its banks, it is then too impetuous to be stemmed; it bears down all before it, and brings destruction and desolation wherever it comes. If, then, this is the nature of power, let us at least do our duty, and like wise men who value freedom use our utmost care to support liberty, the only bulwark against lawless power, which in all ages has sacrificed to its wild lust and boundless ambition the blood of the best men that ever lived...

I hope to be pardoned, Sir, for my zeal upon this occasion...While we pay all due obedience to men in authority we ought at the same time to be upon our guard against power wherever we apprehend that it may affect ourselves or our fellow subjects...You see that I labour under the weight of many years, and am bowed down with great infirmities of body. Yet, old and weak as I am, I should think it my duty, if required, to go to the utmost part of the land where my services could be of any use in assisting to quench the flame of prosecutions upon informations, set on foot by the government to deprive a people of the right of remonstrating and complaining, too, of the arbitrary attempts of men in power...But to conclude: The question before the Court and you, Gentlemen of the jury, is not of small or private concern. It is not the cause of one poor printer, nor of New York alone, which you are now trying. No! It may in its consequence affect every free man that lives under a British government on the main of America. It is the best cause. It is the cause of liberty. And I make no doubt but your upright conduct this day will not only entitle you to the love and esteem of your fellow citizens, but every man who prefers freedom to a life of slavery will bless and honour you as men who have baffled the attempt of tyranny, and by an impartial and uncorrupt verdict have laid a noble foundation for securing to ourselves, our posterity, and our neighbours, that to which nature and the laws of our country have given us a right to liberty of both exposing and opposing arbitrary power (in these parts of the world at least) by speaking and writing truth.'

# JONATHAN EDWARDS
## 5 October 1703 – 22 March 1758

*Sinners in the Hands of an Angry God*
8 July 1741

**This preacher and missionary** to Native Americans is acknowledged as America's most important philosophical theologian, who played an important part in shaping the 'First Great Awakening', a religious revitalization movement that swept the Atlantic world, and especially the American colonies in the 1730s and 1740s. This sermon preached at Enfield, Connecticut is considered a classic of early American literature, delivered during another wave of religious revival with vivid imagery of the Hell that awaits sinners.

'And now you have an extraordinary opportunity, a day wherein Christ has thrown the door of mercy wide open, and stands in calling and crying with a loud voice to poor sinners; a day wherein many are flocking to him, and pressing into the kingdom of God. Many are daily coming from the east, west, north and south; many that were very lately in the same miserable condition that you are in, are now in a happy state, with their hearts filled with love to him who has loved them, and washed them from their sins in his own blood, and rejoicing in hope of the glory of God. How awful is it to be left behind at such a day! To see so many others feasting, while you are pining and perishing! To see so many rejoicing and singing for joy of heart, while you have cause to mourn for sorrow of heart, and howl for vexation of spirit! How can you rest one moment in such a condition? Are not your souls as precious as the souls of the people at Suffield *[a neighbouring town]*, where they are flocking from day to day to Christ? Are there not many here who have lived long in the world, and are not to this day born again?...Do you not see how generality persons of your years are passed over and left, in the present remarkable and wonderful dispensation of God's mercy? You had need to consider yourselves, and awake thoroughly out of sleep. You cannot bear the fierceness and wrath of the infinite God. And you, young men, and young women, will you neglect this precious season which you now enjoy, when so many others of your age are renouncing all youthful vanities, and flocking to Christ? You especially have now an extraordinary opportunity; but if you neglect it, it will soon be with you as with those persons who spent all the precious days of youth in sin, and are now come to such a dreadful pass in blindness and hardness. And you, children, who are unconverted, do not you know that you are going down to hell, to bear the dreadful wrath of that God, who is now angry with you every day and every night? Will you be content to be the children of the devil, when so many other children in the land are converted, and are become the holy and happy children of the King of kings?

And let everyone that is yet out of Christ, and hanging over the pit of hell, whether they be old men and women, or middle aged, or young people, or little children, now hearken to the loud calls of God's Word and providence. This acceptable year of the Lord, that is a day of such great favour to some, will doubtless be a day of as remarkable vengeance to others. Men's hearts harden, and their guilt increases apace at such a day as this, if they neglect their souls: and never was there so great danger of such persons being given up to hardness of heart, and blindness of mind. God seems now to be hastily gathering in his elect in all parts of the land; and probably the bigger part of adult persons that ever shall be saved, will be brought in now in a little time, and that it will be as it was on that great outpouring of the Spirit upon the Jews in the apostles' days, the election will obtain, and the rest will be blinded. If this should be the case with you, you will eternally curse this day, and will curse the day that ever you was born, to see such a season of the pouring out of God's Spirit; and will wish that you had died and gone to hell before you had seen it. Now undoubtedly it is, as it was in the days of John the Baptist, the axe is in an extraordinary manner laid at the root of the trees, that every tree that brings not forth good fruit, may be hewn down, and cast into the fire. Therefore let everyone that is out of Christ, now awake and fly from the wrath to come. The wrath of almighty God is now undoubtedly hanging over great part of this congregation: let everyone fly out of Sodom. Haste and escape for your lives, look not behind you, escape to the mountain, lest you be consumed *[Genesis: 19:17].*'

# KING FREDERICK II, FREDERICK THE GREAT
## 24 January 1712 – 17 August 1786

*'…shortly we have either beaten the Enemy, or we never see
one another again'*
3 December 1757

**Frederick became king of Prussia** and invaded
Silesia in 1740. After defeating Austria in 1741, 1742 and 1745,
Frederick invaded Saxony in 1756, so beginning the Seven Years'
War, and he defeated the Austrians again. He invaded Bohemia
in 1757, defeated the Austrians at Prague, but he was defeated at
Kolin and driven out of Bohemia in 1757. Also in 1757 Frederick
defeated the French at Rossbach and the Austrians at Leuthen
on 4 December, before beating the Russians at Zorndorf in 1758. This is his speech
to his generals before Leuthen. In 1772 he engineered the partition of Poland. This
united most of his disconnected realm and formed the foundations of Germany. He
was familiarly known as *'Old Fritz'* by his troops and by people of across Europe.

'…Let me apprise you, then: I intend, in spite of the Rules of Art, to attack
Prince Karl's Army, which is nearly thrice our strength, wherever I find
it. The question is not of his numbers or the strength of his position: all
this, by courage, by the skill of our methods, we will try to make good.
This step I must risk, or everything is lost. We must beat the enemy,
or perish all of us before his batteries. So I read the case; so I will act
in it. Make this my determination known to all Officers of the Army;
prepare the men for what work is now to ensue, and say that I hold
myself entitled to demand exact fulfilment of orders. For you, when I
reflect that you are Prussians, can I think that you will act unworthily?
But if there should be one or another who dreads to share all dangers
with me, he can have his Discharge this evening, and shall not suffer the
least reproach from me – Hah, I knew it, none of you would desert me! I
depend on your help, then; and on victory as sure. The Cavalry regiment
that does not on the instant, on order given, dash full plunge into the
enemy, I will, directly after the Battle, unhorse, and make it a Garrison
regiment. The Infantry battalion which, meet with what it may, shows
the least sign of hesitating, loses its colours and its sabres, and I cut the
trimmings from its uniform! Now good-night. Gentlemen: shortly we
have either beaten the Enemy, or we never see one another again.'

# GENERAL JAMES WOLFE
## 2 January 1727 – 13 September 1759

*'The impossibility of a retreat makes no difference in the situation of men resolved to conquer or die'*

13 September 1759

**The speech was said to have** been delivered on the Plains of Abraham, after his soldiers had secretly scaled cliffs at night to begin their assault to take the city of Quebec. Wolfe then drew his army up in six battalions facing Quebec and gave this stirring speech before the battle. Wolfe died in the hour of victory, knowing that the French, whose own general, Montcalm was also killed, were fleeing the battlefield. Wolfe's victory secured British control over Canada.

'I congratulate you, my brave countrymen and fellow soldiers, on the spirit and success with which you have executed this important part of our enterprise. The formidable Heights of Abraham are now surmounted; and the city of Quebec, the object of all our toils, now stands in full view before us. A perfidious enemy, who have dared to exasperate you by their cruelties, but not to oppose you on equal ground, are now constrained to face you on the open plain, without ramparts or entrenchments to shelter them. You know too well the forces which compose their army to dread their superior numbers. A few regular troops from old France, weakened by hunger and sickness, who, when fresh, were unable to withstand the British soldiers, are their general's chief dependence. Those numerous companies of Canadians, insolent, mutinous, unsteady, and ill-disciplined, have exercised his utmost skill to keep them together to this time; and, as soon as their irregular ardour is damped by one firm fire, they will instantly turn their backs...As for those savage tribes of Indians...you have experienced how little their ferocity is to be dreaded by resolute men upon fair and open ground... This day puts it into your power to terminate the fatigues of a siege which has so long employed your courage and patience. Possessed with a full confidence of the certain success which British valour must gain over such enemies, I have led you up these steep and dangerous rocks, only solicitous to show you the foe within your reach. The impossibility of a retreat makes no difference in the situation of men resolved to conquer or die; and, believe me, my friends, if your conquest could be bought with the blood of your general, he would most cheerfully resign a life which he has long devoted to his country.'

# WILLIAM PITT, 1ST EARL OF CHATHAM
## 15 November 1708 – 11 May 1778

*'The kingdom is undone!'*
20 January 1775

**William Pitt the Elder** was a Whig statesman who had led the country through the successful Seven Years' War during which Canada was captured. He was semi-retired, in his sixties when he realized the danger of the American situation. He asked Benjamin Franklin to work with him and took Franklin with him to the House of Lords to watch proceedings. Several members argued for conciliatory measures to end the war. Pitt then appealed eloquently and passionately for General Thomas Gage's troops to withdraw immediately from America, as Pitt presciently recognized that England could not win a war there. This is Pitt's unsuccessful plea to the House of Lords for a Bill of Reconciliation with the rebelling American colonies. The news that '*the Great Commoner*', as Pitt was known, was supporting them was a major boost to American morale. In April 1775 the first battles of the Revolutionary War took place at Lexington and Concord, followed on 17 June by the British loss at Bunker Hill. On 5 July 1775 Congress endorsed a proposal asking for recognition of American rights, the 'Olive Branch Petition', which was spurned by George III. On 23 August he declared the colonies to be in open rebellion.

'It is not repealing this or that act of Parliament, – it is not repealing a piece of parchment, – that can restore America to our bosom. You must repeal her fears and her resentments; and you may then hope for her love and her gratitude. But, now, insulted with an armed force posted at Boston, irritated with a hostile array before her eyes, her concessions, if you could force them, would be suspicious and insecure, – the dictates of fear, and the extortions of force! But it is more than evident that you cannot force them, principled and united as they are, to your unworthy terms of submission. Repeal, therefore, my Lords, I say! But bare repeal will not satisfy this enlightened and spirited People. You must go through the work. You must declare you have no right to tax. Then they may trust you. There is no time to be lost. Every moment is big with dangers. While I am speaking, the decisive blow may be struck, and millions involved in the consequence. The very first drop of blood shed in civil and unnatural war will make a wound which years, perhaps ages, may not heal.

When your Lordships look at the papers transmitted to us from America – when you consider their decency, firmness and wisdom, – you cannot but respect their cause, and wish to make it your own. I must declare and avow that, in the master States of the world, I know not the People nor the Senate, who, under such a complication of difficult circumstances, can stand in preference to the delegates of America assembled in General Congress at Philadelphia. For genuine sagacity, for singular moderation, for solid wisdom, manly spirit, sublime sentiment, and simplicity of language, – for everything respectable – and honourable – they stand unrivalled. I trust it is obvious to your Lordships that all attempts to impose servitude upon such men, to establish despotism over such a mighty Continental Nation, must be vain, must be fatal. This wise People speak out. They do not hold the language of slaves. They tell you what they mean. They do not ask you to repeal your laws as a favour. They claim it as a right – they demand it. They tell you they will not submit to them. And I tell you the acts must be repealed. We shall be forced ultimately to retract. Let us retract while we can, not when we must. I say we must necessarily undo these violent, oppressive, acts. They must be repealed. You WILL repeal them. I stake my reputation on it. I will consent to be taken for an idiot, if they are not finally repealed. Avoid, then, this humiliating, this disgraceful necessity. Every motive of justice and of policy, of dignity and of prudence, urges you to allay the ferment in America, by a removal of your troops from Boston, by a repeal of your acts of Parliament. On the other hand, every danger and every hazard impend, to deter you from perseverance in your present ruinous measures: foreign war hanging over your heads by a slight and brittle thread, – France and Spain watching your conduct, and waiting the maturity of our errors! To conclude, my Lords: if the Ministers thus persevere in misadvising and misleading the King, I will not say that they can alienate the affections of his subjects from the Crown, but I will affirm that they will make his Crown not worth his wearing; I will not say that the King is betrayed, but I will pronounce that the kingdom is undone!'

# JOHN WILKES
## 17 October 1725 – 26 December 1797

*'This I know: a successful resistance is a revolution, not a rebellion!'*
6 February 1775

**A journalist and radical politician**, Wilkes fought for better representation of the people, being imprisoned for criticizing King George III in 1763 and 1769. On 10 May 1768 a crowd of around 15,000 arrived outside the prison where Wilkes was being held, chanting *'Wilkes and Liberty'*, *'No Liberty, No King'*, and *'Damn the King! Damn the Government! Damn the Justices!'* Fearing that the crowd would attempt to rescue Wilkes, troops opened fire killing seven people. This so-called *Massacre of St George's Fields* led to riots all over London. In 1771 Wilkes was instrumental in obliging the government to allow printers to publish verbatim accounts of parliamentary debates. In October 1774, as Lord Mayor of London, he presented George III with a plea to change his coercive policies in America. Wilkes then made this first speech to the House of Commons opposing British measures in America, thus encouraging the rebellious colonists that there was support for them in England. Wilkes was expelled from Parliament twice, and in 1776 he introduced the first Bill for Parliamentary Reform. Throughout his Parliamentary career, he supported the American colonies in their disputes with the Crown.

'The address to the king, upon the disturbances in North America, now reported from the Committee of the whole House, appears to be unfounded, rash, and sanguinary. It draws the sword unjustly against America. It mentions, sir, the particular Province of Massachusetts Bay as in a state of actual rebellion. The other provinces are held out to our indignation as aiding and abetting. Arguments have been employed to involve them in all the consequences of an open, declared rebellion, and to obtain the fullest orders for our officers and troops to act against them as rebels. Whether their present state is that of rebellion, or of a fit and just resistance to unlawful acts of power – resistance to our attempts to rob them of their property and liberties, as they imagine – I shall not declare. This I know: a successful resistance is a revolution, not a rebellion! Rebellion indeed appears on the back of a flying enemy; but revolution flames on the breast-plate of the victorious warrior. Who can tell, sir, whether, in consequence of this day's violent and mad address to his majesty, the scabbard may not be thrown away by them as well as by us; and, should success attend them, whether, in a few years, the independent Americans may not celebrate the glorious era of the Revolution of 1775, as we do that of 1688?

The policy, sir, of this measure, I can no more comprehend, than I can acknowledge the justice of it. Is your force adequate to the attempt? I am satisfied it is not. Boston, indeed, you may lay in ashes, or it may be made a strong garrison; but the province will be lost to you. Boston will be like Gibraltar. You will hold, in the Province of Massachusetts Bay, as you do in Spain, a single town, while the whole country remains in the power and possession of the enemy. Where your fleets and armies are stationed, the possession will be secured, while they continue; but all the rest will be lost. In the great scale of empire, you will decline, I fear, from the decision of this day; and the Americans will rise to independence, to power, to all the greatness of the most renowned states! For they build on the solid basis of general public liberty. I tremble, sir, at the almost certain consequences of such an address, founded in cruelty and injustice, equally contrary to the sound maxims of true policy, and the unerring rule of natural right. The Americans will certainly defend their property and their liberties with the spirit which our ancestors exerted, and which, I hope, we should exert, on a like occasion. They will sooner declare themselves independent, and risk every consequence of such a contest, than submit to the galling yoke which administration is preparing for them. An address of this sanguinary nature can not fail of driving them to despair. They will see that you are preparing, not only to draw the sword, but to burn the scabbard. In the most harsh manner you are declaring them rebels! Every idea of a reconciliation will now vanish. They will pursue the most vigorous course in their own defence. The whole continent of North America will be dismembered from Great Britain, and the wide arch of the raised empire will fall. But may the just vengeance of the people overtake the authors of these pernicious counsels! May the loss of the first province of the empire be speedily followed by the loss of the heads of those ministers who have persisted in these wicked, these fatal, these most disastrous measures!'

# EDMUND BURKE
## 12 January 1729 – 9 July 1797

### 'Slavery they can have anywhere'
22 March 1775

**William Pitt's impassioned proposal** had failed to remove British troops from Boston. As MP for Bristol, the Irish statesman and orator Edmund Burke now proposed to the House of Commons 13 resolutions for reconciliation with the American colonies. He spoke for three hours against the pro-war administration of Lord North but failed in his objective. Burke is mainly remembered for his fight for the rights of the American colonists, whom he called *'the American English'* and *'our English brethren in the colonies'*. Burke despised the Hanoverian King George III who he said was using *'the hireling sword of German boors and vassals'*, i.e. German mercenaries, to destroy the colonists' English liberties.

'Surely it is an awful subject, or there is none so on this side of the grave...The proposition is peace. Not peace through the medium of war...my opinion is much more in favour of prudent management than of force; considering force not as an odious, but a feeble instrument for preserving a people so numerous, so active, so growing, so spirited as this, in a profitable and subordinate connection with us. First, Sir, permit me to observe that the use of force alone is but temporary. It may subdue for a moment, but it does not remove the necessity of subduing again; and a nation is not governed which is perpetually to be conquered. My next objection is its uncertainty. Terror is not always the effect of force, and an armament is not a victory. If you do not succeed, you are without resource; for, conciliation failing, force remains; but, force failing, no further hope of reconciliation is left. Power and authority are sometimes bought by kindness; but they can never be begged as alms by an impoverished and defeated violence. A further objection to force is, that you impair the object by your very endeavours to preserve it. The thing you fought for is not the thing which you recover; but depreciated, sunk, wasted, and consumed in the contest. Nothing less will content me than WHOLE AMERICA. I do not choose to consume its strength along with our own, because in all parts it is the British strength that I consume. I do not choose to be caught by a foreign enemy at the end of this exhausting conflict; and still less in the midst of it. I may escape; but

I can make no insurance against such an event. Let me add, that I do not choose wholly to break the American spirit; because it is the spirit that has made the country. Lastly, we have no sort of experience in favour of force as an instrument in the rule of our Colonies...

In this character of the Americans, a love of freedom is the predominating feature which marks and distinguishes the whole; and as an ardent is always a jealous affection, your Colonies become suspicious, restive, and untractable whenever they see the least attempt to wrest from them by force, or shuffle from them by chicane, what they think the only advantage worth living for. This fierce spirit of liberty is stronger in the English Colonies probably than in any other people of the earth, and this from a great variety of powerful causes; which, to understand the true temper of their minds and the direction which this spirit takes, it will not be amiss to lay open somewhat more largely. First, the people of the Colonies are descendants of Englishmen. England, Sir, is a nation which still, I hope, respects, and formerly adored, her freedom. The Colonists emigrated from you when this part of your character was most predominant; and they took this bias and direction the moment they parted from your hands. They are therefore not only devoted to liberty, but to liberty according to English ideas, and on English principles...a persuasion not only favourable to liberty, but built upon it...But let it be once understood that your government may be one thing and their privileges another, that these two things may exist without any mutual relation, – the cement is gone, the cohesion is loosened, and everything hastens to decay and dissolution. As long as you have the wisdom to keep the sovereign authority of this country as the sanctuary of liberty, the sacred temple consecrated to our common faith, wherever the chosen race and sons of England worship freedom, they will turn their faces towards you. The more they multiply, the more friends you will have; the more ardently they love liberty, the more perfect will be their obedience. Slavery they can have anywhere. It is a weed that grows in every soil. They may have it from Spain, they may have it from Prussia. But, until you become lost to all feeling of your true interest and your natural dignity, freedom they can have from none but you.'

# PATRICK HENRY
## 29 May 1736 – 6 June 1799

*'Give me liberty or give me death!'*
23 March 1775

**A lawyer, Henry worked with Jefferson** for American independence, serving as a member of the First Continental Congress in 1774 and being elected governor of Virginia in 1776 and 1784. He is best remembered for this speech he made to the House of Burgesses in Richmond. Wirt's description of the oration was made from oral testimony, omitting some graphic name-calling from the only first-hand written version. The father of Chief Justice Marshall gave a similar account of Henry's speech, which he called *'one of the most bold, vehement, and animated pieces of eloquence that had ever been delivered.'* Henry's resolution was adopted, and Patrick Henry, Richard H. Lee, Robert C. Nicholas, Benjamin Harrison, Lemuel Riddick, George Washington, Adam Stevens, Andrew Lewis, William Christian, Edmund Pendleton, Thomas Jefferson and Isaac Zane were appointed a committee to prepare the plan for independence. Less than a month later, on 19 April 1775, the Battle of Lexington was fought between the American republicans and British troops.

'...Has Great Britain any enemy in this quarter of the world, to call for all this accumulation of navies and armies? No, sir: she has none. They are meant for us: they can be meant for no other. They are sent over to bind and rivet upon us those chains, which the British ministry have been so long forging. And what have we to oppose to them? Shall we try argument? Sir, we have been trying that for the last ten years. Have we any thing new to offer upon the subject? Nothing. We have held the subject up in every light of which it is capable; but it has been all in vain. Shall we resort to entreaty and humble supplication? What terms shall we find, which have not been already exhausted? Let us not, I beseech you, sir, deceive ourselves longer. Sir, we have done every thing that could be done, to avert the storm which is now coming on. We have petitioned – we have remonstrated – we have supplicated – we have prostrated ourselves before the throne, and have implored its interposition to arrest the tyrannical hands of the ministry and parliament...There is no longer any room for hope. If we wish to be free – if we mean to preserve inviolate those inestimable privileges for which we have been so long contending – if we mean not basely to abandon the noble struggle in which we have been so long engaged, and which we have pledged ourselves never to abandon, until the glorious object of our contest shall be obtained – we must fight! – I repeat it, sir; we must fight!! An appeal to arms and to the God of Hosts, is all that is left us!

They tell us, sir, that we are weak – unable to cope with so formidable an adversary. But when shall we be stronger? Will it be the next week, or the next year? Will it be when we are totally disarmed; and when a British guard shall be stationed in every house? Shall we gather strength by irresolution and inaction? Shall we acquire the means of effectual resistance, by lying supinely on our back, and hugging the delusive phantom of hope, until our enemies shall have bound us, hand and foot? Sir, we are not weak, if we make a proper use of those means which the God of nature hath placed in our power. Three millions of people, armed in the holy cause of liberty, and in such a country as that which we possess, are invincible by any force which our enemy can send against us. Besides, sir, we shall not fight our battles alone. There is a just God who presides over the destinies of nations; and who will raise up friends to fight our battles for us. The battle, sir, is not to the strong alone; it is to the vigilant, the active, the brave. Besides, sir, we have no election. If we were base enough to desire it, it is now too late to retire from the contest. There is no retreat, but in submission and slavery! Our chains are forged. Their clanking may be heard on the plains of Boston! The war is inevitable – and let it come!! I repeat it, sir; let it come!!! It is in vain, sir, to extenuate the matter. Gentlemen may cry, peace, peace – but there is no peace. The war is actually begun! The next gale that sweeps from the north, will bring to our ears the clash of resounding arms! Our brethren are already in the field! Why stand we here idle? What is it that gentlemen wish? What would they have? Is life so dear; or peace so sweet, as to be purchased at the price of chains, and slavery? Forbid it, Almighty God! – I know not what course others may take; but as for me, give me liberty, or give me death!'

# CHIEF LOGAN OF THE MINGO

*c.*1725 – 1780

## Logan's Lament
after 10 October 1774

**In the Yellow Creek Massacre** of 30 April 1774, a group of Virginia frontiersmen under Daniel Greathouse murdered a number of Mingo (an Iroquoian group of Native Americans), among them Logan's brother, and at least two other close female relatives, one of them pregnant and caring for her infant daughter. The Mingo had been lured to the cabin of Joshua Baker, a settler and rum trader who lived across the Ohio River from their village, and all were killed except for the infant girl. Logan was not present, and was summoned to return by runners. Tribal chiefs, among them Shawnee, Lenape and Seneca, attempted to negotiate a peaceful resolution, but Logan insisted on his right of revenge. Parties of mixed Mingo and Shawnee warriors, including one led by Logan, attacked settlers in several frontier regions, killing and taking captives. Lord Dunmore, governor of Virginia, launched expeditions known as Dunmore's War, in which Logan did not participate, having satisfied his right of retaliation. The Indians withdrew after the Battle of Point Pleasant at West Virginia, and Dunmore's army marched into the Ohio Country and compelled the Ohio Indians to agree to a peace treaty. Logan refused to attend the peace negotiations and instead issued this celebrated speech. He later fought in the American Revolutionary War against the Americans.

'I appeal to any white man to say if he ever entered Logan's cabin hungry, and he gave him not meat; if he ever came cold and naked and he clothed him not. During the course of the last long and bloody war, Logan remained idle in his cabin, an advocate for peace. Such was my love for the whites, that my countrymen pointed as I passed, and said, Logan is a friend of the white man. I have even thought to live with you but for the injuries of one man, Colonel Cresap, who last spring in cold blood and unprovoked murdered the relatives of Logan, not even sparing his wife and children. There runs not a drop of my blood in the veins of any living creature. This has called on me for revenge. I have sought it; I have killed many; I have fully glutted my vengeance. For my country, I rejoice in the beams of peace. But do not harbour a thought that mine is the joy of fear. Logan never felt fear. He will not turn on his heel to save his life. Who is there to mourn for Logan? Not one.'

# GEORGE WASHINGTON
## 22 February 1732 – 14 December 1799

*'The eyes of all our countrymen are now upon us'*
2 July 1776

**Washington gave this speech** shortly before the Battle of Long Island (27 August 1776), the first major battle in the American Revolutionary War following the United States's Declaration of Independence. The arrival of a British fleet threatened to cut him off. He evacuated the island so skillfully, however, that not a man was lost in the overnight manoeuvres and the Continental Army remained intact to fight another day.

'The time is now near at hand which must probably determine whether Americans are to be freemen or slaves; whether they are to have any property they can call their own; whether their houses and farms are to be pillaged and destroyed, and themselves consigned to a state of wretchedness from which no human efforts will deliver them. The fate of unborn millions will now depend, under God, on the courage and conduct of this army. Our cruel and unrelenting enemy leaves us only the choice of a brave resistance, or the most abject submission. We have, therefore, to resolve to conquer or to die. Our own, our country's honor, calls upon us for a vigorous and manly exertion; and if we now shamefully fail, we shall become infamous to the whole world... The eyes of all our countrymen are now upon us; and we shall have their blessings and praises, if happily we are the instruments of saving them from the tyranny meditated against them. Let us, therefore, animate and encourage each other, and show the whole world that a freeman contending for liberty on his own ground is superior to any slavish mercenary on earth. Liberty, property, life and honor, are all at stake. Upon your courage and conduct rest the hopes of our bleeding and insulted country. Our wives, children and parents expect safety from us only; and they have every reason to believe that Heaven will crown with success so just a cause. The enemy will endeavor to intimidate by show and appearance; but remember they have been repulsed on various occasions by a few brave Americans. Their cause is bad, – their men are conscious of it; and, if opposed with firmness and coolness on their first onset, with our advantage of works, and knowledge of the ground, the victory is most assuredly ours. Every good soldier will be silent and attentive, wait for orders, and reserve his fire until he is sure of doing execution.'

# BRIGADIER-GENERAL JOHN NIXON
## 1 March 1724 – 24 March 1815

*'We hold these truths to be self-evident, that all men are created equal...'*
8 July 1776

**Nixon had fought for the English** from 1755 during the French and Indian War. In 1775, he was a captain of the Minutemen fighting the English at Lexington and Concord, and his unit was one of the last to leave the field at Bunker Hill. He was promoted to colonel of the 6th Massachusetts Regiment, and was also commander of the Philadelphia City Guard. The text of the Declaration of Independence was agreed in Congress by the 13 colonies upon 4 July 1776, and copies were sent to state legislatures. On the morning of 8 July Philadelphia's State House bells tolled and expectant crowds gathered in its yard. Nixon has been selected by Sheriff William Dewees to read the proclamation of independence from the balcony of the observatory. It was the first public reading of the declaration of war against England, and crowds celebrated wildly, although it was not until 1941 that Independence Day became an official holiday in the United States. Nixon fought in the New York and New Jersey campaigns of 1776, becoming a brigadier-general in the Continental Army in the American Revolutionary War. He also fought at Saratoga and at Bemis Heights in 1777 a cannonball passed so close to his head that his sight and hearing were affected for the rest of his life.

'A DECLARATION By the REPRESENTATIVES of the UNITED STATES of AMERICA, in GENERAL CONGRESS ASSEMBLED: When, in the Course of human Events, it becomes necessary for one People to dissolve the Political Bands which have connected them with another, and to assume among the Powers of the Earth, the separate & equal Station to which the Laws of Nature and of Nature's God entitle them, a decent Respect to the Opinions of Mankind requires that they should declare the causes which impel them to the Separation...We hold these truths to be self-evident, that all men are created equal, that they are endowed by their Creator with certain unalienable rights, that among these are Life, Liberty and the pursuit of Happiness. That to secure these rights, Governments are instituted among Men, deriving their just powers from the consent of the governed, That whenever any Form of Government becomes destructive of these ends, it is the Right of the People to alter or to abolish it, and to institute new Government, laying its foundation on such principles and organizing its powers in such form, as to them shall seem most likely to effect their Safety and Happiness. Prudence, indeed, will dictate that Governments long established should not be changed for light and transient causes; and accordingly all experience hath shewn, that mankind are more disposed to suffer, while evils are sufferable, than to right themselves by abolishing the forms to which they are accustomed. But when a long train of abuses and usurpations, pursuing invariably the same Object evinces a design to reduce them under absolute Despotism, it is their right, it is their duty, to throw off such Government, and to provide new Guards for their future security... In every stage of these Oppressions We have Petitioned for Redress in the most humble terms: Our repeated Petitions have been answered only by repeated injury. A Prince whose character is thus marked by every act which may define a Tyrant, is unfit to be the ruler of a free people.

...Nor have We been wanting in attentions to our British brethren. We have warned them from time to time of attempts by their legislature to extend an unwarrantable jurisdiction over us. We have reminded them of the circumstances of our emigration and settlement here. We have appealed to their native justice and magnanimity, and we have conjured them by the ties of our common kindred to disavow these usurpations, which would inevitably interrupt our connections and correspondence. They too have been deaf to the voice of justice and of consanguinity. We must, therefore, acquiesce in the necessity, which denounces our Separation, and hold them, as we hold the rest of mankind, Enemies in War, in Peace Friends...We, therefore, the Representatives of the united States of America, in General Congress, Assembled, appealing to the Supreme Judge of the world for the rectitude of our intentions, do, in the Name, and by Authority of the good People of these Colonies, solemnly publish and declare, That these United Colonies are, and of Right ought to be Free and Independent States; that they are Absolved from all Allegiance to the British Crown, and that all political connection between them and the State of Great Britain, is and ought to be totally dissolved; and that as Free and Independent States, they have full Power to levy War, conclude Peace, contract Alliances, establish Commerce, and to do all other Acts and Things which Independent States may of right do. And for the support of this Declaration, with a firm reliance on the protection of divine Providence, we mutually pledge to each other our Lives, our Fortunes and our sacred Honor.'

# SAMUEL ADAMS
### 27 September 1722 – 2 October 1803

*'A nation of shopkeepers are very seldom so disinterested'*
1 August 1776

**This American statesman was one** of the *'Founding Fathers of the United States'*. He was strongly opposed to English attempts to tax the American colonies, and organized the opposition to the Stamp Act in 1765 and founded the *'Sons of Liberty'* (a political group of American patriots seeking independence). A friend of John Hancock and John Adams, Samuel Adams took a leading role in the Boston Tea Party in 1773, which led to more penal taxes. The governor of Massachusetts called Adams the greatest 'incendiary' in the British empire. Adams influenced both the First and Second Continental Congress, and in the former worked for a boycott on the import of British goods. His speech promoting American independence was delivered from the steps of the State House in Philadelphia, the meeting place of the Continental Congress. Adams declares that by voting for the Declaration of Independence, Americans restored *'the Sovereign to Whom alone all men ought to be obedient'* (God) to the *'throne of America'*. The vote for independence was on 2 July. The decision to use the Declaration written by Thomas Jefferson as the tool to announce the decision publicly was made on 4 July. This speech was delivered the day before the parchment copy of the Declaration of Independence was signed by the members of the Continental Congress on 2 August.

'Countrymen and brethren: I would gladly have declined an honor, to which I find myself unequal. I have not the calmness and impartiality which the infinite importance of this occasion demands. I will not deny the charge of my enemies, that resentment for the accumulated injuries of our country, and an ardor for her glory, rising to enthusiasm, may deprive me of that accuracy of judgment and expression which men of cooler passions may Possess. Let me beseech you, then, to hear me with caution, to examine without prejudice, and to correct the mistakes into which I may be hurried by my zeal. Truth loves an appeal to the common-sense of mankind. Your unperverted understandings can best determine on subjects of a practical nature. The positions and plans which are said to be above the comprehension of the multitude may be always suspected to be visionary and fruitless. He who made all men hath made the truths necessary to human happiness obvious to all.

Our forefathers threw off the yoke of popery in religion: for you is reserved the honor of leveling the popery of politics...

Men who content themselves with the semblance of truth, and a display of words, talk much of our obligations to Great Britain for protection! Had she a single eye to our advantage? A nation of shopkeepers are very seldom so disinterested. Let us not be so amused with words: the extension of her commerce was her object. When she defended our coasts, she fought for her customers, and convoyed our ships loaded with wealth, which we had acquired for her by our industry. She has treated us as beasts of burden, whom the lordly masters cherish that they may carry a greater load...Who among you, my countrymen, that is a father, would claim authority to make your child a slave because you had nourished him in his infancy?...To unite the supremacy of Great Britain and the liberty of America, is utterly impossible. So vast a continent and of such a distance from the seat of empire will every day grow more unmanageable. The motion of so unwieldy a body cannot be directed with any despatch and uniformity, without committing to the Parliament of Great Britain powers inconsistent with our freedom. The authority and force which would be absolutely necessary for the preservation of the peace and good order of this continent, would put all our valuable rights within the reach of that nation...You have now in the field armies sufficient to repel the whole force of your enemies, and their base and mercenary auxiliaries. The hearts of your soldiers beat high with the spirit of freedom – they are animated with the justice of their cause, and while they grasp their swords, can look up to heaven for assistance. Your adversaries are composed of wretches who laugh at the rights of humanity, who turn religion into derision, and would, for higher wages, direct their swords against their leaders or their country. Go on, then, in your generous enterprise, with gratitude to heaven, for past success, and confidence of it in the future. For my own part, I ask no greater blessing than to share with you the common danger and common glory. If I have a wish dearer to my soul, than that my ashes may be mingled with those of a Warren and Montgomery – it is – that these American States may never cease to be free and independent!'

# WILLIAM PITT, 1ST EARL OF CHATHAM
## 15 November 1708 – 11 May 1778

*'...you can not conquer America'*
18 November 1777

**Advanced in years, Pitt struggled to his feet** in the House of Lords to speak on a motion for an address to the throne at the opening of Parliament (see also page 74). This wonderful speech arguing against the continuance of the war with America had no effect, as the amendment was rejected by a vote of 97 to 24 and the war dragged on for another six years.

'...This, my Lords, is a perilous and tremendous moment! It is not a time for adulation. The smoothness of flattery can not now avail – can not save us in this rugged and awful crisis. It is now necessary to instruct the Throne in the language of truth. We must dispel the illusion and the darkness which envelop it, and display, in its full danger and true colours, the ruin that is brought to our doors. This, my Lords, is our duty...No advice is asked from the sober and enlightened care of Parliament! But the Crown, from itself and by itself, declares an unalterable determination to pursue measures – and what measures, my Lords? The measures that have produced the imminent perils that threaten us; the measures that have brought ruin to our doors. Can the minister of the day now presume to expect a continuance of support in this ruinous infatuation? Can Parliament be so dead to its dignity and its duty as to be thus deluded into the loss of the one and the violation of the other? To give an unlimited credit and support for the steady perseverance in measures not proposed for our parliamentary advice, but dictated and forced upon us – in measures, I say, my Lords which have reduced this late flourishing empire to ruin and contempt!...My Lords, this ruinous and ignominious situation, where we can not act with success, nor suffer with honour, calls upon us to remonstrate in the strongest and loudest language of truth, to rescue the ear of majesty from the delusions which surround it. The desperate state of our arms abroad is in part known. No man thinks more highly of them than I do. I love and honour the English troops. I know their virtues and their valour. I know they can achieve any thing except impossibilities; and I know that the conquest of English America is an impossibility. You can not, I venture to say it, you can not conquer America. Your armies'

last war effected every thing that could be effected; and what was it? It cost a numerous army, under the command of a most able general [Lord Amherst], now a noble Lord in this House, a long and laborious campaign, to expel five thousand Frenchmen from French America. My Lords, you can not conquer America. What is your present situation there? We do not know the worst; but we know that in three campaigns we have done nothing and suffered much. Besides the sufferings, perhaps total loss of the Northern force, the best appointed army that ever took the field, commanded by Sir William Howe, has retired from the American lines. He was obliged to relinquish his attempt, and with great delay and danger to adopt a new and distant plan of operations. We shall soon know, and in any event have reason to lament, what may have happened since.

...As to conquest, therefore, my Lords, I repeat, it is impossible. You may swell every expense and every effort still more extravagantly; pile and accumulate every assistance you can buy or borrow; traffic and barter with every little pitiful German prince that sells and sends his subjects to the shambles of a foreign prince; your efforts are forever vain and impotent – doubly so from this mercenary aid on which you rely; for it irritates, to an incurable resentment, the minds of your enemies, to overrun them with the mercenary sons of rapine and plunder, devoting them and their possessions to the rapacity of hireling cruelty! If I were an American, as I am an Englishman, while a foreign troop was landed in my country, I never would lay down my arms – never – never – never!...My Lords, this awful subject, so important to our honour, our Constitution, and our religion, demands the most solemn and effectual inquiry. And I again call upon your Lordships, and the united powers of the state, to examine it thoroughly and decisively, and to stamp upon it an indelible stigma of the public abhorrence. And I again implore those holy prelates of our religion to do away these iniquities from among us. Let them perform a lustration; let them purify this House, and this country, from this sin. My Lords, I am old and weak, and at present unable to say more; but my feelings and indignation were too strong to have said less. I could not have slept this night in my bed, nor reposed my head on my pillow, without giving this vent to my eternal abhorrence of such preposterous and enormous principles.'

# WILLIAM PITT, 1ST EARL OF CHATHAM
## 15 November 1708 – 11 May 1778

*'If we must fall, let us fall like men'*
7 April 1778

**After his speech arguing that America** could not be conquered, Pitt further declined in health, but forced himself to return to the Lords to oppose the Duke of Richmond's proposal for American independence. Pitt did not know the real situation in America, and hoped that the colonies could stay in the empire, or he feared England would be ruined. The dying Pitt rose with difficulty to speak in the House of Lords, being supported by two relations. After struggling to complete his speech, he collapsed in convulsions. His 17-year-old son, William Pitt the Younger, helped carry him away, and his father died four days later. After recounting the events of the war, Pitt concluded:

'My Lords, I rejoice that the grave has not closed upon me; that I am still alive, to lift up my voice against the dismemberment of this ancient and most noble monarchy! Pressed down as I am by the hand of infirmity, I am little able to assist my country in this most perilous conjuncture;... Shall we tarnish the lustre of this nation by an ignominious surrender of its rights and fairest possessions? Shall this great nation, that has survived, whole and entire, the Danish depredations, the Scottish inroads, the Norman Conquest – that has stood the threatened invasion of the Spanish Armada, now fall prostrate before the house of Bourbon? Surely, my Lords, this nation is no longer what it was! Shall a people that seventeen years ago was the terror of the world, now stoop so low as to tell its ancient inveterate enemy, Take all we have, only give us peace? It is impossible! I wage war with no man or set of men. I wish for none of their employments; nor would I co-operate with men who still persist in unretracted error, or who, instead of acting on a firm, decisive line of conduct, halt between two opinions, where there is no middle path. In God's name, if it is absolutely necessary to declare either for peace or war, and the former can not be preserved with honour, why is not the latter commenced without delay? I am not, I confess, well informed as to the resources of this kingdom, but I trust it has still sufficient to maintain its just rights, though I know them not. But, my Lords, any state is better than despair. Let us at least make one effort, and, if we must fall, let us fall like men!'

# CHIEF BUCKONGAHELAS OF THE LENAPE
## c.1720 – May 1805

*'Are they now, do you think, better men than they were?'*
April 1781

**Buckonghelas, a Lenape chief**, had a son named Mahonegon who was killed by Captain William White in West Virginia in June 1773. In the American Revolutionary War, Buckongahelas led some of his people against the American settlers, and did so again in the Northwest Indian War. He established a village near his ally Blue Jacket of the Shawnee, while White Eyes led the pro-American Delawares. Some Delawares had converted to Christianity, and lived in exposed frontier villages run by Moravian missionaries. In April 1781, at the Ohio village of Gnadenhütten , Buckongahelas warned these Christian Delawares that an American militia from Pennsylvania would execute any Indians found in their way. He urged them in this speech (recorded by a Moravian missionary, John Heckewelder) to follow him and move further west away from encroaching Americans, where his warriors would protect them. They did not believe him, and on 8 March 1782 his warning was fulfilled. In the Gnadenhütten Massacre, 96 Christian Indians, including 60 women and children were killed by settlers. Buckonghelas kept moving his people westwards, but was later forced to sign treaties giving up his new lands.

'Friends, listen to what I have to say to you: You see a great and powerful nation divided. You see the father fighting against the son, the son against the father. The father has called on his Indian children to assist him in punishing his children, the Americans, who have become refractory *[resistant to authority]*. I took time to consider what I should do – whether or not I should receive the hatchet of the father to assist him. At first, I looked upon it as a family quarrel in which I was not interested. At length, it appeared to me that the father was right – that his children deserved to be punished a little. That this must be the case I concluded from the many cruel acts his offspring have committed from time to time against his Indian children, by encroaching on their lands, stealing their property, shooting at and even murdering without cause men, women, and children. Yes, even murdering those who at all times had been friendly to them. Look back at the murders committed by the long knives on many of our relations who lived peaceably as neighbors to them on the Ohio. Did not they kill them without the least provocation? Are they now, do you think, better men than they were?'

# GEORGE WASHINGTON
## 22 February 1732 – 14 December 1799

*Preventing the Revolt of his Officers*
15 March 1783

**At the end of the Revolutionary War,** officers of the Continental Army met in Newburgh, New York, to discuss grievances and consider a possible insurrection against the rule of Congress. They were impatient over the failure of Congress to deliver its promises to the army regarding back pay, bounties and life pensions. The officers had heard from Philadelphia that the American government was going bankrupt and that they might not be compensated at all, so were intent upon confronting Congress. Most fighting had ended in 1781, so they had been waiting two years for their grievances to be resolved. On 10 March 1783, an anonymous letter was circulated among the officers of General Washington's main camp at Newburgh, calling for an unauthorized meeting of officers to be held the next day to consider possible military solutions to the problems of the civilian government. Washington found out, and forbade the meeting, but suggested that matters should be discussed four days later at the regular military meeting. Washington spent the intervening time interviewing each officer individually, telling him of the fatal consequences of an action against Congress. When the officers assembled, Washington prepared to read his address, but found his eyesight was failing him, and so produced his spectacles:

'My eyes have grown dim in my country's service, but I never doubted its justice. Gentlemen: By an anonymous summons, an attempt has been made to convene you together; how inconsistent with the rules of propriety, how unmilitary, and how subversive of all order and discipline, let the good sense of the army decide...But as I was among the first who embarked in the cause of our common country; as I have never left your side one moment, but when called from you on public duty, as I have been the constant companion and witness of your distresses, and not among the last to feel and acknowledge your merits; as I have ever considered my own military reputation as inseparably connected with that of the army...While I give you these assurances, and pledge myself in the most unequivocal manner to exert whatever ability I am possessed of in your favor, let me entreat you, gentlemen, on your part, not to take any measures which, viewed in the calm light of reason, will lessen the dignity and sully the glory you have hitherto maintained;

let me request you to rely on the plighted faith of your country, and place a full confidence in the purity of the intentions of Congress; that, previous to your dissolution as an army, they will cause all your accounts to be fairly liquidated, as directed in their resolutions, which were published to you two days ago, and that they will adopt the most effectual measures in their power to render ample justice to you, for your faithful and meritorious services. And let me conjure you, in the name of our common country, as you value your own sacred honor, as you respect the rights of humanity, and as you regard the military and national character of America, to express your utmost horror and detestation of the man who wishes, under any specious pretences, to overturn the liberties of our country, and who wickedly attempts to open the floodgates of civil discord and deluge our rising empire in blood. By thus determining and thus acting, you will pursue the plain and direct road to the attainment of your wishes. You will defeat the insidious designs of our enemies, who are compelled to resort from open force to secret artifice. You will give one more distinguished proof of unexampled patriotism and patient virtue, rising superior to the pressure of the most complicated sufferings. And you will, by the dignity of your conduct, afford occasion for posterity to say, when speaking of the glorious example you have exhibited to mankind, "Had this day been wanting, the world had never seen the last stage of perfection to which human nature is capable of attaining."'

He had addressed their grievances, and withdrew from the meeting to allow discussion, leaving an irresistible impression. No officer opposed the advice he had given. Few of Washington's officers knew that he wore glasses, and were surprised to see them. Seeing his humility and vulnerability, his men were deeply moved, feeling affection for this ageing man who had led them through so much. The officers then cast a unanimous vote, effectively agreeing to the rule of Congress. Thus civilian government in the infant United States of America was preserved, and the experiment of democracy continued. Six months later, by the Treaty of Paris in September 1783, Britain finally recognized American independence. Washington's speech in itself did not prevent a military coup, but his actions in intercepting the officers' revolt, and the manner of his giving the speech, shows his deep feeling for his infant country, helping to secure the future of democracy across the world.

# WILLIAM PITT THE YOUNGER
## 28 May 1759 – 23 January 1806

*'It was conceived in injustice'*
12 June 1781

**Pitt had been the youngest person** to enter Cambridge University, and entered Parliament aged only 21, almost immediately denouncing the continuation of the American War of Independence. He proposed that the prime minister, Lord North, should make immediate peace with the colonies. Just four months after the date of this speech, Cornwallis surrendered at Yorktown. In 1783, Pitt became the youngest British prime minister, aged just 24.

'Gentlemen have passed the highest eulogiums on the American war. Its justice has been defended in the most fervent manner. A noble lord, in the heat of his zeal, has called it a holy war. For my part, although the honourable gentleman who made this motion, and some other gentlemen, have been, more than once, in the course of the debate, severely reprehended for calling it a wicked and accursed war, I am persuaded, and would affirm, that it was a most accursed, wicked, barbarous, cruel, unnatural, unjust and diabolical war! It was conceived in injustice; it was nurtured and brought forth in folly; its footsteps were marked with blood, slaughter, persecution and devastation – in truth, everything which went to constitute moral depravity and human turpitude was to be found in it. It was pregnant with misery of every kind.

The mischief, however, recoiled on the unhappy people of this country, who were made the instruments by which the wicked purposes of the authors of the war were effected. The nation was drained of its best blood, and of its vital resources of men and money. The expense of the war was enormous – much beyond any former experience. And yet, what has the British nation received in return? Nothing but a series of ineffective victories, or severe defeats – victories celebrated only by a temporary triumph over our brethren, whom we would trample down and destroy; victories, which filled the land with mourning for the loss of dear and valued relatives, slain in the impious cause of enforcing unconditional submission...Where was the Englishman, who on reading the narratives of those bloody and well-fought contests, could refrain from lamenting the loss of so much British blood spilt in such a cause, or from weeping, on whatever side victory might be declared?'

# GEORGE WASHINGTON
## 22 February 1732 – 14 December 1799

---

### 'I retire from the great theater of Action'
23 December 1783

**When the Revolutionary War** was drawing to an end, there was speculation that George Washington, then major-general and commander-in-chief, would become the king of a new nation. Following the end of the war in 1783, George III asked what Washington would do next and was told of rumours that he would return to his farm at Mount Vernon. The king replied: *'If he does that, he will be the greatest man in the world.'* Washington indeed followed the example of the Roman general Cincinnatus, rejecting the temptations of power and resigning his position as commander-in-chief. As Washington read his speech, he trembled so much that he had to hold the parchment with two hands to keep it steady. *'The spectators all wept, and there was hardly a member of Congress who did not drop tears. His voice faltered and sunk, and the whole house felt his agitations.'* As soon as he finished, Washington advanced and delivered to President Thomas Mifflin his commission, with a copy of his resignation address, and resumed his place. Mifflin made a short and heartfelt speech of thanks, then Washington rushed through the door of the Annapolis State House, mounted his horse, and rode away at speed.

'The great events on which my resignation depended having at length taken place; I have now the honor of offering my sincere Congratulations to Congress and of presenting myself before them to surrender into their hands the trust committed to me, and to claim the indulgence of retiring from the Service of my Country. Happy in the confirmation of our Independence and Sovereignty, and pleased with the opportunity afforded the United States of becoming a respectable Nation, I resign with satisfaction the Appointment I accepted with diffidence. A diffidence in my abilities to accomplish so arduous a task, which however was superseded by a confidence in the rectitude of our Cause, the support of the Supreme Power of the Union, and the patronage of Heaven...I consider it an indispensable duty to close this last solemn act of my Official life, by commending the Interests of our dearest Country to the protection of Almighty God, and those who have the superintendence of them, to his holy keeping. Having now finished the work assigned me, I retire from the great theater of Action; and bidding an Affectionate farewell to this August body under whose orders I have so long acted, I here offer my Commission, and take my leave of all the employments of public life.'

# BENJAMIN FRANKLIN
## 17 January 1706 – 17 April 1790

*'I agree to this Constitution with all its faults'*
17 September 1787

**Franklin was a polymath and diplomat** with an international reputation, and was called 'the First American' for his campaigning for the union of the American colonies. This speech was given on the last day of the Constitutional Convention. Pennsylvania delegate and 'Founding Father', the 81-year-old Franklin, wanted to give a short speech to the Convention prior to the signing of the final draft of the Constitution. Too weak to give the speech himself, he had fellow Pennsylvanian James Wilson deliver this masterpiece.

'Mr. President – I confess that there are several parts of this constitution which I do not at present approve, but I am not sure I shall never approve them. For, having lived long, I have experienced many instances of being obliged by better information, or fuller consideration, to change opinions even on important subjects, which I once thought right, but found to be otherwise. It is therefore that the older I grow, the more apt I am to doubt my own judgment, and to pay more respect to the judgment of others. Most men indeed as well as most sects in Religion, think themselves in possession of all truth, and that wherever others differ from them, it is so far error. Steele, a Protestant, in a Dedication tells the Pope, that the only difference between our Churches in their opinions of the certainty of their doctrines is, the Church of Rome is infallible and the Church of England is never in the wrong. But though many private persons think almost as highly of their own infallibility as of that of their sect, few express it so naturally as a certain French lady, who in a dispute with her sister, said "I don't know how it happens, Sister but I meet with no body but myself, that's always in the right – *Il n'y a que moi qui a toujours raison.*"

In these sentiments, Sir, I agree to this Constitution with all its faults, if they are such; because I think a general Government necessary for us, and there is no form of Government but what may be a blessing to the people if well administered, and believe farther that this is likely to be well administered for a course of years, and can only end in Despotism, as other forms have done before it, when the people shall become so corrupted as to need despotic Government, being incapable of any other. I doubt too whether any other Convention we can obtain, may be able to make a better Constitution. For when you assemble a number of men to have the advantage of their joint wisdom, you inevitably assemble with those men, all their prejudices, their passions, their errors of opinion, their local interests, and their selfish views. From such an assembly can a perfect production be expected? It therefore astonishes me, Sir, to find this system approaching so near to perfection as it does; and I think it will astonish our enemies, who are waiting with confidence to hear that our councils are confounded like those of the Builders of Babel; and that our States are on the point of separation, only to meet hereafter for the purpose of cutting one another's throats. Thus I consent, Sir, to this Constitution because I expect no better, and because I am not sure, that it is not the best. The opinions I have had of its errors, I sacrifice to the public good. I have never whispered a syllable of them abroad. Within these walls they were born, and here they shall die. If every one of us in returning to our Constituents were to report the objections he has had to it, and endeavor to gain partisans in support of them, we might prevent its being generally received, and thereby lose all the salutary effects and great advantages resulting naturally in our favor among foreign Nations as well as among ourselves, from our real or apparent unanimity. Much of the strength and efficiency of any Government in procuring and securing happiness to the people, depends, on opinion, on the general opinion of the goodness of the Government, as well as of the wisdom and integrity of its Governors. I hope therefore that for our own sakes as a part of the people, and for the sake of posterity, we shall act heartily and unanimously in recommending this Constitution (if approved by Congress and confirmed by the Conventions) wherever our influence may extend, and turn our future thoughts and endeavors to the means of having it well administered. On the whole, Sir, I can not help expressing a wish that every member of the Convention who may still have objections to it, would with me, on this occasion doubt a little of his own infallibility, and to make manifest our unanimity, put his name to this instrument.'

# EDMUND BURKE
## 12 January 1729 – 9 July 1797

### 'Mr. Hastings has no refuge here'
15 February 1788

**Burke resigned his seat in Parliament** to bring charges of impeachment against Warren Hastings (1732–1818), for his crimes when serving in India where he was the first governor-general. The charges of indictment were read in the House of Commons by Burke on 13 and 14 February – the 20 counts took four sittings of the Commons for Burke to read them. Of Burke's accusatory speech that followed Hastings said, *'For the first half hour, I looked up to the orator in a reverie of wonder, and during that time I felt myself the most culpable man on earth.'* On 4 April 1786 Burke had presented the Commons with the *Article of Charge of High Crimes and Misdemeanours* against Hastings. The trial, which did not begin until 14 February 1788, would be the *'first major public discursive event of its kind in England,'* bringing the morality and duty of imperialism to the forefront of public debate. Burke's indictment called Hastings the *'captain-general of iniquity'*; who never dined without *'creating a famine'*; his heart being *'gangrened to the core'* with Hastings resembling both a *'spider of Hell'* and a *'ravenous vulture devouring the carcasses of the dead'*. Burke's philippic was so venomous that it actually provoked public sympathy for Hastings. The house sat for a total of 148 days over a period of seven years during the investigation, the costs of which virtually bankrupted Hastings. He is supposed to have complained that his punishment would have been less extreme if he had pleaded guilty. In April 1795 he was acquitted on all charges, but the trial helped to establish the principle that the empire had moral responsibilities, rather than merely facilitating the wholesale looting of colonies.

'There is a sacred veil to be drawn over the beginning of all governments. Ours in India had an origin like those which time has sanctified by obscurity. Time, in the origin of most governments, has thrown this mysterious veil over them; prudence and discretion make it necessary to throw something of the same drapery over more recent foundations, in which otherwise the fortune, the genius, the talents, and military virtue of this nation never shone more conspicuously. But whatever necessity might hide or excuse or palliate, in the acquisition of power, a wise nation, when it has once made a revolution upon its own principles and for its own ends, rests there. The first step to empire is revolution, by which power is conferred; the next is good laws, good order, good institutions, to give that power stability. I am sorry to say that the reverse of this policy was the principle on which the gentlemen in India acted. It was such as tended to make the new government as unstable as the old. By the vast sums of money acquired by individuals upon this occasion, by the immense sudden prodigies of fortune, it was discovered that a revolution in Bengal was a mine much more easily worked and infinitely more productive than the mines of Potosi and Mexico. It was found that the work was not only very lucrative, but not at all difficult. Where Clive [the great general] forded a deep water upon an unknown bottom, he left a bridge for his successors, over which the lame could hobble and the blind might grope their way...Law and arbitrary power are in eternal enmity. Name me a magistrate, and I will name property; name me power, and I will name protection. It is a contradiction in terms, it is blasphemy in religion, it is wickedness in politics, to say that any man can have arbitrary power. In every patent of office the duty is included... Mr. Hastings has no refuge here. Let him run from law to law; let him fly from the Common Law and the sacred institutions of the country in which he was born; let him fly from acts of Parliament, from which his power originated; let him plead his ignorance of them, or fly in the face of them. Will he fly to the Mahomedan law? That condemns him. Will he fly to the high magistracy of Asia to defend the taking of presents? Padishah and the Sultan would condemn him to a cruel death. Will he fly to the Sufis, to the laws of Persia, or to the practice of those monarchs? I cannot utter the pains, the tortures, that would be inflicted on him, if he were to govern there as he has done in a British province. Let him fly where he will, from law to law; law, I thank God meets him everywhere, and enforced, too, by the practice of the most impious tyrants, which he quotes as if it would justify his conduct. I would as willingly have him tried by the law of the Koran, or the Institutes of Tamerlane, as on the Common Law or Statute Law of this Kingdom...'

# WILLIAM WILBERFORCE
## 24 August 1759 – 29 July 1833

*'How can we bear to think of such a scene as this?'*
12 May 1789

**By 1783, the 'triangular trade' accounted** for 80 per cent of Britain's foreign income. British-made goods were sailed to Africa to buy slaves, which were then transported to the West Indies and Americas where they were sold into labour. On the third leg of the voyage, slave-grown products, such as sugar, tobacco and cotton, were brought to Britain. The British supplied French, Spanish, Dutch, Portuguese and British colonies, and in peak years carried 40,000 men, women and children annually across the Atlantic in horrific conditions with about 13 per cent dying en route. This leg of the triangle was called the *'Middle Passage'*. In the 1780s an anti-slavery campaign began, with the first slave trade petition being issued in 1783. In that year, the young MP William Wilberforce met ship's surgeon and clergyman James Ramsay, who told him about the treatment of slaves at sea and in the plantations. Horrified, Wilberforce became the leading light in the abolitionist campaign, and decided to concentrate on ending the slave trade, rather than eliminating slavery itself. He reasoned that the abolition of the trade would logically lead to the end of slavery. Before the House of Commons, he passionately made his case why this despicable trade must cease. Wilberforce introduced a bill to abolish the slave trade, but it failed. Yet he never gave up, reintroducing the bill year after year. A vote for 'gradual abolition' was eventually carried and succeeding legislation secured abolition in 1807 with the Slave Trade Act. A superb singer, Wilberforce used his voice to dramatic effect when speaking. The diarist James Boswell recounts seeing Wilberforce declaim in the Commons: *'I saw what seemed a mere shrimp mount upon the table; but as I listened, he grew, and grew, until the shrimp became a whale.'*

'...Let any one imagine to himself six or seven hundred of these wretches chained two and two, surrounded with every object that is nauseous and disgusting, diseased, and struggling under every kind of wretchedness! How can we bear to think of such a scene as this? One would think it had been determined to heap on them all the varieties of bodily pain, for the purpose of blunting the feelings of the mind; and yet, in this very point (to show the power of human prejudice), the situation of the slaves has been described by Mr. Norris, one of the Liverpool delegates, in a manner which I am sure will convince the House how interest can draw a film over the eyes, so thick that total blindness could do no more; and how it is our duty therefore to trust not to the reasonings of interested men, nor to their way of colouring a transaction...Mr. Norris talks of frankincense and lime juice: when the surgeons tell you the slaves are stored so close that there is not room to tread among them; and when you have it in evidence from Sir George Young, that even in a ship which wanted two hundred of her complement, the stench was intolerable. The song and the dance are promoted, says Mr. Norris. It had been more fair, perhaps, if he had explained that word "promoted". The truth is, that for the sake of exercise, these miserable wretches, loaded with chains, oppressed with disease and wretchedness, are forced to dance by the terror of the lash, and sometimes by the actual use of it. "I" says one of the other evidences, "was employed to dance the men, while another person danced the women." Such, then, is the meaning of the word "promoted"; and it may be observed, too, with respect to food, that an instrument is sometimes carried out in order to force them to eat, which is the same sort of proof how much they enjoy themselves in that instance also.

...It will be found, upon an average of all ships of which evidence has been given at the Privy Council, that exclusive of those who perish before they sail, not less than twelve and one-half per cent perish in the passage. Besides these, the Jamaica report tells you that not less than four and one-half per cent die on shore before the day of sale, which is only a week or two from the time of landing. One-third more die in the seasoning, and this in a country exactly like their own, where they are healthy and happy, as some of the evidences would pretend. The diseases, however, which they contract on shipboard, the astringent washes which are to hide their wounds, and the mischievous tricks used to make them up for sale, are, as the Jamaica report says – a most precious and valuable report, which I shall often have to advert to – one principal cause of this mortality. Upon the whole, however, here is a mortality of about fifty per cent, and this among negroes who are not bought unless quite healthy at first, and unless (as the phrase is with cattle) they are sound in wind and limb...'

# CAMILLE DESMOULINS
## 2 March 1760 – 5 April 1794

*'It is I who call my brothers to liberty!'*
12 July 1789

**An impoverished radical lawyer**, he was in the midst of a crowd of 6,000 Parisians dismayed by the abrupt dismissal of the politician and finance minister Jacques Necker by Louis XVI. Desmoulins had been circulating among the milling crowds urging the people to take up arms against the monarchy. Failing to rouse them, he leapt on a table outside a café in the gardens of the Palais Royal. In his excitement, he lost his normal stammer, and shouted:

> 'Citizens! You know that the nation has demanded that Necker should retain office, that a monument should be raised to him; he has been dismissed! Could they defy you more insolently? After this, they will dare anything, and for this night they meditate, they prepare perhaps, a St. Bartholomew for the patriots. To arms! To arms! Take, all of you, green cockades, the colour of hope. The infamous police are here. Ah, well, let them watch me, let them observe me carefully. Yes, it is I who call my brothers to liberty!' *Lifting two pistols from his coat, Desmoulins carried on:* 'At least, they shall not take me alive, and I shall know how to die gloriously. Only one misfortune can touch me, it is that of seeing France become enslaved.'

Desmoulins was embraced by the crowd, and riots spread across Paris. By the following day the mob had procured arms and was set up as the Parisian militia, eventually becoming the National Guard. The following day, 14 July, the Bastille was stormed. Elected a deputy to the Convention in 1792, Desmoulins voted for the death of the king, becoming one of the most radical of the revolutionaries. Indeed, in the early days of the Revolution he was known as '*The Lantern Lawyer*' for his advocacy of hanging aristocrats from the lamp posts. He fell foul of Robespierre as he began to moderate his views, asking for clemency for victims and becoming closely associated with Danton. Robespierre proposed burning an edition of a leaflet asking for calm, and Desmoulins responded, '*Burning is not answering*', the same riposte Robespierre's hero Rousseau had made to an archbishop who had proposed the burning of his works. During his trial, Desmoulins was asked his age, and replied '*I am 33, the age of the "sans-culotte" Jesus.*' The accused were not allowed to defend themselves. Desmoulins and Danton were guillotined on the same day. Desmoulins's wife Lucile Duplessis was guillotined, also on false charges, eight days after his execution.

# ANTOINE PIERRE JOSEPH MARIE BARNAVE
## 22 October 1761 – 29 November 1793

*'It is not enough that one should desire to be free'*
1 August 1791

**Elected to the States-General in 1789**, Barnave advocated the Proclamation of the Rights of Man, the emancipation of Jews and the abolition of slavery. He led the fight for the sequestration of the property of the church, and became one of the finest orators of the early years of the Revolution. He was president of the National Assembly from 1790. When he saw, however, that mob law was about to usurp the place of the Republican institutions for which he had striven, he feared political chaos and argued in favour of the restoration of the king as a constitutional monarch. On the arrest of the king and the royal family while attempting to escape from France in June 1791, Barnave was one of the three people appointed to conduct them back to Paris. On the journey he was deeply affected by the fate of Marie-Antoinette, and resolved to do what he could to help the royal family. This speech was delivered to the National Assembly, maintaining the inviolability of the king's person and the need for democratic government. His public career came to an end with the close of the Assembly, and he retired to Grenoble at the beginning of 1792. Barnave was impeached for correspondence with Marie-Antoinette. He told his Revolutionary Tribunal *'Better to suffer and die than lose one shade of my moral and political character.'* The following day he was guillotined.

'It is not enough that one should desire to be free – one must know how to be free. I shall speak briefly, for after the success of our deliberations, I await with confidence the spirit and action of this Assembly. I wish only to announce my opinions on a question, the rejection of which must sooner or later mean the loss of our liberties. This question should leave no doubt in the minds of those who reflect on governments and are guided by impartial judgments. Those who have combated the committee have made a fundamental error. They have confounded democratic government with representative government; they have confounded the rights of the people with the qualifications of an elector, which society dispenses for its well understood interest. Where the government, is representative, where there exists in intermediary degree of electors, society, which elects them, has essentially the right to determine the conditions of their eligibility. There is one right existing in our Constitution, that of the active citizen, but the function of an elector is not a right...'

# RICHARD PRICE
## 23 February 1723 – 19 April 1791

*'Tremble all ye oppressors of the world!'*
4 November 1789

**Price was a Welsh preacher**, statistician and moral philosopher, active in radical causes such as the American and French revolutions, and honoured in both of those countries. He was known in his time as *'the Friend of the Universe'* and *'the Great Apostle of Liberty'*. The year 1789 was a pivotal time in which the Ancien Régime was destroyed, and the French Revolution marks the beginning of the Modern Age of Enlightenment. In Britain, the French Revolution created a radicalism that was embraced by Christian dissenters. Price's address was occasioned by the 100th anniversary of the bloodless 'Glorious Revolution' of 1688, and he fervently gave thanks for the American and French revolutions.

'We are met to thank God for that event in this country to which the name of *The Revolution* has been given; and which, for more than a century, it has been usual for the friends of freedom, and more especially Protestant Dissenters, under the title of the Revolution Society, to celebrate with expressions of joy and exultation...By a bloodless victory, the fetters which despotism had been long preparing for us were broken; the rights of the people were asserted, a tyrant expelled, and a Sovereign of our own choice appointed in his room. Security was given to our property, and our consciences were emancipated...Let us, in particular, take care not to forget the principles of the Revolution. This Society has, very properly, in its Reports, held out these principles, as an instruction to the public. I will only take notice of the three following: First: The right to liberty of conscience in religious matters. Secondly: The right to resist power when abused. And, Thirdly: The right to choose our own governors; to cashier them for misconduct; and to frame a government for ourselves... I would farther direct you to remember, that though the Revolution was a great work, it was by no means a perfect work; and that all was not then gained which was necessary to put the kingdom in the secure and complete possession of the blessings of liberty...You should remember that a representation in the legislature of a kingdom is the basis of constitutional liberty in it, and of all legitimate government; and that without it a government is nothing but an usurpation. When the representation is fair and equal, and at the same time vested with such powers as our House of Commons possesses, a kingdom may be said to govern itself, and consequently to possess true liberty. When the representation is partial, a kingdom possesses liberty only partially; and if extremely partial, it only gives a semblance of liberty; but if not only extremely partial, but corruptly chosen, and under corrupt influence after being chosen, it becomes a nuisance, and produces the worst of all forms of government — a government by corruption, a government carried on and supported by spreading venality and profligacy through a kingdom. May heaven preserve this kingdom from a calamity so dreadful!

What an eventful period is this! I am thankful that I have lived to it; and I could almost say, Lord, now lettest thou thy servant depart in peace, for mine eyes have seen thy salvation *[Luke: 2.29–30]*. I have lived to see a diffusion of knowledge, which has undermined superstition and error – I have lived to see the rights of men better understood than ever; and nations panting for liberty, which seemed to have lost the idea of it. – I have lived to see thirty millions of people, indignant and resolute, spurning at slavery, and demanding liberty with an irresistible voice; their king led in triumph, and an arbitrary monarch surrendering himself to his subjects. – After sharing in the benefits of one Revolution, I have been spared to be a witness to two other Revolutions, both glorious. – And now, methinks, I see the ardour for liberty catching and spreading; a general amendment beginning in human affairs; the dominion of kings changed for the dominion of laws, and the dominion of priests giving way to the dominion of reason and conscience. Be encouraged, all ye friends of freedom, and writers in its defence! The times are auspicious. Your labours have not been in vain. Behold kingdoms, admonished by you, starting from sleep, breaking their fetters, and claiming justice from their oppressors! Behold, the light you have struck out, after setting America free, reflected to France, and there kindled into a blaze that lays despotism in ashes, and warms and illuminates Europe! Tremble all ye oppressors of the world! Take warning all ye supporters of slavish governments, and slavish hierarchies! Call no more (absurdly and wickedly) reformation, innovation. You cannot now hold the world in darkness. Struggle no longer against increasing light and liberality. Restore to mankind their rights; and consent to the correction of abuses, before they and you are destroyed together.'

# GEORGES JACQUES DANTON
## 26 October 1759 – 5 April 1794

*'We must dare, dare again, always dare...'*
2 September 1792

**Danton's speeches were an exception** during the French Revolution as they were delivered without previous preparation. Other orators carefully wrote out and read their speeches but Danton always improvised; he never drew up a precis or published a single speech. Thus, for the text of Danton's speeches we have to rely on the reports in the *Moniteur*. He led the attack on the Tuileries in 1792, and became a member of the Committee of Public Safety, but was overthrown by Robespierre and guillotined along with Desmoulins. The French revolutionary forces at Verdun were besieged from 29 August to 2 September, and they surrendered to the Austrians and Prussians on the day that this speech was made.

'It is gratifying to the ministers of a free people to have to announce to them that their country will be saved. All are stirred, all are excited, all burn to fight. You know that Verdun is not yet in the power of our enemies. You know that its garrison swears to immolate the first who breathes a proposition of surrender. One portion of our people will proceed to the frontiers, another will throw up entrenchments, and the third with pikes will defend the hearts of our cities. Paris will second these great efforts. The commissioners of the Commune will solemnly proclaim to the citizens the invitation to arm and march to the defence of the country. At such a moment you can proclaim that the capital deserves well of all France. At such a moment this National Assembly becomes a veritable committee of war. We ask that you concur with us in directing this sublime movement of the people, by naming commissioners who will second us in these great measures. We ask that any one refusing to give personal service or to furnish arms shall be punished with death. We ask that a set of instructions be drawn up for the citizens to direct their movements. We ask that couriers be sent to all the departments to notify them of the decrees that you proclaim here. The tocsin we are about to ring is not an alarm signal; it sounds the charge on the enemies of our country. To conquer them we must dare, dare again, always dare, and France is saved!'

# JEAN-PAUL MARAT
## 24 May 1743 – 13 July 1793

*In his own Defence*
April 1793

**Marat made regular attacks** on the more conservative French revolutionary leaders. In a pamphlet from 26 July 1790, entitled *'C'en est fait de nous'* (*'We're done for!'*), he wrote: *'Five or six hundred heads would have guaranteed your freedom and happiness but a false humanity has restrained your arms and stopped your blows. If you don't strike now, millions of your brothers will die, your enemies will triumph and your blood will flood the streets. They'll slit your throats without mercy and disembowel your wives. And their bloody hands will rip out your children's entrails to erase your love of liberty forever.'* On 21 January 1793 Louis XVI was guillotined, which caused political turmoil in France. From January to May, Marat fought bitterly with the Girondins, whom he believed to be covert enemies of republicanism. The Girondins won the first round when the Convention ordered that Marat should be tried before the Revolutionary Tribunal in April. He began his defence speech to the Convention as follows, before accusing the Girondins of malicious lies. Marat was acquitted, and with great popular support was carried back to the Convention in triumph. He was one of the three most important men in France, along with Danton and Robespierre, but he became a target for his bitter, and more extreme, enemies. Marat was murdered in his bath by Charlotte Corday, a Girondin sympathizer, three months after this trial.

'If, therefore, I appear before my judges, it is only that I may rise triumphant and confound imposture; it is to unseal the eyes of that part of the nation which has already been led astray on my account; it is to go out a conqueror from this imbroglio, to reassure public opinion, to do a good service in the fatherland, and to strengthen the cause of liberty. Full of confidence in the enlightenment, equity, and civic spirit of this tribunal, I myself urge the most rigorous examination into this affair. Strong as I am in the testimony of my own conscience, in the rectitude of my intentions, in the purity of my civic spirit, I seek no indulgence, but demand strict justice. The decree of accusation brought against me was carried without discussion, in violation of law and in contradiction to the principles of order, liberty, and justice. For it is a principle of right that no citizen shall be censured without having first been heard.'

# MARIE-ANNE CHARLOTTE de CORDAY d'ARNANT
## 27 July 1768 – 17 July 1793

*'Let my head, carried through Paris, be a rallying sign for all the friends of law'*
9 July 1793

**Charlotte Corday blamed Marat** for the September Massacres and the killing of Louis XVI, and believed that only Marat's death would prevent civil war in France. On 9 July she went to Paris, took a hotel room and bought a kitchen knife. News of Marat's illness upset her plans to kill him in his seat at the Convention. She then wrote her manifesto explaining her motives for killing him, knowing that it would be unlikely that she would be allowed to read it at her trial. On 13 July she went to Marat's house and stabbed him as he lay in his bath – he spent much time in the bath in an attempt to alleviate the pain of a debilitating skin condition. She was unrepentant at her trial, saying that it was for the good of France, and she was guillotined. Her body was sent for autopsy by the Jacobins to see if she was a virgin, as they wished to find proof that she shared her bed with another plotter. However, there had been no man in her life – she acted alone. 'The Mountain' refers to the Montagnards, a left-wing political group which largely controlled the Assembly.

'How long, O unhappy Frenchmen, will you delight in strife and division? Too long already have party leaders and other scoundrels preferred the interests of their ambition to the public weal. Oh, why, ye unfortunate victims of their fury, will ye kill one another, and by annihilating yourselves, help to establish the edifice of their tyranny upon broken-hearted France? Upon every side the various factions are breaking asunder, the Mountain alone triumphs by the strength of its wickedness and despotism; its vile plots are hatched by monsters gorged with your blood, who are dragging us to destruction by a thousand different roads. We are working at our own undoing with greater energy than we ever put into the conquest of liberty. Oh, Frenchmen! In a little while there will remain of you only the memory of your existence. Even now the indignant departments are marching upon Paris, and the fire of discord and civil war is already kindled throughout one half of this vast realm; there is yet a possibility of extinguishing it, but the means must be prompt. That vilest of all wretches, Marat, whose name alone suffices to conjure up an image of every crime, in falling beneath the avenging steel has shaken the Mountain, has made Danton and Robespierre grow pale, and terrified the other villains who are seated on this throne of blood. But they are encompassed by bolts which the avenging gods of humanity only suspend in order to render their final fall more terrible, and to warn others who might be tempted to build their fortunes on the ruins of an oppressed people. Frenchmen, you know your enemies; arise, then, and march upon them. Let the Mountain be annihilated and only brothers and friends will remain! I know not whether Heaven holds in reserve for us a republican form of government, but only in the very excess of its anger could it give us a ruler from the Mountain.

Oh, France! Your happiness depends upon the proper execution of your laws; but I break none in killing Marat. Condemned by the whole world, he stands outside the pale of the law. What just tribunal would condemn me? If I am guilty, so was Alcides when he destroyed the monsters; yet did he encounter any as odious as Marat? Oh, friends of humanity, you will not regret a wild beast who has fattened on your blood! And you sad aristocrats, whom the Revolution has treated too roughly, you will not regret him either; you and he had nothing in common. Oh, my country, thy misfortunes tear my heart! I can only offer thee my life, and I thank Heaven for the liberty I have to dispose of it. No one will lose by my death. In killing myself, I shall not be like Paris. I desire my last breath to be useful to my fellow-citizens. Let my head, carried through Paris, be a rallying sign for all the friends of law; let the Mountain – already tottering – see its fall written with my blood; let me be their last victim, and the avenged universe will declare that I have deserved well of humanity. For the rest, if some should view my conduct in a different light, I care little...My relatives and friends ought not to be molested, for no one knew of my plans. I add my register of baptism to this address, to show what the most feeble hand can accomplish when nerved by true self-sacrifice. Frenchmen! Should I fail in my enterprise, I have at least pointed the way: you know your enemies – arise, march, and strike!'

# MAXIMILIEN MARIE ISIDORE DE ROBESPIERRE
## 6 May 1758 – 28 July 1794

*'Terror is nothing else than swift, severe, indomitable justice'*
5 February 1794

**This chilling exhortation was delivered** before the National Convention in Paris. Louis XVI had been executed in January 1793, and Robespierre led the Jacobins against the more moderate Girondins in a power struggle. The Jacobins now used the power of the mob to take control of the city and Girondin leaders were systematically executed. Control of the country passed to the Committee of Public Safety, of which Robespierre became the dominant force. Against a backdrop of the threat of foreign invasion and increasing disorder in the country, the committee unleashed the '*Reign of Terror*', eliminating all those considered enemies of the revolution.

'It is time to mark clearly the aim of the Revolution and the end towards which we wish to move. It is time to take stock of ourselves, of the obstacles which we still face, and of the means which we ought to adopt to attain our objectives...But to found and to consolidate among us this democracy, to realize the peaceable rule of constitutional laws, it is necessary to conclude the war of liberty against tyranny and to pass successfully through the storms of revolution. Such is the aim of the revolutionary system which you have set up...Now what is the fundamental principle of democratic, or popular government, that is to say, the essential mainspring upon which it depends and which makes it function? It is virtue. I mean public virtue...That virtue is nothing else but love of fatherland and its laws...The splendour of the goal of the French Revolution is simultaneously the source of our strength and of our weakness: our strength, because it gives us an ascendancy of truth over falsehood, and of public rights over private interests; our weakness, because it rallies against us all vicious men, all those who in their hearts seek to despoil the people...It is necessary to stifle the domestic and foreign enemies of the Republic or perish with them. Now in these circumstances, the first maxim of our politics ought to be to lead the people by means of reason and the enemies of the people by terror. If the basis of popular government in time of peace is virtue, the basis of popular government in time of revolution is both virtue and terror. Virtue without which terror is murderous, terror without which virtue is powerless. Terror is nothing else than swift, severe, indomitable justice; it flows, then, from virtue.'

# MAXIMILIEN MARIE ISIDORE DE ROBESPIERRE
## 6 May 1758 – 28 July 1794

*'Our blood flows for the cause of humanity'*
8 June 1794

**The leader of the Extreme Left** in the Assembly, Robespierre was one of the chief Jacobin orators and a fierce opponent of the Girondins. He became a member of the Committee of Public Safety and was strongly identified with the horrors of the Reign of Terror. His desire for revolutionary change was not confined to politics and sovereignty, as he wished to inspire a spiritual resurgence in France. The revolutionaries rejected the power of the Roman Catholic Church, and on 7 May 1794 Robespierre had a decree passed by the Convention, establishing state religion, the Cult of the Supreme Being. In honour of the Supreme Being, a celebration was to be held annually on 8 June. Robespierre, as president of the Convention, led the first festival procession in 1794 when he delivered this speech. In late May, Robespierre had introduced a decree which permitted the guillotining of citizens thought to be counter-revolutionaries without extensive trials, enabling the pace of executions to be quickened. This measure, along with his ostentation in leading this expensive procession through Paris, marked the beginning of Robespierre's downfall.

'The day forever fortunate has arrived, which the French people have
consecrated to the Supreme Being. Never has the world which He created
offered to Him a spectacle so worthy of His notice. He has seen reigning
on the earth tyranny, crime, and imposture. He sees at this moment
a whole nation, grappling with all the oppressions of the human race,
suspend the course of its heroic labours to elevate its thoughts and vows
toward the great Being who has given it the mission it has undertaken
and the strength to accomplish it. Is it not He whose immortal hand,
engraving on the heart of man the code of justice and equality, has
written there the death sentence of tyrants? Is it not He who, from the
beginning of time, decreed for all the ages and for all peoples liberty,
good faith, and justice?...The monster which the genius of kings had
vomited over France has gone back into nothingness...Frenchmen, you
war against kings; you are therefore worthy to honour Divinity...Hatred
of bad faith and tyranny burns in our hearts, with love of justice and the
fatherland. Our blood flows for the cause of humanity. Behold our prayer.
Behold our sacrifices. Behold the worship we offer Thee.'

# MAXIMILIEN MARIE ISIDORE DE ROBESPIERRE
## 6 May 1758 – 28 July 1794

*'Death is the commencement of immortality!'*
26 July 1794

His last speech was delivered in the Convention the day before Robespierre's arrest and two days before his execution. In the *Moniteur* only a brief account of it was given at the time of its delivery. The next day in the Convention, one deputy after another accused Robespierre of being a dictator, and he tried to shoot himself while being arrested, but only succeeded in shattering his jaw. He was guillotined facing upwards. When placed on the block his executioner removed the bandage holding Robespierre's injured jaw in place, causing him to scream in pain until the blade dropped. The speech was printed a few weeks after Robespierre's death, from a draft found among his papers.

'The enemies of the Republic call me tyrant! Were I such they would grovel at my feet. I should gorge them with gold, I should grant them impunity for their crimes, and they would be grateful. Were I such, the kings we have vanquished, far from denouncing Robespierre, would lend me their guilty support. There would be a covenant between them and me. Tyranny must have tools. But the enemies of tyranny – whither does their path tend? To the tomb, and to immortality! ...My life? Oh, my life I abandon without a regret! I have seen the Past; and I foresee the Future. What friend of his country would wish to survive the moment when he could no longer serve it – when he could no longer defend innocence against oppression? Wherefore should I continue in an order of things, where intrigue eternally triumphs over truth; where justice is mocked; where passions the most abject, or fears the most absurd, override the sacred interests of humanity?...

Question history, and learn how all the defenders of liberty, in all times, have been overwhelmed by calumny. But their traducers died also. The good and the bad disappear alike from the earth; but in very different conditions. O Frenchmen! O my countrymen! Let not your enemies, with their desolating doctrines, degrade your souls, and enervate your virtues! ...Citizens!... "Death is the commencement of immortality!" I leave to the oppressors of the people a terrible testament, which I proclaim with the independence befitting one whose career is so nearly ended; it is the awful truth: "Thou shalt die!"'

# FISHER AMES
## 19 April 1758 – 4 July 1808

---

### 'What is patriotism?'
### 25 April 1796

**Ames is best known for his opposition** to Jeffersonian democracy, favouring a constitutional republic. He believed that *'the United States must lash itself to a constitution of laws, not the whim of democratic preference'*. He is one of the *'forgotten Founding Fathers'*, and both Daniel Webster and Abraham Lincoln memorized the speech from which the extract below is taken, his greatest declamation. On 19 November 1794, a *'treaty of amity, commerce, and navigation'* (the 'Jay Treaty') with Great Britain had been concluded, and in March 1796 it was proclaimed as the law of the land. Ames's eloquent support of the treaty to preserve peace with England (1794) convinced the House to pass an enabling appropriation. On 25 April a resolution was offered that it would be expedient *'to pass the laws necessary for carrying the treaty into effect'*. Ames's speech was given in favour of this resolution, and it is regarded as one of the first great speeches to the House of Congress. He delivered another of equal merit on 28 April, after which the treaty was accepted.

'What is patriotism? Is it a narrow affection for the spot where a man was born? Are the very clods where we tread entitled to this ardent preference because they are greener? No, sir, this is not the character of the virtue, and it soars higher for its object. It is an extended self-love, mingling with all the enjoyments of life, and twisting itself with the minutest filaments of the heart. It is thus we obey the laws of society, because they are the laws of virtue. In their authority we see not the array of force and terror, but the venerable image of our country's honor. Every good citizen makes that honor his own and cherishes it not only as precious, but as sacred. He is willing to risk his life in its defense, and is conscious that he gains protection while he gives it. For, what rights of a citizen will be deemed inviolable when a State renounces the principles that constitute their security? Or if his life should not be invaded, what would its enjoyments be in a country odious in the eyes of strangers and dishonored in his own? Could he look with affection and veneration to such a country as his parent? The sense of having one would die within him; he would blush for his patriotism, if he retained any, and justly, for it would be a vice. He would be a banished man in his native land...'

# NAPOLÉON BONAPARTE, EMPEROR NAPOLEON I
## 15 August 1769 – 5 May 1821

*'Your country has a right to expect of you great things!'*
10 May 1796

 Napoléon Bonaparte was originally a Corsican nationalist, and he defended the Convention (the Revolutionary legislative assembly) in the Tuileries Palace in Paris from an attack by Royalists in 1795. An artillery officer, he realized that a *'whiff of grapeshot'* would clear the streets – 1,400 Royalists died in this action while the rest fled. Suddenly he had fame and the patronage of the grateful Republican Directorate, and he was given permission to attack Austrian forces in Italy. The Battle of Lodi was won a few days after he gave this speech to the Army of Italy, with the Austrians being driven out of Lombardy. Arcole was won on 15–17 November, and in March 1797 Napoléon led his army into Austria, forcing it to negotiate peace. By clever use of spies and the arts of deception, he won battles by concealment of his troop deployments and by concentration of his forces on the 'hinge' of his enemy's weakened front. In this Italian campaign, Bonaparte's army eventually captured 150,000 prisoners, 540 cannons and 170 standards. During the campaign, Bonaparte became increasingly influential in French politics. His speeches were generally proclamations; but in form and spirit they were orations.

'Soldiers! You have, in 15 days, gained six victories, taken 21 standards
of colours, 50 pieces of cannon, several fortified places, made 1,500
prisoners, and killed or wounded over 10,000 men. You are the equals of
the conquerors of Holland and of the Rhine. Destitute of everything, you
have supplied yourselves with everything. You have won battles without
cannon, crossed rivers without bridges, made forced marches without
shoes, bivouacked without spirituous liquor, and often without bread.
The Republican phalanxes – the soldiers of liberty, were alone capable of
enduring what you have suffered. Thanks to you, soldiers! Your country
has a right to expect of you great things. You have still battles to fight,
cities to take, rivers to pass. Is there one among you whose courage flags?
One who would prefer returning to the sterile summits of the Apennines
and the Alps, to undergo patiently the insults of that slavish soldiery? No,
there is not one such among the victors of Montenotte, of Millesimo, of
Diego, and of Mondovi! Friends, I promise you that glorious conquest:
but be the liberators of peoples, be not their scourges!'

# NAPOLÉON BONAPARTE, EMPEROR NAPOLEON I
## 15 August 1769 – 5 May 1821

*'The French people, free and respected by the whole world, shall give to Europe a glorious peace'*
15 May 1796

**Bonaparte delivered this speech** to the Army of Italy, five days after the victorious Battle of Lodi.

'Soldiers! You have precipitated yourselves like a torrent from the Apennines. You have overwhelmed or swept before you all that opposed your march. Piedmont, delivered from Austrian oppression, has returned to her natural sentiments of peace and friendship towards France. Milan is yours, and over all Lombardy floats the flag of the Republic...The army which proudly threatened you finds no remaining barrier of defence against your courage. The Po, the Tessino, the Adda, could not stop you a single day. Those vaunted ramparts of Italy proved insufficient; you traversed them as rapidly as you did the Apennines. Successes so numerous and brilliant have carried joy to the heart of your country! Your representatives have decreed a festival, to be celebrated in all the communes of the Republic, in honour of your victories. There will your fathers, mothers, wives, sisters, all who hold you dear, rejoice over your triumphs, and boast that you belong to them.

...Let those who have sharpened the poniards of civil war in France, who have pusillanimously assassinated our ministers, who have burned our vessels at Toulon – let them now tremble! The hour of vengeance has knolled! But let not the people be disquieted. We are the friends of every people: and more especially of the descendants of the Brutuses, the Scipios, and other great men to whom we look as bright exemplars. To re-establish the Capitol; to place there with honour the statues of the heroes who made it memorable; to rouse the Roman people, unnerved by many centuries of oppression – such will be some of the fruits of our victories. They will constitute an epoch for posterity. To you, soldiers, will belong the immortal honour of redeeming the fairest portion of Europe. The French people, free and respected by the whole world, shall give to Europe a glorious peace, which shall indemnify it for all the sacrifices which it has borne the last six years. Then, by your own firesides you shall repose; and your fellow citizens, when they point out any one of you, shall say: "He belonged to the army of Italy!".'

# THEOBALD WOLFE TONE
## 20 June 1763 – 19 November 1798

*'...it is no great effort, at this day, to add the sacrifice of my life'*
10 November 1798

**Tone is regarded as the Father** of Irish Republicanism, and in October 1791 he helped found the Society of United Irishmen. By 1794, he realized that the dream of universal suffrage and equal electoral districts could not happen under English rule, and began helping to plan a French invasion. Tone issued an 'Invasion Manifesto' (Address to the People of Ireland) in 1796. The French Directorate appointed General Hoche to command an Irish expedition with Tone as adjutant-general. They sailed on 15 December 1796 with 43 ships and 15,000 men, but were scattered by storms. Hoche died in 1797, and following news of the outbreak of the the 1798 Rebellion in Ireland, on 12 October Tone sailed with General Hardy and 2,300 men aboard the flagship of Commodore Jean-Baptiste Bompard's new invasion fleet comprising a man-of-war, 16 frigates and a schooner. Tone was captured aboard the man-of-war in Lough Swilly, having turned down the opportunity to escape aboard a fast-sailing frigate on 16 October 1798. His brother Matthew had also been captured and hanged on 29 September. Tone was tried and sentenced by court martial, 10 November 1798, under protest from General Hardy at his ignominious treatment as a criminal. He answered the charges with a plea of guilty – *'I mean not to give the court any useless trouble, and wish to spare them the idle task of examining witnesses. I admit all the facts alleged.'* Tone appeared at his trial in French uniform. The speech was addressed to the court martial assembled to try him in the Dublin barracks. His request that he might be shot, instead of hanged, and thus die a soldier's death, was refused. While awaiting execution he tried to commit suicide by slitting his throat, and when discovered on the morning of his execution, said *'I find then I am but a bad anatomist.'* Tone took eight days to die in agony from his wound on 19 November, and his immediate interment was ordered by the English Government to prevent a huge funeral and probable riots. During his trial the judge advocate had called on the prisoner to plead guilty or not guilty to the charge of having acted traitorously and hostilely against the king. Tone replied:

'I mean not to give the court any useless trouble, and wish to spare them the idle task of examining witnesses. I admit all the facts alleged, and only request leave to read an address which I have prepared for this occasion...Mr. President and Gentlemen of the Court-Martial, I mean not to give you the trouble of bringing judicial proof to convict me legally of having acted in hostility to the government of his Britannic majesty in Ireland. I admit the fact. From my earliest youth I have regarded the connection between Great Britain and Ireland as the curse of the Irish nation, and felt convinced that, while it lasted, this country could never be free nor happy. My mind has been confirmed in this opinion by the experience of every succeeding year, and the conclusions which I have drawn from every fact before my eyes. In consequence, I was determined to employ all the powers which my individual efforts could move, in order to separate the two countries. That Ireland was not able of herself to throw off the yoke, I knew; I therefore sought for aid wherever it was to be found. In honourable poverty I rejected offers which, to a man in my circumstances, might be considered highly advantageous. I remained faithful to what I thought the cause of my country, and sought in the French Republic an ally to rescue three millions of my countrymen.

...After such a sacrifice, in a cause which I have always considered – conscientiously considered – as the cause of justice and freedom, it is no great effort, at this day, to add the sacrifice of my life. But I hear it is said that this unfortunate country has been a prey to all sorts of horrors. I sincerely lament it. I beg, however, that it may be remembered that I have been absent four years from Ireland. To me those sufferings can never be attributed. I designed by fair and open war to procure a separation of two countries. For open war I was prepared, but instead of that a system of private assassination has taken place. I repeat, while I deplore it, that it is not chargeable on me. Atrocities, it seems, have been committed on both sides. I do not less deplore them. I detest them from my heart; and to those who know my character and sentiments, I may safely appeal for the truth of this assertion: with them I need no justification. In a case like this success is everything. Success, in the eyes of the vulgar, fixes its merits. Washington succeeded, and Kosciusko *[a national hero in Poland, Belarus and Lithuania who led an uprising against Prussia and Russia]* failed...'

# HENRY GRATTAN
### 3 July 1746 – 6 June 1820

---

*'It was the act of a coward, who raises his arm to strike,
but has not courage to give the blow'*
14 February 1800

**Grattan, an Irishman with unsurpassed** oratorical powers, returned to parliament in 1800 to wage a vigorous but unsuccessful campaign against Prime Minister William Pitt's plans for the legislative union of the Irish and English parliaments. Grattan had secured the restoration of independence to the Irish parliament in 1782, and had retired in 1797. On 15 January 1800 the Irish parliament met for its last-ever session.

At seven o'clock on the following morning Grattan entered the Irish House of Commons and took the oaths. Shortly afterwards he rose to speak. Finding himself too weak to stand, with the leave of the house he addressed it from a seated position. Grattan spoke for over two hours with astounding eloquence, denouncing the proposed union, exclaiming, *'The thing he proposes to buy is what cannot be sold – liberty'*. In spite of the enthusiasm of his supporters, his amendment was defeated by 138 to 96. On 14 February Isaac Corry, the chancellor of the exchequer, moved the first of the resolutions in favour of the union, and made a violent personal attack upon Grattan, whom he charged with encouraging the rebellion. Grattan, in a scathing reply, denied the charge, and on the following morning a duel took place between them at Ball's Bridge, Dublin, with the result being that Corry was wounded in the arm. The following is part of the splendid piece of invective from Grattan which led to the duel.

'Has the gentleman done? Has he completely done? He was unparliamentary from the beginning to the end of his speech. There was scarce a word he uttered that was not a violation of the privileges of the House; but I did not call him to order – Why? Because the limited talents of some men render it impossible for them to be severe without being unparliamentary. But before I sit down I shall show him how to be severe and parliamentary at the same time. On any other occasion I should think myself justifiable in treating with silent contempt anything which might fall from that honourable member; but there are times when the insignificance of the accuser is lost in the magnitude of the accusation. I know the difficulty the honourable gentleman laboured under when he attacked me, conscious that, on a comparative view of our characters, public and private, there is nothing he could say which would injure me. The public would not believe the charge. I despise the falsehood. If such a charge were made by an honest man, I would answer it in the manner I shall do before I sit down. But I shall first reply to it when not made by an honest man.

The right honourable gentleman has called me "an unimpeached traitor". I ask, why not "traitor", unqualified by any epithet? I will tell him: it was because he dare not. It was the act of a coward, who raises his arm to strike, but has not courage to give the blow. I will not call him villain, because it would be unparliamentary, and he is a privy counsellor. I will not call him fool, because he happens to be Chancellor of the Exchequer. But I say he is one who has abused the privilege of Parliament and freedom of debate to the uttering language, which, if spoken out of the House, I should answer only with a blow. I care not how high his situation, how low his character, how contemptible his speech; whether a privy counsellor or a parasite, my answer would be a blow. He has charged me with being connected with the rebels: the charge is utterly, totally, and meanly false...I have returned, not as the right honourable member has said, to raise another storm; I have returned to discharge an honourable debt of gratitude to my country, that conferred a great reward for past services, which, I am proud to say, was not greater than my desert. I have returned to protect that Constitution, of which I was the parent and founder, from the assassination of such men as the honourable gentleman and his unworthy associates. They are corrupt; they are seditious; and they, at this very moment, are in a conspiracy against their country. I have returned to refute a libel as false as it is malicious, given to the public under the appellation of a report of a committee of the lords. Here I stand ready for impeachment or trial; I dare accusation. I defy the honourable gentleman; I defy the government; I defy their whole phalanx; let them come forth. I tell the ministers I will neither give them quarter nor take it. I am here to lay the shattered remains of my Constitution on the floor of this House in defence of the liberties of my country.'

# THOMAS JEFFERSON
## 13 April 1743 – 4 July 1826

*'I advance with obedience to the work'*
4 March 1801

**Thomas Jefferson was inaugurated** as the third president of the United States after one of the nation's closest presidential contests. In this First Inaugural Address, Jefferson tried to reach out to his political opponents and heal the breach between Federalists and Republicans. Strongly criticized as a deist or even an atheist, Jefferson strongly stated his belief in the importance of religion, and listed the *'freedom of religion'* prominently among the constitutional freedoms. In these days where all politicians have teams of speech-writers and spin-doctors to manipulate and express the thoughts of their advisers, it is refreshing to read the self-penned words of a polymath.

'...About to enter, fellow-citizens, on the exercise of duties which comprehend everything dear and valuable to you, it is proper you should understand what I deem the essential principles of our Government, and consequently those which ought to shape its Administration. I will compress them within the narrowest compass they will bear, stating the general principle, but not all its limitations. Equal and exact justice to all men, of whatever state or persuasion, religious or political; peace, commerce, and honest friendship with all nations, entangling alliances with none; the support of the State governments in all their rights, as the most competent administrations for our domestic concerns and the surest bulwarks against antirepublican tendencies; the preservation of the General Government in its whole constitutional vigor, as the sheet anchor of our peace at home and safety abroad; a jealous care of the right of election by the people – a mild and safe corrective of abuses which are lopped by the sword of revolution where peaceable remedies are unprovided; absolute acquiescence in the decisions of the majority, the vital principle of republics, from which is no appeal but to force, the vital principle and immediate parent of despotism; a well-disciplined militia, our best reliance in peace and for the first moments of war till regulars may relieve them; the supremacy of the civil over the military authority; economy in the public expense, that labor may be lightly burdened; the honest payment of our debts and sacred preservation of the public faith;

encouragement of agriculture, and of commerce as its handmaid; the diffusion of information and arraignment of all abuses at the bar of the public reason; freedom of religion; freedom of the press, and freedom of person under the protection of the habeas corpus, and trial by juries impartially selected. These principles form the bright constellation which has gone before us and guided our steps through an age of revolution and reformation. The wisdom of our sages and blood of our heroes have been devoted to their attainment. They should be the creed of our political faith, the text of civic instruction, the touchstone by which to try the services of those we trust; and should we wander from them in moments of error or of alarm, let us hasten to retrace our steps and to regain the road which alone leads to peace, liberty, and safety.

I repair, then, fellow-citizens, to the post you have assigned me. With experience enough in subordinate offices to have seen the difficulties of this the greatest of all, I have learnt to expect that it will rarely fall to the lot of imperfect man to retire from this station with the reputation and the favor which bring him into it. Without pretensions to that high confidence you reposed in our first and greatest revolutionary character, whose preeminent services had entitled him to the first place in his country's love and destined for him the fairest page in the volume of faithful history, I ask so much confidence only as may give firmness and effect to the legal administration of your affairs. I shall often go wrong through defect of judgment. When right, I shall often be thought wrong by those whose positions will not command a view of the whole ground. I ask your indulgence for my own errors, which will never be intentional, and your support against the errors of others, who may condemn what they would not if seen in all its parts. The approbation implied by your suffrage is a great consolation to me for the past, and my future solicitude will be to retain the good opinion of those who have bestowed it in advance, to conciliate that of others by doing them all the good in my power, and to be instrumental to the happiness and freedom of all. Relying, then, on the patronage of your good will, I advance with obedience to the work, ready to retire from it whenever you become sensible how much better choice it is in your power to make. And may that Infinite Power which rules the destinies of the universe lead our councils to what is best, and give them a favorable issue for your peace and prosperity.'

# JOHN QUINCY ADAMS
## 11 July 1767 – 23 February 1848

*'Man, therefore, was not made for himself alone.*
*No, he was made for his country'*
22 December 1802

**After graduating from Harvard College**, this son of President John Adams became a lawyer. Aged 26 he was appointed minister to the Netherlands, then was promoted to the Berlin Legation. In 1802 he was elected to the United States Senate, and made this speech at Plymouth to commemorate the landing of the Pilgrim Fathers. Six years later President Madison appointed him minister to Russia, and then Adams became secretary of state and eventually president of the United States.

'Among the sentiments of most powerful operation upon the human heart, and most highly honorable to the human character, are those of veneration for our forefathers, and of love for our posterity. They form the connecting links between the selfish and the social passions. By the fundamental principle of Christianity, the happiness of the individual is interwoven, by innumerable and imperceptible ties, with that of his contemporaries. By the power of filial reverence and parental affection, individual existence is extended beyond the limits of individual life, and the happiness of every age is chained in mutual dependence upon that of every other. Respect for his ancestors excites, in the breast of man, interest in their history, attachment to their characters, concern for their errors, involuntary pride in their virtues. Love for his posterity spurs him to exertion for their support, stimulates him to virtue for their example, and fills him with the tenderest solicitude for their welfare. Man, therefore, was not made for himself alone. No, he was made for his country, by the obligations of the social compact; he was made for his species, by the Christian duties of universal charity; he was made for all ages past, by the sentiment of reverence for his forefathers; and he was made for all future times, by the impulse of affection for his progeny. Under the influence of these principles, "Existence sees him spurn her bounded reign." They redeem his nature from the subjection of time and space; he is no longer a "puny insect shivering at a breeze;" he is the glory of creation, formed to occupy all time and all extent; bounded, during his residence upon earth, only to the boundaries of the world, and destined to life and immortality in brighter regions, when the fabric of nature itself shall dissolve and perish. The voice of history has not, in all its compass, a note but answers in unison with these sentiments. The barbarian chieftain, who defended his country against the Roman invasion, driven to the remotest extremity of Britain, and stimulating his followers to battle by all that has power of persuasion upon the human heart, concluded his persuasion by an appeal to these irresistible feelings: "Think of your forefathers and of your posterity."

The Romans themselves, at the pinnacle of civilization, were actuated by the same impressions, and celebrated, in anniversary festivals, every great event which had signalized the annals of their forefathers. To multiply instances where it were impossible to adduce an exception would be to waste your time and abuse your patience; but in the sacred volume, which contains the substances of our firmest faith and of our most precious hopes, these passions not only maintain their highest efficacy, but are sanctioned by the express injunctions of the Divine Legislator to his chosen people. The revolutions of time furnish no previous example of a nation shooting up to maturity and expanding into greatness with the rapidity which has characterized the growth of the American people. In the luxuriance of youth, and in the vigor of manhood, it is pleasing and instructive to look backward upon the helpless days of infancy; but in the continual and essential changes of a growing subject, the transactions of that early period would be soon obliterated from the memory but for some periodical call of attention to aid the silent records of the historian. Such celebrations arouse and gratify the kindliest emotions of the bosom. They are faithful pledges of the respect we bear to the memory of our ancestors and of the tenderness with which we cherish the rising generation. They introduce the sages and heroes of ages past to the notice and emulation of succeeding times; they are at once testimonials of our gratitude, and schools of virtue to our children. These sentiments are wise; they are honorable; they are virtuous; their cultivation is not merely innocent pleasure, it is incumbent duty. Obedient to their dictates, you, my fellow-citizens, have instituted and paid frequent observance to this annual solemnity, and what event of weightier intrinsic importance, or of more extensive consequences, was ever selected for this honorary distinction? ...Let us unite in ardent supplication to the Founder of nations and the Builder of worlds, that what then was prophecy may continue unfolding into history – that the dearest hopes of the human race may not be extinguished in disappointment, and that the last may prove the noblest empire of time.'

# ROBERT EMMET
## 4 March 1778 – 20 September 1803

*'Let no man write my epitaph'*
19 September 1803

**At the age of 15 in 1793** Robert Emmet entered Trinity College, Dublin, and became secretary to the secret United Irish Committee. As a result he was expelled from the college in 1798, and fled to France to avoid the many arrests that were taking place in Ireland. While in France, he gained the agreement of Napoleon to support an armed Irish rebellion. He took part in the abortive 1798 rising, but no French help was forthcoming. In April 1799 a warrant was issued for his arrest, and he again escaped to France in the hope of securing military aid. His returned to Ireland in October 1802, and in March 1803 began preparations for another rising. He began to manufacture weapons and explosives at a number of premises in Dublin but the rebels failed to take Dublin Castle on the evening of 23 July 1803. In the riots that followed, Emmet tried to call off the rising after witnessing a dragoon being piked to death. Two judges were hacked to death, and around 50 rebels and 20 military died before the fighting stopped. Emmet fled, but was captured on 25 August after moving to be closer to his lady friend's house. He was tried for treason on 19 September, and the Crown bolstered its weak case by buying the assistance of his defence attorney for £200 and a pension. Emmet's trial is remembered for his stirring speech and his jibe at the 'hanging judge' that '*Lord Norbury might easily drown in the blood of those he had sent to the gallows*'. After he had been found guilty of high treason, and sentenced to hanging, drawing and quartering, Emmet delivered this impromptu speech from the dock. An earlier version of the speech was published in 1818, in a biography on his sweetheart's father John Curran:

'I am here ready to die. I am not allowed to vindicate my character; no man shall dare to vindicate my character; and when I am prevented from vindicating myself, let no man dare to calumniate me. Let my character and my motives repose in obscurity and peace, till other times and other men can do them justice. Then shall my character be vindicated; then may my epitaph be written.

My Lords – What have I to say why sentence of death should not be pronounced on me according to law? I have nothing to say that can alter your predetermination, nor that it will become me to say with any view to the mitigation of that sentence which you are here to pronounce, and I must abide by. But I have that to say which interests me more than life, and which you have laboured (as was necessarily your office in the present circumstances of this oppressed country) to destroy. I have much to say why my reputation should be rescued from the load of false accusation and calumny which has been heaped upon it. I do not imagine that, seated where you are, your minds can be so free from impurity as to receive the least impression from what I am going to utter...If the spirits of the illustrious dead participate in the concerns and cares of those who are dear to them in this transitory life – Oh, ever dear and venerated shade of my departed father, look down with scrutiny upon the conduct of your suffering son; and see if I have even for a moment deviated from those principles of morality and patriotism which it was your care to instil into my youthful mind, and for which I am now to offer up my life! My lords, you are impatient for the sacrifice – the blood which you seek is not congealed by the artificial terrors which surround your victim; it circulates warmly and unruffled, through the channels which God created for noble purposes, but which you are bent to destroy, for purposes so grievous, that they cry to heaven. Be yet patient! I have but a few words more to say. I am going to my cold and silent grave: my lamp of life is nearly extinguished: my race is run: the grave opens to receive me, and I sink into its bosom! I have but one request to ask at my departure from this world – it is the charity of its silence! Let no man write my epitaph: for as no man who knows my motives dare now vindicate them, let not prejudice or ignorance asperse them. Let them and me repose in obscurity and peace, and my tomb remain uninscribed, until other times, and other men, can do justice to my character; when my country takes her place among the nations of the earth, then, and not till then, let my epitaph be written. I have done.'

# RED JACKET
### *c.*1758 – 20 January 1830

*'We gave them corn and meat; they gave us poison in return'*
Summer 1805

**Red Jacket was known as Otetiani** in his youth, and as Sagoyewatha (Keeper Awake) after 1780 because of his oratorical skills. A Seneca Native American, he was chief of the Wolf clan, and became famous for speaking in support of the rights of his people. He played a prominent role in negotiations with the new federal government, and in 1792 headed a delegation of 50 people to Philadelphia where George Washington presented him with a large peace medal. Red Jacket wore this medal on his chest in every portrait painted of him. The name Red Jacket referred to an embroidered scarlet jacket presented to him by a British officer during the Revolution. This speech was given in response to a young missionary named Cram who was sent into the country of the Six Nations by the Evangelical Missionary Society of Massachusetts. He wished to establish a missionary station among the Seneca, and a council of their chiefs was convoked at Buffalo Creek to hear his proposals. After about two hours of consultation between the chiefs, Red Jacket responded with this wonderful *'apologetic'*.

'Friend and Brother – It was the will of the Great Spirit that we should meet together this day. He orders all things and has given us a fine day for our council. He has taken His garment from before the sun and caused it to shine with brightness upon us. Our eyes are opened that we see clearly; our ears are unstopped that we have been able to hear distinctly the words you have spoken. For all these favors we thank the Great Spirit, and Him only. Brother, this council fire was kindled by you. It was at your request that we came together at this time. We have listened with attention to what you have said. You requested us to speak our minds freely. This gives us great joy; for we now consider that we stand upright before you and can speak what we think. All have heard your voice and all speak to you now as one man. Our minds are agreed.

Brother, you say you want an answer to your talk before you leave this place. It is right you should have one, as you are a great distance from home and we do not wish to detain you. But first we will look back a little and tell you what our fathers have told us and what we have heard from the white people. Brother, listen to what we say. There was a time when our forefathers owned this great island. Their seats extended from the rising to the setting sun. The Great Spirit had made it for the use of Indians. He had created the buffalo, the deer, and other animals for food. He had made the bear and the beaver. Their skins served us for clothing. He had scattered them over the country and taught us how to take them. He had caused the earth to produce corn for bread. All this He had done for His red children because He loved them. If we had some disputes about our hunting-ground they were generally settled without the shedding of much blood. But an evil day came upon us. Your forefathers crossed the great water and landed on this island. Their numbers were small. They found friends and not enemies. They told us they had fled from their own country for fear of wicked men and had come here to enjoy their religion. They asked for a small seat. We took pity on them, granted their request, and they sat down among us. We gave them corn and meat; they gave us poison in return. The white people, brother, had now found our country. Tidings were carried back and more came among us. Yet we did not fear them. We took them to be friends. They called us brothers. We believed them and gave them a larger seat. At length their numbers had greatly increased. They wanted more land; they wanted our country. Our eyes were opened and our minds became uneasy. War took place. Indians were hired to fight against Indians, and many of our people were destroyed. They also brought strong liquor among us. It was strong and powerful, and has slain thousands. Brother, our seats were once large and yours were small. You have now become a great people, and we have scarcely a place left to spread our blankets. You have got our country, but are not satisfied; you want to force your religion upon us...Brother, you say there is but one way to worship and serve the Great Spirit. If there is but one religion, why do you white people differ so much about it? Why not all agreed, as you can all read the Book?'

# WILLIAM PITT THE YOUNGER
## 28 May 1759 – 23 January 1806

*'Europe is not to be saved by any single man'*
9 November 1805

**From 1803 Britain had been at war** with Napoleon's 'First French Empire'. Prime Minister Pitt had worked himself almost to death securing a 'Third Coalition' of Russia, Austria, Sweden and Britain to defeat Napoleon. The surrender of the Austrians at Ulm (16–19 October 1805) was news of great bitterness to him. However, soon afterwards came the crowning naval victory at Trafalgar on 21 October. In the summer of 1805 Napoleon had been at Boulogne on the northern coast of France, but his invasion plans were wrecked by the failure of the French fleet to reach the English Channel. Britain's supremacy of the seas now ensured that there would be no invasion. Thus Napoleon marched his army into middle Europe to attack the other members of the Third Coalition. Pitt's popularity was enormously enhanced by the event. The lord mayor of London proposed Pitt's health as *'the saviour of Europe'* at London's Guildhall. Pitt stood, responded in just two sentences, and sat down exhausted. The statesman Lord Curzon rates this as one of the three greatest English language speeches in history along with Lincoln's *Second Inaugural Speech* and his *Gettysburg Address*. Pitt was in ill health, suffering from gout, anxiety and exhaustion and went to Bath to take the waters to recuperate. While there, he heard of the destruction of his coalition on 2 December at the Battle of Austerlitz. It was Bonaparte's greatest victory, against a huge Russo-Austrian army, after which Vienna was occupied and the Austrian empire humbled. Pitt was struck down by a severe internal illness (probably a peptic or duodenal ulcer) and he was gravely ill when, on 11 January 1806, he returned home to Putney Heath. It is said that as he walked along to his bedroom, he observed a map of Europe hanging on the wall, at which he turned to his niece and mournfully said: *'Roll up that map. It will not be wanted these ten years.'* He died 12 days later, just six weeks after this last public speech.

'I return you many thanks for the honour you have done me; but Europe is not to be saved by any single man. England has saved herself by her exertions, and will, as I trust, save Europe by her example.'

# CHIEF TECUMSEH
## March 1768 – 5 October 1813

---

*'My forefathers were warriors'*
Council at Vincennes, 12 August 1810

**In 1809 General Harrison**, governor of Indiana (later an American president), purchased a huge tract of land on both sides of the Wabash River. The Shawnee chief Tecumseh was absent from the negotiations. On his return a furious Tecumseh confronted Harrison at a council at Vincennes to demand that these land purchase treaties be rescinded:

'It is true I am a Shawnee. My forefathers were warriors. Their son is a warrior. From them I take only my existence; from my tribe I take nothing...The being within, communing with past ages, tells me that once, nor until lately, there was no white man on this continent; that it then all belonged to red men, children of the same parents, placed on it by the Great Spirit that made them, to keep it, to traverse it, to enjoy its productions, and to fill it with the same race, once a happy race, since made miserable by the white people, who are never contented but always encroaching. The way, and the only way, to check and to stop this evil, is for all the red men to unite in claiming a common and equal right in the land, as it was at first, and should be yet; for it never was divided, but belongs to all for the use of each. For no part has a right to sell, even to each other, much less to strangers – those who want all, and will not do with less. The white people have no right to take the land from the Indians, because they had it first; it is theirs. They may sell, but all must join. Any sale not made by all is not valid. The late sale is bad...*[The land]* belongs to the first who sits down on his blanket or skins which he has thrown upon the ground; and till he leaves it no other has a right.'

Tecumseh now travelled to try and raise a confederation of tribes to oppose land grabs, and in his absence his twin brother was killed by Harrison at Tippecanoe in 1811. Tecumseh joined the British in the War of 1812, capturing Fort Detroit. He commanded the right wing at the Battle of the Thames where he was killed.

# GEORGE GORDON BYRON
## 22 January 1788 – 19 April 1824

*'Are we aware of our obligations to a mob?'*
27 February 1812

**The Romantic poet Lord Byron** took his seat in the House of Lords in 1809. He was a strong advocate of social reform, and one of the very few parliamentary defenders of the Luddite movement, a group of textile workers who protested – often by destroying mechanized looms – against the changes produced by the Industrial Revolution. He lived in Nottinghamshire, a centre for textile manufacture, where Luddite 'frame-breakers' were destroying new textile machines that were putting them out of work. Byron spoke against the death penalty proposed by the government's Framework Bill. This was his first speech before the Lords, and was full of sarcastic references to the 'benefits' of industrialization and automation, which he said was producing inferior material, as well as putting people out of work. (Judge Jeffreys was a notorious 'hanging judge' who dispensed brutal justice after the Monmouth Rebellion of 1685.)

'During the short time I recently passed in Nottinghamshire, not twelve hours elapsed without some fresh act of violence; and on the day I left the county I was informed that forty frames had been broken the preceding evening, as usual, without resistance and without detection... Are we aware of our obligations to a mob? It is the mob that labour in your fields and serve in your houses, – that man your navy, and recruit your army, – that have enabled you to defy all the world, and can also defy you when neglect and calamity have driven them to despair! You may call the people a mob; but do not forget that a mob too often speaks the sentiments of the people...Setting aside the palpable injustice and the certain inefficiency of the Bill, are there not capital punishments sufficient in your statutes? Is there not blood enough upon your penal code, that more must be poured forth to ascend to Heaven and testify against you? How will you carry the Bill into effect? Can you commit a whole county to their own prisons? Will you erect a gibbet in every field, and hang up men like scarecrows? Or will you proceed (as you must to bring this measure into effect) by decimation? Place the county under martial law? Depopulate and lay waste all around you? And restore Sherwood Forest as an acceptable gift to the crown, in its former condition of a royal chase and an asylum for outlaws? Are these the remedies for a starving and desperate populace? Will the famished wretch who has braved your bayonets be appalled by your gibbets? When death is a relief, and the only relief it appears that you will afford him, will he be dragooned into tranquillity? Will that which could not be effected by your grenadiers be accomplished by your executioners? If you proceed by the forms of law, where is your evidence? Those who have refused to impeach their accomplices when transportation only was the punishment, will hardly be tempted to witness against them when death is the penalty.

With all due deference to the noble lords opposite, I think a little investigation, some previous inquiry, would induce even them to change their purpose. That most favourite state measure, so marvellously efficacious in many and recent instances, temporising, would not be without its advantages in this. When a proposal is made to emancipate or relieve, you hesitate, you deliberate for years, you temporise and tamper with the minds of men; but a death-bill must be passed off-hand, without a thought of the consequences. Sure I am, from what I have heard, and from what I have seen, that to pass the Bill under all the existing circumstances, without inquiry, without deliberation, would only be to add injustice to irritation, and barbarity to neglect. The framers of such a bill must be content to inherit the honours of that Athenian law-giver whose edicts were said to be written not in ink but in blood. But suppose it passed; suppose one of these men, as I have seen them, – meagre with famine, sullen with despair, careless of a life which your Lordships are perhaps about to value at something less than the price of a stocking-frame; – suppose this man surrounded by the children for whom be is unable to procure bread at the hazard of his existence, about to be torn for ever from a family which he lately supported in peaceful industry, and which it is not his fault that he can no longer so support; – suppose this man – and there are ten thousand such from whom you may select your victims – dragged into court, to be tried for this new offence, by this new law; still, there are two things wanting to convict and condemn him and these are, in my opinion, – twelve butchers for a jury, and a Jeffreys for a judge!'

# CHIEF TECUMSEH
## March 1768 – 5 October 1813

---

*'In the name of the Indian chiefs and warriors'*
4 or 5 October 1813

**The following speech,** *'to Major-General Procter, in the name of the Indian chiefs and warriors, as the representative of their Great Father, the King,'* is supposed to have been delivered a short time prior to Tecumseh's death at the Battle of the Thames (at Moravian Town, Upper Canada). The Shawnees tried to enlist the support of all the western Indians against the United States, because of encroachment upon their lands by early settlers and disregard of treaties. In autumn 1811 the Shawnees under Tecumseh's twin brother 'The Prophet' were defeated by General Harrison at Tippecanoe. When the War of 1812 broke out, Tecumseh led a body of Shawnees into Canada to support the British, who gave him the rank of a brigadier-general. He was wounded twice in battle, and in Ohio in the summer of 1813 saved the lives of American prisoners. Tecumseh was disillusioned with Major-General Henry Procter's retreat after the British fleet had been destroyed on Lake Erie, and thought him a coward, urging him to stand and fight in the speech recorded below. In the battle on the Thames River, which flows into Lake St. Clair, Tecumseh commanded the right wing of the allied Indian and British forces that were defeated by General Harrison. He bravely died in the battle. Procter had fled the field and was court-martialled and suspended from his rank and pay. Tecumseh's speech was found in Procter's papers after the major-general had deserted his Indian allies.

'Father, listen to your children! You have them now all before you. The war before this our British father gave the hatchet to his red children, when old chiefs were alive. They are now dead. In that war our father was thrown on his back by the Americans, and our father took them by the hand without our knowledge; and we are afraid that our father will do so again at this time. Summer before last, when I came forward with my red brethren and was ready to take up the hatchet in favor of our British father, we were told not to be in a hurry, that he had not yet determined to fight the Americans.

Listen! When war was declared, our father stood up and gave us the tomahawk, and told us that he was ready to strike the Americans; that he wanted our assistance, and that he would certainly get us our lands back, which the Americans had taken from us.

Listen! You told us, at that time, to bring forward our families to this place, and we did so; and you promised to take care of them, and that they should want for nothing while the men would go and fight the enemy. That we need not trouble ourselves about the enemy's garrisons; that we knew nothing about them, and that our father would attend to that part of the business. You also told your red children that you would take good care of your garrison here, which made our hearts glad.

...Listen!...Our ships have gone one way, and we are much astonished to see our father tying up everything and preparing to run away the other, without letting his red children know what his intentions are. You always told us to remain here and take care of our lands. It made our hearts glad to hear that was your wish. Our great father, the King, is the head, and you represent him. You always told us that you would never draw your foot off British ground; but now, father, we see you are drawing back, and we are sorry to see our father doing so without seeing the enemy.

We must compare our father's conduct to a fat animal that carries its tail upon its back, but when frightened it drops it between its legs and runs off. Listen, father! The Americans have not yet defeated us by land; neither are we sure that they have done so by water – we therefore wish to remain here and fight our enemy should they make their appearance. If they defeat us, we will then retreat with our father. At the battle of the Rapids, last war, the Americans certainly defeated us; and when we retreated to our father's fort in that place the gates were shut against us. We were afraid that it would now be the case, but instead of that we now see our British father preparing to march out of his garrison. Father! You have got the arms and ammunition which our great father sent for his red children. If you have an idea of going away, give them to us, and you may go and welcome, for us. Our lives are in the hands of the Great Spirit. We are determined to defend our lands, and if it is his will we wish to leave our bones upon them.'

# NAPOLÉON BONAPARTE, EMPEROR NAPOLEON I
## 15 August 1769 – 5 May 1821

### 'Do not regret my fate'
### 20 April 1814

**Napoleon had ruled France** and the surrounding countries for 20 years. He built a 500,000 strong Grand Army which used modern tactics and bold improvization to sweep across Europe and acquire an empire for France. However, in 1812, Bonaparte made the fateful decision to invade Russia, eventually reaching Moscow in September. Moscow had been burned by the retreating Russians and did not contain enough supplies to support the hungry French army over the long winter. In his long retreat, Napoleon's army shrank to just 20,000 starving men. England, Austria and Prussia then formed an alliance with Russia against Napoleon, who rebuilt his armies and won several minor victories over the Allies, but was then defeated at Leipzig. On 30 March 1814, Paris was captured by the Allies. Napoleon lost the support of most of his generals and was forced to abdicate on 6 April 1814. In the courtyard at Fontainebleau, Napoleon said farewell to the remaining officers of the Old Guard:

'Soldiers of my Old Guard: I bid you farewell. For twenty years I have constantly accompanied you on the road to honour and glory. In these latter times, as in the days of our prosperity, you have invariably been models of courage and fidelity. With men such as you our cause could not be lost; but the war would have been interminable; it would have been civil war, and that would have entailed deeper misfortunes on France. I have sacrificed all of my interests to those of the country. I go, but you, my friends, will continue to serve France. Her happiness was my only thought. It will still be the object of my wishes. Do not regret my fate; if I have consented to survive, it is to serve your glory. I intend to write the history of the great achievements we have performed together. Adieu, my friends. Would I could press you all to my heart.'

The Allies banished him into exile on the island of Elba off Italy, but ten months later, in March of 1815, he escaped and returned to France. Accompanied by a thousand men from his Old Guard he marched toward Paris and gathered an army of supporters around him along the way. Once again Napoleon assumed the position of emperor, but his new reign lasted only 100 days until his defeat at the Battle of Waterloo on 18 June 1815. A month later he was sent into his final exile on the island of St Helena off the coast of Africa where he died in 1821.

# CHIEF RED EAGLE OF THE CREEK INDIANS
## 1781 – 24 March 1824

*'I fear no man, for I am a Creek warrior'*
9 August 1814

**William 'Red Eagle' Weatherford** was a Creek (Muskogee) who led the tribe in the Creek War. On 30 August 1813 he led a war party of the *'Red Sticks'* faction of Creeks against Fort Mims on the lower Alabama River. Hundreds of settlers, mixed-blood Creeks and militia died there. He fought in several other battles, escaping the Battle of Horseshoe Bend which effectively ended the Creek War. Red Eagle voluntarily turned himself in at Fort Toulouse (later Fort Jackson) to General Andrew Jackson, where he made the following speech. On 9 August 1814 Andrew Jackson forced the Creeks to sign the Treaty of Fort Jackson, ceding 23 million acres (9.3 million ha), half of Alabama and part of southern Georgia to the United States.

'General Jackson, I am not afraid of you. I fear no man, for I am a Creek warrior. I have nothing to request in behalf of myself; you can kill me, if you desire. But I come to beg you to send for the women and children of the war party who are now starving in the woods. Their fields and cribs have been destroyed by your people, who have driven them to the woods without an ear of corn. I hope that you will send out parties who will safely conduct them here in order that they may be fed. I exerted myself in vain to prevent the massacre of the women and children at Fort Mims. I am now done fighting. The Red Sticks are nearly all killed. I have done the white people all the harm I could. I have fought them, and fought them bravely. If I had an army I would yet fight, and contend to the last. But I have none. My people are all gone. I can now do no more than weep over the misfortunes of my Nation. There was a time when I had a choice and could have answered you; I have none now. Even hope has ended. Once I could animate my warriors to battle, but I cannot animate the dead. My warriors can no longer hear my voice. Their bones are at Talladega, Tallashatchie, Emunckfow and Tohopeka. If I had been left to contend with the Georgia Army, I would have raised corn on one bank of the river and fought them on the other. But your people have destroyed my Nation. I rely on your generosity.'

# SIMÓN BOLÍVAR
## 24 July 1783 – 17 December 1830

*'...the triple yoke of ignorance, tyranny and vice'*
15 February 1919

**Simón Bolívar, the celebrated Venezuelan** military and political leader, led the fight in Hispanic America's movement for independence from the Spanish empire. He made this speech at the Congress of Angostura (now called Ciudad Bolívar), which he summoned during the wars of Independence of Venezuela and Colombia. At the opening of its first meeting Bolívar gave this famous '*Address at Angostura*'. This event was the foundation of the first union of independent nations in Latin America, called Gran Colombia, of which he became president. Remembered across South America as '*the Liberator*', he helped Venezuela, Colombia, Bolivia, Ecuador, Panama and Peru to gain independence.

'The people of America, having been held under the triple yoke of ignorance, tyranny and vice, have not been in a position to acquire either knowledge, power or virtue. Disciples of such pernicious masters, the lessons we have received and the examples we have studied, are most destructive. We have been governed more by deception than by force, and we have been degraded more by vice than by superstition. Slavery is the offspring of Darkness; an ignorant people is a blind tool, turned to its own destruction; ambition and intrigue exploit the credulity and inexperience of men foreign to all political, economical or civil knowledge; mere illusions are accepted as reality, licence is taken for liberty, treachery for patriotism, revenge for justice. Even as a sturdy blind man who, relying on the feeling of his own strength, walks along with the assurance of the most wide-awake man and, striking against all kinds of obstacles, can not steady his steps. A perverted people, should it attain its liberty, is bound to lose this very soon, because it would be useless to try to impress upon such people that happiness lies in the practice of righteousness; that the reign of law is more powerful than the reign of tyrants, who are more inflexible, and all ought to submit to the wholesome severity of the law; that good morals, and not force, are the pillars of the law and that the exercise of justice is the exercise of liberty. Thus, Legislators, your task is the more laborious because you are to deal with men misled by the illusions of error, and by civil incentives.

Liberty, says Rousseau, is a succulent food, but difficult to digest. Our feeble fellow-citizens will have to strengthen their mind much before they will be ready to assimilate such wholesome nourishment. Their limbs made numb by their fetters, their eyesight weakened in the darkness of their dungeons and their forces wasted away through their foul servitude, will they be capable of marching with a firm step towards the august temple of Liberty? Will they be capable of coming close to it, and admiring the light it sheds, and of breathing freely its pure air? Consider well your decision. Legislators. Do not forget that you are about to lay the foundations of a new people, which may some day rise to the heights that Nature has marked out for it, provided you make those foundations proportionate to the lofty place which that people is to fill. If your selection be not made under the guidance of the Guardian Angel of Venezuela, who must inspire you with wisdom to choose the nature and form of government that you choose to adopt for the welfare of the people; if you should fail in this, I warn you, the end of our venture would be slavery. The annals of past ages display before you thousands of governments. Recall to mind the nations which have shone most highly on the earth and you will be grieved to see that almost the entire world has been, and still is, a victim of bad government. You will find many systems of governing men, but all are calculated to oppress them, and if the habit of seeing the human race, led by shepherds of peoples, did not dull the horror of such a revolting sight, we would be astonished to see our social species grazing on the surface of the globe, even as lowly herds destined to feed their cruel drivers. Nature, in truth, endows us at birth with the instinctive desire for liberty; but whether because of negligence, or because of an inclination inherent in humanity, it remains still under the bonds imposed on it. And as we see it in such a state of debasement we seem to have reason to be persuaded that the majority of men hold as a truth the humiliating principle that it is harder to maintain the balance of liberty than to endure the weight of tyranny. Would to God that this principle, contrary to the morals of Nature, were false! Would to God that this principle were not sanctioned by the indolence of man as regards his most sacred rights!'

# JOHN QUINCY ADAMS
## 11 July 1767 – 23 February 1848

### *Freedom, Independence, Peace*
4 July 1821

**The son of President John Adams**, he was the sixth president of the United States from 1825 to 1829, and one of the greatest diplomats in American history. In President Monroe's cabinet, John Quincy Adams served as secretary of state from 1817–25, and was responsible for formulating the 'Monroe Doctrine' warning European governments not to interfere in affairs of the western hemisphere. After the Napoleonic Wars, Spain lost control of most of her American colonies, which revolted and declared independence. The Floridas, still Spanish territory, lacked a real Spanish presence or controlling force. Monroe sent General Andrew Jackson to Georgia in 1817 to fight the Seminole and Creek Indians, and to stop Florida from becoming a refuge for runaway slaves. Jackson forced the Seminole Indians south in Florida, executed two British merchants who were supplying weapons to them, and left an American garrison in occupation. President Monroe and all his cabinet, except Adams, believed Jackson had exceeded his instructions, and the Spanish minister demanded '*suitable punishment*'. Adams replied '*Spain must immediately [decide] either to place a force in Florida adequate at once to the protection of her territory... or cede to the United States a province, of which she retains nothing but the nominal possession...*' Adams used the occasion to get Spain to cede Florida and Louisiana by the Adams–Onis Treaty of 1819. On Independence Day 1821, in response to those who advocated American support for Spanish America's independence from Spanish rule, he gave this speech, insisting that American policy amounted to moral support for, but not armed intervention on behalf of, independence movements. Adams confirmed that the United States would not tolerate European interference in the western hemisphere. He also said that that America '*goes not abroad in search of monsters to destroy*' and this policy of isolationism and non-interference in other countries' internal affairs was pursued until the 20th century.

'And now, friends and countrymen, if the wise and learned philosophers of the elder world, the first observers of nutation and aberration, the discoverers of maddening ether and invisible planets, the inventors of Congreve rockets and shrapnel shells, should find their hearts disposed to enquire what has America done for the benefit of mankind? Let our answer be this: America, with the same voice which spoke herself into existence as a nation, proclaimed to mankind the inextinguishable rights of human nature, and the only lawful foundations of government. America, in the assembly of nations, since her admission among them, has invariably, though often fruitlessly, held forth to them the hand of honest friendship, of equal freedom, of generous reciprocity. She has uniformly spoken among them, though often to heedless and often to disdainful ears, the language of equal liberty, of equal justice, and of equal rights. She has, in the lapse of nearly half a century, without a single exception, respected the independence of other nations while asserting and maintaining her own. She has abstained from interference in the concerns of others, even when conflict has been for principles to which she clings, as to the last vital drop that visits the heart. She has seen that probably for centuries to come, all the contests of that Aceldama [the 'field of blood' where Judas Iscariot was supposed to have died] the European world, will be contests of inveterate power, and emerging right.

Wherever the standard of freedom and Independence has been or shall be unfurled, there will her heart, her benedictions and her prayers be. But she goes not abroad, in search of monsters to destroy. She is the well-wisher to the freedom and independence of all. She is the champion and vindicator only of her own. She will commend the general cause by the countenance of her voice, and the benignant sympathy of her example. She well knows that by once enlisting under other banners than her own, were they even the banners of foreign independence, she would involve herself beyond the power of extrication, in all the wars of interest and intrigue, of individual avarice, envy, and ambition, which assume the colors and usurp the standard of freedom. The fundamental maxims of her policy would insensibly change from liberty to force. The frontlet on her brows would no longer beam with the ineffable splendor of freedom and independence; but in its stead would soon be substituted an imperial diadem, flashing in false and tarnished luster the murky radiance of dominion and power. She might become the dictatress of the world; she would be no longer the ruler of her own spirit...Her glory is not dominion, but liberty. Her march is the march of the mind. She has a spear and a shield: but the motto upon her shield is, Freedom, Independence, Peace. This has been her Declaration: this has been, as far as her necessary intercourse with the rest of mankind would permit, her practice.'

# EDWARD EVERETT
## 11 April 1794 – 15 January 1865

*'The Jubilee of America is turned into mourning'*
1 August 1826

**Edward Everett was a US senator**, representative, secretary of state, Massachusetts governor and president of Harvard University. In 1863, he had been the main speaker at the dedication of the National Cemetery at Gettysburg, giving a two-hour address, as he was an outstanding orator. However, his speech was eclipsed by the short address given immediately afterwards by Abraham Lincoln, whom Everett congratulated warmly. This speech in Boston was made 50 years after American independence upon the occasion of both Thomas Jefferson and John Adams dying on the same day, 4 July 1826.

'We are assembled, beneath the weeping canopy of the heavens, in the exercise of feelings in which the whole family of Americans unites with us...The Jubilee of America is turned into mourning. Its joy is mingled with sadness; its silver trumpet breathes a mingled strain. Henceforward, while America exists among the nations of the earth, the first emotion of the fourth of July will be of joy and triumph in the great event which immortalizes the day; the second will be one of chastened and tender recollection of the venerable men who departed on the morning of the jubilee...The men who did so much to make you so are no more. The men who gave nothing to pleasure in youth, nothing to repose in age, but all to that country, whose beloved name filled their hearts, as it does ours, with joy, can now do no more for us; nor we for them. But their memory remains, we will cherish it; their bright example remains, we will strive to imitate it; the fruit of their wise counsels and noble acts remains, we will gratefully enjoy it. They have gone to the companions of their cares, of their dangers, and their toils. It is well with them. The treasures of America are now in heaven. How long the list of our good, and wise, and brave, assembled there! How few remain with us!...The fabric of American freedom, like all things human, however firm and fair, may crumble into dust. But the cause in which these our fathers shone is immortal. They did that to which no age, no people of civilized men, can be indifferent. Their eulogy will be uttered in other languages, when those we speak, like us who speak them, shall be all forgotten. And when the great account of humanity shall be closed, in the bright list of those who have best adorned and served it, shall be found the names of our Adams and our Jefferson!'

# DANIEL WEBSTER
## 18 January 1782 – 24 October 1852

*Second reply to Hayne*
27 January 1830

**Webster was a Whig leader**, secretary of state and leading statesman and lawyer in the United States in the period leading up to the Civil War. He was officially named by the Senate in 1957 as one of its five most outstanding members. Webster had prepared no written copy of this long speech to the Senate, having with him only a few notes jotted down on a few sheets of paper. Lodge, one of his biographers, says its delivery *'was practically extemporaneous'*. Webster, answering enquiries about what he had done to prepare himself, is reported to have said that *'his whole life had been a preparation for the reply to Hayne'*. Lincoln believed this to be the greatest example of American oratory. The debate between Senator Hayne of South Carolina and Webster of Massachusetts had begun the previous day with arguments on federal land policy and widened into South Carolina's disagreement with federal tariffs. The following speech argues against the proposed doctrine of nullification (the right of a state to defy or refuse to obey a federal law) and is considered one of the greatest ever delivered during the first half of the 19th century, Webster's *'greatest peroration'*.

'...Mr. President, I shall enter on no encomium upon Massachusetts; she needs none. There she is. Behold her, and judge for yourselves. There is her history; the world knows it by heart. The past, at least, is secure. There is Boston, and Concord, and Lexington, and Bunker Hill; and there they will remain for ever. The bones of her sons, falling in the great struggle for Independence, now lie mingled with the soil of every State from New England to Georgia; and there they will lie for ever. And Sir, where American Liberty raised its first voice, and where its youth was nurtured and sustained, there it still lives, in the strength of its manhood, and full of its original spirit. If discord and disunion shall wound it, if party strife and blind ambition shall hawk at and tear it, if folly and madness, if uneasiness under salutary and necessary restraint, shall succeed in separating it from that Union, by which alone its existence is made sure, it will stand, in the end, by the side of that cradle in which its infancy was rocked; over the friends who gather round it; and it will fall at last, if fall it must, amidst the proudest monuments of its own glory, and on the very spot of its origin...'

# BLACK HAWK (MAKATAIMESHEKIAKIAK)
## Spring 1767 – 3 October 1838

*'My warriors fell around me'*
27 August 1832

**Black Hawk was a Sauk Indian** war chief in Illinois. Because of American pressure on his ancestral lands, he fought on the side of the British in the War of 1812. The Native American population was troubled by continued occupation of the land by white settlers, and following a disputed treaty made in his absence, Black Hawk began the 'Black Hawk War' in 1831, leading bands of Fox, Kickapoo and Sauk Indians. Their homelands having been taken, they found that they could not move west away from the white man because of the hostile Sioux. After leading raids across the Mississippi, Black Hawk offered peace, which was rejected. Thus he gathered a small group of warriors for what he thought would be a last stand. However, Major Isaiah Stillman's Illinois volunteers fled at the Battle of Stillman's Run on 14 May 1832. Illinois militia and the Michigan territory militia then defeated Black Hawk's 'British Band' on 21 July at the Battle of Wisconsin Heights. On 1–2 August 1832 at the mouth of the Bad Axe River, hundreds of Indian men, women and children were killed by the pursuing militia and their Indian allies supported by a US gunboat. Black Hawk was captured after the battle and the following extract records his sad speech when he surrendered at Prairie du Chien, Wisconsin to General Henry Atkinson.

'You have taken me prisoner, with all my warriors. I am much grieved; for I expected, if I did not defeat you, to hold out much longer, and give you more trouble, before I surrendered. I tried hard to bring you into ambush, but your last general understood Indian fighting. I determined to rush on you, and fight you face to face. I fought hard. But your guns were well aimed. The bullets flew like birds in the air, and whizzed by our ears like the wind through the trees in winter. My warriors fell around me; it began to look dismal. I saw my evil day at hand. The sun rose dim on us in the morning, and at night it sank in a dark cloud, and looked like a ball of fire. That was the last sun that shone on Black Hawk. His heart is dead, and no longer beats quick in his bosom. He is now a prisoner of the white men; they will do with him as they wish. But he can stand torture, and is not afraid of death. He is no coward. Black Hawk is an Indian. He has done nothing for which an Indian ought to be ashamed. He has fought for his countrymen, against white men, who came, year after year, to cheat them and take away their lands.

You know the cause of our making war. It is known to all white men. They ought to be ashamed of it. The white men despise the Indians, and drive them from their homes. They smile in the face of the poor Indian, to cheat him; they shake him by the hand, to gain his confidence, to make him drunk, and to deceive him. We told them to let us alone, and keep away from us; but they followed on and beset our paths, and they coiled themselves among us like the snake. They poisoned us by their touch. We were not safe. We lived in danger. We looked up to the Great Spirit. We went to our father. We were encouraged. His great council gave us fair words and big promises, but we got no satisfaction: things were growing worse. There were no deer in the forest. The opossum and beaver were fled. The springs were drying up, and our squaws and papooses were without food to keep them from starving. We called a great council and built a large fire. The spirit of our fathers arose, and spoke to us to avenge our wrongs or die. We set up the war-whoop, and dug up the tomahawk; our knives were ready, and the heart of Black Hawk swelled high in his bosom, when he led his warriors to battle. He is satisfied. He will go to the world of spirits contented. He has done his duty. His father will meet him there, and commend him.

Black Hawk is a true Indian, and disdains to cry like a woman. He feels for his wife, his children, and his friends. But he does not care for himself. He cares for the Nation and the Indians. They will suffer. He laments their fate. Farewell, my Nation! Black Hawk tried to save you, and avenge your wrongs. He drank the blood of some of the whites. He has been taken prisoner, and his plans are crushed. He can do no more. He is near his end. His sun is setting, and he will rise no more. Farewell to Black Hawk!'

# SEARGENT SMITH PRENTISS
### 30 September 1808 – 1 July 1850

## 'Lafayette is dead!'
### August 1834

**Prentiss was a Whig leader** and congressman for Mississippi from 1838. He was a master of extempore oratory, whom Wendell Phillips called *'the most eloquent of all Southerners – he wielded a power few men ever had.'* Daniel Webster said that Prentiss was the most powerful speaker he had seen. Prentiss had previously fought two duels with Henry Stuart Foote, governor of Mississippi. This eulogy was given to mark the death of the Marquis de Lafayette, a hero of both the American Revolutionary War and of the French Revolution.

'...Death who knocks with equal hand at the door of the cottage and the palace gate, has been busy at his appointed work. Mourning prevails throughout the land, and the countenances of all are shrouded in the mantle of regret. Far across the wild Atlantic, amid the pleasant vineyards in the sunny land of France, there, too, is mourning; and the weeds of sorrow are alike worn by prince and peasant. Against whom has the monarch of the tomb turned his remorseless dart that such widespread sorrow prevails? Hark, and the agonized voice of Freedom, weeping for her favorite son, will tell you in strains sadder than those with which she "shrieked when Kosciusko fell", that Lafayette – the gallant and the good – has ceased to live.

The friend and companion of Washington is no more. He who taught the eagle of our country, while yet unfledged, to plume his young wing and mate his talons with the lion's strength, has taken his flight far beyond the stars, beneath whose influence he fought so well. Lafayette is dead! The gallant ship, whose pennon has so often bravely streamed above the roar of battle and the tempest's rage, has at length gone slowly down in the still and quiet waters. Well mightest thou, O Death, now recline beneath the laurels thou hast won; for never since, as the grim messenger of Almighty Vengeance, thou earnest into this world, did a more generous heart cease to heave beneath thy chilling touch, and never will thy insatiate dart be hurled against a nobler breast! Who does not feel at the mournful intelligence, as if he had lost something cheering from his own path through life; as if some bright star, at which he had been accustomed frequently and fondly to gaze, had been suddenly extinguished in the firmament?...'

# JOHN QUINCY ADAMS
## 11 July 1767 – 23 February 1848

*'Pronounce him one of the first men of his age, and you have
yet not done him justice'*
31 December 1834

**President from 1825–9**, Adams then became a congressman from 1831 until his death. Lafayette had died on 20 May 1834, having been a general in the American Revolutionary War and then a leader of the Garde Nationale in the French Revolution.

'Pronounce him one of the first men of his age, and you have yet not done him justice. Try him by that test to which he sought in vain to stimulate the vulgar and selfish spirit of Napoleon; class him among the men who, to compare and seat themselves, must take in the compass of all ages; turn back your eyes upon the records of time; summon from the creation of the world to this day the mighty dead of every age and every clime – and where, among the race of merely mortal men, shall one he found, who, as the benefactor of his kind, shall claim to take precedence of Lafayette?

There have doubtless been, in all ages, men, whose discoveries or inventions, in the world of matter or of mind, have opened new avenues to the dominion of man over the material creation; have increased his means or his faculties of enjoyment; have raised him in nearer approximation to that higher and happier condition, the object of his hopes and aspirations in his present state of existence. Lafayette discovered no new principle of politics or of morals. He invented nothing in science. He disclosed no new phenomenon in the laws of nature. Born and educated in the highest order of feudal Nobility, under the most absolute Monarchy of Europe, in possession of an affluent fortune, and master of himself and of all his capabilities at the moment of attaining manhood, the principle of republican justice and of social equality took possession of his heart and mind, as if by inspiration from above. He devoted himself, his life, his fortune, his hereditary honors, his towering ambition, his splendid hopes, all to the cause of liberty. He came to another hemisphere to defend her. He became one of the most effective champions of our Independence; but, that once achieved, he returned to his own country, and thenceforward took no part in the controversies which have divided us. In the events of our Revolution, and in the forms of policy which we have adopted for the establishment and perpetuation of our freedom, Lafayette found the most perfect form of government. He wished to add nothing to it.'

# DANIEL O'CONNELL (DÓNAL Ó CONAILL)
## 6 August 1775 – 15 May 1847

*Equal justice for Ireland*
4 February 1836

**Daniel O'Connell was known in Ireland** as *The Liberator,* or *The Emancipator.* He was a lawyer who campaigned for the repeal of the Act of Union that linked Ireland and Great Britain. O'Connell's non-violent philosophy and career have inspired leaders all over the world, including Martin Luther King and Mahatma Gandhi. William Thackeray told him '*you have done more for your nation than any man since Washington ever did*', and Gladstone described him as '*the greatest popular leader the world has ever seen*'. His first major success had been the Catholic Emancipation Act of 1829, which allowed Roman Catholics to become members of Parliament in Britain. Elected an MP, O'Connell gave this speech calling for equal justice for Irish citizens:

'...I have not fatigued myself, but the House, in coming forward upon this occasion. I may be laughed and sneered at by those who talk of my power; but what has created it but the injustice that has been done in Ireland? That is the end and the means of the magic, if you please – the groundwork of my influence in Ireland. If you refuse justice to that country, it is a melancholy consideration to me to think that you are adding substantially to that power and influence, while you are wounding my country to its very heart's core; weakening that throne, the monarch who sits upon which, you say you respect; severing that union which, you say, is bound together by the tightest links, and withholding that justice from Ireland which she will not cease to seek till it is obtained; every man must admit that the course I am taking is the legitimate and proper course – I defy any man to say it is not. Condemn me elsewhere as much as you please, but this you must admit. You may taunt the ministry with having coalesced me, you may raise the vulgar cry of "Irishman and Papist" against me, you may send out men called ministers of God to slander and calumniate *[charge falsely]* me; they may assume whatever garb they please, but the question comes into this narrow compass. I demand, I respectfully insist: on equal justice for Ireland, on the same principle by which it has been administered to Scotland and England. I will not take less. Refuse me that if you can.'

# RICHARD LALOR SHEIL
## 17 August 1791 – 23 May 1851

*On the Irish as 'aliens'*
23 February 1837

**The speech was delivered** in the House of Commons by the Irish MP, writer and lawyer Richard Lalor Sheil during a debate on the Irish Municipal Bill. It was prompted by a remark made some days earlier in the House of Lords by Lord Lyndhurst, who referred to the Irish as *'aliens in blood and religion'*. Lord Lyndhurst was present in the House when Sheil rose to speak. Sheil pointed indignantly at him, which caused every member to turn his eyes on Lyndhurst, while shouts arose from the two sides and continued for some minutes. The Duke of Wellington, referred to in the speech, was Irish, and many of his troops during the Napoleonic Wars were also Irish.

'...There is, however, one man of great abilities not a member of this House, but whose talents and whose boldness have placed him in the topmost place in his party – who, disdaining all imposture, and thinking it the best course to appeal directly to the religious and national antipathies of the people of this country, – abandoning all reserve, and flinging off the slender veil by which his political associates affect to cover, although they can not hide, their motives, – distinctly and audaciously tells the Irish people that they are not entitled to the same privileges as Englishmen; and pronounces them, in any particular which could enter his minute enumeration of the circumstances by which fellow citizenship is created, in race, identity and religion, to be aliens; – to be aliens in race, to be aliens in country, to be aliens in religion! Aliens! Good God! Was Arthur, Duke of Wellington, in the House of Lords, – and did he not start up and exclaim, "HOLD, I HAVE SEEN THE ALIENS DO THEIR DUTY!" The Duke of Wellington is not a man of an excitable temperament. His mind is of a cast too martial to be easily moved; but, notwithstanding his habitual inflexibility, I can not help thinking that, when he heard his Roman Catholic countrymen (for we are his countrymen) designated by a phrase as offensive as the abundant vocabulary of his eloquent confederate could supply, – I can not help thinking that he ought to have recollected the many fields of fight in which we have been contributors to his renown. "The battles, sieges, fortunes that he has passed", ought to have come back upon him...'

# HENRY BROUGHAM, 1ST BARON BROUGHAM AND VAUX
## 19 September 1778 – 7 May 1868

*'Our whole punishments smell of blood. Let the treadmill stop'*
29 January 1838

**Brougham was an Independent MP** who gained fame as counsel for Queen Caroline in 1820–1. He served as Lord Chancellor in 1830–4, and strongly supported the 1832 Reform Act and the 1833 Slavery Abolition Act. From entering the House of Commons in 1810 he had fought against the slave trade, and as Lord Chancellor effected legal reforms and established the Central Criminal Court. He held the House of Commons record for speaking non-stop for six hours. Away from politics, he designed the brougham, a four-wheeled horse-drawn carriage, and was responsible for making Cannes 'the sanatorium of Europe' after he had built a property there and recommended the health-giving properties of its climate. In 1838 he realized that British colonies continued to obstruct the emancipation of slaves and to discriminate against ex-slaves. As he result he gave this wonderful speech in the House of Lords:

'...My lords, we fill up the measure of this injustice by executing laws wickedly conceived, in a yet more atrocious spirit of cruelty. Our whole punishments smell of blood. Let the treadmill stop, from the weary limbs and exhausted frames of the sufferers no longer having the power to press it down the requisite number of turns in a minute, the lash instantly resounds through the mansion of woe! Let the stone spread out to be broken not crumble fast enough beneath the arms already scarred, flayed, and wealed by the whip, again the scourge tears afresh the half-healed flesh! I hasten to a close. There remains little to add. It is, my lords, with a view to prevent such enormities as I have feebly pictured before you, to correct the administration of justice, to secure the comforts of the negroes, to restrain the cruelty of the tormentors, to amend the discipline of the prisons, to arm the governors with local authority over the police; it is with those views that I have formed the first five of the resolutions now upon your table, intending they should take effect during the very short interval of a few months which must elapse before the sixth shall give complete liberty to the slave.

From the instant that glad sound is wafted across the ocean, what a blessed change begins; what an enchanting prospect unfolds itself!

The African, placed on the same footing with other men, becomes in reality our fellow citizen – to our feelings, as well as in his own nature, our equal, our brother. No difference of origin or colour can now prevail to keep the two castes apart. The negro, master of his own labour – only induced to lend his assistance if you make it his interest to help you, yet that aid being absolutely necessary to preserve your existence – becomes an essential portion of the community, nay, the very portion upon which the whole must lean for support. So now the fullness of time is come for at length discharging our duty to the African captive. I have demonstrated to you that everything is ordered – every previous step taken – all safe, by experience shown to be safe, for the long-desired consummation. The time has come, the trial has been made, the hour is striking; you have no longer a pretext for hesitation, or faltering, or delay. The slave has shown, by four years' blameless behaviour and devotion to the pursuits of peaceful industry, that he is as fit for his freedom as any English peasant, aye, or any lord whom I now address.

...I demand his rights; I demand his liberty without stint. In the name of justice and of law, in the name of reason, in the name of God, who has given you no right to work injustice, I demand that your brother be no longer trampled upon as your slave! I make my appeal to the Commons, who represent the free people of England, and I require at their hands the performance of that condition for which they paid so enormous a price – that condition which all their constituents are in breathless anxiety to see fulfilled! I appeal to this House! Hereditary judges of the first tribunal in the world, to you I appeal for justice! Patrons of all the arts that humanize mankind, under your protection I place humanity herself! To the merciful sovereign of a free people, I call aloud for mercy to the hundreds of thousands for whom half a million of her Christian sisters have cried out; I ask their cry may not have risen in vain. But, first, I turn my eye to the Throne of all justice, and, devoutly humbling myself before Him who is of purer eyes than to behold such vast iniquities, I implore that the curse hovering over the head of the unjust and the oppressor be averted from us, that your hearts may be turned to mercy, and that over all the earth His will may at length be done!'

# RICHARD LALOR SHEIL
## 17 August 1791 – 23 May 1851

## *On the Disabilities of the Jews*
### 7 February 1848

**This powerful oration to the House of Commons** was delivered when the election of Baron Rothschild to Parliament had revived the hopes of Jewish emancipation. Jews at this time were excluded from Parliament because only Christians were legally entitled to take the oath of office. However, it was not until 1858 that the Jewish 'disabilities' were entirely removed.

'...It has been said in the course of these discussions that a Jew is not subject to penalties, but to privations. But what is privation but a synonym for penalty? Privation of life, privation of liberty, privation of property, privation of country, privation of right, privation of privilege – these are degrees widely distant indeed, but still degrees in the graduated scale of persecution. The parliamentary disability that affects the Jew has been designated in the course of these debates by the mollified expressions to which men who impart euphemism to severity are in the habit of resorting; but most assuredly an exclusion from the House of Commons ought in the House of Commons itself to be regarded as a most grievous detriment. With the dignity and the greatness and the power of this, the first assembly in the world, the hardship of exclusion is commensurate. Some of the most prominent opponents of this measure are among the last by whom a seat in Parliament ought to be held in little account. On this branch of the case – the hardship of an exclusion from this House – I can speak as a witness as well as an advocate. I belong to that great and powerful community which was a few years ago subject to the same disqualification that affects the Jew, and I felt that disqualification to be most degrading. Of myself I will not speak, because I can speak of the most illustrious person by whom that community was adorned. I have sat under the gallery of the House of Commons by the side of Mr. O'Connell during a great discussion on which the destiny of Ireland was dependent. I was with him when Plunket convinced, and Brougham surprised, and Canning charmed, and Peel instructed, and Russell exalted and improved. How have I seen him repine at his exclusion from the field of high intellectual encounter in those lists in which so many competitors for glory were engaged, and into which, with an injurious tardiness, he was afterward admitted! How have I seen him chafe the chain which bound him down, but which, with an effort of gigantic prowess, he burst at last to pieces! He was at the head of millions of an organized and indissoluble people. The Jew comes here with no other arguments than those which reason and truth supply; but reason and truth are of counsel with him; and in this assembly, which I believe to represent not only the high intelligence but the high-mindedness of England, reason will not long be baffled, and truth, in fulfilment of its great aphorism, will at last prevail...

What is it you fear? What is the origin of this Hebrewphobia? Do you tremble for the Church? The Church has something perhaps to fear from eight millions of Catholics and from three millions of Methodists and more than a million of Scotch seceders...but from the synagogue – the neutral, impartial, apathetic, and unproselytizing synagogue – the Church has nothing to apprehend...It was not by persecution, but despite of it – despite of imprisonment, and exile, and spoliation, and shame, and death, despite the dungeon, the wheel, the bed of steel, and the couch of fire – that the Christian religion made its irresistible and superhuman way. And is it not repugnant to common reason, as well as to the elementary principles of Christianity itself, to hold that it is to be maintained by means diametrically the reverse of those by which it was propagated and diffused? But, alas! For our frail and fragile nature, no sooner had the professors of Christianity become the co-partners of secular authority than the severities were resorted to which their persecuted predecessors had endured. The Jew was selected as an object of special and peculiar infliction. The history of that most unhappy people is, for century after century, a trail of chains and a track of blood. Men of mercy occasionally arose to interpose in their behalf. St. Bernard – the great St. Bernard, the last of the Latin Fathers – with a most pathetic eloquence took their part. But the light that gleamed from the ancient turrets of the Abbey of Clairvaux was transitory and evanescent. New centuries of persecution followed; the Reformation did nothing for the Jew. The infallibility of Geneva was sterner than the infallibility of Rome. But all of us – Calvinists, Protestants, Catholics – all of us who have torn the seamless garment into pieces have sinned most fearfully in this terrible regard...'

# ABRAHAM LINCOLN
## 12 February 1809 – 15 April 1865

*'Mr. Speaker, did you know I am a military hero?'*
27 July 1848

**When a new member of Congress**, Lincoln made this superbly amusing speech in the House of Representatives. He ridiculed the claims to heroism of General Lewis Cass of Michigan, who was campaigning for the Democratic nomination for the presidency against General Zachary Taylor. Some of his asides castigating the expenses claims of politicians have relevance today. This speech was addressing Taylor's policy that presidents should not use the veto. Lincoln had been one of the first volunteers, and a captain in the Black Hawk War.

'...Yes, sir; all his *[Cass's]* biographies (and they are legion) have him in hand, tying him to a military tail, like so many mischievous boys tying a dog to a bladder of beans. True, the material they have is very limited, but they drive at it might and main. He invaded Canada without resistance, and he outvaded it without pursuit. As he did both under orders, I suppose there was to him neither credit nor discredit in them; but they constitute a large part of the tail. He was not at Hull's surrender, but he was close by; he was volunteer aid to General Harrison on the day of the battle of the Thames; and as you said in 1840 Harrison was picking huckleberries two miles off while the battle was fought, I suppose it is a just conclusion with you to say Cass was aiding Harrison to pick huckleberries. This is about all, except the mooted question of the broken sword. Some authors say he broke it, some say he threw it away, and some others, who ought to know, say nothing about it. Perhaps it would be a fair historical compromise to say, if he did not break it, he did not do anything else with it.

...Mr. Speaker, did you know I am a military hero? Yes, Sir; in the days of the Black Hawk War I fought, bled, and came away. Speaking of General Cass's career reminds me of my own. I was not at Stillman's defeat, but I was about as near it as Cass was to Hull's surrender; and, like him, I saw the place very soon afterward. It is quite certain I did not break my sword, for I had none to break, but I bent a musket pretty badly on one occasion. If Cass broke his sword, the idea is he broke it in desperation; I bent the musket by accident. If General Cass went in advance of me in picking huckleberries, I guess I surpassed him in charges upon the wild onions. If he saw any live, fighting Indians, it was more than I did, but I had a good many bloody struggles with the mosquitoes, and although I never fainted from the loss of blood, I can truly say I was often very hungry. Mr. Speaker, if I should ever conclude to doff whatever our Democratic friends may suppose there is of black-cockade federalism about me, and therefore they shall take me up as their candidate for the Presidency, I protest they shall not make fun of me, as they have of General Cass, by attempting to write me into a military hero...

Mr. Speaker, I adopt the suggestion of a friend, that General Cass is a general of splendidly successful charges – charges, to be sure, not upon the public enemy, but upon the public treasury. He was Governor of Michigan territory, and ex-officio Superintendent of Indian Affairs, from the 9th of October, 1813, till the 31st of July, 1831 – a period of seventeen years, nine months, and twenty-two days. During this period he received from the United States treasury, for personal services and personal expenses, the aggregate sum of ninety-six thousand and twenty eight dollars, being an average of fourteen dollars and seventy-nine cents per day for every day of the time. This large sum was reached by assuming that he was doing service at several different places, and in several different capacities in the same place, all at the same time...But I have introduced General Cass's accounts here chiefly to show the wonderful physical capacities of the man. They show that he not only did the labor of several men at the same time, but that he often did it at several places, many hundreds of miles apart, at the same time. And at eating, too, his capacities are shown to be quite as wonderful. From October, 1821, to May, 1822, he eat ten rations a day in Michigan, ten rations a day here in Washington, and near five dollars' worth a day on the road between the two places! And then there is an important discovery in his example – the art of being paid for what one eats, instead of having to pay for it...'

# GIUSEPPE GARIBALDI
### 4 July 1807 – 2 June 1882

*'I offer hunger, thirst, forced marches, battles, and death'*
2 July 1849

**Garibaldi returned to Italy** from commanding the 'Italian Legion' in the Uruguayan civil war to fight in the 'Revolutions of 1848'. He led his men to victory twice in the First Italian Civil War of Independence. In March 1849 he moved to Rome to support the republic proclaimed on 5 February in the Papal States (today's Marche, Lazio, Romagna and Umbria regions). He took command of the defence of Rome against the French, defeating their larger army on 30 April. French reinforcements arrived, and the siege of Rome began on 1 June, with the French prevailing on 29 June. On 30 June the Roman Assembly met and debated the options of surrender, continuing fighting in the streets, or retreating from Rome to continue resistance from the Apennine Mountains. Garibaldi made a speech favouring the third option and said: '*Wherever we may be, there will be Rome*'. Pressured by an arriving French army, the Roman constituent assembly decreed the surrender of Rome and the Republic on 1 July 1849. On 2 July, a wounded Garibaldi was in St Peter's Square in Rome, his mistress Anita at his side, exhorting anybody who was willing to continue the fight to follow him:

> 'Soldiers, I am going out from Rome. Let those who wish to continue the war against the stranger, come with me. I offer neither pay, nor quarters, nor provisions. I offer hunger, thirst, forced marches, battles, and death. Let him who loves his country follow me.'

According to his biographer Giuseppe Guerzoni, the exact words of Garibaldi's complete speech differ from historian to historian, and the only quotation we can be sure of is '*I offer hunger, thirst, forced marches, battles, and death*', a phrase which became the core of one of Winston Churchill's key war speeches. By 8 p.m., Garibaldi had gathered almost 4,000 soldiers, 800 horses, supplies of ammunition and basic equipment, and his small army marched out of Rome. The French army entered Rome on the morning of 3 July, and Garibaldi was hunted by French, Austrian, Spanish and Neapolitan troops. He fled north, trying to reach Venice, which the Austrians were besieging. Anita, who was carrying their fifth child, died during the retreat, and only 250 men remained with him when he arrived at the Republic of San Marino on 29 July 1849. He escaped to Tangier and then to America, and it would be 1854 before he set foot on Italian soil again to raise an army for independence.

# SOJOURNER TRUTH (ISABELLA BAUMFREE)
## 1797 – 26 November 1883

### 'Ain't I a woman?'
29 May 1851

**Born into slavery in New York State** as Isabella Baumfree, she was an abolitionist and women's rights activist who changed her name in 1843. Suffering a terrible upbringing, she escaped from slavery with her baby daughter in late 1826. She met Abraham Lincoln and helped to recruit black troops to the Union cause, spending all her life travelling and speaking for freedom. This speech was delivered in 1851 at the Ohio Women's Rights Convention in Akron, Ohio.

'Well, children, where there is so much racket there must be something out of kilter. I think that 'twixt the Negroes of the South and the women at the North, all talking about rights, the white men will be in a fix pretty soon. But what's all this here talking about? That man over there says that women need to be helped into carriages, and lifted over ditches, and to have the best place everywhere. Nobody ever helps me into carriages, or over mud-puddles, or gives me any best place! And ain't I a woman? Look at me! Look at my arm! I have plowed and planted, and gathered into barns, and no man could head me! And ain't I a woman? I could work as much and eat as much as a man – when I could get it – and bear the lash as well! And ain't I a woman? I have borne thirteen children, and seen most all sold off to slavery, and when I cried out with my mother's grief, none but Jesus heard me! And ain't I a woman? Then they talk about this thing in the head; what's this they call it? [*A member of audience whispered 'intellect'*]. That's it, honey. What's that got to do with women's rights or negroes' rights? If my cup won't hold but a pint, and yours holds a quart, wouldn't you be mean not to let me have my little half measure full? Then that little man in black there, he says women can't have as much rights as men, 'cause Christ wasn't a woman! Where did your Christ come from? Where did your Christ come from? From God and a woman! Man had nothing to do with Him. If the first woman God ever made was strong enough to turn the world upside down all alone, these women together ought to be able to turn it back, and get it right side up again! And now they is asking to do it, the men better let them. Obliged to you for hearing me, and now old Sojourner ain't got nothing more to say.'

# DANIEL WEBSTER
## 18 January 1782 – 24 October 1852

### 'An American no longer?'
7 March 1850

**Aged 68, the secretary of state** made this famous 'seventh of March speech' in favour of the Compromise Measures of 1850. Delivered in the United States Senate, it was his last great speech and one of the most notable of his life. He rebuked the North for agitating about the slavery question and for violating the Fugitive Slave Law, and advocated real concessions to the South. The speech aroused general indignation in the North, and Webster endured an avalanche of criticism from anti-slavery campaigners. He was accused of pandering to the South in order to gain support for his candidacy for the office of president. However, his line of reasoning agrees with all his earlier speeches, his argument always being in favour of 'liberty and union', which he considered the compromise necessary to preserve the Union without armed conflict.

'...Secession! Peaceable secession! Sir, your eyes and mine are never destined to see that miracle. The dismemberment of this vast country without convulsion! The breaking up of the fountains of the great deep without ruffing the surface! Who is so foolish, I beg every body's pardon, as to expect to see any such thing? Sir, he who sees these States, now revolving in harmony around a common center, and expects to see them quit their places and fly off without convulsion, may look the next hour to see heavenly bodies rush from their spheres, and jostle against each other in the realms of space, without causing the wreck of the universe. There can be no such thing as peaceable secession. Peaceable secession is an utter impossibility. Is the great Constitution under which we live, covering this whole country, is it to be thawed and melted away by secession, as the snows on the mountain melt under the influence of a vernal sun, disappear almost unobserved, and run off? No, Sir! No, Sir! I will not state what might produce the disruption of the Union; but, Sir, I see as plainly as I see the sun in heaven what that disruption itself must produce; I see that it must produce war, and such a war as I will not describe, in its twofold character.

Peaceable secession! Peaceable secession! The concurrent agreement of all the members of this great republic to separate! A voluntary separation, with alimony on one side and on the other. Why, what would be the result? Where is the line to be drawn? What States are to be seceded? What is to remain American? What am I to be? An American no longer? Am I to become a sectional man, a local man, a separatist, with no country in common with the gentlemen who sit around me here, or who fill the other house of Congress? Heaven forbid! Where is the flag of the republic to remain? Where is the eagle still to tower? Or is he to cower, and shrink, and fall to the ground? Why, Sir, our ancestors, our fathers and our grandfathers, those of them that are yet living amongst us with prolonged lives, would rebuke and reproach us; and our children and our grandchildren would cry out shame upon us, if we of this generation should dishonor these ensigns of the power of the government and the harmony of that Union which is every day felt among us with so much joy and gratitude.

What is to become of the army? What is to become of the navy? What is to become of the public lands? How is each of the thirty States to defend itself? I know, although the idea has not been stated distinctly, there is to be, or it is supposed possible that there will be, a Southern Confederacy. I do not mean, when I allude to this statement, that any one seriously contemplates such a state of things. I do not mean to say that it is true, but I have heard it suggested elsewhere, that the idea has been entertained, that, after the dissolution of this Union, a Southern Confederacy might be formed. I am sorry, Sir, that it has ever been thought of, talked of, or dreamed of, in the wildest flights of human imagination. But the idea, so far as it exists, must be of a separation, assigning the slave States to one side and the free States to the other. Sir, I may express myself too strongly, perhaps, but there are impossibilities in the natural as well as in the physical world, and I hold the idea of a separation of these States, those that are free to form one government, and those that are slave-holding to form another, as such an impossibility. We could not separate the States by any such line, if we were to draw it. We could not sit down here to-day and draw a line of separation that would satisfy any five men in the country. There are natural causes that would keep and tie us together, and there are social and domestic relations which we could not break if we would, and which we should not if we could...'

# VICTOR-MARIE HUGO
### 26 February 1802 – 22 May 1885

*'...if there is a culprit here, it is not my son, – it is I!'*
11 June 1851

**The poet, playwright, statesman** and human rights activist is best remembered for his novels *Les Misérables* and *The Hunchback of Notre Dame*. More than two million people attended his funeral and he lies in Paris's Pantheon alongside Alexandre Dumas and Émile Zola. His 25-year-old son Charles was put on trial in 1851, charged with *'disrespect to the laws'*. Charles had written an article in *L'Evenement* criticizing the sentence and barbaric execution of Claude Montcharmont on 10 May. Victor Hugo asked to defend his son, and this is part of his speech. Charles was sentenced to six months in prison and fined 500 francs.

'Gentlemen of the jury, if there is a culprit here, it is not my son, – it is I! – I, who for these twenty-five years have opposed capital punishment, – have contended for the inviolability of human life, – have committed this crime for which my son is now arraigned. Here I denounce myself, Mr. Advocate-General! I have committed it under all aggravated circumstances; deliberately, repeatedly, tenaciously. Yes, this old and absurd lex talionis – this law of blood for blood – I have combated all my life – all my life, gentlemen of the jury! And, while I have breath, I will continue to combat it, by all my efforts as a writer, by all my words and all my votes as a legislator! I declare it before the crucifix; before that Victim of the penalty of death, who sees and hears us; before that gibbet, in which, two thousand years ago, for the eternal instruction of the generations, the human law nailed the divine!

In all that my son has written on the subject of capital punishment and for writing and publishing which he is now on trial – in all that he has written, he has merely proclaimed the sentiments with which, from his infancy, I have inspired him. Gentlemen jurors, the right to criticize a law, and to criticize it severely – especially a penal law – is placed beside the duty of amelioration, like the torch beside the work under the artisan's hand. The right of the journalist is as sacred, as necessary, as exempt from prescription, as the right of the legislator.

What are the circumstances? A man, a convict, a sentenced wretch, is dragged, on a certain morning, to one of our public squares. There he finds the scaffold! He shudders, he struggles, he refuses to die. He is young yet – only twenty-nine. Ah! I know what you will say, – "He is a murderer!" But hear me. Two officers seize him. His hands, his feet are tied. He throws off the two officers. A frightful struggle ensues. His feet, bound as they are, become entangled in the ladder. He uses the scaffold against the scaffold! The struggle is prolonged. Horror seizes the crowd! The officers, – sweat and shame on their brows, – pale, panting, terrified, despairing, – despairing with I know not what horrible despair, – shrinking under that public reprobation which ought to have visited the penalty, and spared the passive treatment, the executioner, – the officers strive savagely. The victim clings to the scaffold and shrieks for pardon. His clothes are torn, – his shoulders bloody, – still he resists. At length, after three-quarters of an hour of this monstrous effort, of this spectacle without a name, of this agony, – agony for all, be it understood, – agony for the assembled spectators as well as for the condemned man – after this age of anguish, gentlemen of the jury, they take back the poor wretch to his prison. The People breathe again. The People, naturally merciful, hope that the man will be spared. But no, – the guillotine, though vanquished, remains standing. There it frowns all day, in the midst of a sickened population. And at night the officers, reinforced, drag forth the wretch again, so bound that he is but an inert weight, – they drag him forth, haggard, bloody, weeping, pleading, howling for life, – calling upon God, calling upon his father and mother, – for like a very child had this man become in the prospect of death, – they drag him forth to execution. He is hoisted on the scaffold and his head falls! And then through every conscience runs a shudder. Never had legal murder appeared with an aspect so indecent, so abominable. All feel jointly implicated in the deed. It is at this very moment that from a young man's breast escapes a cry, wrung from his very heart, – a cry of pity and anguish, – a cry of horror, – a cry of humanity. And this cry you would punish! And in the face of the appalling facts which I have narrated, you would say to the guillotine, "Thou art right!" and to Pity, saintly Pity, "Thou art wrong!" Gentlemen of the jury, it cannot be! Gentlemen, I have finished.'

# DANIEL WEBSTER
### 18 January 1782 – 24 October 1852

---

### *'It was sealed in blood'*
### 4 July 1851

**In Washington D.C., President Millard Fillmore** assisted in the laying of the *'cornerstone of the new Capitol edifice'*, and that brilliant speaker, Secretary of State Daniel Webster, delivered what would prove to be his final Independence Day oration.

'Fellow-Citizens – I greet you well; I give you joy, on the return of this anniversary; and I felicitate you, also, on the more particular purpose of which this ever-memorable day has been chosen to witness the fulfilment. Hail! All hail! I see before and around me a mass of faces, glowing with cheerfulness and patriotic pride. I see thousands of eyes turned towards other eyes, all sparkling with gratification and delight. This is the New World! This is America! This is Washington! And this the Capitol of the United States! And where else, among the nations, can the seat of government be surrounded, on any day of any year, by those who have more reason to rejoice in the blessings which they possess? Nowhere, fellow-citizens! Assuredly, nowhere! Let us, then, meet this rising sun with joy and thanksgiving! This is that day of the year which announced to mankind the great fact of American Independence. This fresh and brilliant morning blesses our vision with another beholding of the birthday of our nation; and we see that nation, of recent origin, now among the most considerable and powerful, and spreading over the continent from sea to sea...

On the 4th of July, 1776, the Representatives of the United States of America, in Congress assembled, declared that these United Colonies are, and of right ought to be, free and independent States. This Declaration, made by most patriotic and resolute men, trusting in the justice of their cause and the protection of Heaven, and yet made not without deep solicitude and anxiety, has now stood for seventy-five years, and still stands. It was sealed in blood. It has met dangers, and overcome them; it has had enemies, and conquered them; it has had detractors, and abashed them all; it has had doubting friends, but it has cleared all doubts away; and now, to-day, raising its august form higher than the clouds, twenty millions of people contemplate it with hallowed love, and the world beholds it, and the consequences which have followed from it, with profound admiration. This anniversary animates and gladdens and unites all American hearts. On other days of the year we may be party men, indulging in controversies, more or less important to the public good; we may have likes and dislikes, and we may maintain our political differences, often with warm, and sometimes with angry feelings. But to-day we are Americans all; and all nothing but Americans. As the great luminary over our heads, dissipating mists and fogs, now cheers the whole hemisphere, so do the associations connected with this day disperse all cloudy and sullen weather in the minds and hearts of true Americans. Every man's heart swells within him; every man's port and bearing become somewhat more proud and lofty, as he remembers that seventy-five years have rolled away, and that the great inheritance of liberty is still his; his, undiminished and unimpaired; his in all its original glory; his to enjoy, his to protect, and his to transmit to future generations. Fellow-citizens, this inheritance which we enjoy to-day is not only an inheritance of liberty, but of our own peculiar American liberty...

That liberty is characteristic, peculiar, and altogether our own. Nothing like it existed in former times, nor was known in the most enlightened states of antiquity; while with us its principles have become interwoven into the minds of individual men, connected with our daily opinions, and our daily habits, until it is, if I may so say, an element of social as well as of political life; and the consequence is, that to whatever region an American citizen carries himself, he takes with him, fully developed in his own understanding and experience, our American principles and opinions, and becomes ready at once, in co-operation with others, to apply them to the formation of new governments... Fellow-citizens, fifty-eight years ago Washington stood on this spot to execute a duty like that which has now been performed. He then laid the corner-stone of the original Capitol. He was at the head of the government, at that time weak in resources, burdened with debt, just struggling into political existence and respectability, and agitated by the heaving waves which were overturning European thrones. But even then, in many important respects, the government was strong. It was strong in Washington's own great character; it was strong in the wisdom and patriotism of other eminent public men, his political associates and fellow-laborers; and it was strong in the affections of the people. Since that time astonishing changes have been wrought in the condition and prospects of the American people; and a degree of progress witnessed with which the world can furnish no parallel...'

# FREDERICK DOUGLASS (born FREDERICK AUGUSTUS WASHINGTON BAILEY)
## c.1817/18 – 20 February 1895

*'What to the American slave is your Fourth of July?'*
4 July 1852

**Born a slave, he escaped from servitude** in 1838, and became a leading abolitionist, women's suffragist, editor, author, statesman and reformer. His *Narrative of the Life of Frederick Douglass, an American Slave*, published in 1845, was attacked as it was not thought that a black man could have produced such an eloquent work of literature. He was fond of saying, '*I would unite with anybody to do right and with nobody to do wrong.*' Douglass settled in Rochester, New York, where he published *The North Star*, an abolitionist newspaper. He directed the local underground which smuggled escaped slaves into Canada and also worked to end racial segregation in Rochester's public schools. In 1852, the leading citizens of Rochester asked Douglass to give a speech as part of their Fourth of July celebrations, in a meeting sponsored by the Rochester Ladies' Anti-Slavery Society. In his speech, however, Douglass delivered a scathing attack on the hypocrisy of a nation celebrating freedom and independence on 4 July with speeches, parades and platitudes, while, within its borders, nearly four million humans were still being kept as slaves.

'Fellow citizens, pardon me, and allow me to ask, why am I called upon to speak here today? What have I or those I represent to do with your national independence? Are the great principles of political freedom and of natural justice, embodied in that Declaration of Independence, extended to us? And am I, therefore, called upon to bring our humble offering to the national altar, and to confess the benefits, and express devout gratitude for the blessings resulting from your independence to us?...My subject, then, fellow citizens, is "American Slavery." I shall see this day and its popular characteristics from the slave's point of view. Standing here, identified with the American bondman, making his wrongs mine, I do not hesitate to declare, with all my soul, that the character and conduct of this nation never looked blacker to me than on this Fourth of July...How should I look today in the presence of Americans, dividing and subdividing a discourse, to show that men have a natural right to freedom, speaking of it relatively and positively, negatively and affirmatively? To do so would be to make myself ridiculous, and to offer an insult to your understanding. There is not a man beneath the canopy of heaven who does not know that slavery is wrong for him.

What! Am I to argue that it is wrong to make men brutes, to rob them of their liberty, to work them without wages, to keep them ignorant of their relations to their fellow men, to beat them with sticks, to flay their flesh with the lash, to load their limbs with irons, to hunt them with dogs, to sell them at auction, to sunder their families, to knock out their teeth, to burn their flesh, to starve them into obedience and submission to their masters? Must I argue that a system thus marked with blood and stained with pollution is wrong? No – I will not. I have better employment for my time and strength than such arguments would imply...At a time like this, scorching irony, not convincing argument, is needed. Oh! had I the ability, and could I reach the nation's ear, I would today pour out a fiery stream of biting ridicule, blasting reproach, withering sarcasm, and stern rebuke. For it is not light that is needed, but fire; it is not the gentle shower, but thunder. We need the storm, the whirlwind, and the earthquake. The feeling of the nation must be quickened; the conscience of the nation must be roused; the propriety of the nation must be startled; the hypocrisy of the nation must be exposed; and its crimes against God and man must be denounced.

What to the American slave is your Fourth of July? I answer, a day that reveals to him more than all other days of the year, the gross injustice and cruelty to which he is the constant victim. To him your celebration is a sham; your boasted liberty an unholy license; your national greatness, swelling vanity; your sounds of rejoicing are empty and heartless; your shouts of liberty and equality, hollow mock; your prayers and hymns, your sermons and thanksgivings, with all your religious parade and solemnity, are to him mere bombast, fraud, deception, impiety, and hypocrisy – a thin veil to cover up crimes which would disgrace a nation of savages. There is not a nation of the earth guilty of practices more shocking and bloody than are the people of these United States at this very hour. Go search where you will, roam through all the monarchies and despotisms of the Old World, travel through South America, search out every abuse and when you have found the last, lay your facts by the side of the everyday practices of this nation, and you will say with me that, for revolting barbarity and shameless hypocrisy, America reigns without a rival.'

# JOHN BRIGHT
### 16 November 1811 – 27 March 1889

## 'The Angel of Death has been abroad throughout the land'
### 23 February 1855

**Bright was a strong critic** of Britain's foreign policy and one of the greatest orators of his generation. A Quaker, he fought for social reforms and was strongly anti-war. An MP for 46 years, he coined the phrase '*England is the Mother of Parliaments*'. The following wonderful speech was made in the House of Commons after Prime Minister Lord Palmerston and four members of his Government, including Gladstone, had resigned. The House had disapproved of their conduct during the Crimean War. Disraeli told Bright that '*I would give all that I ever had to have made that speech.*' A British mission was in Vienna negotiating peace, and the House was packed when Bright made his statement, knowing that the vast majority of the members were pro-war. When Bright finished, the House fell silent. Despite his powers of oratory, some politicians and the general public still broadly supported the Anglo-French war against Russia, which was eventually concluded at peace negotiations held in Paris a year later.

'...I know not, sir, who it is that says, "No, no," but I should like to see any man get up and say that the destruction of 200,000 human lives lost on all sides during the course of this unhappy conflict is not a sufficient sacrifice. You are not pretending to conquer territory – you are not pretending to hold fortified or unfortified towns; you have offered terms of peace which, as I understand them, I do not say are not moderate; and breathes there a man in this House or in this country whose appetite for blood is so insatiable that, even when terms of peace have been offered and accepted, he pines for that assault in which of Russian, Turk, French, and English, as sure as one man dies, 20,000 corpses will strew the streets of Sebastopol?...I cannot but notice, in speaking to gentlemen who sit on either side of this House, or in speaking to any one I meet, between this House and any of those localities we frequent when this House is up – I cannot, I say, but notice that an uneasy feeling exists as to the news which may arrive by the very next mail from the East. I do not suppose that your troops are to be beaten in actual conflict with the foe, or that they will be driven into the sea; but I am certain that many homes in England in which there now exists a fond hope that the distant one may return – many such homes may be rendered desolate when the next mail shall arrive. The Angel of Death has been abroad throughout the land; you may almost hear the beating of his wings. There is no one, as when the first-born were slain of old, to sprinkle with blood the lintel and the two side-posts of our doors, that he may spare and pass on; he takes his victims from the castle of the noble, the mansion of the wealthy and the cottage of the poor and the lowly, and it is on behalf of all these classes that I make this solemn appeal...

I tell the noble lord that, if he be ready honestly and frankly to endeavour, by the negotiations about to be opened at Vienna, to put an end to this war, no word of mine, no vote of mine, will be given to shake his power for one single moment, or to change his position in this House. I am sure that the noble lord is not inaccessible to appeals made to him from honest motives and with no unfriendly feeling. The noble lord has been for more than forty years a member of this House. Before I was born he sat upon the Treasury Bench, and he has spent his life in the service of his country. He is no longer young, and his life has extended almost to the term allotted to man. I would ask, I would entreat, the noble lord to take a course which, when he looks back upon his whole political career – whatever he may therein find to be pleased with, whatever to regret – cannot but be a source of gratification to him. By adopting that course he would have the satisfaction of reflecting that having obtained the object of his laudable ambition – having become the foremost subject of the Crown, the director of, it may be, the destinies of his country, and the presiding genius in her councils – he had achieved a still higher and nobler ambition: that he had returned the sword to the scabbard – that at his word torrents of blood had ceased to flow – that he had restored tranquillity to Europe, and saved this country from the indescribable calamities of war.'

# JEFFERSON FINIS DAVIS
## 3 June 1808 – 6 December 1889

*At the Belfast encampment, Maine*
Summer 1858

**A war hero, he served as president** of the Confederate States of America for its entire history, 1861 to 1865, during the American Civil War. Senator for Mississippi, he was influential in holding the states together, and when the Kansas-Nebraska bill was passed, which established that settlers could vote to decide whether to allow slavery, Davis wrote to his constituents that it was *'the triumph of all for which he had contended'*. Davis believed that the danger of sectional discord was over, that peace would reign, and that the Union could be saved through the policy pursued by the Buchanan administration. Around 1858–9, he was nationally acknowledged as a senior statesman, a leader of the people, ranking among the most eminent living Americans. As such, he was introduced to the Union Army in 1858, and gave this hopeful speech, not realizing the conflict to come that would tear America apart.

'Citizen Soldiers...My friends, your worthy General has alluded to my connection with the military service of the country. The memory arose to myself when the troops this day marched past me, and when I looked upon their manly bearing and firm step. I thought could I have seen them thus approaching the last field of battle on which I served, where the changing tide several times threatened disaster to the American flag, with what joy I would have welcomed those striped and starred banners, the emblem and the guide of the free and the brave, and with what pride would the heart have beaten when welcoming the danger's hour, brethren from so remote an extremity of our expanded territory... one of the evidences of the fraternal confidence and mutual reliance of our fathers was to be found in their compact or mutual protection and common defence. So long as their sons preserve the spirit and appreciate the purpose of their fathers, the United States will remain invincible, their power will grow with the lapse of time, and their example show brighter and brighter as revolving ages roll over the temple our fathers dedicated to constitutional liberty, and founded upon truths announced to their sons, but intended for mankind. I thank you, citizen soldiers, for this act of courtesy. It will long and gratefully be remembered, as a token of respect to the distant State of which I am a citizen, and I trust will be noted by others, as indicating that national sentiment which made, and which alone can preserve us a nation.'

# JOHN BROWN
## 9 May 1800 – 2 December 1859

*'...mingle my blood further with the blood of my children'*
2 November 1859

**This leading abolitionist advocated** and practised armed insurrection to end all slavery. He seized the arsenal at Harper's Ferry, Virginia in October 1859, to arm slaves for an insurrection. He was captured two days later, tried by the Commonwealth of Virginia and hanged. This was his last speech to the court at Charles Town, Virginia. President Lincoln called Brown a *'misguided fanatic'*, and the raid at Harper's Ferry escalated tensions leading eventually to secession and the American Civil War.

'I have, may it please the court, a few words to say. In the first place, I deny everything but what I have all along admitted – the design on my part to free the slaves. I intended certainly to have made a clean thing of that matter, as I did last winter when I went into Missouri and there took slaves without the snapping of a gun on either side, moved them through the country, and finally left them in Canada. I designed to have done the same thing again on a larger scale. That was all I intended.
I never did intend murder, or treason, or the destruction of property, or to excite or incite slaves to rebellion, or to make insurrection...This court acknowledges, as I suppose, the validity of the law of God. I see a book kissed here which I suppose to be the Bible, or at least the New Testament. That teaches me that all things whatsoever I would that men should do to me, I should do even so to them. It teaches me, further, to "remember them that are in bonds, as bound with them". I endeavored to act up to that instruction. I say I am yet too young to understand that God is any respecter of persons. I believe that to have interfered as I have done – as I have always freely admitted I have done – in behalf of His despised poor was not wrong, but right. Now, if it is deemed necessary that I should forfeit my life for the furtherance of the ends of justice, and mingle my blood further with the blood of my children and with the blood of millions in this slave country whose rights are disregarded by wicked, cruel, and unjust enactments – I submit; so let it be done!

# WILLIAM LLOYD GARRISON
## 13 December 1805 – 24 May 1879

*On the Death of John Brown*
2 December 1859

**Formerly imprisoned in Baltimore** in the pro-slavery state of Maryland for his writings, Garrison began to publish the radical abolitionist newspaper *The Liberator* in 1831. The following year he founded an Abolition Society in Boston, and was president of the American Antislavery Society between 1843–65. In 1844, Garrison publicly burned a copy of the Constitution, declaring it '*a Covenant with Death, an Agreement with Hell*', referring to the compromise that had written slavery into the Constitution. The State of Georgia offered a reward of $5,000 for his arrest. Garrison was also a prominent voice for the women's suffrage movement.

'...God forbid that we should any longer continue the accomplices of thieves and robbers, of men-stealers and women-whippers! We must join together in the name of freedom. As for the Union – where is it and what is it? In one-half of it no man can exercise freedom of speech or the press – no man can utter the words of Washington, of Jefferson, of Patrick Henry – except at the peril of his life; and Northern men are everywhere hunted and driven from the South if they are supposed to cherish the sentiment of freedom in their bosoms. We are living under an awful despotism – that of a brutal slave oligarchy. And they threaten to leave us if we do not continue to do their evil work, as we have hitherto done it, and go down in the dust before them! Would to heaven they would go! It would only be the paupers clearing out from the town, would it not? But, no, they do not mean to go; they mean to cling to you, and they mean to subdue you. But will you be subdued? I tell you our work is the dissolution of this slavery-cursed Union, if we would have a fragment of our liberties left to us! Surely between freemen, who believe in exact justice and impartial liberty, and slaveholders, who are for cleaning down all human rights at a blow, it is not possible there should be any Union whatever. "How can two walk together except they be agreed?" The slaveholder with his hands dripping in blood – will I make a compact with him? The man who plunders cradles – will I say to him, "Brother, let us walk together in unity?"'

# GIUSEPPE GARIBALDI
## 4 July 1807 – 2 June 1882

*'This people is its own master'*
8 November 1860

**In April 1860, Garibaldi gathered** a thousand volunteers (*I Mille*, or the *Red Shirts*) and claimed Sicily in the name of the king of Piedmont-Sardinia, Victor Emmanuel II. He won an action at Calatafimi and then besieged Palermo. Thousands more volunteers joined him as he invaded mainland Italy. On 7 September he entered Naples, and fought a stalemate with the army of the Neapolitan provinces on 30 September. In October Garibaldi recognized Victor Emanuel as the new king of Italy, granting him control over all of Garibaldi's gains in southern Italy. After turning over Naples to Victor Emmanuel II, he made this speech to his soldiers at Naples, before resuming a humble life and temporary retirement on the island of Caprera.

'We must now consider the period which is just drawing to a close as almost the last stage of our national resurrection, and prepare ourselves to finish worthily the marvellous design of the elect of twenty generations, the completion of which Providence has reserved for this fortunate age.

Yes, young men, Italy owes to you an undertaking which has merited the applause of the universe. You have conquered and you will conquer still, because you are prepared for the tactics that decide the fate of battles. You are not unworthy of the men who entered the ranks of a Macedonian phalanx, and who contended not in vain with the proud conquerors of Asia. To this wonderful page in our country's history another more glorious still will be added, and the slave shall show at last to his free brothers a sharpened sword forged from the links of his fetters. To arms, then, all of you! all of you! And the oppressors and the mighty shall disappear like dust. You, too, women, cast away all the cowards from your embraces; they will give you only cowards for children, and you who are the daughters of the land of beauty must bear children who are noble and brave. Let timid doctrinaires depart from among us to carry their servility and their miserable fears elsewhere. This people is its own master. It wishes to be the brother of other peoples, but to look on the insolent with a proud glance, not to grovel before them imploring its own freedom. It will no longer follow in the trail of men whose hearts are foul. No! No! No!'

# JEFFERSON FINIS DAVIS
## 3 June 1808 – 6 December 1889

*On withdrawing from the Union*
21 January 1861

**Elected to Congress in 1845,** Davis served in the Mexican War in 1846–7 and was elected a United States senator. On 4 July 1858, Davis delivered an anti-secessionist speech on board a ship near Boston. He again urged the preservation of the Union on 11 October in Boston, and returned to the Senate soon after. As Davis explained in his memoir, *The Rise and Fall of the Confederate Government,* he believed that each state was sovereign and had an unquestionable right to secede from the Union. He counselled delay among his fellow Southerners, however, because he did not think that the North would permit the peaceable exercise of the right to secession. He also knew that the South lacked the military and naval resources necessary to defend itself if war were to break out. Following the election of Abraham Lincoln in 1860, events accelerated. Davis, as senator for Mississippi, went to the Senate. Days earlier, the states of Mississippi, Florida and Alabama had joined South Carolina in deciding to secede from the Union. Rumours flew that Georgia, Louisiana and Texas would soon follow. In meetings of his own Mississippi legislature, Davis had argued against secession, but when a majority of the delegates opposed him, he gave in. All gallery seats were taken in the Senate, and people attempted to enter the already crowded cloakrooms and lobby adjacent to the chamber. Davis was the acknowledged leader of the Southern states, and was in great pain, suffering from facial neuralgia. As he proceeded with his valedictory address, his voice gained in volume and force. Absolute silence met the conclusion of his six-minute address. Then there was a small burst of applause and the sounds of open weeping swept the chamber. The vice-president immediately rose to his feet, followed by the 58 senators and the mass of spectators as Davis and his four colleagues solemnly walked up the centre aisle and rode away from the Capitol. Later, describing the *'unutterable grief'* of the occasion, Davis said that his words had been *'not my utterances but rather leaves torn from the book of fate'*. Four days later, Davis was commissioned a major-general of Mississippi troops, and on 9 February 1861, a convention at Montgomery, Alabama named him provisional president of the Confederate States of America. After the Civil War, Davis was arrested in May 1865 and imprisoned until 1867.

'I rise, Mr. President, for the purpose of announcing to the Senate that I have satisfactory evidence that the State of Mississippi, by a solemn ordinance of her people in convention assembled, has declared her separation from the United States. Under these circumstances, of course my functions are terminated here. It has seemed to me proper, however, that I should appear in the Senate to announce that fact to my associates, and I will say but very little more. The occasion does not invite me to go into argument, and my physical condition would not permit me to do so if it were otherwise; and yet it seems to become me to say something on the part of the State I here represent, on an occasion so solemn as this. It is known to senators who have served with me here that I have for many years advocated, as an essential attribute of State sovereignty, the right of a State to secede from the Union. Therefore, if I had not believed there was justifiable cause; if I had thought that Mississippi was acting without sufficient provocation, or without an existing necessity, I should still, under my theory of the government, because of my allegiance to the State of which I am a citizen, have been bound by her action. I, however, may be permitted to say that I do think that she has justifiable cause, and I approve of her act. I conferred with her people before the act was taken, counselled them then that if the state of things which they apprehended should exist when the convention met, they should take the action which they have now adopted...I see now around me some with whom I have served long; there have been points of collision; but whatever of offense there has been to me, I leave here; I carry with me no hostile remembrance. Whatever offense I have given which has not been redressed, or for which satisfaction has not been demanded, I have, senators, in this hour of our parting, to offer you my apology for any pain which, in heat of discussion, I have inflicted. I go hence unencumbered of the remembrance of any injury received, and having discharged the duty of making the only reparation in my power for any injury offered. Mr. President and senators, having made the announcement which the occasion seemed to me to require, it only remains for me to bid you a final adieu.'

# ALEXANDER HAMILTON STEPHENS
## 11 February 1812 – 4 March 1883

### The Cornerstone Speech
21 March 1861

**Stephens, as US representative for Georgia** and a member of the Georgia state senate, was elected in 1861 as a delegate to the Georgia special convention to decide on secession from the United States, where he supported the Union. By the time of the Civil War, Stephens owned 34 slaves and several thousand acres. However, he was elected to the Confederate Congress, and was chosen as vice-president of the provisional government in February 1861. On the brink of the Civil War, Stephens gave this famous speech in Savannah, declaring that slavery was the natural condition of blacks and the foundation of the confederacy. Throughout the Civil War he opposed many of Jefferson Davis's policies.

'...The constitution, it is true, secured every essential guarantee to the institution while it should last, and hence no argument can be justly urged against the constitutional guarantees thus secured, because of the common sentiment of the day. Those ideas, however, were fundamentally wrong. They rested upon the assumption of the equality of races. This was an error...Our new [Confederate] government is founded upon exactly the opposite idea; its foundations are laid, its cornerstone rests, upon the great truth that the negro is not equal to the white man; that slavery subordination to the superior race is his natural and normal condition. This, our new government, is the first, in the history of the world, based upon this great physical, philosophical, and moral truth. This truth has been slow in the process of its development, like all other truths in the various departments of science. It has been so even amongst us. Many who hear me, perhaps, can recollect well, that this truth was not generally admitted, even within their day. The errors of the past generation still clung to many as late as twenty years ago. Those at the North, who still cling to these errors, with a zeal above knowledge, we justly denominate fanatics. All fanaticism springs from an aberration of the mind from a defect in reasoning. It is a species of insanity. One of the most striking characteristics of insanity, in many instances, is forming correct conclusions from fancied or erroneous premises; so with the anti-slavery fanatics. Their conclusions are right if their premises were. They assume that the negro is equal, and hence conclude that he is entitled to equal privileges and rights with the white man...'

# CAMILLO PAOLO FILIPPO GIULIO BENSO, COUNT OF CAVOUR
## 10 August 1810 – 6 June 1861

*'Rome should be the capital of Italy'*
April–May 1861

**Cavour, as he is known**, was a leading figure in the movement towards Italian unification, and the first prime minister of Italy from 23 March 1861 until his death ten weeks later. Cavour became prime minister of Piedmont–Sardinia in 1852. Under him, Piedmont joined the Alliance in the Crimean War, sending 18,000 troops and earning Piedmont a place at the Peace Congress in Paris. He cooperated with Napoleon III in 1858–9 in the war against Austria. Cavour secretly supported the expedition of Garibaldi of 1860, and managed to make Piedmont a new power in Europe, controlling a nearly united Italy that was five times as large as Piedmont had been before he came to power. Cavour effectively secured the unification of Italy under Victor Emmanuel of Piedmont–Sardinia in 1861. On 17 March 1861 the first Italian parliament met in Turin and proclaimed Victor Emmanuel II king of Italy. As prime minister, Cavour urged with all his power that Rome should be made the permanent capital of the country. In May a vote to that effect was passed, but Cavour did not live to see either Rome (controlled by France and the pope) or Venice (controlled by Austria) included in Italy. He died on 6 June following the passing of the vote to declare Rome the capital of Italy. His last words were reportedly *'L'Italia è fatta, tutto è a posto' (Italy is made. All is safe)*. The Papal States came under the protection of Napoleon III, but with the outbreak of the Franco-Prussian War in 1870, Italian troops managed to capture Rome on 20 September. The pope declared himself a prisoner in the Vatican, and in 1871 the capital was at last moved from Florence to Rome.

'Rome should be the capital of Italy. Without the acceptance of this premise by Italy and all Europe there can be no solution of the Roman question. If any one could conceive of a united Italy having any degree of stability, without Rome for its capital, I would declare the Roman question difficult, if not impossible, of solution. And why have we the right, the duty of insisting that Rome shall be united to Italy? Because without Rome as the capital of Italy, Italy can not exist...'

# OTTO EDUARD LEOPOLD VON BISMARCK
## 1 April 1815 – 30 July 1898

*'Iron and blood'*
30 September 1862

During the revolutions of 1848–9, German unification had been a major objective. Representatives of the German states met in Frankfurt to draft a constitution creating a federal union, with a national parliament to be elected by universal male suffrage. In April 1849, the Frankfurt parliament offered the title of emperor to King Friedrich Wilhelm IV of Prussia. Fearing the opposition of the other German princes and military intervention from Austria and Russia against a united Germany, Friedrich refused to accept the title. In 1861, King Wilhelm I succeeded upon Friedrich's death, and he often came into conflict with the increasingly liberal Prussian Diet (parliament). A crisis occurred in 1862, when the Diet refused to authorize funding for a proposed re-organization of the army. The king's ministers could not convince legislators to pass the budget, and the king was unwilling to make concessions. Wilhelm threatened to abdicate and believed that Bismarck was the only politician capable of handling the crisis. However, Bismarck demanded absolute control over foreign affairs, so Wilhelm prevaricated about appointing him to power. In September 1862, the House of Deputies overwhelmingly rejected the proposed budget, and Wilhelm urgently recalled Bismarck, who was then ambassador to Russia. On 23 September 1862, Wilhelm appointed Bismarck minister president (prime minister) and also foreign minister. Bismarck made this speech to the Budget Committee of the Prussian Chamber of Deputies in Berlin. As minister president of Prussia from 1862–90, Bismarck oversaw the unification of Germany. In 1867 he was chancellor of the North German Confederation, and oversaw the creation of the German empire in 1871. He was the first chancellor of the German empire and his diplomacy of *Realpolitik* (political realism) and powerful rule gained him the name of 'The Iron Chancellor'.

> '...Germany is not looking to Prussia's liberalism, but to its power. Bavaria, Württemberg, Baden may indulge liberalism, and yet no one will assign them Prussia's role. Prussia has to coalesce and concentrate its power for the opportune moment, which has already been missed several times. Prussia's borders according to the Vienna Treaties of 1814–15 are not favourable for a healthy, vital state. It is not by speeches and majority resolutions that the great questions of the time are decided – that was the big mistake of 1848 and 1849 – but by iron and blood...'

# ABRAHAM LINCOLN
## 12 February 1809 – 15 April 1865

---

## The Gettysburg Address
19 November 1863

**Abraham Lincoln was the first Republican** president, and his speech was delivered at the dedication of the Soldiers' National Cemetery in Gettysburg, Pennsylvania, after Edward Everett had made the formal speech of the day. Gettysburg had been the bloodiest battle of the civil war, dealing a blow to Lincoln's war effort. More soldiers were desperately needed by the Northern states, but Lincoln's 1863 military drafts were unpopular, particularly among immigrants. Thus Lincoln's principal aim was to sustain public support for the war effort, and he carefully focused his Gettysburg speech to be a two-minute call to rally support for the principles of the Declaration of Independence. This address, that totals just 272 words, has been hailed as the greatest speech in history, and the political journalist William Safire called it *'the best short speech since the Sermon on the Mount'*.

'Four score and seven years ago our fathers brought forth upon this continent a new nation, conceived in liberty, and dedicated to the proposition that all men are created equal. Now we are engaged in a great civil war, testing whether that nation, or any nation so conceived and so dedicated, can long endure. We are met on a great battle-field of that war. We have come to dedicate a portion of that field as a final resting-place for those who here gave their lives that that nation might live. It is altogether fitting and proper that we should do this.

But in a larger sense, we can not dedicate – we can not consecrate – we can not hallow – this ground. The brave men, living and dead, who struggled here, have consecrated it far above our poor power to add or detract. The world will little note, nor long remember, what we say here, but it can never forget what they did here. It is for us, the living, rather, to be dedicated here to the unfinished work which they who fought here thus far so nobly advanced. It is rather for us to be here dedicated to the great task remaining before us – that from these honored dead we take increased devotion to that cause for which they gave the last full measure of devotion – that we here highly resolve that these dead shall not have died in vain – that this nation, under God, shall have a new birth of freedom – and that government of the people, by the people, and for the people, shall not perish from the earth.'

# DANIEL WILLIAM CAHILL
## 28 November 1796 – 28 October 1864

*'There was a time when there was no earth, no sun, no moon, no stars'*
Sunday 29 November 1863

**Born in Ireland**, Cahill became a celebrated preacher in New York, and this powerful sermon was delivered in the last year of his life.

'There was a time when there was no earth, no sun, no moon, no stars; when all the eye now beholds had no existence; when there was nothing, – all darkness, chaos, – when the Divinity reigned alone; when no created voice was heard through God's territories to break the silence of illimitable space. Six thousand years only have elapsed since he built the present world and peopled the skies with the myriad spheres that hang in the arched roof above us. The mere shell, the mere framework of this world may, perhaps, be somewhat older, but we know when Adam was created with the certainty of a parish register. It may be about six thousand years ago: and since that period the history of man is one unbroken page of wickedness and infidelity. Heaven once, in anger, nearly extirpated our race; and once, in mercy, forgave us. Yet, since, the earth is stained with guilt red as scarlet; and the patience of a God – patience infinite – can alone bear it. Who can tell the amount of the crime of even one city for one day? But who can conceive the infinite guilt of all peoples, of all nations, and all ages, ascending and accumulating before God's throne since the beginning? God is great in power, great in goodness, great in mercy, great in wisdom; but he is more than great in patience, to bear the congregated offenses of countless millions, daily, hourly, provoking his anger and opposing his will. But, as the hour of man's creation and man's redemption was arranged by God, and in due time occurred, so the moment for man's total extinction on earth is approaching, and when the time written in the records of heaven shall have arrived, that unerring decree will be executed. By one word he made this world; by one word he can destroy it. By one stroke of his omnipotent pencil he drew the present picture of creation; by one dash of the same brush he can blot it out again and expunge all the work of the skies. Who can limit his power? In one second he can reduce all things to their original chaos, and live again as he did before creation began. He can, when he pleases, destroy all things – the soul excepted. The soul he cannot annihilate. He made the world himself – of course, he can himself destroy it. But Christ is the redeemer of the soul, and, therefore, its immortal existence is as indestructible as the eternity of God...

A mighty conflagration bursts from the melting earth, rages like a hurricane roundabout, devouring all things in its storm and flood of fire, consuming the crumbling wreck of the condemned world. The heavens become terrible, as the kindling earth and seas show their overwhelming flashes on the crimson skies. The sun muffled, the moon black, the stars fallen, floating masses like clouds of blood sweep the skies in circling fury. The Omnipotence which, in the beginning of time, formed all creation, is now concentrated in a point; and, as it were, intensifies the infinity of his wrath, till his anger can swell no higher; and his voice is heard like thunder in the distance. With what eloquent terror does the Saviour paint this scene in his own words: "Men fainting away with fear, running in wild distraction, calling on the ground to open and swallow them, and the rocks to fall on them and hide them from the face of the Lord." The earth on fire: the skies faded: the sun and the stars darkened or extinguished: mankind burning, dying: the angry voice of God coming to judge the world: and Jesus Christ describing the scene, – are realities which the history of God has never seen before; and which never again will be repeated during the endless round of eternity. Reason asks: Oh, who is God? And what is nature? And whence is man? And where is heaven? And why is hell? And what is our destiny? Was the world made in pleasure, moved for a moment in trial and suffering, and then blotted out in anger? In one revolution of the earth on fire it is a blank. Like a burning ship at sea, sinking to the bottom on fire, the earth vanishes into nonexistence under the blue vault, where it once careered in its brilliant circle. Not a vestige remains of its omnipotent path. Its wide territory is a tenantless, dark waste – the myriad lamps of the skies extinguished: all former existences crumbled: silent forever: all chaos: things are as if they had never been: the history of Earth and Time a mere record of the forgotten past: a mere hollow vault in the infinitude of space.'

# ABRAHAM LINCOLN
## 12 February 1809 – 15 April 1865

*'With malice toward none, with charity to all'*
4 March 1865

**Lincoln issued the** *Emancipation Proclamation* on 22 September 1862, freeing slaves in territories not already under Union control. This made the abolition of slavery in the rebel states an official war aim. As Union armies advanced south, more slaves were liberated until over three million in Confederate territories had been freed. Many of them enlisted to fight for the North. However, his Republican Party now feared that Lincoln would be defeated in 1864 when he sought a second term of office, as the country longed for peace. Fortunately for Lincoln, the Democrat candidate, General George B. McClellan supported the war and denounced the Democrats' peace policy. With the Democrats split, Lincoln won all but three states. This second inaugural address was Lincoln's favourite of all his speeches. Victory over the Confederates came just five weeks later, slavery was broken, and Lincoln was firmly in power. Six weeks after this address, he was assassinated.

'At this second appearing to take the oath of the presidential office, there is less occasion for an extended address than there was at first... The progress of our arms, upon which all else chiefly depends, is as well known to the public as to myself, and it is, I trust, reasonably satisfactory and encouraging to all. With high hope for the future, no prediction in regard to it is ventured. On the occasion corresponding to this four years ago, all thoughts were anxiously directed to an impending civil war. All dreaded it; all sought to avoid it. While the inaugural address was being delivered from this place, devoted altogether to saving the Union without war, insurgent agents were in the city seeking to destroy it with war – seeking to dissolve the Union and divide the effects by negotiation. Both parties deprecated war, but one of them would make war rather than let the nation survive, and the other would accept war rather than let it perish, and the war came. One-eighth of the whole population were colored slaves, not distributed generally over the Union, but localized in the Southern part of it. These slaves constituted a peculiar and powerful interest. All knew that this interest was somehow the cause of the war. To strengthen, perpetuate, and extend this interest was the object for which the insurgents would rend the Union by war, while the government claimed no right to do more than to restrict the Territorial enlargement of it.

Neither party expected for the war the magnitude or the duration which it has already attained. Neither anticipated that the cause of the conflict might cease when, or even before the conflict itself should cease. Each looked for an easier triumph, and a result less fundamental and astounding. Both read the same Bible and pray to the same God, and each invokes His aid against the other. It may seem strange that any men should dare to ask a just God's assistance in wringing their bread from the sweat of other men's faces, but let us judge not, that we be not judged. The prayer of both could not be answered. That of neither has been answered fully. The Almighty has His own purposes. "Woe unto the world because of offenses, for it must needs be that offenses come; but woe to that man by whom the offenses cometh!"

If we shall suppose that American slavery is one of those offenses which, in the providence of God, must needs come, but which having continued through His appointed time, He now wills to remove, and that He gives to both North and South this terrible war as the woe due to those by whom the offense came, shall we discern there any departure from those divine attributes which the believers in a living God always ascribe to Him? Fondly do we hope, fervently do we pray, that this mighty scourge of war may speedily pass away. Yet if God wills that it continue until all the wealth piled by the bondsman's two hundred and fifty years of unrequited toil shall be sunk, and until every drop of blood drawn with the lash shall be paid by another drawn with the sword, as was said three thousand years ago, so still it must be said, that the judgments of the Lord are true and righteous altogether. With malice toward none, with charity for all, with firmness in the right as God gives us to see the right, let us finish the work we are in, to bind up the nation's wounds, to care for him who shall have borne the battle, and for his widow and his orphans, to do all which may achieve and cherish a just and a lasting peace among ourselves and with all nations.'

# HENRY WARD BEECHER
## 24 June 1813 – 8 March 1887

*'...cast down but not destroyed'*
4 April 1865

**The brother of Harriet Beecher Stowe**, the novelist who wrote *Uncle Tom's Cabin*, was a social reformer, suffragist, abolitionist and clergyman. President Lincoln was influenced by Beecher to emancipate the slaves before and during the American Civil War, and chose him to be the main speaker when the Stars and Stripes was raised again at Fort Sumter, South Carolina, where the civil war had started.

'On this solemn and joyful day, we again lift to the breeze, our father's flag, now, again, the banner of the United States, with the fervent prayer that God would crown it with honor, protect it from treason, and send it down to our children, with all the blessings of civilization, liberty and religion. Terrible in battle, may it be beneficent in peace. Happily, no bird or beast of prey has been inscribed upon it. The stars that redeem the night from darkness, and the beams of red light that beautify the morning, have been united upon its folds. As long as the sun endures, or the stars, may it wave over a nation neither enslaved nor enslaving. Once, and but once, has treason dishonored it. In that insane hour, when the guiltiest and bloodiest rebellion of time hurled their fires upon this fort, you, sir, *[turning to General Anderson]* and a small heroic band, stood within these now crumbled walls, and did gallant and just battle for the honor and defense of the nation's banner.

In that cope *[strife]* of fire this glorious flag still peacefully waved to the breeze above your head, unconscious of harm as the stars and skies above it. Once it was shot down. A gallant hand, in whose care this day it has been, plucked it from the ground, and reared it again, – "cast down but not destroyed". After a vain resistance, with trembling hand and sad heart, you withdrew it from its height, closed its wings, and bore it far away, sternly to sleep amid the tumults of rebellion and the thunder of battle. The first act of war had begun. The long night of four years had set in...What grim batteries crowd the burdened shores! What scenes have filled this air and disturbed these waters! These shattered heaps of shapeless stone are all that is left of Fort Sumter. Desolation broods in yonder sad city – solemn retribution hath avenged our dishonored banner!...'

# BENJAMIN DISRAELI, 1st EARL of BEACONSFIELD
## 21 December 1804 – 19 April 1881

*'Assassination has never changed the history of the world...'*
1 May 1865

**Disraeli's first speech in the House** of Commons, aged 33, was a disaster. A literary success, he was unprepared when he was repeatedly interrupted. The uproar of cries and laughter overpowered him and he abandoned attempting to speak, shouting at the top of his voice '*You shall hear me!*' Within ten years he had become the leading Conservative orator in the campaign against the Liberals and their Corn Law policy. So great was the impression produced by his speeches that in 1852 he was made chancellor of the exchequer, and twice became prime minister. Earl Russell moved an address to the Crown in the House of Commons expressing sorrow and indignation on Lincoln's murder, and the following is the speech of one of the greatest parliamentary orators, after which the motion was put and agreed unanimously, to loud cheers.

'There are rare instances when the sympathy of a nation approaches those tenderer feelings which are generally supposed to be peculiar to the individual and to be the happy privilege of private life; and this is one. Under any circumstances we should have bewailed the catastrophe at Washington; under any circumstances we should have shuddered at the means by which it was accomplished. But in the character of the victim *[Lincoln]*, and even in the accessories of his last moments, there is something so homely and innocent that it takes the question, as it were, out of all the pomp of history and the ceremonial of diplomacy, – it touches the heart of nations and appeals to the domestic sentiment of mankind. Whatever the various and varying opinions in this house, and in the country generally, on the policy of the late President of the United States, all must agree that in one of the severest trials which ever tested the moral qualities of man he fulfilled his duty with simplicity and strength. Nor is it possible for the people of England at such a moment to forget that he sprang from the same fatherland and spoke the same mother tongue. When such crimes are perpetrated the public mind is apt to fall into gloom and perplexity, for it is ignorant alike of the causes and the consequences of such deeds. But it is one of our duties to reassure them under unreasoning panic and despondency. Assassination has never changed the history of the world...It is with these feelings that I second the address to the crown.'

# GOLDWIN SMITH
### 13 August 1823 – 7 June 1910

## *The Secret beyond Science*
### c.1866

**Smith was Regius Professor** of Modern History at Oxford (1858–66), and he supported the North during the American Civil War. Pamphlets such as *'Does the Bible sanction American Slavery?'*(1863) helped to sway British public opinion. Smith held the professorship of English and Constitutional History at Cornell University before moving to Toronto in 1871 to pursue a career in journalism. Smith is credited with the quotation *'Above all nations is humanity'*, an inscription that was engraved in a stone bench he gave to Cornell when he left there. His reasoning in this speech underlines the Victorian dilemma of how to reconcile scientific discoveries with belief in God.

'What is the sum of physical science? Compared with the comprehensible universe and with conceivable time, not to speak of infinity and eternity, it is the observation of a mere point, the experience of an instant. Are we warranted in founding anything upon such data, except that which we are obliged to found upon them – the daily rules and processes necessary for the natural life of man? We call the discoveries of science sublime; and truly. But the sublimity belongs not to that which they reveal, but to that which they suggest. And that which they suggest is, that through this material glory and beauty, of which we see a little and imagine more, there speaks to us a being whose nature is akin to ours, and who has made our hearts capable of such converse. Astronomy has its practical uses, without which man's intellect would scarcely rouse itself to those speculations; but its greatest result is a revelation of immensity pervaded by one informing mind; and this revelation is made by astronomy only in the same sense in which the telescope reveals the stars to the eye of the astronomer. Science finds no law for the thoughts which, with her aid, are ministered to man by the starry skies. Science can explain the hues of sunset, but she can not tell from what urns of pain and pleasure its pensiveness is poured. These things are felt by all men, felt the more in proportion as the mind is higher. They are a part of human nature; and why should they not be as sound a basis for philosophy as any other part? But if they are, the solid wall of material law melts away, and through the whole order of the material world pours the influence, the personal influence, of a spirit corresponding to our own. Again, is it true that the fixed or the unvarying is the last revelation of science? These risings in the scale of created beings, this gradual evolution of planetary systems from their centre – do they bespeak mere creative force? Do they not rather bespeak something which, for want of an adequate word, we must call creative effort, corresponding to the effort by which man raises himself and his estate? And where effort can be discovered, does not spirit reign again?

A creature whose sphere of vision is a speck, whose experience is a second, sees the pencil of Raphael moving over the canvas of the transfiguration. It sees the pencil moving over its own speck, during its own second of existence, in one particular direction, and it concludes that the formula expressing that direction is the secret of the whole... Reason, no doubt, is our appointed guide to truth. The limits set to it by each dogmatist, at the point where it comes into conflict with his dogma, are human limits; its providential limits we can learn only by dutifully exerting it to the utmost. Yet reason must be impartial in the acceptance of data and in the demand of proof. Facts are not the less facts because they are not facts of sense; materialism is not necessarily enlightenment; it is possible to be at once chimerical and gross. We may venture, without any ingratitude to science as the source of material benefits and the training school of inductive reason, to doubt whether the great secret of the moral world is likely to be discovered in her laboratory, or to be revealed to those minds which have been imbued only with her thoughts, and trained in her processes alone. Some, indeed, among the men of science who have given us sweeping theories of the world, seem to be not only one-sided in their view of the facts, leaving out of sight the phenomena of our moral nature, but to want one of the two faculties necessary for sound investigation. They are acute observers, but bad reasoners. And science must not expect to be exempt from the rules of reasoning. We can not give credit for evidence which does not exist, because if it existed it would be of a scientific kind; nor can we pass at a bound from slight and precarious premises to a tremendous conclusion, because the conclusion would annihilate the spiritual nature and annul the divine origin of man.'

# CHARLES FRANCIS ADAMS, JR.
## 27 May 1835 – 20 May 1915

### *'Gettysburg was immortal'*
### 4 July 1869

 **The grandson of John Quincy Adams** and the great-grandson of John Adams, he inherited their oratorical skills. A lawyer, Adams fought for the Union at Gettysburg, ending the war as a brevet-brigadier general. The battle lasted from 1 July to 3 July 1863 and his commemorative Independence Day speech given almost exactly six years later is a magnificent retelling of that terrible battle which caused the largest number of casualties in the American Civil War. Gettysburg is celebrated as the turning-point in the war.

'...When those great bodies of infantry drove together in the crash of battle, the clouds of cavalry which had hitherto covered up their movements were swept aside to the flanks. Our work for the time was done, nor had it been an easy or a pleasant work. The road to Gettysburg had been paved with our bodies and watered with our blood. Three weeks before, in the middle days of June, I, a captain of cavalry, had taken the field at the head of one hundred mounted men, the joy and pride of my life. Through twenty days of almost incessant conflict the hand of death had been heavy upon us, and now, upon the eve of Gettysburg, thirty-four of the hundred only remained, and our comrades were dead on the field of battle, or languishing in hospitals, or prisoners in the hands of the enemy. Six brave young fellows we had buried in one grave where they fell on the heights of Aldie *[a battle of 17 June 1863 in Virginia]*. It was late on the evening of the first of July, that there came to us rumors of heavy fighting at Gettysburg, nearly forty miles away. The regiment happened then to be detached, and its orders for the second were to move in the rear of Sedgwick's corps and see that no man left the column. All that day we marched to the sound of the cannon. Sedgwick, very grim and stern, was pressing forward his tired men, and we soon saw that for once there would be no stragglers from the ranks. As the day grew old and as we passed rapidly up from the rear to the head of the hurrying column, the roar of battle grew more distinct, until at last we crowned a hill, and the contest broke upon us. Across the deep valley, some two miles away, we could see the white smoke of the bursting shells, while below the sharp incessant rattle of the musketry told of the fierce struggle that was going on. Before us ran the straight, white, dusty road, choked with artillery, ambulances, caissons, ammunition trains, all pressing forward to the field of battle, while mixed among them, their bayonets gleaming through the dust like wavelets on a river of steel, tired, foot-sore, hungry, thirsty, begrimed with sweat and dust, the gallant infantry of Sedgwick's corps hurried to the sound of the cannon as men might have flocked to a feast. Moving rapidly forward, we crossed the brook which ran so prominently across the map of the field of battle, and halted on its further side to await our orders. Hardly had I dismounted from my horse when, looking back, I saw that the head of the column had reached the brook and deployed and halted on its other bank, and already the stream was filled with naked men shouting with pleasure as they washed off the sweat of their long day's march.

Even as I looked, the noise of the battle grew louder, and soon the symptoms of movement were evident. The rappel was heard, the bathers hurriedly clad themselves, the ranks were formed, and the sharp, quick snap of the percussion caps told us the men were preparing their weapons for action. Almost immediately a general officer rode rapidly to the front of the line, addressed to it a few brief, energetic words, the short sharp order to move by the flank was given, followed immediately by the "double-quick;" the officer placed himself at the head of the column, and that brave infantry which had marched almost forty miles since the setting of yesterday's sun, – which during that day had hardly known either sleep, or food, or rest, or shelter from the July heat, – now, as the shadows grew long, hurried forward on the run to take its place in the front of battle and to bear up the reeling fortunes of the day...Twenty-four hours later we stood on that same ground. Many dear friends had yielded up their young lives during the hours which had elapsed, but, though twenty thousand fellow-creatures were wounded or dead around us, though the flood gates of heaven seemed opened and the torrents fell upon the quick and the dead, yet the elements seemed electrified with a certain magic influence of victory, and as the great army sank down over-wearied in its tracks it felt that the crisis and danger was passed, – that Gettysburg was immortal...'

# SUSAN BROWNELL ANTHONY
## 15 February 1820 – 13 March 1906

## *Is it a Crime for a Citizen of the United States to Vote?*
### January – June 1873

**Anthony travelled around the United States** and Europe giving 75 to 100 speeches on women's rights every year for 45 years. Anthony decided to vote in the 1872 presidential election. She argued that the recently adopted Fourteenth Amendment gave women the constitutional right to vote in federal elections. The Amendment said that *'all persons born and naturalized in the United States...are citizens of the United States'*, and as citizens they were entitled to the *'privileges'* of US citizens. To Anthony, those privileges obviously included the right of females to vote. On 1 November 1872, Anthony and her three sisters entered a voter registration office, part of a group of 50 women Anthony had organized to register in her home town of Rochester. The election inspectors refused Anthony's request to vote, but she persisted, quoting the Fourteenth Amendment's citizenship provision and the relevant article from the New York Constitution pertaining to voting, which contained no sex qualification. The inspectors were unmoved until Anthony threatened them with criminal court proceedings. Seven or eight other Rochester women also managed to vote. On 18 November she was arrested, and on 24 January was indicted to stand trial for illegally voting. She used the months before her trial to make this stump speech in all 29 postal districts of Monroe County, New York. When the trial was deferred until 17 June, she then launched her suffrage lecture tour in Ontario County. Anthony spoke for 21 days in a row, ending her tour in Canandaigua, the county seat, on the night before the opening of her trial.

'Friends and fellow citizens: I stand before you tonight under indictment for the alleged crime of having voted at the last presidential election, without having a lawful right to vote. It shall be my work this evening to prove to you that in thus voting, I not only committed no crime, but, instead, simply exercised my citizen's rights, guaranteed to me and all United States citizens by the National Constitution, beyond the power of any state to deny. The preamble of the Federal Constitution says: "We, the people of the United States, in order to form a more perfect union, establish justice, insure domestic tranquility, provide for the common defense, promote the general welfare, and secure the blessings of liberty to ourselves and our posterity, do ordain and establish this

Constitution for the United States of America." It was we, the people; not we, the white male citizens; nor yet we, the male citizens; but we, the whole people, who formed the Union. And we formed it, not to give the blessings of liberty, but to secure them; not to the half of ourselves and the half of our posterity, but to the whole people – women as well as men. And it is a downright mockery to talk to women of their enjoyment of the blessings of liberty while they are denied the use of the only means of securing them provided by this democratic-republican government – the ballot. For any state to make sex a qualification that must ever result in the disfranchisement of one entire half of the people, is to pass a bill of attainder, or, an *ex post facto* law, and is therefore a violation of the supreme law of the land. By it the blessings of liberty are forever withheld from women and their female posterity.

To them this government has no just powers derived from the consent of the governed. To them this government is not a democracy. It is not a republic. It is an odious aristocracy; a hateful oligarchy of sex; the most hateful aristocracy ever established on the face of the globe; an oligarchy of wealth, where the rich govern the poor. An oligarchy of learning, where the educated govern the ignorant, or even an oligarchy of race, where the Saxon rules the African, might be endured; but this oligarchy of sex, which makes father, brothers, husband, sons, the oligarchs over the mother and sisters, the wife and daughters, of every household – which ordains all men sovereigns, all women subjects, carries dissension, discord, and rebellion into every home of the nation. Webster, Worcester, and Bouvier all define a citizen to be a person in the United States, entitled to vote and hold office. The only question left to be settled now is: Are women persons? And I hardly believe any of our opponents will have the hardihood to say they are not. Being persons, then, women are citizens; and no state has a right to make any law, or to enforce any old law, that shall abridge their privileges or immunities. Hence, every discrimination against women in the constitutions and laws of the several states is today null and void, precisely as is every one against Negroes.'

# CHIEF JOSEPH (HINMUUTTU-YALATLAT)
## 3 March 1840 – 21 September 1904

*'From where the sun now stands I will fight no more forever'*
5 October 1877

The last great war between the US government and an Indian nation ended at 4 p.m., 5 October 1877, in the Bear Paw Mountains of northern Montana. In 1877, the US Government had sent General Oliver Howard to force the Nez Percé Indians to move to an Idaho reservation, breaking an 1873 treaty it had signed with the Nez Percé. Chief Joseph and his band left for the reservation, but before they could reach it, several Nez Percé youths, disillusioned by broken treaty promises and white encroachment on their land, attacked and killed some white settlers. For 11 weeks, Chief Joseph led his people on a 1,600-mile (2,500km) retreat towards Canada. The chief and his party repeatedly turned the tables on numerically superior forces. They eluded and outfought 2,000 Army soldiers, engaging ten separate US commands in 13 battles and skirmishes, and in nearly every instance either defeated the American forces or fought them to a standstill. Finally, the Nez Percé proved no match for Gatling guns, howitzers and cannons. During the final battle, General Miles attempted to seize Chief Joseph under a flag of truce, but the chief had to be exchanged when the Nez took a white lieutenant prisoner. Chief Joseph of the Nez Percé nation surrendered 87 men, 184 women and 147 children to units of the US cavalry. A total of 382 members of his tribe had died or been killed. At that moment, Joseph delivered one of the most eloquent speeches in American history. Having handed his rifle to Colonel Nelson Miles, Joseph heartbreakingly said:

'Tell General Howard I know his heart. What he told me before, I have it in my heart. I am tired of fighting. Our Chiefs are killed; Looking Glass is dead, Ta Hool Hool Shute is dead. The old men are all dead. It is the young men who say yes or no. He who led on the young men *[Olikut or Alikut, Chief Joseph's brother]* is dead. It is cold, and we have no blankets; the little children are freezing to death. My people, some of them, have run away to the hills, and have no blankets, no food. No one knows where they are – perhaps freezing to death. I want to have time to look for my children, and see how many of them I can find. Maybe I shall find them among the dead. Hear me, my Chiefs! I am tired; my heart is sick and sad. From where the sun now stands I will fight no more forever.'

# CHIEF JOSEPH (HINMUUTTU-YALATLAT)
## 3 March 1840 – 21 September 1904

*'Words do not pay for my dead people'*
14 January 1879

**Joseph continued to lead his band** of Wallowa Nez Percé for another 25 years after surrendering in 1877. Joseph spoke against the injustice of United States's policy towards his people and hoped that America's promise of freedom and equality might one day be fulfilled for Native Americans as well. According to his doctor he died *'of a broken heart'*. This is part of a speech he made at Lincoln Hall in 1879 on a visit to Washington, D.C.

'Words do not pay for my dead people. They do not pay for my country now overrun by white men. They do not protect my father's grave. They do not pay for my horses and cattle. Good words do not give me back my children. Good words will not make good the promise of your war chief, General Miles. Good words will not give my people a home where they can live in peace and take care of themselves. I am tired of talk that comes to nothing. It makes my heart sick when I remember all the good words and all the broken promises. There has been too much talking by men who had no right to talk. Too many misinterpretations have been made; too many misunderstandings have come up between the white men and the Indians. If the white man wants to live in peace with the Indian he can live in peace. There need be no trouble. Treat all men alike. Give them the same laws. Give them all an even chance to live and grow. All men were made by the same Great Spirit Chief. They are all brothers. The earth is the mother of all people, and all people should have equal rights upon it. You might as well expect all rivers to run backward as that any man who was born a free man should be contented penned up and denied liberty to go where he pleases. If you tie a horse to a stake, do you expect he will grow fat? If you pen an Indian up on a small spot of earth and compel him to stay there, he will not be contented nor will he grow and prosper. I have asked some of the Great White Chiefs where they get their authority to say to the Indian that he shall stay in one place, while he sees white men going where they please. They cannot tell me.'

# WILLIAM EWART GLADSTONE
## 29 December 1809 – 19 May 1898

### 'Remember the rights of the savage'
26 November 1879

**Following his electoral defeat in 1874**, Gladstone resigned the Liberal leadership and hoped to spend the rest of his life in retirement. The Balkan Massacres of 1876 drew him back to politics and while campaigning in 1879, he outlined what he called '*the right policies of foreign policy*', which included the preservation of peace, the love of liberty and respect for the equal rights of all minorities and nations. Gladstone skilfully and angrily attacked Disraeli's foreign policies and leadership. The following speech was occasioned by British military action in the Khost Valley in southeastern Afghanistan. After speaking at the Corn Exchange, Gladstone received a presentation at the Foresters Hall, Dalkeith, Scotland where he made this speech. Gladstone saw the Anglo-Afghan War as a 'huge dishonour' and spoke against it passionately. On becoming prime minister for his second term, he promptly ended it in 1880.

'Remember the rights of the savage, as we call him. Remember that the happiness of his humble home, remember that the sanctity of life in the hill villages of Afghanistan among the winter snows, is as inviolable in the eye of Almighty God as can be your own. Remember that He who has united you together as human beings in the same flesh and blood, has bound you by the law of mutual love; that that mutual love is not limited by the shores of this island, is not limited by the boundaries of Christian civilization; that it passes over the whole surface of the earth, and embraces the meanest along with the greatest in its unmeasured scope. And, therefore, I think that in appealing to you ungrudgingly to open your own feelings, and bear your own part in a political crisis like this, we are making no inappropriate demand, but are beseeching you to fulfil a duty which belongs to you, which, so far from involving any departure from your character as women, is associated with the fulfilment of that character, and the performance of its duties; the neglect of which would in future times be to you a source of pain and just mortification, and the fulfilment of which will serve to gild your own future years with sweet remembrances, and to warrant you in hoping that, each in your own place and sphere, you have raised your voice for justice, and have striven to mitigate the sorrows and misfortunes of mankind.'

# FREDERICK DOUGLASS (born FREDERICK AUGUSTUS WASHINGTON BAILEY)
## c.1817/18 – 20 February 1895

### '...did John Brown fail?'
### 30 May 1881

**Born a slave, this journalist, orator and editor** fought both for the abolition of slavery and for women's rights. At the 1888 Republican National Convention, he became the first African-American to receive a vote as a nominated candidate for president of the United States in a major party's roll call vote. Douglass made this speech at Storer College, of which he was a trustee. The college was located at Harpers Ferry in West Virginia, and operated from 1867 as a mission school for former slaves, growing into a degree-granting college open to all races, creeds, and colours. Harpers Ferry was symbolic for a number of reasons. It was here in 1859 that John Brown's raid against slavery struck a blow for freedom. Some, like Douglass, felt it was John Brown who had fired the first shot of the American Civil War.

'...But the question is, did John Brown fail? He certainly did fail to get out of Harpers Ferry before being beaten down by United States soldiers; he did fail to save his own life, and to lead a liberating army into the mountains of Virginia. But he did not go to Harpers Ferry to save his life...The true question is, did John Brown draw his sword against slavery and thereby lose his life in vain? And to this I answer ten thousand times, No! No man fails, or can fail, who so grandly gives himself and all he has to a righteous cause. No man, who in his hour of extremest need, when on his way to meet an ignominious death, could so forget himself as to stop and kiss a little child, one of the hated race for whom he was about to die, could by any possibility fail...Did John Brown fail?...If John Brown did not end the war that ended slavery, he did at least begin the war that ended slavery. If we look over the dates, places and men for which this honor is claimed, we shall find that not Carolina, but Virginia, not Fort Sumter, but Harpers Ferry, and the arsenal, not Col. Anderson, but John Brown, began the war that ended American slavery and made this a free Republic. Until this blow was struck, the prospect for freedom was dim, shadowy, and uncertain. The irrepressible conflict was one of words, votes, and compromises...'

# CHESTER ALAN ARTHUR
### 5 October 1829 – 18 November 1886

*'All hearts are filled with grief and horror'*
22 September 1881

**Arthur had been nominated** for vice-president of the United States as a representative of the *'Stalwart'* Republicans, but that faction of the party was defeated in the National Convention by the element known as the *'Half-Breeds'*. After Charles Guiteau's assassination of President Garfield in 1881, the Republican Party and the nation waited to hear what Vice-President Arthur would say upon assuming the presidency. Arthur disarmed political factions in this Inaugural Address of genius and conciliatory statesmanship. As president, Arthur did more than anyone to reunite a country still divided after the Civil War, in which he had served as quartermaster-general of New York troops.

'For the fourth time in the history of the Republic its chief magistrate has been removed by death. All hearts are filled with grief and horror at the hideous crime which has darkened our land, and the memory of the murdered President, his protracted sufferings, his unyielding fortitude, the example and achievements of his life and the pathos of his death will forever illumine the pages of our history. For the fourth time, the officer elected by the people and ordained by the constitution to fill a vacancy so created, is called to assume the executive chair. The wisdom of our fathers, foreseeing even the most dire possibilities, made sure that the government should never be imperilled because of the uncertainty of human life. Men may die but the fabric of our free institutions remains unshaken. No higher or more assuring proof could exist of the strength and permanence of popular government than the fact that though the chosen of the people be struck down, his constitutional successor is peacefully installed without shock or strain except that of the sorrow which mourns the bereavement. All the noble aspirations of my lamented predecessor...will be garnered in the hearts of the people and it will be my earnest endeavor to profit and to see that the nation shall profit by his example and experience...Summoned to these high duties and responsibilities, and profoundly conscious of their magnitude and gravity, I assume the trust imposed by the constitution, relying for aid on divine guidance and on the virtue, patriotism, and intelligence of the American people.'

# OTTO EDUARD LEOPOLD VON BISMARCK
## 1 April 1815 – 30 July 1898

*'We Germans fear God and nothing else in the world!'*
6 February 1888

**This is an extract from one of** 'the Iron Chancellor's' most famous addresses to the Reichstag. This stirring call to the new nation comes at end of the speech. It was preceded by Bismarck's declaration that the German empire, a *'satiated nation'*, must not get involved in dangerous coalitions and conflicts. The famous line above is immediately followed by one that many forget: *'It is this fear of God which makes us love and cherish peace.'* This was Bismarck's last major Reichstag speech on foreign policy before his dismissal from office in March 1890.

'If we Germans wish to wage a war with the full effect of our national strength, it must be a war which satisfies all who take part in it, all who sacrifice anything for it, in short the whole nation. It must be a national war, a war carried on with the enthusiasm of 1870, when we were foully attacked. I still remember the ear-splitting, joyful shouts in the station at Köln *[Cologne]*. It was the same all the way from Berlin to Köln, in Berlin itself. The waves of popular approval bore us into the war, whether or no we wished it. That is the way it must be, if a popular force like ours is to show what it can do...People should not do this. It would then be easier for us to be more obliging to our two neighbours. Every country after all is sooner or later responsible for the windows which its press has smashed. The bill will be rendered some day, and will consist of the ill-feeling of the other country. We are easily influenced – perhaps too easily – by love and kindness, but quite surely never by threats! We Germans fear God, and nothing else in the world! It is this fear of God which makes us love and cherish peace. If in spite of this anybody breaks the peace, he will discover that the ardent patriotism of 1813, which called to the standards the entire population of Prussia – weak, small, and drained to the marrow as it then was – has today become the common property of the whole German nation. Attack the German nation anywhere, and you will find it armed to a man, and every man with the firm belief in his heart: God will be with us.'

# BENJAMIN HARRISON
## 20 August 1833 – 13 March 1910

*'I believe that patriotism has been blown into a higher and holier flame in many hearts'*
30 April 1889

**Benjamin Harrison was the** 23rd president of the United States. He made this speech at a banquet in New York City to commemorate the 100th anniversary of the inauguration of George Washington as the first president of the United States. Harrison was known as the *'Centennial President'* because of this distinction.

'Congratulations to you today, as one of the instructive and interesting features of this occasion, that these great thoroughfares, dedicated to trade, have closed their doors and covered the insignia of commerce with the Stars and Stripes; that your great exchanges have closed, and that into the very heart of Wall Street the flag has been carried. Upon this old, historic spot the men who give their time and energies to trade have given these days to their country, to the cause of her glory, and to the aspiration of her honor and development. I have great pleasure in believing that the love of country has been intensified in many hearts here; not only of you who might be called, and some who have been called, to witness your love for the flag in battlefields by sea and land, but in these homes, among these fair women who look down upon us to-night, and in the thoughts of those little children who mingled their piping cries with the hoarser acclaims as we moved along your streets to-day. I believe that patriotism has been blown into a higher and holier flame in many hearts...It is a glorious history. It is the fireside and the home. It is the high thoughts that are in the heart, born of the inspiration which comes by the stories of their fathers, the martyrs to liberty; it is the graveyards into which our careful country has gathered the unconscious dust of those who have died. Here, in these things, is that thing we love and call our country rather than in anything that can be touched or handled...To elevate the morals of our people; to hold up the law as that sacred thing, which, like the ark of God of old, cannot be touched by irreverent hands, and frowns upon every attempt to displace its supremacy; to unite our people in all that makes home pure and honorable, as well as to give our energies in the direction of our material advancement, – these services ye may render, and out of this great demonstration do we not all feel like re-consecrating ourselves to the love and service of our country ?'

# FRANCES ELIZABETH CAROLINE WILLARD
## 28 September 1839 – 17 February 1898

*'...there is nothing new under the sun'*
1890

**After graduating from North Western** Female College at Evanston, Illinois, Willard taught and travelled until 1874, when she became secretary of the Women's Christian Temperance Union, and in 1883 she founded the World's Women's Christian Temperance Union. Her efforts for women's suffrage and the cause of prohibition included a 50-day speaking tour in 1874. She travelled an average of 30,000 miles (48,000 km) a year, and gave an average of 400 lectures annually for a decade, mostly with her longtime companion Anna Adams Gordon. Willard was greatly respected and honoured, and was the first woman represented among the United States's greatest leaders in Statuary Hall in the United States Capitol.

'...I wish we were all more thorough students of the mighty past, for we should thus be rendered braver prophets of the future, and more cheerful workers in the present. History shows us with what tenacity the human race survives. Earthquake, famine, and pestilence have done their worst, but over them rolls a healing tide of years and they are lost to view; on sweeps the great procession, and hardly shows a scar. Rulers around whom clustered new forms of civilization pass away; but greater men succeed them. Nations are rooted up; great hopes seem blighted; revolutions rise and rivers run with the blood of patriots; the globe itself seems headed toward the abyss; new patriots are born; higher hopes bloom out like stars; humanity emerges from the dark ages vastly ahead of what it was on entering that cave of gloom, and ever the right comes uppermost; and now is Christ's kingdom nearer than when we first believed. Only those who have not studied history lose heart in great reforms; only those unread in the biography of genius imagine themselves to be original. Except in the realm of material invention, there is nothing new under the sun...Love and friendship form a beautiful rainbow over his landscape and reach up toward his sky. But the only two great environments of the soul are work for humanity and faith in God. Those wounded in love will find that affection, dear and vital as it is, comes to us not as the whole of life, not as its wide wondrous landscape of the earth, not as its beautiful vision of the sky, but as its beautiful embellishment, its rainbow fair and sweet. But were it gone there would still remain the two greatest and most satisfying pictures on which the soul can gaze – humanity and God.'

# RUSSELL HERMAN CONWELL
## 15 February 1843 – 6 December 1925)

*Acres of Diamonds*
Lecture delivered variously around 6,000 times, 1890–1925

**This Baptist minister, orator, philanthropist**, lawyer and writer is remembered as the founder and first president of Philadelphia's Temple University, and for this inspirational lecture. Conwell's ability to establish Temple University and other civic projects was largely derived from the income that he earned from this speech. Its central idea is that one need not look elsewhere for opportunity, achievement or fortune as the resources to achieve all good things are present in one's own community. His theme is developed from an anecdote told to Conwell by an Arab guide. A man wanted to find diamonds so badly that he sold his property and went off in futile search for them. However, the new owner of his home discovered that a rich diamond mine was located right there on the property. Conwell elaborates on the theme through examples of success, genius, service or other virtues asking ordinary Americans to: '*Dig in your own back-yard!*' This section of the speech describes how the young army officer Conwell and his soldiers were introduced to a welcoming crowd by a stuttering mayor who lacked the gift of oratory.

'We are especially pleased to see with us to-day this young hero...who in imagination we have seen leading – we have seen leading – leading. We have seen leading his troops on the deadly breach. We have seen his shining – we have seen his shining – his shining – his shining sword flashing. Flashing in the sunlight, as he shouted to his troops, "Come on!" Oh dear, dear, dear! How little that good man knew about war. If he had known anything about war at all he ought to have known what any of my G.A.R. *[Grand Army of the Republic – a Civil War Union veterans' confederation]* comrades here to-night will tell you is true, that it is next to a crime for an officer of infantry ever in time of danger to go ahead of his men. I, with my shining sword flashing in the sunlight, shouting to my troops, "Come on!" I never did it. Do you suppose I would get in front of my men to be shot in front by the enemy and in the back by my own men? That is no place for an officer. The place for the officer in actual battle is behind the line. How often, as a staff officer, I rode down the line, when our men were suddenly called to the line of a battle, and the Rebel yells were coming out of the woods, and shouted: "Officers to the rear! Officers to the rear!" Then every officer gets behind the line of private soldiers, and the higher the officer's rank the farther behind he goes. Not because he is any less brave, but because the laws of war require that.

And yet he shouted, "I, with my shining sword" – In that house there sat the company of my soldiers who had carried that boy across the Carolina rivers that he might not wet his feet. Some of them had gone far out to wet his feet. Some of them had gone far out to get a pig or a chicken. Some of them had gone to death under the shell-swept pines in the mountains of Tennessee, yet in the good man's speech they were scarcely known. He did refer to them, but only incidentally. The hero of the hour was this boy. Did the nation owe him anything? No, nothing then and nothing now. Why was he the hero? Simply because that man fell into that same human error – that this boy was great because he was an officer and these were only private soldiers. Oh, I learned the lesson then that I will never forget so long as the tongue of the bell of time continues to swing for me. Greatness consists not in the holding of some future office, but really consists in doing great deeds with little means, and the accomplishment of vast purposes from the private ranks of life. To be great at all one must be great here, now, in Philadelphia. He who can give to this city better streets and better sidewalks, better schools and more colleges, more happiness and more civilization, more of God, he will be great anywhere. Let every man or woman here, if you never hear me again, remember this, that if you wish to be great at all, you must begin where you are and what you are, in Philadelphia, now. He that can give to his city any blessing, he who can be a good citizen while he lives here, he that can make better homes, he that can be a blessing whether he works in the shop or sits behind the counter or keeps house, whatever be his life, he who would be great anywhere must first be great in his own Philadelphia.'

# ROBERT GREEN 'BOB' INGERSOLL
## 11 August 1833 – 21 July 1899

*'He is the gentlest memory of our world'*
1895

**Ingersoll was a Civil War colonel**, a Republican political leader, and was acknowledged as one of the greatest orators of his age.

'Lincoln was not a type. He stands alone – no ancestors, no fellows, and no successors. He had the advantage of living in a new country, of social equality, of personal freedom, of seeing in the horizon of his future the perpetual star of hope. In a new country, a man must possess at least three virtues – honesty, courage, and generosity. In a new country, character is essential; in the old, reputation is sufficient. In the new, they find what a man really is; in the old, he generally passes for what he resembles. Lincoln never finished his education. So to the night of his death he was a pupil, a learner, an inquirer, a seeker after knowledge. Lincoln was a many-sided man, acquainted with smiles and tears, complex in brain, single in heart. He was never afraid to ask – never too dignified to admit that he did not know. No man had keener wit or kinder humor. He had intellect without arrogance, genius without pride, and religion without cant – that is to say, without bigotry and without deceit. He was an orator – clear, sincere, natural. If you wish to know the difference between an orator and an elocutionist – between what is felt and what is said – between what the heart and brain can do together and what the brain can do alone – read Lincoln's wondrous words at Gettysburg, and then the speech of Edward Everett. The oration of Lincoln will never be forgotten. It will live until languages are dead and lips are dust. Wealth could not purchase, power could not awe this divine, this loving man. He knew no fear except the fear of doing wrong. Hating slavery, pitying the master – seeking to conquer, not persons, but prejudices – he was the embodiment of the self-denial, the courage, the hope, and the nobility of a nation. He spoke, not to inflame, not to upbraid, but to convince. He raised his hands, not to strike, but in benediction. He longed to pardon. He loved to see the pearls of joy on the cheeks of a wife whose husband he had rescued from death. Lincoln was the grandest figure of the fiercest civil war. He is the gentlest memory of our world.'

# BOOKER TALIAFERRO WASHINGTON
## 5 April 1856 – 14 November 1915

*'One-third of the population of the South is of the Negro race'*
18 September 1895

**Booker Washington was the dominant** figure in the African-American community and this is the statement of what he called the 'accommodationist' strategy of black response to southern racial tensions. Washington promised that he would encourage blacks to become proficient in agriculture, commerce and domestic service, and to encourage them to *'dignify and glorify common labor'*. He assured whites that blacks were loyal people who believed they would prosper in proportion to their hard work. Washington asked whites to trust blacks and provide them with opportunities so that both races could advance in industry and agriculture. This shared responsibility came to be known as the *Atlanta Compromise*. The speech was greeted by thunderous applause and a standing ovation.

'One-third of the population of the South is of the Negro race. No enterprise seeking the material, civil, or moral welfare of this section can disregard this element of our population and reach the highest success. I but convey to you, Mr. President and directors, the sentiment of the masses of my race when I say that in no way have the value and manhood of the American negro been more fittingly and generously recognized than by the managers of this magnificent Exposition at every stage of its progress. It is a recognition that will do more to cement the friendship of the two races than any occurrence since the dawn of our freedom...Here bending, as it were, over the altar that represents the struggles of your race and mine, both starting practically empty-handed three decades ago, I pledge that in your effort to work out the great and intricate problem which God has laid at the doors of the South, you shall have at all times the patient, sympathetic help of my race; only let this be constantly in mind, that, while from representations in these buildings of the product of field, of forest, of mine, of factory, letters and art, much good will come, yet far above and beyond material benefits will be that higher good, that, let us pray God, will come, in a blotting out of sectional differences and racial animosities and suspicions, in a determination to administer absolute justice, in a willing obedience among all classes to the mandates of the law. This, this, coupled with our material prosperity, will bring into our beloved South a new heaven and a new earth...'

# WILLIAM JENNINGS BRYAN
## 19 March 1860 – 26 July 1925

## Concluding lines from his *Cross of Gold* speech
Delivered at the Democratic National Convention, Chicago, 8 July 1896

**Because of Bryan's faith** in the goodness and rightness of the people, he was nicknamed 'The Great Commoner'. This was in its time thought to be the most famous speech in American political history. The issue was whether to endorse the free coinage of silver at a ratio of silver to gold of 16 to 1. This would have increased the amount of money in circulation and aided cash-poor and debt-burdened farmers, but the measure was opposed by financial interests. The 36-year-old former Congressman from Nebraska aspired to be the Democratic nominee for president, and he had been building support for himself among the delegates. At the conclusion of the electrifying speech, Bryan stretched out his arms in a Christ-like manner for five seconds, while the crowd remained quiet. According to the *New York World*, at that point everyone seemed to go mad at once and shrieked and rushed the stage. The response, wrote one reporter, *'came like one great burst of artillery'*. The *New York Times* commented that *'a wild, raging irresistible mob'* had been unleashed. Men and women screamed and waved their hats and canes: *'Some, like demented things, divested themselves of their coats and flung them high in the air.'* Despite the widespread opposition of the press, the next day the Democratic Convention nominated Bryan for president on the fifth ballot. The Republican William McKinley won the election and the Gold Standard Act came about in 1900.

'...If the gold standard is the standard of civilization, why, my friends, should we not have it? Mr. Carlisle said in 1878 that this was a struggle between the idle holders of idle capital and the struggling masses who produce the wealth and pay the taxes of the country; and my friends, it is simply a question that we shall decide upon which side shall the Democratic Party fight. Upon the side of the idle holders of idle capital, or upon the side of the struggling masses? That is the question that the party must answer first; and then it must be answered by each individual hereafter. The sympathies of the Democratic Party, as described by the platform, are on the side of the struggling masses, who have ever been the foundation of the Democratic Party. There are two ideas of government. There are those who believe that if you just legislate to make the well-to-do prosperous, that their prosperity will leak through on those below. The Democratic idea has been that if you legislate to make the masses prosperous their prosperity will find its way up and through every class that rests upon it. You come to us and tell us that the great cities are in favor of the gold standard. I tell you that the great cities rest upon these broad and fertile prairies. Burn down your cities and leave our farms, and your cities will spring up again as if by magic. But destroy our farms and the grass will grow in the streets of every city in the country.

My friends, we shall declare that this nation is able to legislate for its own people on every question without waiting for the aid or consent of any other nation on earth, and upon that issue we expect to carry every single state in the Union. I shall not slander the fair state of Massachusetts nor the state of New York by saying that when citizens are confronted with the proposition, "Is this nation able to attend to its own business?" – I will not slander either one by saying that the people of those states will declare our helpless impotency as a nation to attend to our own business. It is the issue of 1776 over again. Our ancestors, when but three million, had the courage to declare their political independence of every other nation upon earth. Shall we, their descendants, when we have grown to 70 million, declare that we are less independent than our forefathers? No, my friends, it will never be the judgment of this people. Therefore, we care not upon what lines the battle is fought. If they say bimetallism is good but we cannot have it till some nation helps us, we reply that, instead of having a gold standard because England has, we shall restore bimetallism, and then let England have bimetallism because the United States have. If they dare to come out in the open field and defend the gold standard as a good thing, we shall fight them to the uttermost, having behind us the producing masses of the nation and the world. Having behind us the commercial interests and the laboring interests and all the toiling masses, we shall answer their demands for a gold standard by saying to them, you shall not press down upon the brow of labor this crown of thorns. You shall not crucify mankind upon a cross of gold.'

# ÉMILE FRANÇOIS ZOLA
## 2 April 1840 – 29 September 1902

*'I swear that Dreyfus is innocent'*
22 February 1898

**The novelist Zola became the champion** of Captain Alfred Dreyfus against the French authorities, which had falsely convicted Dreyfus, a Jew, of selling military secrets to a foreign power. On 10 January 1898, Major Walsin-Esterhazy was acquitted after a secret trial by court-martial on charges preferred by the brother of Captain Dreyfus, who argued that the major was the real author of the memorandum which Captain Dreyfus was accused of having prepared for the German Government. Three days after the acquittal of Walsin-Esterhazy, Zola published the celebrated *'J'accuse'* (*'I accuse'*) letter addressed to President Félix Faure. The letter resulted, as Zola had expected, in his own arrest. Zola's trial for libel was really the first public hearing of the Dreyfus case, and it began on 2 February. On 22 February, Zola delivered this celebrated appeal to the jury. Convicted of libel on 23 February, Zola absented himself from Paris, but carried on agitating on behalf of Dreyfus which finally forced the rehearing of the case and the pardon of that victim of French militarism and anti-Semitism. Zola's address to the jury is one of the most important documents in the political history of the last quarter of the 19th century.

'...Dreyfus is innocent. I swear it! I stake my life on it – my honour! At this solemn moment, in the presence of this tribunal which is the representative of human justice, before you, gentlemen, who are the very incarnation of the country, before the whole of France, before the whole world, I swear that Dreyfus is innocent. By my forty years of work, by the authority that this toil may have given me, I swear that Dreyfus is innocent. By all I have now, by the name I have made for myself, by my works which have helped for the expansion of French literature, I swear that Dreyfus is innocent. May all that melt away, may my works perish if Dreyfus be not innocent! He is innocent. All seems against me – the two Chambers, the civil authority, the most widely-circulated journals, the public opinion which they have poisoned. And I have for me only an ideal of truth and justice. But I am quite calm; I shall conquer. I was determined that my country should not remain the victim of lies and injustice. I may be condemned here. The day will come when France will thank me for having helped to save her honour.'

# THEODORE (TEDDY) ROOSEVELT
## 27 October 1858 – 6 January 1919

*'...not the doctrine of ignoble ease, but the doctrine of the strenuous life'*
10 April 1899

**Based upon his personal experience**, Roosevelt argued that strenuous effort and overcoming hardship was the key for all Americans to make the nation fit for the 20th century. He reasoned that any individual who worked hard and was not lazy would be a success. To get the empathy of the audience, he used the example of the citizens of Chicago and Illinois. Those who do not embrace 'the strenuous life' do not live meaningful lives. The speech is about self-actualization – working hard to make the most of our lives. Two years after this speech, Vice-President Roosevelt became the youngest president of the United States, upon the assassination of William McKinley.

'In speaking to you, men of the greatest city of the West *[Chicago]*, men of the State which gave to the country Lincoln and Grant, men who pre-eminently and distinctly embody all that is most American in the American character I wish to preach, not the doctrine of ignoble ease, but the doctrine of the strenuous life. The life of toil and effort, of labor and strife; to preach that highest form of success which comes, not to the man who desires mere easy peace, but to the man who does not shrink from danger, from hardship or from bitter toil, and who out of these wins the splendid ultimate triumph...I preach to you, then, my countrymen, that our country calls not for the life of ease but for the life of strenuous endeavor. The twentieth century looms before us big with the fate of many nations. If we stand idly by, if we seek merely swollen, slothful ease and ignoble peace, if we shrink from the hard contests where men must win at hazard of their lives and at the risk of all they hold dear, then the bolder and stronger peoples will pass us by, and will win for themselves the domination of the world. Let us therefore boldly face the life of strife, resolute to do our duty well and manfully; resolute to uphold righteousness by deed and by word; resolute to be both honest and brave, to serve high ideals, yet to use practical methods. Above all, let us shrink from no strife, moral or physical, within or without the nation, provided we are certain that the strife is justified, for it is only through strife, through hard and dangerous endeavor, that we shall ultimately win the goal of true national greatness.'

# JOHN DILLON
### 4 September 1851 – 4 August 1927

*'Amid the obstructions and the cynicism of a materialistic age*
*he never lost his hold on the "ideal"'*
20 May 1898

**A leader of the Irish Nationalist party**, Dillon entered Parliament in 1880, being re-elected in 1892, 1895, 1897 and 1900. He was imprisoned in 1881–2 and again in 1891, in all being imprisoned six times. He became chairman of the Irish National Federation in 1896. An MP for over 35 years, he was the last leader of the Irish Parliamentary Party. In 1881 Dillon had denounced Gladstone's Land Act, and in 1897 he opposed in the House of Commons the Address to Queen Victoria on the occasion of the Diamond Jubilee, on the ground that her reign had not been a blessing to Ireland. However, Dillon had a special regard for Gladstone, who died the day before this speech in the House of Commons. Gladstone had served four times as prime minister and had championed a bill proposing Home Rule for Ireland.

'As an Irishman I feel that I have a special right to join in paying a tribute to the great Englishman who died yesterday, because the last and, as all men will agree, the most glorious years of his strenuous and splendid life were dominated by the love which he bore to our nation, and by the eager and even passionate desire to serve Ireland and give her liberty and peace. By virtue of the splendid quality of his nature, which seemed to give him perpetual youth, Mr Gladstone's faith in a cause to which he had once devoted himself never wavered, nor did his enthusiasm grow cold. Difficulties and the weight of advancing years were alike ineffectual to blunt the edge of his purpose or to daunt his splendid courage, and even when racked with pain, and when the shadow of death was darkening over him, his heart still yearned toward the people of Ireland, and his last public utterance was a message of sympathy for Ireland and of hope for her future. His was a great and deep nature. He loved the people with a wise and persevering love. His love of the people and his abiding faith in the efficacy of liberty and of government based on the consent of the people, as an instrument of human progress, was not the outcome of youthful enthusiasm, but the deep-rooted growth of long years, and drew its vigour from an almost unparalleled experience of men and of affairs. Above all men I have ever known or read of, in his case the lapse of years seemed to have no influence to narrow his sympathies or to contract his heart. Young men felt old beside him. And to the last no generous cause, no suffering people, appealed to him in vain, and that glorious voice which had so often inspirited the friends of freedom and guided them to victory was to the last at the service of the weak and the oppressed of whatever race or nation. Mr Gladstone was the greatest Englishman of his time.

He loved his own people as much as any Englishman that ever lived. But through communion with the hearts of his own people he acquired that wider and greater gift – the power of understanding and sympathizing with other peoples. He entered into their sorrows and felt for their oppressions. And with splendid courage he did not hesitate, even in the case of his much-loved England, to condemn her when he thought she was wronging others, and in so doing he fearlessly faced odium and unpopularity among his own people, which it must have been bitter for him to bear; and so he became something far greater than a British statesman, and took a place amid the greatest leaders of the human race. Amid the obstructions and the cynicism of a materialistic age he never lost his hold on the "ideal". And so it came to pass that wherever throughout the civilized world a race or nation of men were suffering from oppression, their thoughts turned toward Gladstone, and when that mighty voice was raised in their behalf Europe and the civilized world listened, and the breathing of new hopes entered into the hearts of men made desperate by long despair. In the years that have gone by England has lost many men who served their country splendidly and round whose graves the British people deeply mourned; but round the death-bed of Gladstone the people of this island are joined in their sorrow by many peoples, and to-day throughout the Christian world – in many lands and in many tongues – prayers will be offered to that God on whom in his last supreme hour of trial Mr Gladstone humbly placed his firm reliance, begging that He will remember to His great servant how ardently he loved his fellow men, without distinction of race, while he lived among them, and how mightily he laboured for their good.'

# STEPHEN GROVER CLEVELAND
### 18 March 1837 – 24 June 1908

*'...let us determine to meet the call of patriotic duty in every time of our country's danger or need'*
19 September 1901

**The 22nd and 24th president** of the United States, this lawyer is the only president to serve two non-consecutive terms (1885–9 and 1893–7). He won the popular vote three times, in 1884, 1888 and 1892. However, in 1888 the Republican Benjamin Harrison won because of fraudulent voting in the swing state of Indiana, which Cleveland lost by only 2,348 votes. The Democrats wanted Cleveland to run again in 1896, but he refused. He had been the only Democrat president in the era of Republican political domination from 1860 to 1912. A lawyer, Cleveland had been elected mayor of Buffalo in 1882, and served as governor of New York in 1883–4. Cleveland's admirers praised him for his honesty and integrity, and he worked against corruption and patronage. After leaving the White House, Cleveland lived in retirement at his estate in Princeton, New Jersey, becoming a trustee of the university. Thus he was asked to give the following eulogy. William McKinley Jr (29 January 1843–14 September 1901) was elected president in both 1896 and 1900, but he had been assassinated by an anarchist just five days earlier.

'Today the grave closes over the dead body of the man but lately chosen by the people of the United States from among their number to represent their nationality, preserve, protect and defend their Constitution, to faithfully execute the laws ordained for their welfare, and safely to hold and keep the honor and integrity of the Republic. His time of service is ended, not by the expiration of time, but by the tragedy of assassination. He has passed from public sight, not joyously bearing the garlands and wreaths of his countrymen's approving acclaim, but amid the sobs and tears of a mourning nation. He has gone to his home, not the habitation of earthly peace and quiet, bright with domestic comfort and joy, but to the dark and narrow house appointed for all the sons of men, there to rest until the morning light of the resurrection shall gleam in the East. All our people loved their dead president. His kindly nature and lovable traits of character and his amiable consideration for all about him will long be in the minds and hearts of his countrymen....

The man who is universally mourned to-day achieved the highest distinction which his great country can confer on any man, and he lived a useful life. He was not deficient in education, but with all you will hear of his grand career, and of his services to his country and his fellow citizens, you will not hear that either the high place he reached or what he accomplished was due entirely to his education. You will instead constantly hear as accounting for his great success that he was obedient and affectionate as a son, patriotic and faithful as a soldier, honest and upright as a citizen, tender and devoted as a husband, and truthful, generous, unselfish, moral and clean in every relation of life. He never thought any of these things too weak for manliness. Make no mistake. Here was a most distinguished man, a great man, a useful man – who became distinguished, great and useful because he had, and retained unimpaired, the qualities of heart which I fear university students sometimes feel like keeping in the background or abandoning.

There is a most serious lesson for all of us in the tragedy of our late president's death. The shock of it is so great that it is hard at this time to read this lesson calmly. We can hardly fail to see, however, behind the bloody deed of the assassin, horrible figures and faces from which it will not do to turn away. If we are to escape further attack upon our peace and security, we must boldly and resolutely grapple with the monster of anarchy. It is not a thing that we can safely leave to be dealt with by party or partisanship. Nothing can guarantee us against its menace except the teaching and the practice of the best citizenship, the exposure of the ends and aims of the gospel of discontent and hatred of social order, and the brave enactment and execution of repressive laws. Our universities and colleges can not refuse to join in the battle against the tendencies of anarchy. Their help in discovering and warning against the relationship between the vicious councils and deeds of blood, and their steadying influence upon the elements of unrest, can not fail to be of inestimable value. By the memory of our murdered president, let us resolve to cultivate and preserve the qualities that made him great and useful; and let us determine to meet the call of patriotic duty in every time of our country's danger or need.'

# THEODORE ROOSEVELT
## 27 October 1858 – 6 January 1919

*'No people on earth have more cause to be thankful than ours'*
4 March 1905

**Roosevelt led the Rough Riders** (a small cavalry regiment that saw action in the Spanish–American War of 1898), becoming their colonel and achieving national fame. He was elected governor of New York in 1899, before becoming McKinley's vice-president in 1900. On the president's assassination in 1901, Roosevelt became the youngest ever president of the United States at the age of 42. He led the Progressive Movement in the Republican Party, with a 'cowboy' image deriving from his reputation as a soldier, explorer and hunter. Roosevelt was a noted 'trust-buster', increasing regulation of businesses and he pushed a 'Square Deal' policy aimed at improving the lot of the average citizen. His foreign policies could be summarized by his famous phrase '*Speak softly and carry a big stick*', and he won a Nobel Peace Prize for negotiating the end of the Russo-Japanese War. His inaugural address shows how important he felt it was for the American example of free self-government to succeed as an example to the rest of the world.

'No people on earth have more cause to be thankful than ours, and this is said reverently, in no spirit of boastfulness in our own strength, but with gratitude to the Giver of Good, Who has blessed us with the conditions which have enabled us to achieve so large a measure of well-being and of happiness. To us as a people it has been granted to lay the foundations of our national life in a new continent. We are the heirs of the ages, and yet we have had to pay few of the penalties which in old countries are exacted by the dead hand of a bygone civilization. We have not been obliged to fight for our existence against any alien race; and yet our life has called for the vigor and effort without which the manlier and hardier virtues wither away...Much has been given to us, and much will rightfully be expected from us. We have duties to others and duties to ourselves – and we can shirk neither. We have become a great nation, forced by the fact of its greatness into relation to the other nations of the earth, and we must behave as beseems a people with such responsibilities. Toward all other nations, large and small, our attitude must be one of cordial and sincere friendship. We must show not only in our words but in our deeds that we are earnestly desirous of securing their good will by acting toward them in a spirit of just and generous recognition of all their rights. But justice and generosity in a nation, as in an individual, count most when shown not by the weak but by the strong. While ever careful to refrain from wronging others, we must be no less insistent that we are not wronged ourselves. We wish peace; but we wish the peace of justice, the peace of righteousness. We wish it because we think it is right, and not because we are afraid. No weak nation that acts rightly and justly should ever have cause to fear, and no strong power should ever be able to single us out as a subject for insolent aggression.

Our relations with the other powers of the world are important; but still more important are our relations among ourselves. Such growth in wealth, in population, and in power, as a nation has seen during the century and a quarter of its national life, is inevitably accompanied by a like growth in the problems which are ever before every nation that rises to greatness. Power invariably means both responsibility and danger. Our forefathers faced certain perils which we have outgrown. We now face other perils the very existence of which it was impossible that they should foresee. Modern life is both complex and intense, and the tremendous changes wrought by the extraordinary industrial development of the half century are felt in every fiber of our social and political being. Never before have men tried so vast and formidable an experiment as that of administering the affairs of a continent under the forms of a democratic republic...But we have faith that we shall not prove false to memories of the men of the mighty past. They did their work; they left us the splendid heritage we now enjoy. We in our turn have an assured confidence that we shall be able to leave this heritage unwasted and enlarged to our children's children. To do so, we must show, not merely in great crises, but in the every-day affairs of life, the qualities of practical intelligence, of courage, of hardihood, and endurance, and, above all, the power of devotion to a lofty ideal, which made great the men who founded this Republic in the days of Washington; which made great the men who preserved this Republic in the days of Abraham Lincoln.'

# MARY CHURCH TERRELL
### 23 September 1863 – 24 July 1954

*'...our people are sacrificed on the altar of prejudice*
*in the capital of the United States'*
10 October 1906

**The daughter of two former slaves**, Terrell was an educator, political activist and professional lecturer, honoured for her tremendous work as an early civil rights leader, women's rights advocate, founder of the National Association of Colored Women, and charter member of the NAACP. She was one of the first African-American women to gain a college degree. In 1904 Terrell was invited to speak at the International Congress of Women, held in Berlin, the only black woman at the conference. Terrell received an enthusiastic ovation when she honoured the host nation by delivering her address in German. She then proceeded to repeat the speech in French, and ended with the English version. In 1950 Terrell started what would be a successful fight to integrate eating places in the District of Columbia. After the age of 80, Terrell continued to participate in picket lines, protesting at the segregation of restaurants and theatres. She lived to see the Supreme Court's decision that it was unconstitutional to segregate schools by race. She died two months later at the age of 90, after a lifetime of work towards equality of race and gender.

'Washington, D.C., has been called "The Colored Man's Paradise." Whether this soubriquet was given to the national capital in bitter irony by a member of the handicapped race, as he reviewed some of his own persecutions and rebuffs, or whether it was given immediately after the war by an ex-slaveholder who for the first time in his life saw colored people walking about like free men, minus the overseer and his whip, history saith not. It is certain that it would be difficult to find a worse misnomer for Washington than "The Colored Man's Paradise" if so prosaic a consideration as veracity is to determine the appropriateness of a name. For fifteen years I have resided in Washington, and while it was far from being a paradise for colored people when I first touched these shores it has been doing its level best ever since to make conditions for us intolerable. As a colored woman I might enter Washington any night, a stranger in a strange land, and walk miles without finding a place to lay my head. Unless I happened to know colored people who live here or ran across a chance acquaintance who could recommend a colored boarding-house to me, I should be obliged to spend the entire night wandering about. Indians, Chinamen, Filipinos, Japanese, and representatives of any other dark race can find hotel accommodations, if they can pay for them. The colored man alone is thrust out of the hotels of the national capital like a leper...

The colored laborer's path to a decent livelihood is by no means smooth. Into some of the trades unions here he is admitted, while from others he is excluded altogether. By the union men this is denied, although I am personally acquainted with skilled workmen who tell me they are not admitted into the unions because they are colored. But even when they are allowed to join the unions they frequently derive little benefit, owing to certain tricks of the trade. When the word passes round that help is needed and colored labourers apply, they are often told by the union officials that they have secured all the men they needed, because the places are reserved for white men, until they have been provided with jobs, and colored men must remain idle, unless the supply of white men is too small...And so I might go on citing instance after instance to show the variety of ways in which our people are sacrificed on the altar of prejudice in the capital of the United States and how almost insurmountable are the obstacles which block his path to success...It is impossible for any white person in the United States, no matter how sympathetic and broad, to realize what life would mean to him if his incentive to effort were suddenly snatched away. To the lack of incentive to effort, which is the awful shadow under which we live, may be traced the wreck and ruin of scores of colored youth. And surely nowhere in the world do oppression and persecution based solely on the color of the skin appear more hateful and hideous than in the capital of the United States, because the chasm between the principles upon which this Government was founded, in which it still professes to believe, and those which are daily practiced under the protection of the flag, yawn so wide and deep.'

# EMMELINE PANKHURST
## 15 July 1858 – 14 June 1928

*'There are women lying at death's door...'*
13 November 1913

**Pankhurst was a major leader of the** British suffragette movement before the First World War, and it was between spells in prison that she travelled to America and gave the speech reproduced here. It was not until 1928 that women were granted fully equal rights of voting as men in Britain. In 1907 she moved to London and joined her three daughters in the struggle for the vote, being imprisoned many times and subjected to force-feeding on ten occasions in just one 18-month period while she was on hunger strike. In her fifties, Pankhurst's actions inspired many other women to follow her example of committing acts of civil disobedience as a political protest. In 1999, *Time* named her as one of the 100 Most Important People of the 20th Century: *'she shaped an idea of women for our time; she shook society into a new pattern from which there could be no going back'*. She spoke out against the conditions of her confinement, including vermin, meagre food and the *'civilized torture of solitary confinement and absolute silence'* she endured. During one trial in 1908, she told the court: *'We are here not because we are law-breakers; we are here in our efforts to become law-makers.'* This is one of the finest speeches in this book.

'...I have seen men smile when they heard the words "hunger strike", and yet I think there are very few men today who would be prepared to adopt a "hunger strike" for any cause. It is only people who feel an intolerable sense of oppression who would adopt a means of that kind. It means you refuse food until you are at death's door, and then the authorities have to choose between letting you die, and letting you go; and then they let the women go. Now, that went on so long that the government felt that they were unable to cope. It was *[then]* that, to the shame of the British government, they set the example to authorities all over the world of feeding sane, resisting human beings by force. There may be doctors in this meeting: if so, they know it is one thing to feed by force an insane person; but it is quite another thing to feed a sane, resisting human being who resists with every nerve and with every fibre of her body the indignity and the outrage of forcible feeding. Now, that was done in England, and the government thought they had crushed us. But they found that it did not quell the agitation, that more and more women came in and even passed that terrible ordeal, and they were obliged to let them go.

Then came the legislation – the "Cat and Mouse Act". The Home Secretary said: "Give me the power to let these women go when they are at death's door, and leave them at liberty under licence until they have recovered their health again and then bring them back." It was passed to repress the agitation, to make the women yield – because that is what it has really come to, ladies and gentlemen. It has come to a battle between the women and the government as to who shall yield first, whether they will yield and give us the vote, or whether we will give up our agitation. Well, they little know what women are. Women are very slow to rouse, but once they are aroused, once they are determined, nothing on earth and nothing in heaven will make women give way; it is impossible. And so this "Cat and Mouse Act" which is being used against women today has failed. There are women lying at death's door, recovering enough strength to undergo operations, who have not given in and won't give in, and who will be prepared, as soon as they get up from their sick beds, to go on as before. There are women who are being carried from their sick beds on stretchers into meetings. They are too weak to speak, but they go amongst their fellow workers just to show that their spirits are unquenched, and that their spirit is alive, and they mean to go on as long as life lasts. Now, I want to say to you who think women cannot succeed, we have brought the government of England to this position, that it has to face this alternative: either women are to be killed or women are to have the vote. I ask American men in this meeting, what would you say if in your state you were faced with that alternative, that you must either kill them or give them their citizenship? Well, there is only one answer to that alternative, there is only one way out – you must give those women the vote...I come to ask you to help to win this fight.'

# KING ALBERT I OF BELGIUM
## 8 April 1875 – 17 February 1934

*'It is the moment for action'*
4 August 1914

In 1914 Germany had declared war on Russia, and now illegally demanded free passage of its troops across neutral Belgium to pursue its war with France. Belgium declined Germany's request, and two days later King Albert made this speech to the Belgian parliament. On the same day Great Britain entered the war to comply with the 1839 Treaty of London that pledged action in defence of Belgian neutrality.

'Never, since 1839, has a more solemn hour struck for Belgium: the integrity of our territory is threatened. The very force of our righteous cause, the sympathy which Belgium, proud of her free institutions and her moral victories, has always received from other nations, and the necessity of our autonomous existence in respect of the equilibrium of Europe, make us still hopeful that the dreaded emergency will not be realized. But if our hopes are betrayed, if we are forced to resist the invasion of our soil, and to defend our threatened homes, this duty, however hard it may be, will find us armed and resolved upon the greatest sacrifices. Even now, in readiness for any eventuality, our valiant youth is up in arms, firmly resolved, with the traditional tenacity and composure of the Belgians, to defend our threatened country...Everywhere in Flanders and Wallonia, in the towns and in the countryside, one single feeling binds all hearts together: the sense of patriotism. One single vision fills all minds: that of our independence endangered. One single duty imposes itself upon our wills: the duty of stubborn resistance. In these solemn circumstances two virtues are indispensable: a calm but unshaken courage, and the close union of all Belgians...It is the moment for action...No one in this country will fail in his duty. If the foreigner, in defiance of that neutrality whose demands we have always scrupulously observed, violates our territory, he will find all the Belgians gathered about their sovereign, who will never betray his constitutional oath, and their Government, invested with the absolute confidence of the entire nation. I have faith in our destinies; a country which is defending itself conquers the respect of all; such a country does not perish!'

# JEAN RAPHAËL ADRIEN RENÉ VIVIANI
## 8 November 1863 – 7 September 1925

*'We are without reproach'*
4 August 1914

**The French prime minister's official** statement to parliament recounts the lead-up to the First World War, drawing attention to Germany's absolute determination to engineer conflict. Viviani went on to praise those nations which had either declared neutrality, i.e. Italy, or had else indicated support for France, including Russia and Britain (members of an alliance with France called the Triple Entente), before ending his statement with an appeal to his countrymen to do their duty.

 '...This attack, which has no excuse, and which began before we were notified of any declaration of war, is the last act of a plan, whose origin and object I propose to declare before our own democracy and before the opinion of the civilized world...Gentlemen, we proclaim loudly the object of their attack – it is the independence, the honour, the safety, which the Triple Entente has regained in the balance of power for the service of peace. The object of attack is the liberties of Europe, which France, her allies, and her friends, are proud to defend. We are going to defend these liberties, for it is they that are in dispute, and all the rest is but a pretext. France, unjustly provoked, did not desire war, she has done everything to avert it. Since it is forced upon her, she will defend herself against Germany and against every Power which has not yet declared its intentions, but joins with the latter in a conflict between the two countries. A free and valiant people that sustains an eternal ideal, and is wholly united to defend its existence; a Democracy which knows how to discipline its military strength, and was not afraid a year ago to increase its burden as an answer to the armaments of its neighbour; a nation armed, struggling for its own life and for the independence of Europe – here is a sight which we are proud to offer to the onlookers in this desperate struggle, that has for some days been preparing with the greatest calmness and method. We are without reproach. We shall be without fear. France has often proved in less favourable circumstances that she is a most formidable adversary when she fights, as she does today, for liberty and for right. In submitting our actions to you, gentlemen, who are our judges, we have, to help us in bearing the burden of our heavy responsibility, the comfort of a clear conscience and the conviction that we have done our duty.'

# HERBERT HENRY ASQUITH
## 12 September 1852 – 15 February 1928

*'...this war has been forced upon us'*
6 August 1914

**Asquith gave this address to the House** of Commons two days after Britain had entered the war with Germany in defence of Belgium. This Liberal prime minister recounted the background to the outbreak of general war in Europe in July/August 1914, placing great emphasis on the efforts of the British foreign secretary, Sir Edward Grey, to secure continued peace in the face of German aggression. The German invasion in violation of treaties angered the nation and raised the spectre of German control of the entire continent, so Asquith led the nation to war in alliance with France. Asquith finished his speech by stating that Britain would throw her entire empire's resources into the war to ensure victory. On 5 December 1916, no longer enjoying the support of the press or of leading Conservatives in his War Coalition, Asquith resigned, declining to serve under any other prime minister. David Lloyd George became head of the coalition two days later, in accordance with his demands, heading a much smaller War Cabinet and prosecuting the war with more vigour.

'With the utmost reluctance and with infinite regret, His Majesty's Government have been compelled to put this country in a state of war with what for many years and indeed generations past has been a friendly Power...I am entitled to say, and I do so on behalf of this country – I speak not for a party, I speak for the country as a whole – that we made every effort any Government could possibly make for peace. But this war has been forced upon us. What is it we are fighting for? Every one knows, and no one knows better than the Government, the terrible, incalculable suffering, economic, social, personal and political, which war, and especially a war between the Great Powers of the world, must entail. There is no man amongst us sitting upon this bench in these trying days – more trying perhaps than any body of statesmen for a hundred years have had to pass through – there is not a man amongst us who has not, during the whole of that time, had clearly before his vision the almost unequalled suffering which war, even in a just cause, must bring about, not only to the people who are for the moment living in this country and in the other countries of the world, but to posterity and to the whole prospects of European civilization. Every step we took we took with that vision before our eyes, and with a sense of responsibility which it is impossible to describe.

Unhappily, if in spite of all our efforts to keep the peace, and with that full and overpowering consciousness of the result, if the issue be decided in favour of war, we have, nevertheless, thought it to be the duty as well as the interest of this country to go to war, the House may be well assured it was because we believe, and I am certain the country will believe, that we are unsheathing our sword in a just cause. If I am asked what we are fighting for I reply in two sentences: In the first place, to fulfil a solemn international obligation, an obligation which, if it had been entered into between private persons in the ordinary concerns of life, would have been regarded as an obligation not only of law but of honour, which no self-respecting man could possibly have repudiated. I say, secondly, we are fighting to vindicate the principle which, in these days when force, material force, sometimes seems to be the dominant influence and factor in the development of mankind, we are fighting to vindicate the principle that small nationalities are not to be crushed, in defiance of international good faith, by the arbitrary will of a strong and overmastering Power. I do not believe any nation ever entered into a great controversy – and this is one of the greatest history will ever know – with a clearer conscience and a stronger conviction that it is fighting, not for aggression, not for the maintenance even of its own selfish interest, but that it is fighting in defence of principles the maintenance of which is vital to the civilization of the world. With a full conviction, not only of the wisdom and justice, but of the obligations which lay upon us to challenge this great issue, we are entering into the struggle. Let us now make sure that all the resources, not only of this United Kingdom, but of the vast Empire of which it is the centre, shall be thrown into the scale.'

# DAVID LLOYD GEORGE
## 17 January 1863 – 26 March 1945

## *'A dark day for humanity'*
### 19 September 1914

This is an excerpt from one of the greatest speeches of all time, given to an audience of fellow Welshmen in London. Then chancellor of the exchequer in Asquith's government, Lloyd George was the greatest orator of the day, and after listening to what he called *'the greatest war song in the world' (The March of the Men of Harlech)*, this was his first speech that was made in favour of the Great War:

'There is no man in this room who has always regarded the prospect of engaging in a great war with greater reluctance and with greater repugnance than I have done throughout the whole of my political life. There is no man either inside or outside of this room more convinced that we could not have avoided it without national dishonour. I am fully alive to the fact that every nation who has ever engaged in any war has always invoked the sacred name of honour. Many a crime has been committed in its name; there are some being committed now. All the same, national honour is a reality, and any nation that disregards it is doomed. Why is our honour as a country involved in this war? Because, in the first instance, we are bound by honourable obligations to defend the independence, the liberty, the integrity, of a small neighbour that has always lived peaceably. She could not have compelled us; she was weak; but the man who declines to discharge his duty because his creditor is too poor to enforce it is a blackguard. We entered into a treaty – a solemn treaty – two treaties – to defend Belgium and her integrity. Our signatures are attached to the documents. Our signatures do not stand alone there; this country was not the only country that undertook to defend the integrity of Belgium. Russia, France, Austria, Prussia – they are all there. Why are Austria and Prussia not performing the obligations of their bond? It is suggested that when we quote this treaty it is purely an excuse on our part – it is our low craft and cunning to cloak our jealousy of a superior civilization – that we are attempting to destroy...

It is the interest of Prussia today to break the treaty, and she has done it. She avows it with cynical contempt for every principle of justice. She says: "Treaties only bind you when your interest is to keep them."

"What is a treaty?" says the German Chancellor, "A scrap of paper."...
This doctrine of the scrap of paper, this doctrine which is proclaimed
by Bernhardi *[the influential German general who wrote* 'Germany and
the Next War' *in 1911]*, that treaties only bind a nation as long as it is to
its interest, goes under the root of all public law. It is the straight road
to barbarism...We are fighting against barbarism, and there is only one
way of putting it right. If there are nations that say they will only respect
treaties when it is to their interest to do so, we must make it to their
interest to do so for the future...Belgium has been treated brutally...
Hundreds and thousands of her people, their neat, comfortable little
homes burned to the dust, are wandering homeless in their own land.
What was their crime? Their crime was that they trusted to the word of
a Prussian King...But Belgium is not the only little nation that has been
attacked in this war, and I make no excuse for referring to the case of
the other little nation, the case of Servia *[Serbia]*...That is the story of two
little nations. The world owes much to little nations – and to little men!
This theory of bigness, this theory that you must have a big empire, and
a big nation, and a big man – well, long legs have their advantage in a
retreat. The Kaiser's ancestor chose his warriors for their height, and
that tradition has become a policy in Germany. Germany applies that
ideal to nations, and will only allow six-foot-two nations to stand in the
ranks. But ah! the world owes much to the little five-foot-five nations. The
greatest art in the world was the work of little nations; the most enduring
literature of the world came from little nations; the greatest literature of
England came when she was a nation of the size of Belgium fighting a
great empire. The heroic deeds that thrill humanity through generations
were the deeds of little nations fighting for their freedom. Yes, and
the salvation of mankind came through a little nation...But Germany
insists that this is an attack by a lower civilization upon a higher one.
As a matter of fact, the attack was begun by the civilization which
calls itself the higher one...That is what we are fighting – that claim to
predominancy of a material, hard civilization, a civilization which if it
once rules and sways the world, liberty goes, democracy vanishes.
And unless Britain and her sons come to the rescue it will be a dark
day for humanity.'

# THOMAS WOODROW WILSON
## 28 December 1856 – 3 February 1924

*'It is a war against all nations'*
2 April 1917

**Woodrow Wilson was narrowly re-elected** as president of the United States in 1916 on the platform of *'He kept us out of the War'*. However, US neutrality was compromised in 1917 when Germany proposed a military alliance with Mexico against the USA, and began unrestricted submarine attacks on all forms of shipping, causing American deaths. President Wilson outlined the case for declaring war upon Germany in this speech to the joint Houses of Congress. A formal declaration followed four days later, on 6 April 1917.

'On the third of February last I officially laid before you the extraordinary announcement of the Imperial German Government that on and after the first day of February it was its purpose to put aside all restraints of law or of humanity and use its submarines to sink every vessel that sought to approach either the ports of Great Britain and Ireland or the western coasts of Europe or any of the ports controlled by the enemies of Germany within the Mediterranean...Even hospital ships and ships carrying relief to the sorely bereaved and stricken people of Belgium, though the latter were provided with safe conduct through the proscribed areas by the German Government itself and were distinguished by unmistakable marks of identity, have been sunk with the same reckless lack of compassion or of principle. I was for a little while unable to believe that such things would in fact be done by any government that had hitherto subscribed to the humane practices of civilized nations. International law had its origin in the attempt to set up some law which would be respected and observed upon the seas, where no nation had right of dominion and where lay the free highways of the world...

It is a war against all nations. American ships have been sunk, American lives taken, in ways which it has stirred us very deeply to learn of, but the ships and people of other neutral and friendly nations have been sunk and overwhelmed in the waters in the same way. There has been no discrimination. The challenge is to all mankind. Each nation must decide for itself how it will meet it. The choice we make for ourselves must be made with a moderation of counsel and a temperateness for judgement befitting our character and our motives as a nation. We must put excited feeling away. Our motive will not be revenge or the victorious assertion of the physical might of the nation, but only the vindication of right, of human right, of which we are only a single champion. When I addressed the Congress on the twenty-sixth of February last I thought that it would suffice to assert our neutral rights with arms, our right to use the seas against unlawful interference, our right to keep our people safe against unlawful violence...But armed neutrality, it now appears, is impracticable. Because submarines are in effect outlaws when used as the German submarines have been used against merchant shipping, it is impossible to defend ships against their attacks as the law of nations has assumed that merchantmen would defend themselves against privateers or cruisers, visible craft giving chase upon the open sea. It is common prudence in such circumstances, grim necessity indeed, to endeavor to destroy them before they have shown their own intention...

We have no quarrel with the German people. We have no feeling toward them but one of sympathy and friendship. It was not upon their impulse that their government acted in entering this war. It was not with their previous knowledge or approval...It is a distressing and oppressive duty, Gentlemen of the Congress, which I have performed in thus addressing you. There are, it may be, many months of fiery trial and sacrifice ahead of us. It is a fearful thing to lead this great peaceful people into war, into the most terrible and disastrous of all wars, civilization itself seeming to be in the balance. But the right is more precious than peace, and we shall fight for the things which we have always carried nearest our hearts – for democracy, for the right of those who submit to authority to have a voice in their own Governments, for the rights and liberties of small nations, for a universal dominion of right by such a concert of free peoples as shall bring peace and safety to all nations and make the world itself at last free. To such a task we can dedicate our lives and our fortunes, everything that we are and everything that we have, with the pride of those who know that the day has come when America is privileged to spend her blood and her might for the principles that gave her birth and happiness and the peace which she has treasured. God helping her, she can do no other.'

# DAVID LLOYD GEORGE
## 17 January 1863 – 26 March 1945

*'Today we wage the most devastating war earth has ever seen'*
12 April 1917

**One can almost sense the prime minister's** relief at the decision of the United States to enter the First World War six days earlier, as Britain was just about exhausted after four years of battle. Lloyd George was one of Britain's most capable prime ministers, the man whom Hitler later said won the Great War. As minister for munitions in 1915, secretary of state for war in 1916, and then prime minister and war leader from 1916–18, Lloyd George had fought tirelessly to convince Woodrow Wilson that the United States should join the Allies, against strong opposition in America. This speech of gratitude was widely reported in all the US media to help support their resolution to become an ally.

'I am in the happy position of being, I think, the first British Minister of the Crown who, speaking on behalf of the people of this country, can salute the American Nation as comrades in arms. I am glad; I am proud. I am glad not merely because of the stupendous resources which this great nation will bring to the succour of the alliance, but I rejoice as a democrat that the advent of the United States into this war gives the final stamp and seal to the character of the conflict as a struggle against military autocracy throughout the world. That was the note that ran through the great deliverance of President Wilson. It was echoed, Sir, in your resounding words today. The United States of America have the noble tradition, never broken, of having never engaged in war except for liberty. And this is the greatest struggle for liberty that they have ever embarked upon. I am not at all surprised, when one recalls the wars of the past, that America took its time to make up its mind about the character of this struggle...The fact that the United States of America has made up its mind finally makes it abundantly clear to the world that this is no struggle of that character, but a great fight for human liberty...

I can see peace coming now – not a peace which will be the beginning of war; not a peace which will be an endless preparation for strife and bloodshed; but a real peace. The world is an old world. It has never had peace. It has been rocking and swaying like an ocean, and Europe – poor Europe! – has always lived under the menace of the sword. When this war began two-thirds of Europe were under autocratic rule. It is the other way about now, and democracy means peace. The democracy of France did not want war; the democracy of Italy hesitated long before they entered the war; the democracy of this country shrank from it – shrank and shuddered – and never would have entered the cauldron had it not been for the invasion of Belgium. The democracies sought peace; strove for peace. If Prussia had been a democracy there would have been no war. Strange things have happened in this war. There are stranger things to come, and they are coming rapidly. There are times in history when this world spins so leisurely along its destined course that it seems for centuries to be at a standstill; but there are also times when it rushes along at a giddy pace, covering the track of centuries in a year. Those are the times we are living in now. Today we wage the most devastating war earth has ever seen; tomorrow – perhaps not a distant tomorrow – war may be abolished forever from the category of human crimes. This may be something like the fierce outburst of winter which we are now witnessing before the complete triumph of the sun. It is written of those gallant men who won that victory on Monday – men from Canada, from Australia, and from this old country, which has proved that in spite of its age it is not decrepit – it is written of those gallant men that they attacked with the dawn – fit work for the dawn! – to drive out of forty miles of French soil those miscreants who had defiled it for three years. "They attacked with the dawn." Significant phrase! The breaking up of the dark rule of the Turk, which for centuries has clouded the sunniest land in the world, the freeing of Russia from an oppression which has covered it like a shroud for so long, the great declaration of President Wilson coming with the might of the great nation which he represents into the struggle for liberty are heralds of the dawn. "They attacked with the dawn," and these men are marching forward in the full radiance of that dawn, and soon Frenchmen and Americans, British, Italians, Russians, yea, and Serbians, Belgians, Montenegrins, will march into the full light of a perfect day.'

# ALEXANDER FYODOROVICH KERENSKY
## 4 May 1881 – 11 June 1970

*'They died, but they were never slaves'*
14 May 1917

**After the February Revolution** of 1917 in Petrograd (St Petersburg), Kerensky became minister of justice in the Russian Provisional Government. The war minister had stated that the Russian army was on the verge of disintegrating. Kerensky argued that while Russia's allies were continuing to fight successfully on their various fronts, Russia should likewise continue its fight on the Eastern Front, described by Kerensky as the 'Allied Front'. He toured the front lines, exhorting the troops to stay and fight, and launched the 'Kerensky Offensive' in June 1917 against the German–Austrian–Hungarian army. After a short period as prime minister of the new Republic, Kerensky was overthrown by the Bolsheviks and fled into exile.

'I came to you because my strength is exhausted. I no longer feel my former courage, nor have my former belief that we are conscientious citizens, not slaves in revolt. I am sorry I did not die two months ago, when the dream of a new life was growing in the hearts of the Russian people, when I was sure the country could govern itself without the whip. As affairs are going now, it will be impossible to save the country...Are not enemy forces being thrown over on to the Anglo-French front, and is not the Anglo-French advance already halted? There is no such thing as a "Russian front", there is only one general allied front. We are marching towards peace and I should not be in the ranks of the Provisional Government if the ending of the war were not the aim of the whole Provisional Government; but if we are going to propose new war aims we must see we are respected by friend as well as by foe. If the tragedy and desperateness of the situation are not realized by all in our State, if our organization does not function like a machine, then all our dreams of liberty, all our ideals, will be thrown back for decades and perhaps will be drowned in blood. Beware! The time has now come when every one in the depth of his conscience must reflect where he is going and where he is leading others who were kept in ignorance by the old regime and still regard every printed word as law. The fate of the country is in your hands, and it is in most extreme peril. History must be able to say of us, "They died, but they were never slaves".'

# DAVID LLOYD GEORGE
## 17 January 1863 – 26 March 1945

*'Germany expected to find a lamb and found a lion'*
June 1917

**The British prime minister here rebutted** arguments that Britain bore responsibility for the outbreak of war. He argued that Britain strove harder than any nation to achieve peace, but that the Germans were absolutely determined to provoke a war.

'It is a satisfaction for Britain in these terrible times that no share of the responsibility for these events rests on her. She is not the Jonah in this storm. The part taken by our country in this conflict, in its origin, and in its conduct, has been as honourable and chivalrous as any part ever taken in any country in any operation. We might imagine from declarations which were made by the Germans...that this terrible war was wantonly and wickedly provoked by England...Wantonly provoked by England to increase her possessions, and to destroy the influence, the power, and the prosperity of a dangerous rival. There never was a more foolish travesty of the actual facts...What are the main facts? There were six countries which entered the war at the beginning. Britain was last, and not the first. Before she entered the war Britain made every effort to avoid it; begged, supplicated, and entreated that there should be no conflict. I was a member of the Cabinet at the time, and I remember the earnest endeavours we made to persuade Germany and Austria not to precipitate Europe into this welter of blood. We begged them to summon a European conference to consider. Had that conference met, arguments against provoking such a catastrophe were so overwhelming that there would never have been a war. Germany knew that, so she rejected the conference, although Austria was prepared to accept it. She suddenly declared war, and yet we are the people who wantonly provoked this war, in order to attack Germany. We begged Germany not to attack Belgium, and produced a treaty, signed by the King of Prussia, as well as the King of England, pledging himself to protect Belgium against an invader, and we said, "If you invade Belgium we shall have no alternative but to defend it". The enemy invaded Belgium, and now they say, "Why, forsooth, you, England, provoked this war." It is not quite the story of the wolf and the lamb. I will tell you why – because Germany expected to find a lamb and found a lion.'

# VLADIMIR ILYICH LENIN
## 22 April 1870 – 21 January 1924

*'Long live the world socialist revolution!'*
25 October 1917

**On 23 October 1917, Lenin led** a rising to capture the Russian Provisional Government offices in Petrograd. By 25 October, Bolshevik forces had occupied key localities and members of the government were either captured or fugitives. In the afternoon, Lenin convened the Petrograd Soviet to announce the triumph of the 'workers' and the completion of a successful revolution.

'Comrades, the workers' and peasants' revolution, about the necessity of which the Bolsheviks have always spoken, has been accomplished. What is the significance of this workers' and peasants' revolution? Its significance is, first of all, that we shall have a Soviet government, our own organ of power, in which the bourgeoisie will have no share whatsoever. The oppressed masses will themselves create a power. The old state apparatus will be shattered to its foundations and a new administrative apparatus set up in the form of the Soviet organizations. From now on, a new phase in the history of Russia begins, and this, the third Russian revolution, should in the end lead to the victory of socialism. One of our urgent tasks is to put an immediate end to the war. It is clear to everybody that in order to end this war, which is closely bound up with the present capitalist system, capital itself must be fought. We shall be helped in this by the world working-class movement, which is already beginning to develop in Italy, Britain and Germany. The proposal we make to international democracy for a just and immediate peace will everywhere awaken an ardent response among the international proletarian masses... A single decree putting an end to landed proprietorship will win us the confidence of the peasants. The peasants will understand that the salvation of the peasantry lies only in an alliance with the workers. We shall institute genuine workers' control over production. We have now learned to make a concerted effort. The revolution that has just been accomplished is evidence of this. We possess the strength of mass organization, which will overcome everything and lead the proletariat to the world revolution. We must now set about building a proletarian socialist state in Russia. Long live the world socialist revolution!'

# VLADIMIR ILYICH LENIN
## 22 April 1870 – 21 January 1924

*'For the power of the people!'*
17 November 1917

**The Marxist revolutionary returned** from Finland to lead the October Revolution of 1917, and as leader of the Bolsheviks, came to be leader of Soviet Russia from that time. The Provisional Government was deposed, and the Winter Palace was stormed, forcing Kerensky to escape the country. A month after this speech, the feared secret service CHEKA was established by Lenin to defend the Revolution, and all media were taken over by the new state. By March 1918 Lenin had extricated Russia from the First World War, losing huge territories in order to consolidate communist control of the state. This speech announced the overthrow of Kerensky and cautioned that the Bolshevik Revolution must beware a military-led counter-revolution.

'We have deposed the Government of Kerensky, which rose against the revolution and the people. The change which resulted in the deposition of the Provisional Government was accomplished without bloodshed... Announcing this to the army at the front, the Revolutionary Committee calls upon the revolutionary soldiers to watch closely the conduct of the men in command. Officers who do not join the accomplished revolution immediately and openly must be arrested at once as enemies. The Petrograd Council of Workmen's and Soldiers' Delegates considers this to be the programme of the new authority: First – The offer of an immediate democratic peace. Second – The immediate handing over of large proprietarial lands to the peasants. Third – The transmission of all authority to the Council of Workmen's and Soldiers' Delegates. Fourth – The honest convocation of a Constitutional Assembly. The national revolutionary army must not permit uncertain military detachments to leave the front for Petrograd. They should use persuasion, but where this fails they must oppose any such action on the part of these detachments by force without mercy. The present order must be read immediately to all military detachments in all arms. The suppression of this order from the rank and file by army organizations is equivalent to a great crime against the revolution and will be punished by all the strength of the revolutionary law. Soldiers! For peace, for bread, for land, and for the power of the people!'

# DAVID LLOYD GEORGE
## 17 January 1863 – 26 March 1945

*'I am certain that the nation will shrink from no sacrifice'*
30 March 1918

**The prime minister made this statement** to confirm the appointment of Marshal Ferdinand Foch of France as Allied Supreme Commander, a position Foch held until 11 November 1918, when he accepted the German request for an armistice. Foch's appointment was in response to sweeping German territorial gains following the opening of their Spring (or Ludendorff) Offensive on 21 March 1918. The Germans had the temporary, but important, advantage of 50 army divisions being released from the Eastern Front because of the Russian surrender. With one man now in overall charge of the Allies, by April the German offensive had been halted and Allied advances led to the collapse of the Hindenburg Line and the surrender of the German empire in November.

'For the first few days after the German Army had launched upon our lines an attack unparalleled in its concentration of troops and guns the situation was extremely critical. Thanks to the indomitable bravery of our troops, who gradually stemmed the enemy advance until reinforcements could arrive and our faithful Ally could enter into the battle, the situation is now improved. The struggle, however, is still only in its opening stages, and no prediction of its future course can yet be made. From the first day the War Cabinet has been in constant session and in communication with Headquarters and with the French and American Governments. A number of measures have been taken in concert between the Governments to deal with the emergency. The enemy has had the incalculable advantage of fighting as one army. To meet this, the Allies have, since the battle began, taken a most important decision. With the cordial cooperation of the British and French Commanders-in-Chief, General Foch has been charged by the British, French and American Governments to coordinate the action of the Allied Armies on the Western Front...It is clear that, whatever may happen in this battle, the country must be prepared for further sacrifices to ensure final victory. I am certain that the nation will shrink from no sacrifice which is required to secure this result, and the necessary plans are being carefully prepared by the Government and will be announced when Parliament meets.'

# HENRI JOSEPH EUGÈNE GOURAUD
## 17 November 1867 – 16 September 1946

*'Kill them, kill them in abundance, until they have had enough'*
16 July 1918

**At the Dardanelles in 1915**, Gouraud had broken his leg and lost an arm. General of the 4th Army from July 1917, this was Gouraud's appeal to his forces, at the beginning of the Second Battle of the Marne (15 July–4 August 1918). This was Germany's final major attempt to achieve a breakthrough on the Western Front before the arrival of ever-increasing US troops in the war tilted the balance in the Allies' favour. The battle began when 23 German divisions attacked the French 4th Army east of Rheims, in the Fourth Battle of Champagne. The US 42nd Division was attached to Gouraud's army, and was commanded by Gouraud at the time. Meanwhile, 17 divisions of the German 7th Army, aided by the 9th Army, attacked the French 6th Army to the west of Rheims, whereby von Ludendorff hoped to split the French in two. Gouraud's troops stopped the German advance on the first day, but the Germans captured a bridgehead 4 miles (6.5 km) deep, west of Rheims. The British XXII Corps and 85,000 American troops joined the French for the battle, and stalled the advance on 17 July. The German Spring Offensive failed because of an American and French counter-attack that inflicted severe casualties. When the attack stalled, Marshal Foch initiated an offensive on 18 July. The Germans had not only failed in their aim to win the war through their offensive, but had in fact lost ground, and a number of German commanders came to realize that the war was lost.

'To the French and American Soldiers of the Army: We may be attacked at any moment. You all feel that a defensive battle was never undertaken under more propitious conditions. We are warned, and we are on our guard. We have received strong reinforcements of infantry and artillery. You will fight on ground which by your hard labour you have transformed into a mighty fortress, into a fortress which is invincible if the passages are well guarded. The bombardment will be terrible. You will endure it without weakness. The attack in a cloud of dust and gas will be fierce, but your positions and your armament are formidable. The strong and brave hearts of free men beat in your breasts. None will look behind, none will give way. Every man will have only one thought – "Kill them, kill them in abundance, until they have had enough." And thus your General tells you it will be a glorious day.'

# GENERAL JOHN JOSEPH 'BLACK JACK' PERSHING
## 13 September 1860 – 15 July 1948

*'You came to the battlefield at a crucial hour'*
27 August 1918

**Pershing had fought against the Sioux** and Apache, and in Cuba, Mexico and the Philippines, rising in the course of his distinguished military career to become the only person to be promoted in his own lifetime to the highest rank ever held in the United States Army, 'General of the Armies'. In the First World War Pershing led the American Expeditionary Forces, which first saw serious action during the summer of 1918, contributing eight divisions, alongside 24 French ones, at the Second Battle of the Marne. Combined with the British 4th Army's victory at Amiens, the Franco-American victory at the Marne marked the turning point of the war on the Western Front. This was Pershing's Order of the Day to US Forces, celebrating the victory.

'It fills me with pride to record in general orders a tribute to the service achievements of the 1st and 3rd Corps, comprising the 1st, 2nd, 3rd, 4th, 26th, 28th, 32nd, and 42nd Divisions of the American Expeditionary Forces. You came to the battlefield at a crucial hour for the Allied cause. For almost four years the most formidable army the world has yet seen had pressed its invasion of France and stood threatening its capital. At no time has that army been more powerful and menacing than when, on July 15th, it struck again to destroy in one great battle the brave men opposed to it and to enforce its brutal will upon the world and civilization. Three days later, in conjunction with our allies, you counter-attacked. The Allied armies gained a brilliant victory that marks the turning point of the war. You did more than to give the Allies the support to which, as a nation, our faith was pledged. You proved that our altruism, our pacific spirit, and our sense of justice have not blunted our virility or our courage. You have shown that American initiative and energy are as fit for the tasks of war as for the pursuits of peace. You have justly won unstinted praise from our allies and the eternal gratitude of our countrymen. We have paid for our success with the lives of many of our brave comrades. We shall cherish their memory always and claim for our history and literature their bravery, achievement, and sacrifice. This order will be read to all organizations at the first assembly formations following its receipt.'

# TOMÁS (THOMAS) GARRIGUE MASARYK
### 7 March 1850 – 14 September 1937

## 'I am too moved to speak'
### 20 December 1918

**A politician, academic, sociologist** and philosopher, the Czech Tomás Masaryk wanted to reform the Austro-Hungarian Habsburg monarchy into a democratic federal state in his homeland. However, when war broke out in 1914, he came to favour the abolition of the monarchy and full independence for Czechs and Slovaks. In August he was lucky to avoid arrest as an agitator. To work for his aims, he fled to Geneva for refuge in December 1914, constantly travelling in the cause to Rome, London, Paris, Russia, the United States and Japan, organizing support. In Russia, he founded the Czechoslovak Legion from former Austro-Hungarian prisoners-of-war to fight for the Allies against the empire, and became professor of Slav Research at King's College, London. His intelligence network of Czech revolutionaries gave vital intelligence to the Allies. His visit to the United States was successful, resulting in the Lansing Declaration of May 1918, which supported in principle the formation of an independent Czech state. With the fall of the Austro-Hungarian empire in 1918, the Allies recognized Masaryk as head of the Provisional Czechoslovak government, and on 14 November 1918, he was elected president of the Czechoslovak Republic by the National Assembly in Prague. Masaryk was re-elected in general elections held in 1920, 1927 and 1934. He held office until December 1935, when he resigned due to bad health. His son Jan Masaryk was Czechoslovakia's foreign minister from 1940–8, and was killed by the Soviet NKVD by being defenestrated (thrown out of a window) in Prague. What follows is Masaryk's address on entering Prague as first president of the Republic.

'I am too moved to speak. This is the first time in four years that I have been so deeply touched. We know how much worked against us and how many difficulties we had to overcome, but we will find a friendly way out. Dr Kramar said that you were impatiently waiting my coming. I also was impatiently awaiting the moment when I should come here to continue your work. How many sleepless nights I have passed during these four years! I knew you were oppressed and how hard was your task. You are all heroic and strong with a strength which showed that you were united behind your leaders, though they were exiled. My heart speaks its thanks. I promise that my efforts will continue without wavering.'

# KAISER WILHELM II
## 27 January 1859 – 4 June 1941

*'The hour is grave!'*
Proclamations to the Army, 6 and 10 October 1918

**In 1888 the 29-year-old Wilhelm II** became the ninth king of Prussia and the third emperor of Germany. Two years later he dismissed the German chancellor, Otto Bismarck, mainly because of his cautious foreign policy. Hating parliamentary democracy, Wilhelm now acted for some years as an autocratic monarch, and was a passionate supporter of German militarism and imperialism. Although he was Queen Victoria's grandson, the kaiser followed an anti-British foreign policy, and also gave support to South Africa during the Boer War. During the Boxer Rebellion, a regiment of German troops was sent to China after hearing Wilhelm exhort them on 27 July 1900: *'Should you encounter the enemy, he will be defeated! No quarter will be given! Prisoners will not be taken! Whoever falls into your hands is forfeited!'* After suffering a nervous breakdown in 1908, he played a less dominant role in government, but strongly supported German imperialism and encouraged Tirpitz's attempts to build up a navy to rival that of Britain. After the assassination of Archduke Franz Ferdinand, Wilhelm encouraged Austro-Hungarian aggression, but did not foresee the situation developing into all-out conflict with the outbreak of the First World War. Wilhelm was commander-in-chief of the armed forces during the war, but the decision to replace the Army chief of staff with von Hindenburg was taken against Wilhelm's wishes. In 1918, the arrival of American troops turned the tide of war against Germany, and its various allies began to surrender. The British–French–American attack on the Hindenburg Line began on 26 September 1918. Belgian gains were lost, Bulgaria signed a separate armistice on 29 September and the Allies gained control of Serbia and Greece. The collapse of the Balkans meant that Germany was about to lose its main supplies of oil and food, and US troops continued to arrive at the rate of 10,000 per day. Having suffered over six million casualties, Germany moved towards peace, and President Wilson demanded the abdication of the kaiser. The German High Command concluded that the war could not be won. It recommended to the Reichstag on 2 October 1918 that a peace be negotiated, a message repeated by Army Chief of Staff von Hindenburg on 3 October. However, the kaiser then appealed on 6 October to the army to maintain their resolve in their 'grave' hour.

'For months past the enemy, with enormous exertions and almost without pause in the fighting, has stormed against your lines. In weeks of the struggle, often without repose, you have had to persevere and resist a numerically far superior enemy. Therein lies the greatness of the task which has been set for you and which you are fulfilling. Troops of all the German States are doing their part and are heroically defending the Fatherland on foreign soil. Hard is the task. My navy is holding its own against the united enemy naval forces and is unwaveringly supporting the army in its difficult struggle. The eyes of those at home rest with pride and admiration on the deeds of the army and navy. I express to you the thanks of myself and the Fatherland. The collapse of the Macedonian front has occurred in the midst of the hardest struggle. In accord with our allies, I have resolved once more to offer peace to the enemy, but I will only extend my hand for an honourable peace. We owe that to the heroes who have laid down their lives for the Fatherland, and we make that our duty to our children. Whether arms will be lowered still is a question. Until then we must not slacken. We must, as hitherto, exert all our strength tirelessly to hold our ground against the onslaught of our enemies. The hour is grave, but, trusting in your strength and in God's gracious help, we feel ourselves to be strong enough to defend our beloved Fatherland.'

Wilhelm II repeated the call on 10 October:

'The hour is grave! We are fighting for the future of the Fatherland and for the protection of the soil of the Homeland. To that end we need the united action of the intellectual, moral, and economic powers of Germany. On the co-operation of those powers our invincibility rests. The will for defence must bind all separate views and separate wishes into one great unity of conception. God grant us something of the spirit of the war of liberation.'

The kaiser dismissed von Ludendorff on 26 October. However, the Social Democrat Philipp Scheidemann declared the death of Imperial Germany on 9 November and the Weimar Republic was established. The kaiser and his family fled to the Netherlands, and on the 11th hour of the 11th day of the 11th month the armistice was signed. With Adolf Hitler's rise to power after 1933, Wilhelm entertained hopes of being restored to his empire but they came to nothing.

# MOHANDAS KARAMCHAND GANDHI
## 2 October 1869 – 30 January 1948

*'Non-violence is the first article of my faith'*
23 March 1922

**Leader of the Indian National Congress** from 1920, Gandhi and his followers in the independence movement practised a policy of non-violent non-cooperation with the British authorities. Gandhi was arrested and charged with sedition for three articles that appeared in his *Young India* magazine. Gandhi pleaded guilty and this is part of his statement to the court, after which he was sentenced to six years imprisonment. Imprisoned three more times in the course of his life, while expressing support for Britain in the Second World War, he also started the 'Quit India' campaign in 1942 in order to help India gain independence from her colonial rulers.

'Non-violence is the first article of my faith. It is the last article of my faith. But I had to make my choice. I had either to submit to a system which I considered has done an irreparable harm to my country or incur the risk of the mad fury of my people bursting forth when they understood the truth from my lips. I know that my people have sometimes gone mad. I am deeply sorry for it; and I am therefore, here, to submit not to a light penalty but to the highest penalty. I do not ask for mercy. I do not plead any extenuating act. I am here, therefore, to invite and submit to the highest penalty that can be inflicted upon me for what in law is a deliberate crime and what appears to me to be the highest duty of a citizen. The only course open to you, Mr Judge, is, as I am just going to say in my statement, either to resign your post or inflict on me the severest penalty if you believe that the system and law you are assisting to administer are good for the people. I do not expect that kind of conversion. But by the time I have finished with my statement you will, perhaps, have a glimpse of what is raging within my breast to run this maddest risk which a sane man can run.

Little do town-dwellers know how the semi-starved masses of Indians are slowly sinking to lifelessness. Little do they know that their miserable comfort represents the brokerage they get for the work they do for the foreign exploiter, that the profits and the brokerage are sucked from the masses. Little do they realize that the government established by law in British India is carried on for this exploitation of the masses. No sophistry, no jugglery in figures can explain away the evidence the skeletons in many villages present to the naked eye. I have no doubt whatsoever that both England and the town-dwellers of India will have to answer, if there is a God above, for this crime against humanity which is perhaps unequalled in history. The law itself in this country has been used to serve the foreign exploiter. My experience of political cases in India leads me to the conclusion that in nine out of every ten the condemned men were totally innocent. Their crime consisted in love of their country. In ninety-nine cases out of a hundred, justice has been denied to Indians as against Europeans in the courts of India. This is not an exaggerated picture. It is the experience of almost every Indian who has had anything to do with such cases. In my opinion the administration of the law is thus prostituted consciously or unconsciously for the benefit of the exploiter.

The greatest misfortune is that Englishmen and their Indian associates in the administration of the country do not know that they are engaged in the crime I have attempted to describe. In fact I believe that I have rendered a service to India and England by showing in non-cooperation the way out of the unnatural state in which both are living. In my humble opinion, non-cooperation with evil is as much a duty as is cooperation with good. But in the past, non-cooperation has been deliberately expressed in violence to the evildoer. I am endeavouring to show to my countrymen that violent non-cooperation only multiplies evil and that as evil can only be sustained by violence, withdrawal of support of evil requires complete abstention from violence. Non-violence implies voluntary submission to the penalty for non-cooperation with evil. I am here, therefore, to invite and submit cheerfully to the highest penalty that can be inflicted upon me for what in law is deliberate crime and what appears to me to be the highest duty of a citizen. The only course open to you, the Judge and the Assessors, is either to resign your posts and thus dissociate yourselves from evil if you feel that the law you are called upon to administer is an evil and that in reality I am innocent, or to inflict on me the severest penalty if you believe that the system and the law you are assisting to administer are good for the people of this country and that my activity is therefore injurious to the public weal.'

# CLARENCE SEWARD DARROW
## 18 April 1857 – 13 March 1938

*'I have spoken about the war. I believed in it.*
*I don't know whether I was crazy or not.'*
10 September 1924

**Clarence Darrow was the finest lawyer** of his day, and a leader in the American Civil Liberties Union. Apart from making a famous defence in the 'Scopes Trial' of 1925, he defended the rich University of Chicago students Richard Loeb and Nathan Leopold Jr in 1924. They had been motivated to commit 'the perfect crime' and had murdered 14-year-old Bobby Franks in a quest for thrills and excitement. Darrow's speech below is notable for its criticism of capital punishment and retribution-based penal systems. He was 67 years old when hired to defend the killers in the so-called *'Trial of the Century'*. The media was expecting a *'not guilty by reason of insanity'* plea, but Darrow astounded everyone by having both plead guilty. By doing so, he avoided a jury trial, and brought all his oratorical skills to bear upon a county circuit court judge. His summarizing speech has been called the finest of Darrow's career. The murderers were sentenced to life imprisonment rather than hanging, as demanded by the state attorney.

'...Now, your Honor, I have spoken about the war. I believed in it. I don't know whether I was crazy or not. Sometimes I think perhaps I was. I approved of it; I joined in the general cry of madness and despair. I urged men to fight. I was safe because I was too old to go. I was like the rest. What did they do? Right or wrong, justifiable or unjustifiable – which I need not discuss today – it changed the world. For four long years the civilized world was engaged in killing men. Christian against Christian, barbarian uniting with Christians to kill Christians; anything to kill. It was taught in every school, aye in the Sunday schools. The little children played at war. The toddling children on the street. Do you suppose this world has ever been the same since? How long, your Honor, will it take for the world to get back the humane emotions that were slowly growing before the war? How long will it take the calloused hearts of men before the scars of hatred and cruelty shall be removed?...We read of killing one hundred thousand men in a day. We read about it and we rejoiced in it – if it was the other fellows who were killed. We were fed on flesh and drank blood. Even down to the prattling babe. I need not tell you how many upright, honorable young boys have come into this court charged with murder, some saved and some sent to their death, boys who fought in this war and learned to place a cheap value on human life. You know it and I know it. These boys were brought up in it. The tales of death were in their homes, their playgrounds, their schools; they were in the newspapers that they read; it was a part of the common frenzy – what was a life? It was nothing. It was the least sacred thing in existence and these boys were trained to this cruelty. It will take fifty years to wipe it out of the human heart, if ever. I know this, that after the Civil War in 1865, crimes of this sort increased, marvellously. No one needs to tell me that crime has no cause. It has as definite a cause as any other disease, and I know that out of the hatred and bitterness of the Civil War crime increased as America had never seen before. I know that Europe is going through the same experience to-day; I know it has followed every war; and I know it has influenced these boys so that life was not the same to them as it would have been if the world had not made red with blood...

I do not know how much salvage there is in these two boys. I hate to say it in their presence, but what is there to look forward to? I do not know but what your Honor would be merciful to them, but not merciful to civilization, and not merciful if you tied a rope around their necks and let them die; merciful to them, but not merciful to civilization, and not merciful to those who would be left behind. To spend the balance of their days in prison is mighty little to look forward to, if anything. Is it anything? They may have the hope that as the years roll around they might be released. I do not know. I do not know. I will be honest with this court as I have tried to be from the beginning. I know that these boys are not fit to be at large. I believe they will not be until they pass through the next stage of life, at forty-five or fifty. Whether they will then, I cannot tell. I am sure of this; that I will not be here to help them. So far as I am concerned, it is over...'

# ADOLF HITLER
## 20 April 1889 – 30 April 1945

*'Work and bread!'*
Appeal to the German nation broadcast 15 July 1932

**Adolf Hitler was born at the** Gasthof zum Pommer, an inn in Braunau am Inn, Austria–Hungary, the fourth of six children to Alois Hitler and Klara Pölzl. He had a troubled childhood and was expelled from school after getting drunk and using his school certificate as toilet paper. Rejected by art colleges, he failed as a painter and became homeless in Vienna in 1910. Moving to Munich, he escaped military service in Austria and was arrested. He was found physically unfit for active service and allowed to return to Germany. However, the 25-year-old misfit and failure was accepted by the Bavarian army in a reserve regiment, when Germany entered the First World War. Hitler was never promoted above being a regimental 'runner' delivering messages. He became convinced that the Jews were the cause of Germany's defeat. In 1919 he became a police spy in the army and then joined the extreme right-wing National Socialist German Workers' Party. His rabble-rousing speeches against Jews, Bolsheviks and bankers, fuelled by venom and hate, powered his rise up the party hierarchy to become one of its leaders. By 1921 he was leader of the National Socialist German Workers' Party (NSDAP or Nazi Party). In 1923, Hitler attempted an unsuccessful armed uprising in Munich and was imprisoned for nine months, during which time he dictated his book *Mein Kampf* outlining his political ideology. The Nazis grew stronger during the 1920s and in the 1932 elections became the largest party in the German parliament. This speech was part of broadcast made after that election success. Hitler became chancellor of Germany in 1933 and its unopposed Führer from 1934 until his suicide at the end of the Second World War. This is not the place for a biography, but such was the early history of a disturbed man who came almost to destroy Western civilization.

'Fate has given those in power today more than 13 years to be tested and proven...Once it was their desire to govern Germany better in the future than in the past, and they are forced to observe that the only real product of their attempts at government is that Germany and the German *Volk* are still alive...If the present parties seriously want to save Germany, why have they not done so already? Had they wanted to save Germany, why has it not happened? Had the men of these parties honestly intended to do so, then their programmes must have been bad.

If, however, their programmes were right, then either their desire cannot have been sincere, or they must have been too foolish or too weak. Now, after 13 years, after they have destroyed everything in Germany, the time has finally arrived for their own elimination. Whether or not today's parliamentary parties exist or not is of no consequence; what is, however, necessary is that the German nation be prevented from collapsing completely into ruin. Therefore it is a duty to defeat these parties, for in order to secure their own existence, they must tear the nation apart over and over again...

Thirteen years ago we National Socialists were laughed at and derided – today our opponents' laughter has turned to tears! A faithful group of people has arisen which will gradually overcome the prejudices of class madness and the arrogance of rank. A faithful community of people which is resolved to take up the fight for the preservation of our race, not because it is made up of Bavarians or Prussians or men from Württemberg or Saxony; not because they are Catholics or Protestants, workers or civil servants, bourgeois or salaried workers, etc, but because all of them are Germans. Within this feeling of inseparable solidarity, mutual respect has grown, and from this respect has grown an understanding, and from this understanding the tremendous power which moves us all. We National Socialists march into every election with the single commitment that we will, the following day, once more face the task of the inner reorganization of our body politic. For we are not fighting merely for the mandates or the ministerial posts, but rather for the German individual, whom we wish to – and shall – join together once more to inseparably share a single common destiny. The Almighty, Who has allowed us in the past to rise from seven men to 13 million in 13 years, will further allow these 13 million to once become a German *Volk*. It is in this *Volk* that we believe, for this *Volk* we fight; and if necessary, it is to this *Volk* that we are willing, as the thousands of comrades before us, to commit ourselves body and soul. If the nation does its duty, then the day will come which restores to us: one Reich in honour and freedom – work and bread!'

# FRANKLIN DELANO ROOSEVELT
## 30 January 1882 – 12 April 1945

*'The only thing we have to fear is fear itself'*
4 March 1933

**In 1932, the United States was deep into** the Great Depression, and the public felt that President Hoover was not doing enough to alleviate it. Roosevelt and the Democratic Party mobilized the poor as well as organized labour, ethnic minorities, urbanites and Southern whites, crafting the New Deal coalition for his 1932 presidential campaign. During the campaign, Roosevelt constantly stated: '*I pledge you, I pledge myself, to a new deal for the American people*', a slogan later adopted for his legislative programme. Roosevelt won 57 per cent of the vote and carried all but six states. No one was clear on what FDR's plan was, but the promise of 'change' and a 'New Deal' had powered his campaign. In this first inaugural address, Roosevelt buoyed up the injured psyche of the American people and presented his case for broader executive powers to tackle the Depression. Two million were homeless. A quarter of the workforce was unemployed, farm prices had dropped by 60 per cent and industrial production had fallen by more than half since 1929. By the evening of 4 March 1933, 32 of the 48 states, as well as the District of Columbia had closed their banks. The New York Federal Reserve Bank was unable to open on the following day, as huge sums had been withdrawn by panicking customers. This is the terrifying background to Roosevelt's inaugural address. Beginning with this speech, Roosevelt blamed the economic crisis on bankers and financiers, the quest for profit, and the self-interest basis of capitalism. Nothing changes. The 2008 recession had the same causes.

'President Hoover, Mr Chief Justice, my friends: This is a day of national consecration. And I am certain that on this day my fellow Americans expect that on my induction into the Presidency, I will address them with a candor and a decision which the present situation of our people impels. This is pre-eminently the time to speak the truth, the whole truth, frankly and boldly. Nor need we shrink from honestly facing conditions in our country today. This great Nation will endure, as it has endured, will revive and will prosper. So, first of all, let me assert my firm belief that the only thing we have to fear is fear itself – nameless, unreasoning, unjustified terror which paralyzes needed efforts to convert retreat into advance. In every dark hour of our national life, a leadership of frankness and of vigor has met with that understanding and support of the people themselves which is essential to victory. And I am convinced that you will again give that support to leadership in these critical days. In such a spirit on my part and on yours we face our common difficulties. They concern, thank God, only material things. Values have shrunk to fantastic levels; taxes have risen; our ability to pay has fallen; government of all kinds is faced by serious curtailment of income; the means of exchange are frozen in the currents of trade; the withered leaves of industrial enterprise lie on every side; farmers find no markets for their produce; and the savings of many years in thousands of families are gone. More important, a host of unemployed citizens face the grim problem of existence, and an equally great number toil with little return. Only a foolish optimist can deny the dark realities of the moment.

And yet our distress comes from no failure of substance. We are stricken by no plague of locusts. Compared with the perils which our forefathers conquered, because they believed and were not afraid, we have still much to be thankful for. Nature still offers her bounty and human efforts have multiplied it. Plenty is at our doorstep, but a generous use of it languishes in the very sight of the supply. Primarily, this is because the rulers of the exchange of mankind's goods have failed, through their own stubbornness and their own incompetence, have admitted their failure, and have abdicated. Practices of the unscrupulous money changers stand indicted in the court of public opinion, rejected by the hearts and minds of men. True, they have tried. But their efforts have been cast in the pattern of an outworn tradition. Faced by failure of credit, they have proposed only the lending of more money. Stripped of the lure of profit by which to induce our people to follow their false leadership, they have resorted to exhortations, pleading tearfully for restored confidence. They only know the rules of a generation of self-seekers. They have no vision, and when there is no vision the people perish. Yes, the money changers have fled from their high seats in the temple of our civilization. We may now restore that temple to the ancient truths. The measure of that restoration lies in the extent to which we apply social values more noble than mere monetary profit. Happiness lies not in the mere possession of money; it lies in the joy of achievement, in the thrill of creative effort.'

# HUEY PIERCE LONG
## 30 August 1893 – 10 September 1935

### 'Every man a king'
23 February 1934

**'Kingfish' Long was the governor** of Louisiana (1928–32) and senator for Louisiana (1932–5), whose rise was compared by President Roosevelt to those of Mussolini and Hitler. His populist policies made politicians and big business scared of him, and he was killed in mysterious circumstances, when planning his own presidential bid. He created the Share Our Wealth programme in 1934, with the motto '*Every man a king*', proposing new wealth distribution measures by taxing large corporations and rich individuals. He believed that this would cut the poverty and crime of the Great Depression, advocating public spending on public works, education and pensions to stimulate the economy. Criticised as a 'communist', he replied that his policies were enshrined in The Bible and the Declaration of Independence. Long stated that his plan was '*the only defense this country's got against communism*'. The Senate would not support his proposals, so Long urged the country to support them – by 1935 his society had 7.5 million members. On his death, many of Long's programmes were admittedly copied by Roosevelt in his 'New Deal' programme to drag America out of recession. This was a wonderful appeal to the American nation contained in Long's speech to launch the 'Share Our Wealth Society.'

'...Is that a right of life, when the young children of this country are being reared into a sphere which is more owned by 12 men that is by 120,000,000 people?...It is not the difficulty of the problem which we have; it is the fact that the rich people of this country – and by rich people I mean the super-rich – will not allow us to solve the problems, or rather the one little problem that is afflicting this country, because in order to cure all of our woes it is necessary to scale down the big fortunes, that we may scatter the wealth to be shared by all of the people. We have a marvellous love for this Government of ours; in fact, it is almost a religion, and it is well that it should be, because we have a splendid form of government and we have a splendid set of laws. We have everything here that we need, except that we have neglected the fundamentals upon which the American Government was principally predicated...

How may of you remember the first thing that the Declaration of Independence said? It said, "We hold these truths to be self-evident, that there are certain inalienable rights of the people, and among them are life, liberty, and the pursuit of happiness"; and it said, further, "We hold the view that all men are created equal." Now, what did they mean by that? Did they mean, my friends, to say that all men were created equal and that that meant that any one man was born to inherit $10,000,000,000 and that another child was to be born to inherit nothing? Did that mean, my friends, that someone would come into this world without having had an opportunity, of course, to have hit one lick of work, should be born with more than it and all of its children and children's children could ever dispose of, but that another one would have to be born into a life of starvation? That was not the meaning of the Declaration of Independence when it said that all men are created equal of "That we hold that all men are created equal." Nor was it the meaning of the Declaration of Independence when it said that they held that there were certain rights that were inalienable – the right of life, liberty, and the pursuit of happiness. Is that right of life, my friends, when the young children of this country are being reared into a sphere which is more owned by 12 men than it is by 120,000,000 people?...

Now, we have organized a society, and we call it "Share Our Wealth Society", a society with the motto "every man a king". Every man a king, so there would be no such thing as a man or woman who did not have the necessities of life, who would not be dependent upon the whims and caprices and ipsi dixit of the financial martyrs for a living. What do we propose by this society? We propose to limit the wealth of big men in the country...We have to limit fortunes. Our present plan is that we will allow no one man to own more than $50,000,000...We will limit hours of work. There is not any necessity of having over-production. I think all you have got to do, ladies and gentlemen, is just limit the hours of work to such an extent as people will work only so long as is necessary to produce enough for all of the people to have what they need...'

# ADOLF HITLER
## 20 April 1889 – 30 April 1945

*'My patience is now at an end!'*
26 September 1938

**Some historians believe this to be Hitler's** finest and most powerful invective. He used crude nationalism and emotions to sway his audience – love, hate, fear, pride and envy amongst them. Germany had annexed Austria and now laid claim to the Sudetenland area of Czechoslovakia, where many ethnic Germans lived. Hitler insisted in this speech that he had no 'territorial problem', only with Sudetenland. Three days after this speech, Britain, France and Italy signed the Munich Pact with Germany, allowing the Sudetenland to be annexed by German troops on 1 October. On 3 September 1939 the Second World War began, after Hitler's fresh claims on European territory and invasion of Poland.

'And now in front of us is the last problem that must be solved and it will be solved. It is the last territorial claim which I have to make in Europe, but it is the claim from which I will not retreat and which, God willing, I will make good...I can here assert: when we occupied Austria, my first order was: no Czech needs to serve, rather he must not serve, in the German Army. I have not forced him to a conflict with his conscience. Mr Benes *[Czech president]* now fixes his hopes on the world! And he and his diplomats make no secret of that fact. They state: we hope that *[Prime Minister]* Chamberlain will be overthrown, that *[French Premier]* Daladier will be removed, that on every hand revolutions will break out. They fix their hope on Soviet Russia. He still thinks then that he will be able to escape the fulfilment of his obligations. And then I can say only one thing: now two men stand arrayed one against the other: there is Mr Benes and here stand I. We are two men of a different constitution. In the great struggle of the peoples while Mr Benes was sneaking about through the world, I as a decent German soldier did my duty. And now today I confront this man as the soldier of my people! I have only a few statements still to make: I am grateful to Mr Chamberlain for all his efforts. I have assured him that the German people desires nothing less than peace, but I have also told him that I cannot pull back from the limits set to our patience. I have further assured him, and I repeat it here, that when this problem is solved there is for Germany no further territorial problem in Europe. And I have further assured him that at the moment when Czechoslovakia solves her problems, that means when the Czechs have come to terms with their other minorities, and in a peaceable way and not through oppression, then I have no further interest in the Czech state. And that is guaranteed to him! We want no Czechs!

But in the same way I want to state to the German people that with regard to the problem of the Sudeten Germans my patience is now at an end! I have made Mr Benes an offer which is nothing but the putting into effect of what he himself has promised. The decision now lies in his hands: Peace or War! He will either accept this offer and at last give the Germans their freedom or we will go and fetch this freedom for ourselves. The world must take note that in four and a half years of war, and through the long years of my political life, there is one thing which no one could ever throw in my teeth: I have never been a coward! Now I go before my people as its first soldier and behind me – that the world should know – there marches a people and a different people from that of 1918! If then a wandering scholar was able to inject the poison of democratic catchwords into our people – the people of today are no longer the people that they were then. Such catchwords are for us like wasp-stings: they cannot hurt us: we are now immune. In this hour the whole German people will unite with me! It will feel my will to be its will. Just as in my eyes it is its future and its fate which give me the commission for my action. And we wish now to make our will as strong as it was in the time of our struggle, the time when I, as a simple unknown soldier, went out to conquer a Reich and never doubted of success and final victory. Then there gathered close about me a band of brave men and brave women, and they went with me. And so I ask you, my German people, to take your stand behind me, man by man, and woman by woman. In this hour we all desire to forge a common will and that will must be firmer than every hardship and every danger. And if this will is firmer than hardship and danger then one day it will break down hardship and danger. We are determined! Now let Mr Benes make his choice!'

# ÉDOUARD DALADIER
## 18 June 1884 – 10 October 1970

## *Nazis' Aim is Slavery*
### Radio broadcast to the people of France, 29 January 1940

**The French premier delivered this** radio address after the Nazis had conquered Poland, and just a few months before Hitler's armies attacked France. He had signed the Munich Agreement under pressure from the British prime minister, Neville Chamberlain, who knew that without it war was inevitable. However, Daladier had told Britain in April 1938 that Hitler's purpose was to achieve '*a domination of the Continent in comparison with which the ambitions of Napoleon were feeble...Today it is the turn of Czechoslovakia. Tomorrow it will be the turn of Poland and Romania...*' Daladier frantically tried to prepare for war, trying to buy American aircraft. War was declared on Germany by France on 4 September 1939, following Britain's declaration on 3 September, but for months there was no fighting. Daladier resigned as prime minister in March 1940 but remained in the government as minister of defence. After the German breakthrough at Sedan, Daladier became foreign minister. Germany lauched its invasion of France on 10 May, and Daladier and other government members quickly escaped to Morocco, believing that the government could operate effectively from North Africa. However, he was arrested and tried by the French Vichy government, and imprisoned until the end of the war. After the war he was an opponent of Charles de Gaulle, who had fled to Britain on 17 June 1940.

'After five months of war one thing has become more and more clear. It is that Germany seeks to establish a domination over the world quite different from any known previously in history. The domination at which the Nazis aim is not limited to the displacement of the balance of power and the imposition of supremacy of one nation. It seeks the systematic and total destruction of those conquered by Hitler, and it does not negotiate with the nations which he has subdued. He destroys them. He takes from them their whole political and economic existence and wants even to deprive them of their history and their culture. He considers them only as vital space and a vacant territory over which he has every right. The human beings who make up these nations are for him just cattle. He orders their massacre or their migration. He compels them to make room for their conquerors. He does not even bother to impose any war tribute on them. He just takes all their wealth, and, to prevent any revolt, he wipes out their leaders and scientifically seeks the physical and moral degradation of those whose independence he has confiscated. Under this domination, in thousands of towns and villages in Europe there are millions of human beings now living in misery which, some months ago, they could never have imagined. Austria, Bohemia, Slovakia and Poland are lands of despair. Their entire peoples have been deprived of the means of moral and material happiness. Subdued by treachery or brutal violence, they have no other recourse than to work for their executioners who grant them scarcely enough to secure for themselves the most miserable existence.

A world of masters and slaves in the image of Germany herself is being created. For, while Germany is crushing beneath her tyranny men of every race and language, she is herself being crushed beneath her own servitude and her domination mania. The German worker and peasant are the slaves of their Nazi masters while the worker and peasant of Bohemia and Poland have in turn become slaves of these slaves. Before this first fulfilment of a mad dream, the whole world may tremble. Nazi propaganda is entirely founded on the exploitation of the weakness of the human heart. It does not address itself to the strong or the heroic. It tells the rich they are going to lose their money. It tells the worker this is a rich man's war. It tells the intellectual and the artist that all he valued is being destroyed by war. It tells the lover of good things that soon he will have none of them. It says to the Christian believer: "How can you accept this massacre?" It tells the adventurer – "a man like you should profit by the misfortunes of your country". It is those who speak this way who have destroyed or confiscated all the wealth they could lay their hands on, who have reduced their workers to slavery, who have destroyed all intellectual freedom, who have imposed terrible privations on millions of men and women and who have made murder their law. What do contradictions matter to them if they can crush the resistance of those who wish to put an obstacle in the way of their ambitions to be masters of the world? For us there is more to do than merely win the war. We shall win it, but we must also win a victory far greater than that of arms. In this world of masters and slaves, which those madmen who rule at Berlin are seeking to forge, we must also save liberty and human dignity.'

# DAVID LLOYD GEORGE
## 17 January 1863 – 26 March 1945

*'The nation is prepared for every sacrifice so long as it has leadership'*
7 May 1940

**Prime minister during the First World War**, Lloyd George still had parliamentary influence in the 1930s.In 1935 he tried to promote a programme emulating Roosevelt's New Deal, but failed. Lloyd George began to realize the threat posed by Germany, and in the late 1930s was sent to dissuade Hitler from pursuing his plans of national expansion. The Norway, or Narvik, debate held on 7 and 8 May 1940 in the House of Commons was ostensibly a debate about the Norwegian campaign, but it soon became a critical condemnation of Prime Minister Chamberlain's conduct of the Second World War. What follows is the last important parliamentary intervention of Lloyd George's career, a powerful speech designed to undermine Chamberlain as prime minister and to pave the way for the ascendancy of Churchill as premier. Lloyd George's speech was the 'nail in the coffin' of Chamberlain's premiership, and he resigned two days after the debate. Churchill offered Lloyd George a place in his cabinet but he refused.

'I intervene with reluctance in this debate...You are not going to rouse the British Empire – because you will have to do it not merely in Britain, but throughout the world...Is there anyone in this House who will say that he is satisfied with the speed and efficiency of the preparations in any respect for air, for army or for navy? Everybody is disappointed. Everybody knows that whatever was done was done half-heartedly, ineffectively, without drive and unintelligently. For three to four years I thought to myself that the facts with regard to Germany were exaggerated by the First Lord, because the then prime minister – not this prime minister – said that they were not true. The First Lord, Mr Churchill, was right about it. Then came the war. The prime minister must remember that he has met this formidable foe of ours in peace and in war. He has always been worsted. He is not in a position to put it on the ground of friendship. He has appealed for sacrifice. The nation is prepared for every sacrifice so long as it has leadership, as long as the Government show clearly what they are aiming at and so long as the nation is confident that those who are leading it are doing their best. I say solemnly that the prime minister should give an example of sacrifice, because there is nothing which can contribute more to victory in this war than that he should sacrifice the seals of office.'

# SIR WINSTON LEONARD SPENCER CHURCHILL
## 30 November 1874 – 24 January 1965

*'I have nothing to offer but blood, toil, tears and sweat'*
13 May 1940

 **Churchill had served in India**, the Sudan, the Boer War and the First World War before embarking upon a political career. On 10 May 1940, hours before the German invasion of France, it was clear that British politicians had no confidence in Prime Minister Neville Chamberlain. Chamberlain resigned, on condition that the next prime minister could command support from all three major parties in the House of Commons. A meeting between Chamberlain, Lord Halifax, Churchill and the government chief whip led to the recommendation that Churchill should lead an all-party coalition government. Churchill had warned of the growing threat of Hitler long before the start of the war. He refused to consider an armistice with Hitler, and his wonderful oratory prepared the British for the rigours of a long war. Churchill kept resistance in Europe and Africa alive until the United States joined the war in 1941, and the Allies could begin counter-attacking in 1942. This was his inspiring first speech upon taking office as prime minister.

'I say to the House as I said to ministers who have joined this government, I have nothing to offer but blood, toil, tears and sweat. We have before us an ordeal of the most grievous kind. We have before us many, many months of struggle and suffering. You ask, what is our policy? I say it is to wage war by land, sea, and air. War with all our might and with all the strength God has given us, and to wage war against a monstrous tyranny never surpassed in the dark and lamentable catalogue of human crime. That is our policy. You ask, what is our aim? I can answer in one word. It is victory. Victory at all costs – Victory in spite of all terrors – Victory, however long and hard the road may be, for without victory there is no survival. Let that be realized. No survival for the British Empire, no survival for all that the British Empire has stood for, no survival for the urge, the impulse of the ages, that mankind shall move forward toward his goal. I take up my task in buoyancy and hope. I feel sure that our cause will not be suffered to fail among men. I feel entitled at this juncture, at this time, to claim the aid of all and to say, "Come then, let us go forward together with our united strength".'

# SIR WINSTON LEONARD SPENCER CHURCHILL
## 30 November 1874 – 24 January 1965

### 'We shall fight on the beaches'
#### 4 June 1940

**This speech was meant to inform** and inspire the nation after the British retreat from Dunkirk. Churchill had been expecting an utter disaster after the Belgians suddenly and unexpectedly capitulated, leaving the British army exposed to the Germans. He told the nation that 30,000 men were lost in the fighting, along with 1,000 pieces of field artillery and all the army's transport vehicles, and that he had only expected about 20–30,000 soldiers to make it back to Britain safely. In what Churchill called a *'miracle of deliverance'*, over nine days a total of 338,226 British and French soldiers were rescued. (140,000 French troops were saved and then repatriated, but the French surrendered within weeks and they consequently became POWs.) However, almost 900 ships and boats had delivered 200,000 Allied soldiers, who would otherwise have been taken prisoner, so that they were still available to defend Britain. For his succinctness in summing up a desperate situation to his call for vigilance against invasion and his final cry that Britain would fight until its last breath, this is a marvellous piece of oratory appealing to the very heart of patriotism. Out of a disaster – the defeat of the British army, the surrender of the Belgians and the defeat of the French – Churchill salvaged a sense of hope that the British would never surrender.

'...Nevertheless, our thankfulness at the escape of our Army and so many men, whose loved ones have passed through an agonizing week, must not blind us to the fact that what has happened in France and Belgium is a colossal military disaster...Turning once again, and this time more generally, to the question of invasion, I would observe that there has never been a period in all these long centuries of which we boast when an absolute guarantee against invasion, still less against serious raids, could have been given to our people. In the days of Napoleon the same wind which would have carried his transports across the Channel might have driven away the blockading fleet. There was always the chance, and it is that chance which has excited and befooled the imaginations of many Continental tyrants. Many are the tales that are told. We are assured that novel methods will be adopted, and when we see the originality of malice, the ingenuity of aggression, which our enemy displays, we may certainly prepare ourselves for every kind of novel stratagem and every kind of brutal and treacherous manoeuvre. I think that no idea is so outlandish that it should not be considered and viewed with a searching, but at the same time, I hope, with a steady eye. We must never forget the solid assurances of sea power and those which belong to air power if it can be locally exercised.

I have, myself, full confidence that if all do their duty, if nothing is neglected, and if the best arrangements are made, as they are being made, we shall prove ourselves once again able to defend our Island home, to ride out the storm of war, and to outlive the menace of tyranny, if necessary for years, if necessary alone. At any rate, that is what we are going to try to do. That is the resolve of His Majesty's Government – every man of them. That is the will of Parliament and the nation. The British Empire and the French Republic, linked together in their cause and in their need, will defend to the death their native soil, aiding each other like good comrades to the utmost of their strength. Even though large tracts of Europe and many old and famous States have fallen or may fall into the grip of the Gestapo and all the odious apparatus of Nazi rule, we shall not flag or fail. We shall go on to the end, we shall fight in France, we shall fight on the seas and oceans, we shall fight with growing confidence and growing strength in the air, we shall defend our Island, whatever the cost may be, we shall fight on the beaches, we shall fight on the landing grounds, we shall fight in the fields and in the streets, we shall fight in the hills; we shall never surrender, and even if, which I do not for a moment believe, this Island or a large part of it were subjugated and starving, then our Empire beyond the seas, armed and guarded by the British Fleet, would carry on the struggle, until, in God's good time, the New World, with all its power and might, steps forth to the rescue and the liberation of the old.'

# SIR WINSTON LEONARD SPENCER CHURCHILL
## 30 November 1874 – 24 January 1965

---

### 'This was their finest hour'
### 18 June 1940

**It is difficult to overestimate the magnificence** of Churchill's oratory in raising the nation's spirits in times of utter disaster – enduring defeats, being bombed, with no apparent prospect of victory. Britain was now fighting alone, with its Commonwealth allies, against the greatest army the world had seen. As usual, he begins with the bad news, but reminds the nation that there were unremitting setbacks for the first four years of the First World War. He is preparing people for a long war, with eventual victory, and his closing sentences are among the most emotionally moving and inspiring in the history of language. He makes the case for Britain and the Commonwealth defending the foundations of civilization against a new Dark Age.

'...If Hitler can bring under his despotic control the industries of the countries he has conquered, this will add greatly to his already vast armament output. On the other hand, this will not happen immediately, and we are now assured of immense, continuous and increasing support in supplies and munitions of all kinds from the United States; and especially of aeroplanes and pilots from the Dominions and across the oceans coming from regions which are beyond the reach of enemy bombers. I do not see how any of these factors can operate to our detriment on balance before the winter comes; and the winter will impose a strain upon the Nazi regime, with almost all Europe writhing and starving under its cruel heel, which, for all their ruthlessness, will run them very hard. We must not forget that from the moment when we declared war on the 3rd September it was always possible for Germany to turn all her Air Force upon this country, together with any other devices of invasion she might conceive, and that France could have done little or nothing to prevent her doing so. We have, therefore, lived under this danger, in principle and in a slightly modified form, during all these months. In the meanwhile, however, we have enormously improved our methods of defence, and we have learned what we had no right to assume at the beginning, namely, that the individual aircraft and the individual British pilot have a sure and definite superiority. Therefore, in casting up this dread balance sheet and contemplating our dangers with a disillusioned eye, I see great reason for intense vigilance and exertion, but none whatever for panic or despair.

During the first four years of the last war the Allies experienced nothing but disaster and disappointment. That was our constant fear: one blow after another, terrible losses, frightful dangers. Everything miscarried. And yet at the end of those four years the morale of the Allies was higher than that of the Germans, who had moved from one aggressive triumph to another, and who stood everywhere triumphant invaders of the lands into which they had broken. During that war we repeatedly asked ourselves the question: How are we going to win? And no one was able ever to answer it with much precision, until at the end, quite suddenly, quite unexpectedly, our terrible foe collapsed before us, and we were so glutted with victory that in our folly we threw it away.

...However matters may go in France or with the French Government, or other French Governments, we in this Island and in the British Empire will never lose our sense of comradeship with the French people. If we are now called upon to endure what they have been suffering, we shall emulate their courage, and if final victory rewards our toils they shall share the gains, aye, and freedom shall be restored to all. We abate nothing of our just demands; not one jot or tittle do we recede. Czechs, Poles, Norwegians, Dutch, Belgians have joined their causes to our own. All these shall be restored. What General Weygand called the Battle of France is over. I expect that the Battle of Britain is about to begin. Upon this battle depends the survival of Christian civilization. Upon it depends our own British life, and the long continuity of our institutions and our Empire. The whole fury and might of the enemy must very soon be turned on us. Hitler knows that he will have to break us in this Island or lose the war. If we can stand up to him, all Europe may be free and the life of the world may move forward into broad, sunlit uplands. But if we fail, then the whole world, including the United States, including all that we have known and cared for, will sink into the abyss of a new Dark Age made more sinister, and perhaps more protracted, by the lights of perverted science. Let us therefore brace ourselves to our duties, and so bear ourselves that, if the British Empire and its Commonwealth last for a thousand years, men will still say, "This was their finest hour".'

# SIR WINSTON LEONARD SPENCER CHURCHILL
## 30 November 1874 – 24 January 1965

*'Never in the field of human conflict was so much owed*
*by so many to so few'*
20 August 1940

**Here Churchill praises the RAF** in the middle of its dogged defence of the homeland in 'the Battle of Britain', which took place in the skies above England from 10 July to 17 September 1940. Hitler wanted control of the airspace over the English Channel to launch Operation Sealion, which was his plan to invade Britain. Germany had 1,600 serviceable warplanes in northwest France, facing 660 serviceable aircraft in Britain. By 17 September, Britain had lost 550 planes, its airfields were almost all destroyed, but the Luftwaffe had lost 1,000 aircraft, and Hitler called off the invasion, deciding to target the Soviet Union instead. Around this time, Churchill disclosed to colleagues that if Germany invaded, he would close his speech with *'The hour has come. Kill the Hun'*. Yet again, here Churchill dredges hope from overwhelmingly bad news, in that this war is somehow better suited to British arms than the mass slaughter of the First World War – *'this new kind of war is well suited to the genius and the resources of the British nation and the British Empire'*. Again the speech begins with bad news – Britain is alone against the might of the Axis – but Churchill goes on to tell the people about the wonderful advances in British military and naval strength, and that Britain can *'out-produce'* its enemies. Churchill tells his people that there are *'solid grounds for the confidence which we feel'*, that sea power makes invasion almost impossible, and ends by informing the nation of deals being made with the mighty United States for the defence of the free world. As was the case in 1917, people knew that if America could be persuaded to join the war, Hitler and Mussolini could yet be defeated.

'...Hitler is now sprawled over Europe. Our offensive springs are being slowly compressed, and we must resolutely and methodically prepare ourselves for the campaigns of 1941 and 1942...The enemy is, of course, far more numerous than we are. But our new production already, as I am advised, largely exceeds his, and the American production is only just beginning to flow in. It is a fact, as I see from my daily returns, that our bomber and fighter strength now, after all this fighting, are larger than they have ever been. We believe that we shall be able to continue the air struggle indefinitely and as long as the enemy pleases, and the longer it continues the more rapid will be our approach, first towards that parity, and then into that superiority in the air, upon which in a large measure the decision of the war depends. The gratitude of every home in our Island, in our Empire, and indeed throughout the world, except in the abodes of the guilty, goes out to the British airmen who, undaunted by odds, unwearied in their constant challenge and mortal danger, are turning the tide of the world war by their prowess and by their devotion. Never in the field of human conflict was so much owed by so many to so few.

All hearts go out to the fighter pilots, whose brilliant actions we see with our own eyes day after day; but we must never forget that all the time, night after night, month after month, our bomber squadrons travel far into Germany, find their targets in the darkness by the highest navigational skill, aim their attacks, often under the heaviest fire, often with serious loss, with deliberate careful discrimination, and inflict shattering blows upon the whole of the technical and war-making structure of the Nazi power. On no part of the Royal Air Force does the weight of the war fall more heavily than on the daylight bombers who will play an invaluable part in the case of invasion and whose unflinching zeal it has been necessary in the meanwhile on numerous occasions to restrain...I have no hesitation in saying that this process of bombing the military industries and communications of Germany and the air bases and storage depots from which we are attacked, which process will continue upon an ever-increasing scale until the end of the war, and may in another year attain dimensions hitherto undreamed of, affords one at least of the most certain, if not the shortest, of all the roads to victory.... The right to guide the course of world history is the noblest prize of victory. We are still toiling up the hill; we have not yet reached the crest-line of it; we cannot survey the landscape or even imagine what its condition will be when that longed-for morning comes. The task which lies before us immediately is at once more practical, more simple and more stern. I hope – indeed I pray – that we shall not be found unworthy of our victory if after toil and tribulation it is granted to us. For the rest, we have to gain the victory. That is our task.'

# FRANKLIN DELANO ROOSEVELT
## 30 January 1882 – 12 April 1945

*'Freedom means the supremacy of human rights everywhere'*
6 January 1941

**This State of the Union speech** on 'four freedoms', delivered to the 77th Congress of the United States, prepared America for Roosevelt's mission to help the Allied cause in the Second World War. His inclusion of the latter two freedoms went beyond traditional values protected by the First Amendment, endorsing a right to economic security and an internationalist perspective on foreign policy. This concept of the *Four Freedoms* became part of the mission undertaken by Eleanor Roosevelt with regard to her inspiration for the United Nations Declaration of Human Rights of 1948. It reads: *'Whereas disregard and contempt for human rights have resulted in barbarous acts which have outraged the conscience of mankind, and the advent of a world in which human beings shall enjoy freedom of speech and belief and freedom from fear and want has been proclaimed the highest aspiration of the common people...'*. With this speech Roosevelt had roused the American public, military and politicians into an expectation of war, and threw America's might firmly behind the Allies. On 7 December 1941, the Japanese attacked the United States naval base at Pearl Harbor.

'I address you, the members of this new Congress, at a moment unprecedented in the history of the union. I use the word "unprecedented" because at no previous time has American security been as seriously threatened from without as it is today...I suppose that every realist knows that the democratic way of life is at this moment being directly assailed in every part of the world – assailed either by arms – or by secret spreading of poisonous propaganda by those who seek to destroy unity and promote discord in nations that are still at peace. During 16 long months this assault has blotted out the whole pattern of democratic life in an appalling number of independent nations, great and small. And the assailants are still on the march, threatening other nations, great and small...Armed defense of democratic existence is now being gallantly waged in four continents. If that defense fails, all the population and all the resources of Europe and Asia, and Africa and Australasia will be dominated by conquerors. And let us remember that the total of those populations in those four continents, the total of those populations and their resources greatly exceed the sum total of the population and the resources of the whole of the western hemisphere – yes, many times over...the future of all the American Republics is today in serious danger. That is why this annual message to the Congress is unique in our history. That is why every member of the executive branch of the government and every member of the Congress face great responsibility, great accountability. The need of the moment is that our actions and our policy should be devoted primarily – almost exclusively – to meeting this foreign peril. For all our domestic problems are now a part of the great emergency. Just as our national policy in internal affairs has been based upon a decent respect for the rights and the dignity of all our fellow men within our gates, so our national policy in foreign affairs has been based on a decent respect for the rights and the dignity of all nations, large and small. And the justice of morality must and will win in the end...Let us say to the democracies: "We Americans are vitally concerned in your defense of freedom. We are putting forth our energies, our resources, and our organizing powers to give you the strength to regain and maintain a free world. We shall send you in ever-increasing numbers, ships, planes, tanks, guns. That is our purpose and our pledge."...

In the future days, which we seek to make secure, we look forward to a world founded upon four essential human freedoms. The first is freedom of speech and expression – everywhere in the world. The second is freedom of every person to worship God in his own way – everywhere in the world. The third is freedom from want, which, translated into world terms, means economic understandings which will secure to every nation a healthy peacetime life for its inhabitants – everywhere in the world. The fourth is freedom from fear, which, translated into world terms, means a world-wide reduction of armaments to such a point and in such a thorough fashion that no nation will be in a position to commit an act of physical aggression against any neighbor – anywhere in the world...This nation has placed its destiny in the hands and heads and hearts of its millions of free men and women, and its faith in freedom under the guidance of God. Freedom means the supremacy of human rights everywhere. Our support goes to those who struggle to gain those rights and keep them. Our strength is our unity of purpose. To that high concept there can be no end save victory.'

# HAROLD LECLAIR ICKES
## 3 March 1874 – 3 February 1952

*What is an American?*

18 May 1941

**Harold Ickes was the longest-serving** US secretary of the interior, from 1933 to 1946, and was responsible for implementing much of Roosevelt's 'New Deal'. A superb orator, he was often used by the administration to rebut the radio broadcasts of John L. Lewis and the United Mine Workers. He fought against segregation, and in 1938 he proposed offering Alaska as a *'haven for Jewish refugees from Germany and other areas in Europe where the Jews are subjected to oppressive restrictions'*. He strongly influenced the United States's entrance into the Second World War, and his remarkable speech was delivered during an *'I am an American Day'* meeting in New York's Central Park. At the time, Hitler looked like achieving world domination, after Austria, Czechoslovakia, Poland, Norway, Denmark, France, Belgium, Luxembourg, the Netherlands and areas in North Africa had all fallen to the Nazis. Britain was suffering from repeated air raids and her merchant shipping was under immense pressure in supplying the country and its war effort. However, there was a strong pacifist movement in the USA, and effective anti-democratic Fascist propaganda was making some decision-makers look with favour at the rise of Fascism. Ickes countered that propaganda, defined what it means to be a free American, and offered a damning assessment of the future the United States would face standing alone against a victorious Hitler. He exhorted America to join the battle for freedom before it was too late during the heated debate over open American support for the Allies. Seven months later, on 8 December 1941, thankfully the United States entered the war.

'...I say that it is time for the great American people to raise its voice and cry out in mighty triumph what it is to be an American. And why it is that only Americans, with the aid of our brave allies – yes, let's call them "allies" – the British, can and will build the only future worth having. I mean a future, not of concentration camps, not of physical torture and mental straitjackets, not of sawdust bread or of sawdust Caesars – I mean a future when free men will live free lives in dignity and in security. This tide of the future, the democratic future, is ours. It is ours if we show ourselves worthy of our culture and of our heritage. But make no mistake about it; the tide of the democratic future is not like the ocean tide – regular, relentless, and inevitable. Nothing in human affairs is mechanical or inevitable. Nor are Americans mechanical. They are very human indeed. What constitutes an American? Not color nor race nor religion. Not the pedigree of his family nor the place of his birth. Not the coincidence of his citizenship. Not his social status nor his bank account. Not his trade nor his profession. An American is one who loves justice and believes in the dignity of man. An American is one who will fight for his freedom and that of his neighbor. An American is one who will sacrifice property, ease and security in order that he and his children may retain the rights of free men. An American is one in whose heart is engraved the immortal second sentence of the Declaration of Independence. Americans have always known how to fight for their rights and their way of life. Americans are not afraid to fight. They fight joyously in a just cause.

We Americans know that freedom, like peace, is indivisible. We cannot retain our liberty if three-fourths of the world is enslaved. Brutality, injustice and slavery, if practiced as dictators would have them, universally and systematically, in the long run would destroy us as surely as a fire raging in our nearby neighbor's house would burn ours if we didn't help to put out his. If we are to retain our own freedom, we must do everything within our power to aid Britain. We must also do everything to restore to the conquered peoples their freedom. This means the Germans too. Such a program, if you stop to think, is selfishness on our part. It is the sort of enlightened selfishness that makes the wheels of history go around. It is the sort of enlightened selfishness that wins victories. Do you know why? Because we cannot live in the world alone, without friends and without allies. If Britain should be defeated, then the totalitarian undertaker will prepare to hang crepe on the door of our own independence. Perhaps you wonder how this could come about? Perhaps you have heard "them" the wavers of the future cry, with calculated malice, that even if Britain were defeated we could live alone and defend ourselves single handed, even against the whole world...We would have to live perpetually as an armed camp, maintaining a huge standing army, a gigantic air force, two vast navies. And we could not do this without endangering our freedom, our democracy, our way of life...'

# VYACHESLAV MIKHAILOVICH MOLOTOV
## 9 March 1890 – 8 November 1986

*'This war has been forced upon us'*
22 June 1941

**A leading politician and protégé of Stalin** from the 1920s, Molotov played a ruthless part in the 'Great Terror', and was the main Soviet signatory of the Nazi–Soviet Non-Aggression Pact of 1939, also known as the Molotov–Ribbentrop Pact. Just two weeks after the Pact was signed, Hitler's armies invaded Poland. Then, in accordance with a secret protocol in the Pact, the Russians themselves invaded Poland from the east and the country was divided up between the Nazis and the Soviets. However, with Europe crushed and Britain too difficult to invade, in June 1941 Hitler surprised Stalin by turning the tables and invading the Soviet Union, declaring a 'war of annihilation'. Molotov announced the attack in a radio broadcast to the Soviet people, and afterwards played a similar role to Churchill in uplifting morale by radio broadcasts throughout the war. He immediately conducted urgent negotiations with Britain (after ignoring past pleas for assistance) and also travelled to the United States as foreign minister, cementing wartime alliances there. He was responsible for post-war negotiations, but was dismissed from the Presidium (Politburo) of the Central Committee by Nikita Khruschev in 1957, as Molotov was the most senior of Stalin's colleagues still alive.

'Citizens of the Soviet Union: The Soviet Government and its head, Comrade Stalin, have authorized me to make the following statement: Today at 4 o'clock a.m., without any claims having been presented to the Soviet Union, without a declaration of war, German troops attacked our country, attacked our borders at many places and bombed with their aircraft our cities; Zhitomir, Kiev, Sevastopol, Kaunas and some others, killing and wounding over 200 persons. There were also enemy air raids and artillery shelling from Rumanian and Finnish territory. This unheard-of attack upon our country is treachery unparalleled in the history of civilized nations. The attack on our country was undertaken despite the fact that a treaty of non-aggression had been signed between the USSR and Germany and that the Soviet Government most faithfully abided by all the provisions of this treaty. The attack upon our country was perpetrated despite the fact that during the entire period of operation of this treaty, the German government could not find grounds for a single complaint against the USSR with regard to observance of this treaty. Entire responsibility for this predatory attack upon the Soviet Union lies fully and completely with Germany's Fascist rulers. At 5:30 a.m. – that is, after the attack had already been perpetrated, Von der Schulenburg, the German ambassador in Moscow, on behalf of his government made the statement to me as People's Commissar of Foreign Affairs to the effect that the German Government had decided to launch war against the USSR in response to the concentration of Red Army units near the eastern German frontier...Now that the attack on the Soviet Union has already been committed, the Soviet Government has ordered our troops to repulse the predatory assault and to drive German troops from the borders of our country.

This war has been forced upon us, not by the German people, not by German workers, peasants and intellectuals, whose sufferings we well understand, but by the clique of bloodthirsty Fascist rulers of Germany who have enslaved Frenchmen, Czechs, Poles, Serbians, Norway, Belgium, Denmark, Holland, Greece and other nations. The government of the Soviet Union expresses its unshakeable confidence that our valiant army and navy and brave falcons of the Soviet Air Force will acquit themselves honourably in performing their duty to the fatherland and to the Soviet people, and will inflict a crushing blow upon the aggressor. This is not the first time that our people have had to deal with an attack by an arrogant foe. At the time of Napoleon's invasion of Russia our people's reply was war for the fatherland, and Napoleon was defeated and met his fate. It will be the same with Hitler, who in his arrogance has proclaimed a new crusade against our country. The Red Army and our whole people will again wage victorious war for the fatherland, for our country, for honour, for liberty. The government of the Soviet Union expresses the firm conviction that the entire population of our country, all workers, peasants and intellectuals, men and women, will perform their duties and do their work conscientiously. Our whole people must now stand solid and united as never before. Each one of us must demand of himself and of others discipline, organization and self-denial worthy of real Soviet patriots, in order to provide for all the needs of the Red Army, Navy and Air Force, to ensure victory over the enemy. The government calls upon you, citizens of the Soviet Union, to rally still more closely around our glorious Bolshevist party, around our Soviet Government, around our great leader and comrade, Stalin. Ours is a righteous cause. The enemy shall be defeated. Victory will be ours.'

# JOSEPH VISSARIONOVICH STALIN
## 18 December 1878 – 5 March 1953

*'The war you are waging is a war of liberation, a just war'*
7 November 1941

**By the end of 1941, Russia had suffered** 4.3 million casualties and German forces had advanced 1,050 miles (1,700 km) in 18 weeks. The battle for Moscow began in October. Stalin addressed the crowds in Red Square to stoke up the people's will to fight for their homeland.

'Comrades, today we celebrate the 24th anniversary of the October Revolution in difficult conditions. The German bandits' treacherous attack and the war that they forced upon us have created a threat to our nation. We have temporarily lost a number of regions, and the enemy stands at the gates of Leningrad and Moscow. The enemy calculated that our army would be scattered at the very first blow and our country forced to its knees. But the enemy wholly miscalculated. Despite temporary reverses, our army and our navy are bravely fending off enemy attacks along the whole front, inflicting heavy losses, while our country – our whole country – has organized itself into a single fighting camp in order, jointly with our army and navy, to rout the German invaders. There was a time when our country was in a still more difficult situation. Recall the year 1918, when we celebrated the first anniversary of the October Revolution. At that time three-quarters of our country was in the hands of foreign interventionists. We had temporarily lost the Ukraine, the Caucasus, Central Asia, the Urals, Siberia and the Far East. We had no allies, we had no Red Army – we had only just begun to create it – and we suffered a shortage of bread, a shortage of arms, a shortage of equipment. At that time 14 states were ranged against our nation, but we did not become despondent or downhearted. In the midst of the fires of war we organized the Red Army and converted our country into a military camp. The spirit of the great Lenin inspired us at that time for the war against the interventionists. And what happened? We defeated the interventionists, regained all our lost territories and gained victory.

Today our country is in a far better position than it was 23 years ago. Today it is many times richer in industry, food and raw materials. Today we have allies who together with us form a united front against the German invaders. Today we enjoy the sympathy and support of all the peoples of Europe fallen under the yoke of Fascist tyranny. Today we have a splendid army and a splendid navy, defending the freedom and independence of our country with their lives. We suffer no serious shortage either of food or of arms or equipment. Our whole country, all the peoples of our country, are backing our army and our navy, helping them to smash the Nazi hordes. Our reserves in manpower are inexhaustible. The spirit of the great Lenin inspires us in our patriotic war today as it did 23 years ago. Is it possible, then, to doubt that we can and must gain victory over the German invaders? The enemy is not as strong as some terror-stricken pseudo-intellectuals picture him. The devil is not as terrible as he is painted. Who can deny that our Red Army has more than once put the much-vaunted German troops to fearful flight? If one judges by Germany's real position and not by the boasts of German propagandists, it is not hard to see that the Nazi German invaders are facing disaster.

Hunger and poverty reign in Germany. In four and a half months of war Germany has lost four and a half million soldiers. Germany is bleeding white; her manpower is expiring. A spirit of revolt is taking hold not only of the nations of Europe under the German invaders' yoke, but of the Germans themselves, who see no end to the war. The German invaders are straining their last forces. There is no doubt that Germany cannot keep up such an effort for much longer. Another few months, another half year, one year perhaps – and Hitlerite Germany must collapse under the weight of its own crimes. Comrades, Red Army and Red Navy men, commanders and political instructors, men and women guerrillas! The whole world is looking to you as a force capable of destroying the brigand hordes of German invaders. The enslaved peoples of Europe under the yoke of the German invaders are looking to you as their liberators. A great mission of liberation has fallen to your lot.

Be worthy of this mission! The war you are waging is a war of liberation, a just war. Let the heroic images of our great ancestors – Alexander Nevsky, Dmitri Donskoi, Kusma Minin, Dmitri Pozharsky, Alexander Suvorov, Mikhail Kutuzov – inspire you in this war! Let the victorious banner of the great Lenin fly over your heads! Utter destruction to the German invaders! Death to the German armies of occupation! Long live our glorious motherland, her freedom and her independence! Under the banner of Lenin – onwards to victory!'

# BLESSED CARDINAL CLEMENS AUGUST, GRAF von GALEN
## 16 March 1878 – 22 March 1946

*'...mentally ill people in Germany have been deliberately killed and more will be killed in the future'*
3 August 1941

A German count, he was the Roman Catholic bishop of Münster, and consistently spoke out against the actions of the Third Reich. In 1941 von Galen gave a series of sermons protesting against Nazi policies on euthanasia, Gestapo terror, forced sterilizations and concentration camps. One Nazi official proposed that the bishop should be executed. On 13 July 1941, von Galen publicly attacked the Gestapo, disappearances without trials, the closing of Catholic institutions and the fear blighting the lives of all honest Germans. In a second sermon, on 20 July 1941, he informed the faithful that all written protests against Nazi hostilities had been useless, and that members of religious orders were still being deported or jailed. In this third sermon von Galen complained of the continued desecration of Catholic churches, the closing of convents and monasteries, and the deportation and euthanasia of mentally ill people, usually inside prison camps. His sermons were reproduced and sent all over Germany, and to German soldiers on the western and eastern fronts. He was carefully monitored for the duration of the war, but escaped execution, probably because of the effect this would have had on the morale of German Catholic troops. Von Galen was made a cardinal in Rome in February 1946, and died a few days after his return to Germany, from an appendix infection.

> '...I am reliably informed that lists are also being drawn up in the asylums of the province of Westphalia of those patients who are to be taken away as so-called "unproductive national comrades" and soon to be killed. The first transport left the Marienthal institution near Münster during this past week...Those patients who are destined to be killed are transported from home to a distant asylum presumably in order to protect those who deliberately kill those poor people, members of our families, from the legal punishment. Some sickness is then given as the cause of death. Since the corpse has been burnt straight away, the relatives and also the police are unable to establish whether the sickness really happened and what the cause of death was. However, I have been assured that the Reich Interior Ministry and the office of the Reich Doctors' Leader, Dr Conti, make no bones about the fact that in reality a large number of mentally ill people in Germany have been deliberately killed and more will be killed in the future.'

# FRANKLIN DELANO ROOSEVELT
## 30 January 1882 – 12 April 1945

---

## 'A date which will live in infamy'
### 8 December 1941

**When the Second World War broke out** in 1939, the United States stayed out of the fighting, despite Prime Minister Churchill's constant appeals for America to save Western democracy. However, in March 1941 Roosevelt began Lend-Lease aid to Britain and its allies, which in turn stimulated the stagnant American economy. Japan's surprise attack on Pearl Harbor in Hawaii, without any declaration of war, followed the pattern of its previous foreign invasions of Russia, China and Korea during the 20th century. On 7 December 1941, the US Pacific Fleet was unexpectedly bombed by Japanese aircraft at Pearl Harbor, and 16 warships were damaged or sunk. Anti-war sentiment in the United States suddenly evaporated, and the country united behind Roosevelt. Three days after Roosevelt made this speech, Hitler declared war on the United States.

'Yesterday, December 7, 1941 – a date which will live in infamy – the United States of America was suddenly and deliberately attacked by naval and air forces of the Empire of Japan. The United States was at peace with that nation, and, at the solicitation of Japan, was still in conversation with its government and its Emperor looking toward the maintenance of peace in the Pacific...It will be recorded that the distance of Hawaii from Japan makes it obvious that the attack was deliberately planned many days or even weeks ago. During the intervening time the Japanese government has deliberately sought to deceive the United States by false statements and expressions of hope for continued peace...Yesterday the Japanese government also launched an attack against Malaya. Last night Japanese forces attacked Hong Kong. Last night Japanese forces attacked Guam. Last night Japanese forces attacked the Philippine Islands. Last night Japanese forces attacked Wake Island. This morning the Japanese attacked Midway Island. Japan has, therefore, undertaken a surprise offensive extending throughout the Pacific area. The facts of yesterday speak for themselves. The people of the United States have already formed their opinions and well understand the implication to the very life and safety of our nation. As commander in chief of the Army and Navy I have directed that all measures be taken for our defense. Always will we remember the character of the onslaught against us.'

# FRANKLIN DELANO ROOSEVELT
## 30 January 1882 – 12 April 1945

*'We are now in this war'*
9 December 1941

**On 7 December, the Japanese attacked** Pearl Harbor, on 8 December
the USA declared war on Japan, and on 9 December Roosevelt made this broadcast
to the American people. Two days later Japan's Axis allies Germany and Italy also
declared war against the USA.

'The sudden criminal attacks perpetrated by the
Japanese in the Pacific provide the climax of a decade
of international immorality. Powerful and resourceful
gangsters have banded together to make war upon the
whole human race. Their challenge has now been flung
at the United States of America. The Japanese have
treacherously violated the long-standing peace between
us. Many American soldiers and sailors have been killed
by enemy action. American ships have been sunk; American airplanes
have been destroyed. The Congress and the people of the United States
have accepted that challenge. Together with other free peoples, we are
now fighting to maintain our right to live among our world neighbors in
freedom and in common decency, without fear of assault. The course that
Japan has followed for the past ten years in Asia has paralleled the course
of Hitler and Mussolini in Europe and Africa. Today, it has become far
more than a parallel. It is collaboration so well calculated that all the
continents of the world, and all the oceans, are now considered by the
Axis strategists as one gigantic battlefield.

In 1931, Japan invaded Manchukuo – without warning. In 1935, Italy
invaded Ethiopia – without warning. In 1938, Hitler occupied Austria
– without warning. In 1939, Hitler invaded Czechoslovakia – without
warning. Later in 1939, Hitler invaded Poland – without warning.
In 1940, Hitler invaded Norway, Denmark, Holland, Belgium, and
Luxembourg – without warning. In 1940, Italy attacked France and
later – Greece – without warning. In 1941, the Axis Powers attacked
Yugoslavia and Greece and they dominated the Balkans – without
warning. In 1941, Hitler invaded Russia – without warning. And now
Japan has attacked Malaya and Thailand – and the United States –
without warning.

It is all of one pattern. We are now in this war. We are all in it – all the way. Every single man, woman, and child is a partner in the most tremendous undertaking of our American history. We must share together the bad news and the good news, the defeats and the victories – the changing fortunes of war...

We may acknowledge that our enemies have performed a brilliant feat of deception, perfectly timed and executed with great skill. It was a thoroughly dishonorable deed, but we must face the fact that modern warfare as conducted in the Nazi manner is a dirty business...Your Government knows that for weeks Germany has been telling Japan that if Japan did not attack the United States, Japan would not share in dividing the spoils with Germany when peace came. She was promised by Germany that if she came in she would receive the complete and perpetual control of the whole of the Pacific area – and that means not only the Far East, not only all of the islands in the Pacific, but also a stranglehold on the west coast of North, Central, and South America. We also know that Germany and Japan are conducting their military and naval operations in accordance with a joint plan, That plan considers all peoples and nations which are not helping the Axis powers as common enemies of each and every one of the Axis powers. That is their simple and obvious grand strategy. That is why the American people must realize that it can be matched only with similar grand strategy...The true goal we seek is far above and beyond the ugly field of battle. When we resort to force, as now we must, we are determined that this force shall be directed toward ultimate good as well as against immediate evil. We Americans are not destroyers – we are builders. We are now in the midst of a war, not for conquest, not for vengeance, but for a world in which this Nation, and all that this Nation represents, will be safe for our children. We expect to eliminate the danger from Japan, but it would serve us ill if we accomplished that and found that the rest of the world was dominated by Hitler and Mussolini. We are going to win the war and we are going to win the peace that follows. And in the dark hours of this day – and through dark days that may be yet to come – we will know that the vast majority of the members of the human race are on our side. Many of them are fighting with us. All of them are praying for us. For, in representing our cause, we represent theirs as well – our hope and their hope for liberty under God.'

# ADOLF HITLER
## 20 April 1889 – 30 April 1945

*'In September 1939 I assured you that neither force of arms
nor time would overcome Germany'*
Declaration of war against the USA, 11 December 1941

**This is said to be Hitler's greatest speech.** Already
at war with the Soviet Union, Britain and its allies, Hitler spoke
to the Reichstag in Berlin, just four days after the Japanese
attack on Pearl Harbor. This 88-minute address, which he had
written himself, was broadcast to the German nation. In it Hitler
recounted the reasons for the outbreak of war in September
1939, went on to explain why he had decided to strike against the
Soviet Union in June 1941, and reviewed the dramatic course of
the war thus far. Then he dealt at length with President Franklin
Roosevelt's 'hostile' policies towards Germany. Hitler detailed the increasingly
belligerent actions of Roosevelt's government. He then dramatically announced that
Germany was now joining Japan in war against the United States.

'...The German people and its soldiers are working and fighting today,
not only for the present, but for the future, nay the most distant,
generations. A historical revision on a unique scale has been imposed on
us by the Creator...But it is a fact that the two conflicts between Germany
and the USA were inspired by the same force and caused by two men
in the USA – Wilson and Roosevelt...The Three Powers have therefore
concluded the following Agreement, which was signed in Berlin today...
Germany, Italy and Japan will wage the common war forced upon them
by the USA and England with all the means of power at their disposal,
to a victorious conclusion...That the Anglo–Saxon–Jewish–Capitalist
World finds itself now in one and the same Front with Bolshevism does
not surprise us National Socialists: we have always found them together.
We have ended the struggle successfully inside Germany and have
destroyed our adversaries after 16 years of struggle for power. When,
23 years ago, I decided to enter political life and to lift this nation out of
its decline, I was a nameless, unknown soldier. Many among you know
how difficult the first few years of this struggle were. From the time
when the Movement consisted of seven men, until we took over power in
January 1933, the path was so miraculous that only Providence itself and
its blessing could have made this possible. Today I am at the head of the

strongest Army in the world, the most gigantic Air Force and of a proud Navy. Behind and around me stands the Party with which I became great and which has become great through me. The enemies I see before me are the same enemies as 20 years ago, but the path along which I look forward cannot be compared with that on which I look back. The German people recognizes the decisive hour of its existence, millions of soldiers do their duty, millions of German peasants and workers, women and girls, bake bread for the home country and produce arms for the Front. We are allied with strong peoples, who in the same need are faced with the same enemies....

You, my fellow party members, know my unflinching determination to pursue a fight once begun to its successful conclusion. You know my determination in such a struggle to be deterred by nothing, to break every resistance which must be broken. In September 1939 I assured you that neither force nor arms nor time would overcome Germany. I will assure my enemies that neither force of arms nor time nor any internal doubts can make us waver in the performance of our duty. When we think of the sacrifices of our soldiers, any sacrifice made by the Home Front is utterly unimportant. When we think of those who in past centuries have fallen for the Reich, then we realize the magnitude of our duty. But anybody who tries to evade this duty has no claim to be regarded in our midst as a fellow German. Just as we were unmercifully hard in our struggle for power, we shall be unmercifully hard in the struggle to maintain our nation. At a time when thousands of our best men are dying, nobody must expect to live who tries to undervalue the sacrifices made at the Front. No matter under what camouflage he tries to disturb this German Front, to undermine the resistance of our people, to weaken the authority of the regime, to sabotage the achievements of the Home Front, he shall die for it! But with the difference that this sacrifice brings the highest honour to the soldier at the Front, whereas the other dies dishonoured and disgraced. Our enemies must not deceive themselves – in the 2,000 years of our German history, our people have never been more united than today. The Lord of the Universe has treated us so well in the past years that we bow in gratitude to a providence which has allowed us to be members of such a great nation. We thank Him that we also can be entered with honour into the ever-lasting book of German history!'

# MOHANDAS KARAMCHAND GANDHI
## 2 October 1869 – 30 January 1948

*'I believe that in the history of the world, there has not been a more
genuinely democratic struggle for freedom than ours'*
8 August 1942

Gandhi was the leader of India's independence
movement, a pioneer of civil disobedience who believed in the
power of non-violence to achieve change. During the Second
World War, Britain desperately needed the citizens of its empire to
help in the war effort, and initially Gandhi favoured 'non-violent
moral support'. Other political leaders were offended by this
unilateral inclusion of India in the war, without consultation with
Congressional representatives, and all Congressmen resigned
from office. Gandhi declared that India could not be party to a war being fought
for democratic freedom, while freedom was denied to India itself. He drafted this
appeal for the British to quit India. Gandhi made it clear that India would not support
the war effort unless it was granted immediate independence. Almost the entire
Congress leadership was put into confinement less than 24 hours after Gandhi's
speech, and the greater number of the Congress leaders were to spend the rest of the
war in jail. '*Quit India*' became the most forceful movement in the history of the fight
for independence. Thousands of freedom fighters were killed or injured by police
gunfire, while hundreds of thousands were arrested. While in jail, Gandhi's wife –
also imprisoned – died in his arms. He was released before the end of the war on 6
May 1944 because of his failing health – for him to die in prison would cause further
civil unrest. At the end of the war, the British gave clear indications that power would
be transferred to Indian hands. Gandhi called off the struggle, and around 100,000
political prisoners were released, including the Congress's leadership.

'...Let me, however, hasten to assure that I am the same Gandhi as I was
in 1920. I have not changed in any fundamental respect. I attach the
same importance to non-violence that I did then. If at all, my emphasis
on it has grown stronger...I believe that in the history of the world,
there has not been a more genuinely democratic struggle for freedom
than ours. I read Carlyle's *French Revolution* while I was in prison, and
Pandit Jawaharlal has told me something about the Russian revolution.
But it is my conviction that inasmuch as these struggles were fought
with the weapon of violence they failed to realize the democratic ideal.
In the democracy which I have envisaged, a democracy established by

non-violence, there will be equal freedom for all. Everybody will be his own master. It is to join a struggle for such democracy that I invite you today. Once you realize this you will forget the differences between the Hindus and Muslims, and think of yourselves as Indians only, engaged in the common struggle for independence.

Then, there is the question of your attitude towards the British. I have noticed that there is hatred towards the British among the people. The people say they are disgusted with their behaviour. The people make no distinction between British imperialism and the British people. To them, the two are one. This hatred would even make them welcome the Japanese. It is most dangerous. It means that they will exchange one slavery for another. We must get rid of this feeling. Our quarrel is not with the British people, we fight their imperialism. The proposal for the withdrawal of British power did not come out of anger. It came to enable India to play its due part at the present critical juncture. It is not a happy position for a big country like India to be merely helping with money and material obtained willy-nilly from her while the United Nations are conducting the war. We cannot evoke the true spirit of sacrifice and valour, so long as we are not free. I know the British Government will not be able to withhold freedom from us, when we have made enough self-sacrifice. We must, therefore, purge ourselves of hatred. Speaking for myself, I can say that I have never felt any hatred. As a matter of fact, I feel myself to be a greater friend of the British now than ever before. One reason is that they are today in distress. My very friendship, therefore, demands that I should try to save them from their mistakes. As I view the situation, they are on the brink of an abyss. It, therefore, becomes my duty to warn them of their danger even though it may, for the time being, anger them to the point of cutting off the friendly hand that is stretched out to help them. People may laugh, nevertheless that is my claim. At a time when I may have to launch the biggest struggle of my life, I may not harbour hatred against anybody.'

# PAUL JOSEPH GOEBBELS
## 29 October 1897 – 1 May 1945

*'Now, people rise up and let the storm break loose!'*
18 February 1943

**The speech was delivered in the Sportpalast** in Berlin by Hitler's minister of propaganda and was broadcast to the German people by radio. Famed for his oratory, Goebbels was possibly Hitler's most faithful follower, an anti-Semite responsible for the *Kristallnacht* (Night of Broken Glass) attack on German Jews in 1938. After the total defeat of the German army at Stalingrad in February 1943, the tide was turning against Germany, and Goebbels intensified his propaganda efforts. In this speech he called for total war and further mobilization of troops. In Hitler's bunker in Berlin in 1945, as the Allies closed in, Hitler killed himself. Goebbels and his wife killed their six children before also committing suicide.

'Only three weeks ago I stood in this place to read the Führer's proclamation on the tenth anniversary of the seizure of power, and to speak to you and to the German people. The crisis we now face on the Eastern Front was at its height. In the midst of the hard misfortunes the nation faced in the battle on the Volga, we joined together in a mass meeting on the 30th of January to display our unity, our unanimity and our strong will to overcome the difficulties we faced in the fourth year of the war. It was a moving experience for me, and probably also for all of you, to be linked by radio with the last heroic fighters in Stalingrad during our powerful meeting here in the Sport Palace. They radioed to us that they had heard the Führer's proclamation, and perhaps for the last time in their lives joined us in raising their hands to sing the national anthems. What an example German soldiers have set in this great age! And what an obligation it puts on us all, particularly the entire German homeland! Stalingrad was and is fate's great alarm call to the German nation! A nation that has the strength to survive and overcome such a disaster, even to draw more strength from it, is unbeatable. In my speech to you and the German people, I shall remember the heroes of Stalingrad, who put me and all of us under a deep obligation. I do not know how many millions are listening to me over the radio tonight, at home and at the front. I want to speak to all of you from the depths of my heart to the depths of yours. I believe that all the German people have a passionate interest in what I have to say tonight. I will therefore speak with holy seriousness and openness, as the hour demands. The German people, raised, educated and disciplined by National Socialism, can bear the whole truth. It knows the gravity of the situation, and its leadership can therefore demand the necessary stern measures, yes even the sternest measures. We Germans are armed against weakness and uncertainty. The blows and misfortunes of the war only give us additional strength, firm resolve, and a spiritual and combative will to overcome all difficulties and obstacles with revolutionary élan...

The most powerful ally on earth, the people itself, stands behind us and is determined to follow the Führer, come what may. They will accept the heaviest burdens to achieve victory. What power on earth can stop us from reaching our goal? Now we must and will succeed! I stand before you not only as the spokesman of the government, but as the spokesman of the people...All the leaders of the party, the army and government join with us also...When the war began, we looked to the nation alone. That which serves its struggle for life is good and must be encouraged. What harms its struggle for life is bad and must be eliminated and cut out. With burning hearts and cool heads we will overcome the major problems of this phase of the war. We are on the road to final victory. That victory rests on our faith in the Führer. This evening I once again remind the whole nation of its duty. The Führer expects us to do deeds which will cast all we have done in the past into the shadows. We do not want to fail him. As we are proud of him, he should be proud of us. The great crises and upsets of national life show who the true men and women are. We have no right any longer to speak of the weaker sex, for both sexes are displaying the same determination and spiritual strength. The nation is ready for anything. The Führer has commanded, and we will follow him. In this hour of national reflection and contemplation, we believe firmly and unshakeably in victory. We see it before us, we need only to reach for it. We must resolve to subordinate everything to it. That is the duty of the hour. Let the slogan be: Now, people rise up and let the storm break loose!'

# GENERAL GEORGE SMITH PATTON JR
## 11 November 1885 – 21 December 1945

*'Americans love a winner'*
5 June 1944

## Commissioned in 1909, in the First World War

Patton was the first officer assigned to the new US Tank Corps, and he became a leading advocate of armoured warfare. In the Second World War, he commanded corps and armies in North Africa, Sicily and Europe, later falling out with Eisenhower over his (correct) fears of Soviet military aggression spreading across Europe. In 1944 he led the 3rd Army 100 miles (160 km) in 48 hours to relieve the French town of Bastogne during the Battle of the Bulge. This is part of his utterly brilliant final pep-talk in England to troops before the Normandy D-Day landings in June. One need not apologise for the language – the vernacular was used by 'Old Blood and Guts' Patton to empathize with his men.

'Men, this stuff that some sources sling around about America wanting out of this war, not wanting to fight, is a crock of bullshit. Americans love to fight, traditionally. All real Americans love the sting and clash of battle. You are here today for three reasons. First, because you are here to defend your homes and your loved ones. Second, you are here for your own self respect, because you would not want to be anywhere else. Third, you are here because you are real men and all real men like to fight. When you, here, everyone of you, were kids, you all admired the champion marble player, the fastest runner, the toughest boxer, the big league ball players, and the All-American football players. Americans love a winner. Americans will not tolerate a loser. Americans despise cowards. Americans play to win all of the time. I wouldn't give a hoot in hell for a man who lost and laughed. That's why Americans have never lost nor will ever lose a war; for the very idea of losing is hateful to an American...You are not all going to die. Only two percent of you right here today would die in a major battle. Death must not be feared. Death, in time, comes to all men. Yes, every man is scared in his first battle. If he says he's not, he's a liar. Some men are cowards but they fight the same as the brave men or they get the hell slammed out of them watching men fight who are just as scared as they are. The real hero is the man who fights even though he is scared. Some men get over their fright in a minute under fire. For some, it takes an hour. For some, it takes days. But a real man will never let his fear of death overpower his honor, his sense of duty to his country, and his innate manhood. Battle is the most magnificent competition in which a human being can indulge. It brings out all that is best and it removes all that is base. Americans pride themselves on being He-Men and they ARE *[emphasized]* He-Men. Remember that the enemy is just as frightened as you are, and probably more so. They are not supermen.

...We have the finest food, the finest equipment, the best spirit, and the best men in the world. *[Patton bent his head in contemplation before looking up and shouting.]* Why, by God, I actually pity those poor sons-of-bitches we're going up against. By God, I do. *[Prolonged applause]* My men don't surrender!...Sure, we want to go home. We want this war over with. The quickest way to get it over with is to go get the bastards who started it. The quicker they are whipped, the quicker we can go home. The shortest way home is through Berlin and Tokyo. And when we get to Berlin *[shouting]* I am personally going to shoot that paper-hanging son-of-a-bitch Hitler. Just like I'd shoot a snake!...From time to time there will be some complaints that we are pushing our people too hard. I don't give a good Goddamn about such complaints. I believe in the old and sound rule that an ounce of sweat will save a gallon of blood. The harder WE push, the more Germans we will kill. The more Germans we kill, the fewer of our men will be killed. Pushing means fewer casualties. I want you all to remember that. *[Pause]* There is one great thing that you men will all be able to say after this war is over and you are home once again. You may be thankful that 20 years from now when you are sitting by the fireplace with your grandson on your knee and he asks you what you did in the great World War II, you WON'T have to cough, shift him to the other knee and say, "Well, your Granddaddy shovelled shit in Louisiana." No, Sir, you can look him straight in the eye and say, "Son, your Granddaddy rode with the Great 3rd Army and a Son-of-a-God-damned-Bitch named Georgie Patton!"

# GENERAL DWIGHT DAVID EISENHOWER
## 14 October 1890 – 28 March 1969

*'The tide has turned. The free men of the world are*
*marching together to victory'*
6 June 1944

**A five-star general, Eisenhower was president** of the United States
from 1953–61. In the Second World War, as Supreme Commander of Allied Forces
in Europe, he was responsible for planning Operation Overlord, the invasion of
Western Europe on 6 June 1944. The success of the Normandy invasion was not
assured. Long after the successful landings on D-Day and the BBC broadcast of
Eisenhower's brief speech below, a second speech was found in a shirt pocket by one
of Eisenhower's aides. It read: *'Our landings in the Cherbourg–Havre area have failed
to gain a satisfactory foothold and I have withdrawn the troops. My decision to attack at
this time and place was based on the best information available. The troops, the air and the
Navy did all that bravery and devotion to duty could do. If any blame or fault attaches to
the attempt, it is mine alone.'* After an initial airborne assault, nearly 160,000 troops
crossed the English Channel in an amphibious attack on 6 June, and more than 3
million troops had landed by the end of August. Once the beachheads were secured,
a three-week military build-up took place on the beaches before Operation Cobra,
the strategy to break out from the Normandy beachhead. With another huge Allied
invasion advancing from the south of France, and Russian pressure from the east,
Germany was doomed.

'You will bring about the destruction of the German war machine, the
elimination of Nazi tyranny over the oppressed peoples of Europe, and
security for ourselves in a free world. Your task will not be an easy one.
Your enemy is well trained, well equipped, and battle-hardened. He will
fight savagely. But this is the year 1944. Much has happened since the
Nazi triumphs of 1940–1. The United Nations have inflicted upon the
Germans great defeat in open battle man to man. Our air offensive has
seriously reduced their strength in the air and their capacity to wage
war on the ground. Our home fronts have given us an overwhelming
superiority in weapons and munitions of war and placed at our disposal
great reserves of trained fighting men. The tide has turned. The free men
of the world are marching together to victory. I have full confidence in
your courage, devotion to duty, and skill in battle. We will accept nothing
less than full victory. Good luck, and let us all beseech the blessings of
Almighty God upon this great and noble undertaking.'

# PASTOR FRIEDRICH GUSTAV EMIL MARTIN NIEMÖLLER
## 14 January 1892 – 6 March 1984

*'First they came for the communists'*
1946

**A successful U-Boat officer** in the First World War, this Lutheran preacher was initially a supporter of Hitler. He became disenchanted with Nazi policies and eventually helped to found the Confessing Church – a Protestant group that opposed the Nazification of the German churches – along with Dietrich Bonhoeffer. Both Hitler and Rudolf Hess personally detested Niemöller. For his opposition, Niemöller was imprisoned in 1937, and was detained in the horrific Sachsenhausen and Dachau concentration camps from 1938–45. After his imprisonment, he expressed his deep regret about not having done enough to stir the 14,000 Protestant pastors before 1937 to help Hitler's victims. From 6 January 1946 he made a series of speeches to representatives of the Confessing Church in Frankfurt and to other congregations:

'God didn't ask me where I was from 1937 to 1945, he asked me where I was from 1933 to 1937. From 1933 to 1937 I didn't have an answer. Maybe I should have said: I was a brave pastor of the Confessing Church in those years, I risked speaking critically and thus risked freedom and my life? But God didn't ask me about all that. God asked: Where were you from 1933 to 1937, when human beings were being burned here? Those weren't my Christian brothers, who were burned there, those were Communists, Jehovah's Witnesses, etc. That's why I didn't do anything.'

A German professor was quoted in 1955 as saying: *'Pastor Niemöller spoke for thousands and thousands of men like me when he...said that, when the Nazis attacked the communists, he was rather uneasy, but, after all, he was not a communist, and so he did nothing; and then they attacked the socialists, and he was a little more uneasy, but, still, he was not a socialist, and he did nothing; and then the schools, the press, the Jews, and so on, and he was always uneasier, but still he did nothing. And then they attacked the Church, and he was a Churchman, and he did something – but by then it was too late.'*
From Niemöller's anguished self-blame arose the well-known lament:
*'First they came for the communists, and I did not speak out – because I was not a communist;*
*Then they came for the trade unionists, and I did not speak out – because I was not a trade unionist;*
*Then they came for the Jews, and I did not speak out – because I was not a Jew;*
*Then they came for me – and there was no one left to speak out for me.'*

# SIR WINSTON LEONARD SPENCER CHURCHILL
## 30 November 1874 – 24 January 1965

*'...an iron curtain has descended across the Continent'*
5 March 1946

**Less than a year after the end** of the Second World War, Churchill delivered this speech during which he coined the term 'Iron Curtain' to describe the line across Europe dividing the self-governing nations of the West from those in Eastern Europe under Soviet Communist control. Churchill gave the speech at Westminster College, in Fulton, Missouri, after receiving an honorary degree and he was introduced by Missourian, President Harry Truman.

'The United States stands at this time at the pinnacle of world power. It is a solemn moment for the American Democracy. For with primacy in power is also joined an awe-inspiring accountability to the future... All this means that the people of any country have the right, and should have the power by constitutional action, by free unfettered elections, with secret ballot, to choose or change the character or form of government under which they dwell; that freedom of speech and thought should reign; that courts of justice, independent of the executive, unbiased by any party, should administer laws which have received the broad assent of large majorities or are consecrated by time and custom. Here are the title deeds of freedom which should lie in every cottage home. Here is the message of the British and American peoples to mankind. Let us preach what we practise – let us practise what we preach...A shadow has fallen upon the scenes so lately lighted by the Allied victory. Nobody knows what Soviet Russia and its Communist international organization intends to do in the immediate future, or what are the limits, if any, to their expansive and proselytising tendencies. I have a strong admiration and regard for the valiant Russian people and for my wartime comrade, Marshal Stalin. There is deep sympathy and goodwill in Britain – and I doubt not here also – towards the peoples of all the Russias and a resolve to persevere through many differences and rebuffs in establishing lasting friendships. We understand the Russian need to be secure on her western frontiers by the removal of all possibility of German aggression. We welcome Russia to her rightful place among the leading nations of the world. We welcome her flag upon the seas. Above all, we welcome constant, frequent and growing contacts between the Russian people and our own people on both sides of the Atlantic. It is my duty however, for I am sure you would wish me to state the facts as I see them to you, to place before you certain facts about the present position in Europe.

From Stettin in the Baltic to Trieste in the Adriatic, an iron curtain has descended across the Continent. Behind that line lie all the capitals of the ancient states of Central and Eastern Europe. Warsaw, Berlin, Prague, Vienna, Budapest, Belgrade, Bucharest and Sofia, all these famous cities and the populations around them lie in what I must call the Soviet sphere, and all are subject in one form or another, not only to Soviet influence but to a very high and, in many cases, increasing measure of control from Moscow. Athens alone – Greece with its immortal glories – is free to decide its future at an election under British, American and French observation. The Russian-dominated Polish Government has been encouraged to make enormous and wrongful inroads upon Germany, and mass expulsions of millions of Germans on a scale grievous and undreamed-of are now taking place. The Communist parties, which were very small in all these Eastern States of Europe, have been raised to pre-eminence and power far beyond their numbers and are seeking everywhere to obtain totalitarian control. Police governments are prevailing in nearly every case, and so far, except in Czechoslovakia, there is no true democracy...The safety of the world requires a new unity in Europe, from which no nation should be permanently outcast. It is from the quarrels of the strong parent races in Europe that the world wars we have witnessed, or which occurred in former times, have sprung. Twice in our own lifetime we have seen the United States, against their wishes and their traditions, against arguments, the force of which it is impossible not to comprehend, drawn by irresistible forces, into these wars in time to secure the victory of the good cause, but only after frightful slaughter and devastation had occurred. Twice the United States has had to send several millions of its young men across the Atlantic to find the war; but now war can find any nation, wherever it may dwell between dusk and dawn. Surely we should work with conscious purpose for a grand pacification of Europe, within the structure of the United Nations and in accordance with its Charter. That I feel is an open cause of policy of very great importance. In front of the iron curtain which lies across Europe are other causes for anxiety...'

# GEORGE CATLETT MARSHALL
## 31 December 1880 – 16 October 1959

*'What must be done?'*
5 June 1947

**George Marshall was the US Army chief** of staff during the Second World War, and chief military adviser to President Roosevelt. He was much valued by Winston Churchill for his organizational capabilities. New president Harry Truman sent Marshall to China after the war to try and broker a peace between Mao Zedong's (Mao Tse-tung's) Communists and Jiang Jie Shi's (Chiang Kai-shek's) Nationalists, but he was not successful. Marshall was US secretary of state in 1947. The USA wanted Europe to be rapidly rebuilt after the destruction of the war years to prevent the spread of communism, and to increase trade and thereby world prosperity. In this speech at Harvard University, Marshall outlined the vital *European Recovery Program* to restore and modernize its economy in line with the American model of capitalism and enterprise. He wanted to call it the *Truman Plan*, but the President insisted that it was called the *Marshall Plan*. For his tremendous work, Marshall received the Nobel Peace Prize in 1953.

'...But to speak more seriously, I need not tell you that the world situation is very serious. That must be apparent to all intelligent people. I think one difficulty is that the problem is one of such enormous complexity that the very mass of facts presented to the public by press and radio make it exceedingly difficult for the man in the street to reach a clear appraisement of the situation. Furthermore, the people of this country are distant from the troubled areas of the earth and it is hard for them to comprehend the plight and consequent reactions of the long-suffering peoples, and the effect of those reactions on their governments in connection with our efforts to promote peace in the world. In considering the requirements for the rehabilitation of Europe, the physical loss of life, the visible destruction of cities, factories, mines, and railroads was correctly estimated, but it has become obvious during recent months that this visible destruction was probably less serious than the dislocation of the entire fabric of European economy. For the past ten years conditions have been abnormal. The feverish preparation for war and the more feverish maintenance of the war effort engulfed all aspects of national economies. Machinery has fallen into disrepair or is entirely obsolete. Under the arbitrary and destructive Nazi rule, virtually every possible enterprise was geared into the German war machine. Long-standing commercial ties, private institutions, banks, insurance companies, and shipping companies disappeared through loss of capital, absorption through nationalization, or by simple destruction. In many countries, confidence in the local currency has been severely shaken. The breakdown of the business structure of Europe during the war was complete. Recovery has been seriously retarded by the fact that two years after the close of hostilities a peace settlement with Germany and Austria has not been agreed upon. But even given a more prompt solution of these difficult problems, the rehabilitation of the economic structure of Europe quite evidently will require a much longer time and greater effort than has been foreseen...

Meanwhile, people in the cities are short of food and fuel, and in some places approaching the starvation levels. So the governments are forced to use their foreign money and credits to procure these necessities abroad. This process exhausts funds which are urgently needed for reconstruction. Thus a very serious situation is rapidly developing which bodes no good for the world. The modern system of the division of labor upon which the exchange of products is based is in danger of breaking down. The truth of the matter is that Europe's requirements for the next three or four years of foreign food and other essential products – principally from America – are so much greater than her present ability to pay that she must have substantial additional help or face economic, social, and political deterioration of a very grave character...It is logical that the United States should do whatever it is able to do to assist in the return of normal economic health in the world, without which there can be no political stability and no assured peace. Our policy is directed not against any country or doctrine but against hunger, poverty, desperation, and chaos. Its purpose should be the revival of a working economy in the world so as to permit the emergence of political and social conditions in which free institutions can exist. Such assistance, I am convinced, must not be on a piecemeal basis as various crises develop...

As I said more formally a moment ago, we are remote from the scene of these trouble...And yet the whole world of the future hangs on a proper judgment. It hangs, I think, to a large extent on the realization of the American people, of just what are the various dominant factors. What are the reactions of the people? What are the justifications of those reactions? What are the sufferings? What is needed? What can best be done? What must be done?'

# JAWARHARLAL NEHRU
## 14 November 1889 – 27 May 1964

*'The light has gone out of our lives'*
30 January 1948

'**Pandit' (Scholar) Nehru was India's** first prime minister, after independence was gained in 1947, and had long been a key player in the struggle for an independent India. He was the political heir to his mentor, Mahatma Gandhi. Gandhi had been the pioneer of mass civil disobedience, a course of non-violence to achieve independence for India, and his honorific '*Mahatma*' means Great Soul. In India he is known as '*Bapu*' (Father) and honoured as the Father of the Nation. On 30 January 1948, Gandhi was shot while having his nightly public walk in New Delhi. His assassin was a Hindu extremist who held Gandhi responsible for weakening India by insisting upon a payment to Pakistan after the partition of India into Muslim Pakistan and Hindu India, a partition that Gandhi never wanted. An emotional Nehru made this announcement to the Indian nation.

'Friends and Comrades, the light has gone out of our lives and there is darkness everywhere. I do not know what to tell you and how to say it. Our beloved leader, Bapu as we called him, the Father of the Nation, is no more. Perhaps I am wrong to say that. Nevertheless, we will never see him again as we have seen him for these many years. We will not run to him for advice and seek solace from him, and that is a terrible blow, not to me only, but to millions and millions in this country. And it is a little difficult to soften the blow by any other advice that I or anyone else can give you. The light has gone out, I said, and yet I was wrong. For the light that shone in this country was no ordinary light. The light that has illumined this country for these many years will illumine this country for many more years, and a thousand years later, that light will be seen in this country and the world will see it and it will give solace to innumerable hearts. For that light represented something more than the immediate past, it represented the living, the eternal truths, reminding us of the right path, drawing us from error, taking this ancient country to freedom.

All this has happened when there was so much more for him to do. We could never think that he was unnecessary or that he had done his task. But now, particularly, when we are faced with so many difficulties, his not being with us is a blow most terrible to bear. A madman has put an end to his life, for I can only call him mad who did it, and yet there has been enough of poison spread in this country during the past years and months, and this poison has had an effect on people's minds. We must face this poison, we must root out this poison, and we must face all the perils that encompass us, and face them not madly or badly, but rather in the way that our beloved teacher taught us to face them. The first thing to remember now is that none of us dare misbehave because he is angry. We have to behave like strong and determined people, determined to face all the perils that surround us, determined to carry out the mandate that our great teacher and our great leader has given us, remembering always that if, as I believe, his spirit looks upon us and sees us, nothing would displease his soul so much as to see that we have indulged in any small behaviour or any violence.

So we must not do that. But that does not mean that we should be weak, but rather that we should, in strength and in unity, face all the troubles that are in front of us. We must hold together, and all our petty troubles and difficulties and conflicts must be ended in the face of this great disaster. A great disaster is a symbol to us to remember all the big things of life and forget the small things of which we have thought too much. In his death he has reminded us of the big things of life, the living truth, and if we remember that, then it will be well with India...And while we pray, the greatest prayer that we can offer is to take a pledge to dedicate ourselves to the truth, and to the cause for which this great countryman of ours lived and for which he has died. That is the best prayer that we can offer him and his memory. That is the best prayer we can offer to India and ourselves.'

# HARRY S. TRUMAN
## 8 May 1884 – 26 December 1972

*'Democracy alone can supply the vitalizing force to stir the*
*peoples of the world into triumphant action'*
20 January 1949

**As vice-president, Truman had first taken** the presidential oath of office on 12 April 1945, upon the death of President Franklin D. Roosevelt. Truman's victory in the 1948 election was so unexpected, however, that many newspapers prematurely declared the Republican candidate, Governor Thomas E. Dewey of New York, the winner. Truman's inaugural address reaffirms American policy of relying on the Marshall Plan, stimulated trade and defence treaties and alliances to make the world safe for democracy.

'Almost a year ago, in company with 16 free nations of Europe, we launched the greatest cooperative economic program in history. The purpose of that unprecedented effort is to invigorate and strengthen democracy in Europe, so that the free people of that continent can resume their rightful place in the forefront of civilization and can contribute once more to the security and welfare of the world. Our efforts have brought new hope to all mankind. We have beaten back despair and defeatism. We have saved a number of countries from losing their liberty. Hundreds of millions of people all over the world now agree with us, that we need not have war – that we can have peace. The initiative is ours...In the coming years, our program for peace and freedom will emphasize four major courses of action. First, we will continue to give unfaltering support to the United Nations and related agencies, and we will continue to search for ways to strengthen their authority and increase their effectiveness. We believe that the United Nations will be strengthened by the new nations which are being formed in lands now advancing toward self-government under democratic principles. Second, we will continue our programs for world economic recovery. This means, first of all, that we must keep our full weight behind the European recovery program. We are confident of the success of this major venture in world recovery. We believe that our partners in this effort will achieve the status of self-supporting nations once again. In addition, we must carry out our plans for reducing the barriers to world trade and increasing its volume. Economic recovery and peace itself depend on increased world trade. Third, we will strengthen freedom-loving nations against the dangers of aggression. We are now working out with a number of countries a joint agreement designed to strengthen the security of the North Atlantic area. Such an agreement would take the form of a collective defense arrangement within the terms of the United Nations Charter. We have already established such a defense pact for the Western Hemisphere by the treaty of Rio de Janeiro. The primary purpose of these agreements is to provide unmistakable proof of the joint determination of the free countries to resist armed attack from any quarter. Each country participating in these arrangements must contribute all it can to the common defense...In addition, we will provide military advice and equipment to free nations which will cooperate with us in the maintenance of peace and security.

Fourth, we must embark on a bold new program for making the benefits of our scientific advances and industrial progress available for the improvement and growth of underdeveloped areas. More than half the people of the world are living in conditions approaching misery. Their food is inadequate. They are victims of disease. Their economic life is primitive and stagnant. Their poverty is a handicap and a threat both to them and to more prosperous areas. For the first time in history, humanity possesses the knowledge and the skill to relieve the suffering of these people. The United States is pre-eminent among nations in the development of industrial and scientific techniques. The material resources which we can afford to use for the assistance of other peoples are limited. But our imponderable resources in technical knowledge are constantly growing and are inexhaustible. I believe that we should make available to peace-loving peoples the benefits of our store of technical knowledge in order to help them realize their aspirations for a better life. And, in cooperation with other nations, we should foster capital investment in areas needing development. Our aim should be to help the free peoples of the world, through their own efforts, to produce more food, more clothing, more materials for housing, and more mechanical power to lighten their burdens...Democracy alone can supply the vitalizing force to stir the peoples of the world into triumphant action, not only against their human oppressors, but also against their ancient enemies – hunger, misery, and despair. On the basis of these four major courses of action we hope to help create the conditions that will lead eventually to personal freedom and happiness for all mankind...To that end we will devote our strength, our resources, and our firmness of resolve. With God's help, the future of mankind will be assured in a world of justice, harmony, and peace.'

# WILLIAM CUTHBERT FAULKNER
## 25 September 1897 – 6 July 1962

*'When will I be blown up?'*
10 December 1950

This is William Faulkner's acceptance speech for the 1949 Nobel Prize in Literature, after which award Faulkner belatedly began to be recognized as one of the most important writers in the history of American literature. As a boy, his family moved to Oxford, Mississippi, the small town that became the setting for much of his fiction. Faulkner never graduated from high school, never received a college degree, and lived in a small town in the poorest state in the nation, simultaneously balancing a growing family of dependents and impending financial ruin. During the Great Depression he wrote a series of novels all set in the same small southern county, including *As I Lay Dying*, *Light in August* and above all, *Absalom, Absalom!*, that would later be applauded as some of the greatest novels ever written by an American. In the 1940s Faulkner was invited by Howard Hawks to Hollywood to collaborate on film scripts, gaining some financial security at last. As well as novels he wrote short stories and poetry. Faulkner drank to excess, often while writing, saying that it helped to fuel his creative process. At the time of his speech, there was a worldwide fear about the threat of atomic warfare, and Faulkner addressed such emotions as they might impact young writers, reminding them of their duty to write whatever the circumstances.

'I feel that this award was not made to me as a man, but to my work – life's work in the agony and sweat of the human spirit, not for glory and least of all for profit, but to create out of the materials of the human spirit something which did not exist before. So this award is only mine in trust. It will not be difficult to find a dedication for the money part of it commensurate with the purpose and significance of its origin. But I would like to do the same with the acclaim too, by using this moment as a pinnacle from which I might be listened to by the young men and women already dedicated to the same anguish and travail, among whom is already that one who will some day stand where I am standing.

Our tragedy today is a general and universal physical fear so long sustained by now that we can even bear it. There are no longer problems of the spirit. There is only the question: When will I be blown up? Because of this, the young man or woman writing today has forgotten the problems of the human heart in conflict with itself which alone can make good writing because only that is worth writing about, worth the agony and the sweat. He must learn them again. He must teach himself that the basest of all things is to be afraid; and, teaching himself that, forget it forever, leaving no room in his workshop for anything but the old verities and truths of the heart, the universal truths lacking which any story is ephemeral and doomed – love and honor and pity and pride and compassion and sacrifice. Until he does so, he labors under a curse. He writes not of love but of lust, of defeats in which nobody loses anything of value, of victories without hope and, worst of all, without pity or compassion. His griefs grieve on no universal bones, leaving no scars. He writes not of the heart but of the glands.

Until he learns these things, he will write as though he stood among and watched the end of man. I decline to accept the end of man. It is easy enough to say that man is immortal simply because he will endure: that when the last ding-dong of doom has clanged and faded from the last worthless rock hanging tideless in the last red and dying evening, that even then there will still be one more sound: that of his puny inexhaustible voice, still talking. I refuse to accept this. I believe that man will not merely endure: he will prevail. He is immortal, not because he alone among creatures has an inexhaustible voice, but because he has a soul, a spirit capable of compassion and sacrifice and endurance. The poet's, the writer's, duty is to write about these things. It is his privilege to help man endure by lifting his heart, by reminding him of the courage and honor and hope and pride and compassion and pity and sacrifice which have been the glory of his past. The poet's voice need not merely be the record of man, it can be one of the props, the pillars to help him endure and prevail.'

# NELSON ROLIHLAHLA MANDELA
## 18 July 1918 –

*'No easy walk to freedom'*
ANC presidential address, 21 September 1953

**Mandela began fighting for civil rights** in South Africa after the 1948 election victory of the Afrikaner-dominated National Party, which actively legislated for racial segregation or *'apartheid'*. Mandela was president of the Youth League when the ANC (African National Congress) launched its *Campaign for the Defiance of Unjust Laws* in 1952, and was elected National Volunteer-in-Chief. The Defiance Campaign was a non-violent civil disobedience campaign, hoping to build on a core of selected volunteers and thereby involve more and more ordinary people, culminating in mass defiance of apartheid. Mandela travelled the country organizing resistance to discriminatory legislation. When brought to trial, he and 19 co-accused were shown to have consistently adopted a non-violent course of action. However, for his part in the Defiance Campaign, Mandela was convicted of contravening the Suppression of Communism Act. Mandela was given a suspended prison sentence, prohibited from attending gatherings and confined to Johannesburg for six months. At this time, Mandela was admitted to the profession of attorney, and opened South Africa's first black law firm in central Johannesburg in 1952. The authorities then demanded that the practice should be moved out of Johannesburg.

In 1953 Mandela was asked to prepare a plan to enable the leadership of the movement to maintain contact with its membership without recourse to public meetings. It was thought that the ANC would, like the Communist Party, be declared illegal and it wanted to be able to operate from underground. The plan outlined was known as the M-Plan, after Mandela. He had been elected as ANC Transvaal president earlier in the year, but had been served with a banning order, so his presidential address was therefore read on his behalf. Mandela played an important part in popularizing the Freedom Charter, which provided the foundation of the anti-apartheid cause, and was adopted by the Congress of the People in 1955. Having been banned again for two years in 1953, Mandela was not able to attend. During the whole of the 1950s, Mandela was the victim of various forms of repression. He was banned, arrested and imprisoned. A five-year banning order was enforced against him in March 1956. In later days he was to be incarcerated for 27 years, 18 of which he spent on Robben Island. The following is an extract from his speech:

'In June, 1952, the African National Congress and the South African Indian Congress, bearing in mind their responsibility as the representatives of the downtrodden and oppressed people of South Africa, took the plunge and launched the Campaign for the Defiance of the Unjust Laws...Factory and office workers, doctors, lawyers, teachers, students and the clergy; Africans, Coloureds, Indians and Europeans, old and young, all rallied to the national call and defied the pass laws and the curfew and the railway apartheid regulations. At the end of the year, more than 8,000 people of all races had defied. The Campaign called for immediate and heavy sacrifices. Workers lost their jobs, chiefs and teachers were expelled from the service, doctors, lawyers and businessmen gave up their practices and businesses and elected to go to jail. Defiance was a step of great political significance. It released strong social forces which affected thousands of our countrymen. It was an effective way of getting the masses to function politically; a powerful method of voicing our indignation against the reactionary policies of the Government. It was one of the best ways of exerting pressure on the Government and extremely dangerous to the stability and security of the State. It inspired and aroused our people from a conquered and servile community of yes-men to a militant and uncompromising band of comrades-in-arms. The entire country was transformed into battle zones where the forces of liberation were locked up in immortal conflict against those of reaction and evil...The cumulative effect of all these measures is to prop up and perpetuate the artificial and decaying policy of the supremacy of the white men. The attitude of the government to us is that: "Let's beat them down with guns and batons and trample them under our feet. We must be ready to drown the whole country in blood if only there is the slightest chance of preserving white supremacy."... You can see "that there is no easy walk to freedom anywhere, and many of us will have to pass through the valley of the shadow [of death] again and again before we reach the mountain tops of our desires." Dangers and difficulties have not deterred us in the past, they will not frighten us now. But we must be prepared for them like men in business who do not waste energy in vain talk and idle action. The way of preparation [for action] lies in our rooting out all impurity and indiscipline from our organization and making it the bright and shining instrument that will cleave its way to freedom.'

# ALBERT SCHWEITZER
14 January 1875 – 4 September 1965

## The Problem of Peace
Nobel Peace Prize acceptance speech, 4 November 1954

**Born near Strasbourg in Alsace**, Germany (now France), Schweitzer was called the greatest Christian of his time. By the time he was 21, Schweitzer had decided on his course for life. For nine years he would dedicate himself to the study of science, music and theology, then he would devote the rest of his life to serving humanity directly. He based this personal philosophy on 'reverence for life' and he possessed a deep commitment to serve humanity through thought and deeds. Before he was 30, Schweitzer was a respected writer on theology, an accomplished organist, and an authority on the life and works of Johann Sebastian Bach. In 1904 he was inspired to become a medical missionary after reading an evangelical paper regarding the needs of medical missions. He then studied medicine from 1905 to 1913 at the University of Strasbourg. Schweitzer also raised money to establish a hospital at Lambaréné in French Equatorial Africa (now Gabon), founding the hospital there in 1913. From 1924, except for relatively short periods of time, he spent the remainder of his life there, working tirelessly as doctor, surgeon, pastor and administrator. Over the years, because of his incessant fund-raising, it expanded and served thousands of Africans. In his 1933 autobiography, he wrote: '*What has been presented as Christianity during these nineteen centuries is only a beginning, full of mistakes, not full blown Christianity springing from the spirit of Jesus.*'

European visitors and journalists travelled to his hospital in the jungle, and were amazed to find patients sitting in the dust outside the hospital, cooking their own meals, and with goats and chickens everywhere. Schweitzer told them that the Africans would not have stayed in hospital beds, and they would not have eaten special hospital foods. Rather than chasing his patients away with 'modern conveniences', Schweitzer decided to treat the Africans in the only way they would accept. Since supplies of food were hard to obtain, the goats and chickens were the only source of meat and eggs. Schweitzer did not try to make sense of the terrible sufferings in Africa, saying: '*We cannot understand what happens in the universe. What is glorious in it is united with what is full of horror. What is full of meaning is united to what is senseless. The spirit of the universe is at once creative and destructive – it creates while it destroys and destroys while it creates, and therefore it remains to us a riddle. And we must inevitably resign ourselves to this.*' Shortly before she died, Schweitzer's wife asked him for how long he planned to stay in Africa. He replied, '*As long as I draw breath.*' For his many years of humanitarian efforts Schweitzer was awarded the 1952 Nobel Peace Prize. Schweitzer's lecture of acceptance, given two years later, is considered one of the best speeches of its kind ever made. With the $33,000 prize money, he built a leper hospital at Lambaréné.

'...Even today, we live in an age characterized by the absence of peace; even today, nations can feel themselves threatened by other nations; even today, we must concede to each nation the right to stand ready to defend itself with the terrible weapons now at its disposal. Such is the predicament in which we seek the first sign of the spirit in which we must place our trust. This sign can be none other than an effort on the part of peoples to atone as far as possible for the wrongs they inflicted upon each other during the last war. Hundreds of thousands of prisoners and deportees are waiting to return to their homes; others, unjustly condemned by a foreign power, await their acquittal; innumerable other injustices still await reparation. In the name of all who toil in the cause of peace, I beg the peoples to take the first step along this new highway. Not one of them will lose a fraction of the power necessary for their own defence. If we take this step to liquidate the injustices of the war which we have just experienced, we will instil a little confidence in all people. For any enterprise, confidence is the capital without which no effective work can be carried on. It creates in every sphere of activity conditions favouring fruitful growth. In such an atmosphere of confidence thus created we can begin to seek an equitable settlement of the problems caused by the two wars. I believe that I have expressed the thoughts and hopes of millions of men who, in our part of the world, live in fear of war to come. May my words convey their intended meaning if they penetrate to the other part of the world – the other side of the trench – to those who live there in the same fear. May the men who hold the destiny of peoples in their hands, studiously avoid anything that might cause the present situation to deteriorate and become even more dangerous...'

# NIKITA SERGEYEVICH KHRUSHCHEV
## 15 April 1894 – 11 September 1971

*'We must abolish the cult of the individual once and for all'*
25 February 1956

**The Soviet dictator Stalin had died in 1953**, and after a power struggle, Khrushchev became first secretary of the Communist Party (1953–64) and also premier (1958–64). Some of Khrushchev's ministers, including Molotov and Malenkov, opposed this speech that denounced Stalin as a monster, and managed to persuade Khrushchev to make it in a closed session, hence it became known as *'the Secret Speech'*. It took four hours to deliver to a shocked audience at the 20th Party Congress and was the first direct attack upon Stalin and his legacy. It caused a sensation across the Soviet Union and its satellites in Eastern Europe, and led to unrest in Czechoslovakia and Hungary. As part of his de-Stalinization policy, Khrushchev had released thousands of political prisoners from the gulag labour camps. His attack on Stalin paved the way for Gorbachev's later reforms and the freeing of Eastern Europe – the significance of this speech for world peace cannot be underestimated.

'Comrades! In the party central committee's report at the 20th congress and in a number of speeches by delegates to the congress much has been said about the cult of the individual. After Stalin's death, the central committee began explaining that it is alien to the spirit of Marxism–Leninism to elevate one person, to transform him into a superman endowed with supernatural characteristics, akin to those of a god. Such a man supposedly knows everything, sees everything, thinks for everyone, can do anything, is infallible in what he does. Such a belief about a man, and specifically about Stalin, was cultivated among us for many years... Comrades! The party congress should learn about new documents, which confirm Stalin's character...Stalin invented the concept of "enemy of the people". This term automatically rendered it unnecessary that the ideological mistakes of a man should be proven. It made possible the use of the cruellest repression, against anyone who disagreed with Stalin, against those who were only suspected of hostile intent, against those who had bad reputations. On the whole, the only proof of guilt actually used was the "confession" of the accused himself. "Confessions" were acquired through physical pressures. Innocent individuals – who in the past had defended the party line – became victims. Mass arrests and deportations of many thousands of people, execution without trial and without proper investigation created a climate of insecurity, fear and even desperation. Vladimir Ilyich demanded uncompromising dealings with the enemies of the revolution. Lenin used such methods, however, only against actual class enemies and not against those who made mistakes. Stalin, on the other hand, used extreme methods and mass repressions at a time when the revolution was already victorious...After Lenin's death, Stalin trampled on the principle of collective party leadership. Of the 139 members and candidates of the central committee who were elected at the 17th congress, 98 people, 70 per cent, were arrested and shot. It is inconceivable that a congress so composed could have elected a central committee in which a majority would prove to be enemies of the party. Delegates were active participants in the building of our socialist state; many of them suffered and fought during the pre-revolutionary years; they fought their enemies courageously and often nervelessly looked death in the face. How, then, can we believe that such people had joined the camps of the enemies of socialism? This was the result of Stalin's abuse of power.

...Stalin was a very distrustful man, sickly suspicious. He could look at a man and say: "Why are your eyes so shifty today?" or "Why are you turning so much today and not wanting to look me directly in the eyes?" The sickly suspicion created in him a general distrust. Everywhere and in everything he saw "enemies", "two-facers" and "spies"...Stalin sanctioned the most brutal violation of socialist legality, torture and oppression... The power accumulated in the hands of one person, Stalin, led to serious consequences during the great patriotic war...Comrades! We must abolish the cult of the individual once and for all. We must correct the views connected with the cult in history, philosophy and sciences, and continue systematically the work done by the party's central committee during the last years, a work characterized by collective leadership and self-criticism. Comrades! The 20th congress of the Communist Party of the Soviet Union has revealed with a new strength the unshakeable unity of our party, its cohesiveness around the central committee, its firm will to accomplish the great task of building communism. And the fact that we present in all their ramifications the basic problems of overcoming the cult of the individual shows the great moral and political strength of our party. We are absolutely certain that our party, armed with the historical resolutions of the 20th congress, will lead the Soviet people along the Leninist path to new successes, to new victories. Long live the victorious banner of our party – Leninism!'

# ANEURIN 'NYE' BEVAN
## 15 November 1897 – 6 July 1960

*'It will take us very many years to live down what we have done'*
5 December 1956

**Bevan was a Labour politician and** former minister, but in opposition when he made this speech against the Suez War. Tellingly, Conservative minister Selwyn Lloyd told Tam Dalyell MP that it was the *'greatest Commons performance'*, *'...and it was at my expense, because as Foreign Secretary, it had been my duty to speak before him and put the Government's case.'* The Anglo–French–Israeli attack on Suez in Egypt has many parallels with the recent invasion of Iraq. President Nasser of Egypt regretted Bevan's early death, as Bevan could see that the Western powers were, by their actions, forcing Arab states to join together against the West. Bevan was vilified by the press for much of his career, but he remains one of the few honest post-war British politicians.

'The speech to which we have just listened is the last of a long succession that the right honourable gentleman, the Secretary of State for Foreign Affairs, has made to the House in the last few months and, if I may be allowed to say so, I congratulate him upon having survived so far. He appears to be in possession of vigorous health, which is obviously not enjoyed by all his colleagues, and he appears also to be exempted from those Freudian lapses which have distinguished the speeches of the Lord Privy Seal, and therefore he has survived so far with complete vigour. However, I am bound to say that the speech by the right honourable gentleman today carries the least conviction of all. I have been looking through the various objectives and reasons that the government have given to the House of Commons for making war on Egypt, and it really is desirable that when a nation makes war upon another nation it should be quite clear why it does so. It should not keep changing the reasons as time goes on. There is, in fact, no correspondence whatsoever between the reasons given today and the reasons set out by the prime minister at the beginning. The reasons have changed all the time. I have got a list of them here, and for the sake of the record I propose to read it. I admit that I found some difficulty in organizing a speech with any coherence because of the incoherence of the reasons. They are very varied.

...I resent most bitterly this unconcern for the lives of innocent men and women. It may be that the dead in Port Said are 100, 200 or 300. If it is only one, we had no business to take it. Do honourable members begin to realize how this is going to revolt the world when it passes into the imagination of men and women everywhere that we – with eight million here in London, the biggest single civilian target in the world, with our crowded island exposed, as no nation in the world is exposed, to the barbarism of modern weapons – we ourselves set the example. We ourselves conscript our boys and put guns and aeroplanes in their hands and say, "Bomb there". Really, this is so appalling that human language can hardly describe it. And for what? The government resorted to epic weapons for squalid and trivial ends, and that is why, all through this unhappy period, ministers, all of them, have spoken and argued and debated well below their proper form – because they have been synthetic villains. They are not really villains. They have only set off on a villainous course, and they cannot even use the language of villainy. Therefore, in conclusion, I say that it is no use honourable members consoling themselves that they have more support in the country than many of them feared they might have. Of course they have support in the country. They have support among many of the unthinking and unreflective who still react to traditional values, who still think that we can solve all these problems in the old ways. Of course they have. Not all the human race has grown to adult state yet. But do not let them take comfort in that thought. The right honourable member for Woodford (Sir Winston Churchill) has warned them before. In the first volume of his *Second World War*, he writes about the situation before the war and he says this: "Thus an administration more disastrous than any in our history saw all its errors and shortcomings acclaimed by the nation. There was, however, a bill to be paid, and it took the new House of Commons nearly 10 years to pay it." It will take us very many years to live down what we have done. It will take us many years to pay the price. I know that tomorrow evening honourable and right honourable members will probably, as they have done before, give the government a vote of confidence, but they know in their heart of hearts that it is a vote which the government do not deserve.'

# MAURICE HAROLD MACMILLAN
## 10 February 1894 – 29 December 1986

### 'The wind of change'
3 February 1960

**Prime minister from 1957–63**, Macmillan's first and second governments deliberately encouraged the movement towards the independence of African nations from Britain, and the following speech made in Cape Town, South Africa on his African tour was a landmark in the strategy of decolonization. Despite considerable opposition from white minorities and British political and commercial interests, 12 countries quickly obtained independence under Macmillan. South Africa left the Commonwealth in 1961 to pursue its policy of apartheid, but its people now knew that Britain wholeheartedly disagreed with segregation, and that other members of the Commonwealth had achieved independence by democratic means.

'...As I've travelled around the Union I have found everywhere, as I expected, a deep preoccupation with what is happening in the rest of the African continent. I understand and sympathize with your interests in these events and your anxiety about them. Ever since the break up of the Roman empire one of the constant facts of political life in Europe has been the emergence of independent nations. They have come into existence over the centuries in different forms, different kinds of government, but all have been inspired by a deep, keen feeling of nationalism, which has grown as the nations have grown. In the 20th century, and especially since the end of the war, the processes which gave birth to the nation states of Europe have been repeated all over the world. We have seen the awakening of national consciousness in peoples who have for centuries lived in dependence upon some other power. Fifteen years ago this movement spread through Asia. Many countries there, of different races and civilizations, pressed their claim to an independent national life. Today the same thing is happening in Africa, and the most striking of all the impressions I have formed since I left London a month ago is of the strength of this African national consciousness. In different places it takes different forms, but it is happening everywhere. The wind of change is blowing through this continent, and whether we like it or not, this growth of national consciousness is a political fact. We must all accept it as a fact, and our national policies must take account of it. Well you understand this better than anyone, you are sprung from Europe, the home of nationalism, here in Africa you have yourselves created a free nation. A new nation. Indeed in the history of our times yours will be recorded as the first of the African nationalists. This tide of national consciousness which is now rising in Africa is a fact, for which both you and we, and the other nations of the Western world are ultimately responsible. For its causes are to be found in the achievements of Western civilization, in the pushing forwards of the frontiers of knowledge, the applying of science to the service of human needs, in the expanding of food production, in the speeding and multiplying of the means of communication, and perhaps above all and more than anything else in the spread of education.

As I have said, the growth of national consciousness in Africa is a political fact, and we must accept it as such. That means, I would judge, that we've got to come to terms with it. I sincerely believe that if we cannot do so we may imperil the precarious balance between the East and West on which the peace of the world depends. The world today is divided into three main groups. First there are what we call the Western Powers. You in South Africa and we in Britain belong to this group, together with our friends and allies in other parts of the Commonwealth. In the United States of America and in Europe we call it the Free World. Secondly there are the Communists – Russia and her satellites in Europe and China whose population will rise by the end of the next ten years to the staggering total of 800 million. Thirdly, there are those parts of the world whose people are at present uncommitted either to Communism or to our Western ideas. In this context we think first of Asia and then of Africa. As I see it the great issue in this second half of the 20th century is whether the uncommitted peoples of Asia and Africa will swing to the East or to the West. Will they be drawn into the Communist camp? Or will the great experiments in self-government that are now being made in Asia and Africa, especially within the Commonwealth, prove so successful, and by their example so compelling, that the balance will come down in favour of freedom and order and justice? The struggle is joined, and it is a struggle for the minds of men. What is now on trial is much more than our military strength or our diplomatic and administrative skill. It is our way of life. The uncommitted nations want to see before they choose.'

# PATRICE ÉMERY LUMUMBA
## 2 July 1925 – 17 January 1961

*'We are going to rule not by the peace of guns and bayonets
but by a peace of the heart and the will'*
30 June 1960

**This Congolese independence leader** was the first legally elected prime minister of the Republic of the Congo, after he helped the country win its independence from Belgium in June 1960. This is his Independence Day speech. Only ten weeks later, Lumumba's government was deposed in a coup and he was imprisoned, tortured and murdered with the direct assistance of Belgium, the USA and the United Nations. An honourable and respected man, the circumstances of his overthrow and death make horrific reading for all lovers of democracy, and have led to an ongoing bloodbath in the region ever since. This is possibly why he has been virtually airbrushed from history. Africa analysts believe that this speech was the spark that led to Lumumba's murder. The murderous President Joseph Mobutu handed Lumumba over to Moise Tshombe, the premier of the province of of Katanga, who killed him. Mobutu later took over the region, which he renamed Zaire. In 1968, Pierre Mulele, Lumumba's minister of education, was lured out of exile in Brazzaville on the assumption that he would be granted an amnesty, but he was instead tortured and killed by Mobutu. While Mulele was still alive, his eyes were gouged out, his genitals were ripped off and his limbs were amputated one by one. The whole central African region is corrupt and dangerous, and much of the ongoing problem stems from the West's callous treatment of Lumumba.

'...For this independence of the Congo, even as it is celebrated today with Belgium, a friendly country with whom we deal as equal to equal, no Congolese worthy of the name will ever be able to forget that it has been won by fighting, a day-to-day fight, an ardent and idealistic fight, a fight in which we were spared neither deprivation nor suffering, and for which we gave our strength and our blood. We are proud of this struggle, of tears, of fire, and of blood, to the core of our being, for it was a noble and just struggle, and indispensable to put an end to the humiliating slavery which was imposed upon us by force. This was our fate for 80 years of a colonial regime; our wounds are still too fresh and too painful for us to wipe them from our memory. We have known harassing work, exacted in exchange for salaries which did not allow us to eat enough to assuage our hunger, or to clothe ourselves, or to house ourselves decently, or to raise our children as creatures dear to us. We have suffered ironies, insults, blows that we endured morning, noon, and night, because we are Negroes...The Republic of the Congo has been proclaimed, and our country is now in the hands of its own children.

...We are going to show the world what the black man can do when he works in freedom, and we are going to make the Congo the focus of the sun's radiance for all of Africa. We are going to keep watch over the lands of our country so that they truly profit her children. We are going to restore ancient laws and make new ones which will be just and noble. We are going to put an end to suppression of free thought and see to it that all our citizens enjoy completely the fundamental liberties enshrined in the Declaration of the Rights of Man. We are going to do away with all discrimination of every variety and assure for each and all the position to which human dignity, work, and dedication entitles him. We are going to rule not by the peace of guns and bayonets but by a peace of the heart and the will...In conclusion, I ask you to respect unconditionally the life and the property of your fellow citizens and of foreigners living in our country. If the conduct of these foreigners leaves something to be desired, our justice will speedily expel them from the territory of the Republic; if, on the contrary, their conduct is good, they must be left in peace, for they also are working for our country's prosperity. The Congo's independence marks a decisive step towards the liberation of the entire African continent. Sire, Excellencies, Mesdames, Messieurs, my dear fellow countrymen, my brothers of race, my brothers of struggle – this is what I wanted to tell you in the name of the Government on this magnificent day that marks our complete independence. Our government, strong, national, popular, will be the health of our country. I call on all Congolese citizens, men, women and children, to apply themselves resolutely to the task of creating a prosperous national economy which will assure our economic independence. Glory to the fighters for national liberation! Long live independence and African unity! Long live the independent and sovereign Congo!'

# JOHN FITZGERALD KENNEDY
## 29 May 1917 – 22 November 1963

*'Ask not what your country can do for you –*
*Ask what you can do for your country'*
20 January 1961

**This is the superb inaugural address** of the 35th president, who served from 1961 until his assassination in 1963. After war service as commander of Motor Torpedo Boat PT-109, Kennedy was groomed by his father for a political career, becoming a Democratic congressional representative from 1947–53, then a senator until 1960, when he fought the presidential election. He defeated the incumbent vice-president Richard Nixon by the narrowest of margins (only 115,000 popular votes), becoming the second-youngest president (after Theodore Roosevelt) and the first Catholic president. Kennedy personified the youth and ambition of the United States, and listening to this speech, the nation felt that a new era and a 'new frontier' were being ushered in.

'Vice-President Johnson, Mr. Speaker, Mr. Chief Justice, President Eisenhower, Vice-President Nixon, President Truman, reverend clergy, fellow citizens, we observe today not a victory of party, but a celebration of freedom – symbolizing an end, as well as a beginning – signifying renewal, as well as change. For I have sworn before you and Almighty God the same solemn oath our forebears prescribed nearly a century and three-quarters ago. The world is very different now. For man holds in his mortal hands the power to abolish all forms of human poverty and all forms of human life. And yet the same revolutionary beliefs for which our forebears fought are still at issue around the globe – the belief that the rights of man come not from the generosity of the state, but from the hand of God. We dare not forget today that we are the heirs of that first revolution. Let the word go forth from this time and place, to friend and foe alike, that the torch has been passed to a new generation of Americans, born in this century, tempered by war, disciplined by a hard and bitter peace, proud of our ancient heritage and unwilling to witness or permit the slow undoing of those human rights to which this Nation has always been committed, and to which we are committed today at home and around the world. Let every nation know, whether it wishes us well or ill, that we shall pay any price, bear any burden, meet any hardship, support any friend, oppose any foe, to assure the survival and the success of liberty. This much we pledge and more...

All this will not be finished in the first 100 days. Nor will it be finished in the first 1,000 days, nor in the life of this administration, nor even perhaps in our lifetime on this planet. But let us begin. In your hands, my fellow citizens, more than mine, will rest the final success or failure of our course. Since this country was founded, each generation of Americans has been summoned to give testimony to its national loyalty. The graves of young Americans who answered the call to service surround the globe. Now the trumpet summons us again – not as a call to bear arms, though arms we need – not as a call to battle, though embattled we are – but a call to bear the burden of a long twilight struggle, year in and year out, "rejoicing in hope, patient in tribulation" – a struggle against the common enemies of man: tyranny, poverty, disease, and war itself. Can we forge against these enemies a grand and global alliance, North and South, East and West, that can assure a more fruitful life for all mankind? Will you join in that historic effort? In the long history of the world, only a few generations have been granted the role of defending freedom in its hour of maximum danger. I do not shrink from this responsibility – I welcome it. I do not believe that any of us would exchange places with any other people or any other generation. The energy, the faith, the devotion which we bring to this endeavor will light our country and all who serve it – and the glow from that fire can truly light the world. And so, my fellow Americans: Ask not what your country can do for you – Ask what you can do for your country. My fellow citizens of the world: ask not what America will do for you, but what together we can do for the freedom of man. Finally, whether you are citizens of America or citizens of the world, ask of us here the same high standards of strength and sacrifice which we ask of you. With a good conscience our only sure reward, with history the final judge of our deeds, let us go forth to lead the land we love, asking His blessing and His help, but knowing that here on earth God's work must truly be our own.'

# DOUGLAS MACARTHUR
## 26 January 1880 – 5 April 1964

*'Duty, Honor, Country'*
12 May 1962

**A veteran of the First World War**, General MacArthur served with distinction in the Second World War, and accepted the surrender of Japan, overseeing its occupation from 1945–51. He led the UN forces in the Korean War, repelling the North Korean invasion of the South, but was controversially removed from command by President Truman in 1951 for wishing to expand the war by attacking China. From 1960 his health deteriorated, and in a meeting with the new President Kennedy he was highly critical of the military advice concerning the abortive Bay of Pigs operation in Cuba. He also cautioned Kennedy and his successor Johnson about the build-up of arms in Vietnam, urging both to concentrate instead upon domestic policy. This brilliant speech made at the Military Academy at West Point was delivered by a frail MacArthur, aged 82, when he accepted the Sylvanus Thayer Award for outstanding service to the nation. It summarizes what he believed to be the necessary virtues, not just of a soldier, but of a citizen.

'...Duty, Honor, Country. Those three hallowed words reverently dictate what you ought to be, what you can be, what you will be. They are your rallying points: to build courage when courage seems to fail; to regain faith when there seems to be little cause for faith; to create hope when hope becomes forlorn. Unhappily, I possess neither that eloquence of diction, that poetry of imagination, nor that brilliance of metaphor to tell you all that they mean. The unbelievers will say they are but words, but a slogan, but a flamboyant phrase. Every pedant, every demagogue, every cynic, every hypocrite, every troublemaker, and, I am sorry to say, some others of an entirely different character, will try to downgrade them even to the extent of mockery and ridicule. Words with lasting impact – But these are some of the things they do. They build your basic character, they mold you for your future roles as the custodians of the nation's defense, they make you strong enough to know when you are weak, and brave enough to face yourself when you are afraid. They teach you to be proud and unbending in honest failure, but humble and gentle in success; not to substitute words for actions, nor to seek the path of comfort, but to face the stress and spur of difficulty and challenge; to learn to stand up in the storm but to have compassion on those who fall; to master yourself before you seek to master others; to have a heart that is clean, a goal that is high; to learn to laugh yet never forget how to weep; to reach into the future yet never neglect the past; to be serious yet never to take yourself too seriously; to be modest so that you will remember the simplicity of true greatness, the open mind of true wisdom, the meekness of true strength. They give you a temper of the will, a quality of the imagination, a vigor of the emotions, a freshness of the deep springs of life, a temperamental predominance of courage over timidity, an appetite for adventure over love of ease.

They create in your heart the sense of wonder, the unfailing hope of what next, and the joy and inspiration of life. They teach you in this way to be an officer and a gentleman. And what sort of soldiers are those you are to lead? Are they reliable, are they brave, are they capable of victory? Their story is known to all of you; it is the story of the American man-at-arms. My estimate of him was formed on the battlefield many, many years ago and has never changed. I regarded him then as I regard him now – as one of the world's noblest figures, not as one of the finest military characters but also as one of the most stainless. His name and fame are the birthright of every American citizen. In his youth and strength, his love and loyalty he gave – all that mortality can give...The shadows are lengthening for me. The twilight is here. My days of old have vanished tone and tint; they have gone glimmering through the dreams of things that were. Their memory is one of wondrous beauty, watered by tears, and coaxed and caressed by the smiles of yesterday. I listen vainly for the witching melody of faint bugles blowing reveille, of far drums beating the long roll. In my dreams I hear again the crash of guns, the rattle of musketry, the strange, mournful mutter of the battlefield. But in the evening of my memory, always I come back to West Point. Always there echoes and re-echoes Duty, Honor, Country. Today marks my final roll call with you, but I want you to know that when I cross the river my last conscious thoughts will be of The Corps, and The Corps, and The Corps. I bid you farewell.'

# JOHN FITZGERALD KENNEDY
## 29 May 1917–22 November 1963

*'We choose to go to the Moon'*
12 September 1962

**Speaking at Rice University, Houston, Texas**
the president defended the enormous expense of the space
programme and reaffirmed America's commitment to landing a
man on the Moon before the end of the 1960s. In 1961 Kennedy
was already eager for the United States to take the lead in the
'space race'. The Soviet Union had forged ahead of the United
States in the development of space technology, and Kennedy
first announced the goal for landing a man on the Moon in the
speech to a Joint Session of Congress on 25 May. On 20 July 1969, almost six years
after Kennedy's assassination, the Apollo Program's goal was realized when the first
Americans landed on the Moon.

'...We meet at a college noted for knowledge, in a city noted for progress,
in a state noted for strength, and we stand in need of all three, for we
meet in an hour of change and challenge, in a decade of hope and fear,
in an age of both knowledge and ignorance. The greater our knowledge
increases, the greater our ignorance unfolds. Despite the striking fact
that most of the scientists that the world has ever known are alive
and working today, despite the fact that this Nation's own scientific
manpower is doubling every 12 years in a rate of growth more than
three times that of our population as a whole, despite that, the vast
stretches of the unknown and the unanswered and the unfinished still
far outstrip our collective comprehension...If this capsule history of our
progress teaches us anything, it is that man, in his quest for knowledge
and progress, is determined and cannot be deterred. The exploration
of space will go ahead, whether we join in it or not, and it is one of the
great adventures of all time, and no nation which expects to be the leader
of other nations can expect to stay behind in this race for space. Those
who came before us made certain that this country rode the first waves
of the industrial revolution, the first waves of modern invention, and
the first wave of nuclear power, and this generation does not intend to
founder in the backwash of the coming age of space. We mean to be a
part of it – we mean to lead it. For the eyes of the world now look into
space, to the Moon and to the planets beyond, and we have vowed that

we shall not see it governed by a hostile flag of conquest, but by a banner of freedom and peace. We have vowed that we shall not see space filled with weapons of mass destruction, but with instruments of knowledge and understanding.

Yet the vows of this Nation can only be fulfilled if we in this Nation are first, and, therefore, we intend to be first. In short, our leadership in science and industry, our hopes for peace and security, our obligations to ourselves as well as others, all require us to make this effort, to solve these mysteries, to solve them for the good of all men, and to become the world's leading space-faring nation...There is no strife, no prejudice, no national conflict in outer space as yet. Its hazards are hostile to us all. Its conquest deserves the best of all mankind, and its opportunity for peaceful cooperation many never come again. But why, some say, the Moon? Why choose this as our goal? And they may well ask why climb the highest mountain? Why, 35 years ago, fly the Atlantic? Why does Rice play Texas? We choose to go to the Moon. We choose to go to the Moon in this decade and do the other things, not because they are easy, but because they are hard, because that goal will serve to organize and measure the best of our energies and skills, because that challenge is one that we are willing to accept, one we are unwilling to postpone, and one which we intend to win, and the others, too. It is for these reasons that I regard the decision last year to shift our efforts in space from low to high gear as among the most important decisions that will be made during my incumbency in the office of the Presidency...Many years ago the great British explorer George Mallory, who was to die on Mount Everest, was asked why did he want to climb it. He said, "Because it is there." Well, space is there, and we're going to climb it, and the Moon and the planets are there, and new hopes for knowledge and peace are there. And, therefore, as we set sail we ask God's blessing on the most hazardous and dangerous and greatest adventure on which man has ever embarked. Thank you.'

# JOHN FITZGERALD KENNEDY
## 29 May 1917 – 22 November 1963

*'Ich bin ein Berliner'*
Rudolph Wilde Platz near the Berlin Wall, 26 June 1963

**Germany had become the major focus** of Cold War political tensions between the United States and the Soviet Union. The former capital Berlin was located in East Germany, and Berlin itself was also divided, with East Berlin under Soviet control and West Berlin under American, English and French jurisdiction. In 1948, Russia blockaded West Berlin's railroads, highways and waterways. For the next 11 months, the USA and Britain conducted a massive airlift, supplying nearly two million tons of food, coal and industrial supplies to the besieged people. In 1961 East German authorities began construction of a 12-foot (3.7-m) high wall stretching for 100 miles (160 km) around the perimeter of West Berlin, preventing anyone in the East from crossing to freedom in the West. Nearly 200 East Germans would be killed trying to climb over or dig under the wall, and thousands more imprisoned for trying to escape. More would have attempted to cross, but the East Germans imprisoned relatives of those who were successful. A massive crowd gathered to listen to the charismatic president delivering this memorable speech, confirming that America would always support Berlin.

'I am proud to come to this city as the guest of your distinguished Mayor, who has symbolized throughout the world the fighting spirit of West Berlin. And I am proud to visit the Federal Republic with your distinguished Chancellor who for so many years has committed Germany to democracy and freedom and progress, and to come here in the company of my fellow American, General Clay, who has been in this city during its great moments of crisis and will come again if ever needed. Two thousand years ago the proudest boast was *"civis Romanus sum"*. Today, in the world of freedom, the proudest boast is *"Ich bin ein Berliner"*. I appreciate my interpreter translating my German! There are many people in the world who really don't understand, or say they don't, what is the great issue between the free world and the Communist world. Let them come to Berlin. There are some who say that Communism is the wave of the future. Let them come to Berlin. And there are some who say in Europe and elsewhere we can work with the Communists. Let them come to Berlin. And there are even a few who say that it is true that Communism is an evil system, but it permits us to make economic progress. "*Lass' sie nach Berlin kommen.*" Let them come to Berlin. Freedom has many difficulties and democracy is not perfect, but we have never had to put a wall up to keep our people in, to prevent them from leaving us. I want to say, on behalf of my countrymen, who live many miles away on the other side of the Atlantic, who are far distant from you, that they take the greatest pride that they have been able to share with you, even from a distance, the story of the last 18 years. I know of no town, no city, that has been besieged for 18 years that still lives with the vitality and the force, and the hope and the determination of the city of West Berlin. While the wall is the most obvious and vivid demonstration of the failures of the Communist system, for all the world to see, we take no satisfaction in it, for it is, as your Mayor has said, an offense not only against history but an offense against humanity, separating families, dividing husbands and wives and brothers and sisters, and dividing a people who wish to be joined together.

What is true of this city is true of Germany – real, lasting peace in Europe can never be assured as long as one German out of four is denied the elementary right of free men, and that is to make a free choice. In 18 years of peace and good faith, this generation of Germans has earned the right to be free, including the right to unite their families and their nation in lasting peace, with good will to all people. You live in a defended island of freedom, but your life is part of the main...Freedom is indivisible, and when one man is enslaved, all are not free. When all are free, then we can look forward to that day when this city will be joined as one and this country and this great Continent of Europe in a peaceful and hopeful globe. When that day finally comes, as it will, the people of West Berlin can take sober satisfaction in the fact that they were in the front lines for almost two decades. All free men, wherever they may live, are citizens of Berlin, and, therefore, as a free man, I take pride in the words "*Ich bin ein Berliner.*"'

# MARTIN LUTHER KING JR
## 15 January 1929 – 4 April 1968

*'I have a dream'*
28 August 1963

**The clergyman was a prominent leader** in the African-American civil rights movement, whose great progress has made him an icon for human rights causes across the world. When President Kennedy brought the Civil Rights Bill before Congress in 1963, King made a speech on television on 11 June, pointing out that: *'The Negro baby born in America today, regardless of the section of the nation in which he is born, has about one-half as much chance of completing high school as a white baby born in the same place on the same day; one third as much chance of completing college; one third as much chance of becoming a professional man; twice as much chance of becoming unemployed; about one-seventh as much chance of earning $10,000 a year; a life expectancy which is seven years shorter; and the prospects of earning only half as much.'* In an attempt to persuade Congress to pass Kennedy's proposed legislation, King and other civil rights leaders organized the famous March on Washington for Jobs and Freedom. Most newspapers condemned the idea, the *New York Herald Tribune* warning: *'If Negro leaders persist in their announced plans to march 100,000-strong on the capital they will be jeopardizing their cause. The ugly part of this particular mass protest is its implication of unconstrained violence if Congress doesn't deliver.'* The march, on 28 August, was a huge success, with estimates of the crowd varying from between 250,000 to 400,000. King was the final speaker and from the steps of the Lincoln Memorial in Washington D.C. he outlined his vision of American racial harmony in an historic piece of oratory. King's style was that of a fervent Baptist preacher, and the live speech is easily accessible today on the Internet. The following year, at the age of 35, King became the youngest man to win the Nobel Peace Prize. Kennedy's Civil Rights bill was still being debated by Congress when the president was assassinated in November 1963. After the act was passed, King concentrated on helping those in poverty. He knew that race and economic issues were closely connected and he began preaching and writing about the need to redistribute wealth. He argued that African-Americans and poor whites were natural allies and if they worked together they could help change society. He was assassinated five years after giving this speech.

'I am happy to join with you today in what will go down in history as the greatest demonstration for freedom in the history of our nation. Five score years ago, a great American, in whose symbolic shadow we stand today, signed the Emancipation Proclamation. This momentous decree came as a great beacon light of hope to millions of Negro slaves who had been seared in the flames of withering injustice. It came as a joyous daybreak to end the long night of their captivity. But one hundred years later, the Negro still is not free. One hundred years later, the life of the Negro is still sadly crippled by the manacles of segregation and the chains of discrimination. One hundred years later, the Negro lives on a lonely island of poverty in the midst of a vast ocean of material prosperity. One hundred years later, the Negro is still languished in the corners of American society and finds himself an exile in his own land. And so we've come here today to dramatize a shameful condition.

...Let us not wallow in the valley of despair, I say to you today, my friends. And so even though we face the difficulties of today and tomorrow, I still have a dream. It is a dream deeply rooted in the American dream. I have a dream that one day this nation will rise up and live out the true meaning of its creed: "We hold these truths to be self-evident, that all men are created equal." I have a dream that one day on the red hills of Georgia, the sons of former slaves and the sons of former slave owners will be able to sit down together at the table of brotherhood. I have a dream that one day even the state of Mississippi, a state sweltering with the heat of injustice, sweltering with the heat of oppression, will be transformed into an oasis of freedom and justice. I have a dream that my four little children will one day live in a nation where they will not be judged by the color of their skin but by the content of their character. I have a dream today! I have a dream that one day, down in Alabama, with its vicious racists, with its governor having his lips dripping with the words of "interposition" and "nullification" – one day right there in Alabama little black boys and black girls will be able to join hands with little white boys and white girls as sisters and brothers.'

# JOHN FITZGERALD KENNEDY
## 29 May 1917 – 22 November 1963

*'Artists are not engineers of the soul'*
26 October 1963

**This is part of a wonderful speech** commemorating the death of the poet Robert Frost, in which the president made clear the need for a nation to represent itself not only through its strength but also through its art and *'full recognition of the place of the artist'*. Two years later, President Lyndon Johnson signed the National Foundation on the Arts and the Humanities Act, creating The National Endowment for the Arts.

'When power leads men toward arrogance, poetry reminds him of his limitations. When power narrows the areas of man's concern, poetry reminds him of the richness and diversity of his existence. When power corrupts, poetry cleanses. For art establishes the basic human truth which must serve as the touchstone of our judgment. The artist, however faithful to his personal vision of reality, becomes the last champion of the individual mind and sensibility against an intrusive society and an officious state. The great artist is thus a solitary figure. He has, as Frost said, a lover's quarrel with the world. In pursuing his perceptions of reality, he must often sail against the currents of his time. This is not a popular role. If Robert Frost was much honored in his lifetime, it was because a good many preferred to ignore his darker truths. Yet in retrospect, we see how the artist's fidelity has strengthened the fiber of our national life. If sometimes our great artists have been the most critical of our society, it is because their sensitivity and their concern for justice, which must motivate any true artist, makes him aware that our Nation falls short of its highest potential. I see little of more importance to the future of our country and our civilization than full recognition of the place of the artist. If art is to nourish the roots of our culture, society must set the artist free to follow his vision wherever it takes him. We must never forget that art is not a form of propaganda; it is a form of truth...In free society art is not a weapon and it does not belong to the spheres of polemic and ideology. Artists are not engineers of the soul. It may be different elsewhere. But democratic society – in it, the highest duty of the writer, the composer, the artist is to remain true to himself and to let the chips fall where they may. In serving his vision of the truth, the artist best serves his nation.'

# MALCOLM X (born MALCOLM LITTLE)
## 19 May 1925 – 21 February 1965

*'The ballot or the bullet'*
3 April 1964

**An advocate for the rights of African-Americans**, he has been described as one of the greatest and most influential African-Americans in history. Growing up in foster homes after his father had died and his mother was committed to a mental hospital, he was sentenced to eight to ten years in prison in 1946. In gaol, he became politicized, joined the Nation of Islam and on his release in 1952 became one of its leaders and spokesmen. Malcolm X was the public face of the Nation of Islam, but he fell out with its leader, Elijah Muhammad, and on 8 March 1964 publicly announced his break from the organization. He became a Sunni Muslim and travelled to Mecca. On his return, he turned away from the racism espoused by Elijah Muhammad and founded Muslim Mosque Inc. and the Black Nationalist Organization of Afro-American Unity. Muhammad had prevented him from liaising with other, more moderate civil rights leaders, but on 26 March Malcolm X finally met Martin Luther King Jr. In this speech, a week later, Malcolm X advised African-Americans to exercise their right to vote wisely. A year later, he was assassinated, and three members of the Nation of Islam were imprisoned for the crime.

'...Now in speaking like this, it doesn't mean that we're anti-white, but it does mean we're anti-exploitation, we're anti-degradation, we're anti-oppression. And if the white man doesn't want us to be anti-him, let him stop oppressing and exploiting and degrading us. Whether we are Christians or Muslims or nationalists or agnostics or atheists, we must first learn to forget our differences...If we don't do something real soon, I think you'll have to agree that we're going to be forced either to use the ballot or the bullet. It's one or the other in 1964. It isn't that time is running out – time has run out!...

No, I'm not an American. I'm one of the 22 million black people who are the victims of Americanism. One of the 22 million black people who are the victims of democracy, nothing but disguised hypocrisy. So, I'm not standing here speaking to you as an American, or a patriot, or a flag- saluter, or a flag-waver – no, not I. I'm speaking as a victim of this American system. And I see America through the eyes of the victim. I don't see any American dream; I see an American nightmare. These 22 million victims are waking up. Their eyes are coming open. They're beginning to see what they used to only look at. They're becoming politically mature...'

# NELSON ROLIHLAHLA MANDELA
## 18 July 1918 –

*'...it is an ideal for which I am prepared to die'*
20 April 1964

**Nelson Mandela had made a defining** African National Congress (ANC) presidential address in his *'No Easy Walk to Freedom'* speech of 1953. It was read on his behalf as he was subject to a banning order. He had been committed to a policy of non-violent resistance, but Mandela and 155 others were arrested in December 1956 and charged with treason. The trial lasted until 1961, when all the defendants were acquitted. As a last resort against continued abuse of black rights, Mandela began coordinating sabotage campaigns against government and military targets, despairing of a peaceful road to equality. After living on the run for 17 months, he was again arrested in August 1962 after a CIA tip-off to the South African authorities. Mandela was now sentenced to five years in prison for having incited workers to strike in 1961, and for leaving South Africa illegally. While imprisoned, he and other ANC leaders were tried again on sabotage charges and crimes equivalent to treason, and Mandela was again brought to court. In his statement for the defence, Mandela described how the ANC had used peaceful means to resist apartheid for years until the 'Sharpeville Massacre' of 1960, when police opened fire on a group of protesters, killing 69 unarmed blacks. This event, along with the referendum establishing the Republic of South Africa (out of British control), the declaration of a 'state of emergency' and the banning of the ANC made it clear that the ANC's only choice was to resist oppression through acts of sabotage. All except one defendant were found guilty, but they escaped the death sentence, being sentenced instead to life imprisonment with hard labour on 12 June 1964.

These are the last words of Mandela's statement from the dock, at the opening of the defence case in the trial at Pretoria Supreme Court. Nelson Mandela was now imprisoned on Robben Island for the next 18 years. Conditions were poor and political prisoners were kept separate from ordinary criminals, receiving fewer privileges. Mandela was allowed just one visitor and one heavily censored letter every six months. In 1969, British intelligence foiled an escape plot hatched by South African intelligence, which wanted Mandela to escape so that they could 'accidentally' shoot him during recapture. In March 1982 Mandela was transferred from Robben Island to Pollsmoor Prison, along with other senior ANC leaders. In February 1985 President Botha offered Mandela conditional release if he would renounce armed struggle. Mandela refused the offer, releasing a statement via his daughter saying

'*What freedom am I being offered while the organization of the people remains banned? Only free men can negotiate. A prisoner cannot enter into contracts.*' In 1988 Mandela was moved to Victor Verster Prison, and the 'Free Nelson Mandela' campaign grew in strength around the world. In 1989 President Botha suffered a stroke, and the new President de Klerk announced Mandela's release in February 1990. Mandela served as president of South Africa from 1994–9. The following is an extract from his speech:

'Some of the things so far told to the Court are true and some are untrue. I do not, however, deny that I planned sabotage. I did not plan it in a spirit of recklessness, nor because I have any love of violence. I planned it as a result of a calm and sober assessment of the political situation that had arisen after many years of tyranny, exploitation, and oppression of my people by the whites...But the violence which we chose to adopt was not terrorism...Above all, we want equal political rights, because without them our disabilities will be permanent. I know this sounds revolutionary to the whites in this country, because the majority of voters will be Africans. This makes the white man fear democracy. But this fear cannot be allowed to stand in the way of the only solution which will guarantee racial harmony and freedom for all. It is not true that the enfranchisement of all will result in racial domination. Political division, based on colour, is entirely artificial and, when it disappears, so will the domination of one colour group by another. The ANC has spent half a century fighting against racialism. When it triumphs it will not change that policy. This then is what the ANC is fighting. Their struggle is a truly national one. It is a struggle of the African people, inspired by their own suffering and their own experience. It is a struggle for the right to live. During my lifetime I have dedicated myself to this struggle of the African people. I have fought against white domination, and I have fought against black domination. I have cherished the ideal of a democratic and free society in which all persons live together in harmony and with equal opportunities. It is an ideal which I hope to live for and to achieve. But if needs be, it is an ideal for which I am prepared to die.'

# LYNDON BAINES JOHNSON
### 27 August 1908 – 22 January 1973

## *The American Promise*
### 15 March 1965

**In the wake of the ugly violence** perpetuated against civil rights marchers in Selma, Alabama in 1965, the new president adopted the '*We Shall Overcome*' slogan of Martin Luther King Jr in this call for the country to end racial discrimination. This special message to a joint session of Congress was broadcast nationally. By throwing the full weight of the presidency behind the Civil Rights movement for the first time, Johnson helped usher in the Voting Rights Act. Johnson, who served as representative and senator for Texas before becoming Kennedy's vice-president and then president after his assassination in 1963, achieved more than any president since Lincoln in advancing the cause of civil rights, worked tirelessly to end poverty and improve health and education. However, his presidency was blighted by the ongoing war in Vietnam.

'...I speak tonight for the dignity of man and the destiny of democracy. I urge every member of both parties, Americans of all religions and of all colors, from every section of this country, to join me in that cause. At times history and fate meet at a single time in a single place to shape a turning point in man's unending search for freedom. So it was at Lexington and Concord. So it was a century ago at Appomattox. So it was last week in Selma, Alabama. There, long-suffering men and women peacefully protested the denial of their rights as Americans. Many were brutally assaulted. One good man, a man of God, was killed. There is no cause for pride in what has happened in Selma. There is no cause for self-satisfaction in the long denial of equal rights of millions of Americans. But there is cause for hope and for faith in our democracy in what is happening here tonight. For the cries of pain and the hymns and protests of oppressed people have summoned into convocation all the majesty of this great Government – the Government of the greatest Nation on earth. Our mission is at once the oldest and the most basic of this country: to right wrong, to do justice, to serve man. In our time we have come to live with moments of great crisis. Our lives have been marked with debate about great issues; issues of war and peace, issues of prosperity and depression. But rarely in any time does an issue lay bare the secret heart of America itself. Rarely are we met with a challenge, not to our growth or abundance, our welfare or our security, but rather to the values and the purposes and the meaning of our beloved Nation. The issue of equal rights for American Negroes is such an issue. And should we defeat every enemy, should we double our wealth and conquer the stars, and still be unequal to this issue, then we will have failed as a people and as a nation. For with a country as with a person, "What is a man profited, if he shall gain the whole world, and lose his own soul?" There is no Negro problem. There is no Southern problem. There is no Northern problem. There is only an American problem. And we are met here tonight as Americans – not as Democrats or Republicans – we are met here as Americans to solve that problem.

...We shall overcome. But even if we pass this bill, the battle will not be over. What happened in Selma is part of a far larger movement which reaches into every section and State of America. It is the effort of American Negroes to secure for themselves the full blessings of American life. Their cause must be our cause too. Because it is not just Negroes, but really it is all of us, who must overcome the crippling legacy of bigotry and injustice. And we shall overcome. As a man whose roots go deeply into Southern soil I know how agonizing racial feelings are. I know how difficult it is to reshape the attitudes and the structure of our society. But a century has passed, more than a hundred years, since the Negro was freed. And he is not fully free tonight. It was more than a hundred years ago that Abraham Lincoln, a great President of another party, signed the Emancipation Proclamation, but emancipation is a proclamation and not a fact. A century has passed, more than a hundred years, since equality was promised. And yet the Negro is not equal. A century has passed since the day of promise. And the promise is unkept. The time of justice has now come. I tell you that I believe sincerely that no force can hold it back. It is right in the eyes of man and God that it should come. And when it does, I think that day will brighten the lives of every American...'

# MARTIN LUTHER KING JR
## 15 January 1929 – 4 April 1968

*'I've been to the mountaintop'*
3 April 1968

**On 3 April 1967, King had made** a major speech expressing opposition to the Vietnam War. His strategy of linking poverty, civil rights and the Vietnam War was made in support of the presidential campaign of Robert F. Kennedy. FBI files show that J. Edgar Hoover, the director of the bureau, reported to President Johnson that Kennedy and King were working together in order to undermine his presidency. King was convinced that the violence that disrupted the anti-Vietnam marches and meetings had been caused by government provocateurs. King returned to Memphis, Tennessee in March 1968 to prepare for a major non-violent march in Washington D.C. He agreed to speak in support of a strike by Memphis's sanitation workers at the Mason Temple, a year to the day after his Vietnam speech. After the meeting King and his party were taken to the Lorraine motel, and the following day he was shot and killed as he stood on the balcony. His death precipitated rioting in 125 cities and resulted in 46 people being killed. Two months later, James Earl Ray was arrested for the crime in London and extradited. He pleaded guilty to King's murder and was sent to jail for 99 years. People close to King are still convinced that the FBI was behind the assassination.

'...Strangely enough, I would turn to the Almighty and say, "If you allow me to live just a few years in the second half of the 20th century, I will be happy." Now that's a strange statement to make because the world is all messed up. The nation is sick, trouble is in the land, confusion all around. That's a strange statement. But I know, somehow, that only when it is dark enough can you see the stars. And I see God working in this period of the 20th century in a way that men in some strange way are responding. Something is happening in our world. The masses of people are rising up. And wherever they are assembled today, whether they are in Johannesburg, South Africa; Nairobi, Kenya; Accra, Ghana; New York City; Atlanta, Georgia; Jackson, Mississippi; or Memphis, Tennessee, the cry is always the same: "We want to be free." And another reason that I'm happy to live in this period is that we have been forced to a point where we are going to have to grapple with the problems that men have been trying to grapple with through history, but the demands didn't force them to do it. Survival demands that we grapple with them. Men for years now have been talking about war and peace. But now, no longer can they just talk about it. It is no longer a choice between violence and non-violence in this world; it's non-violence or non-existence. That is where we are today.

And also, in the human rights revolution, if something isn't done and done in a hurry to bring the colored peoples of the world out of their long years of poverty, their long years of hurt and neglect, the whole world is doomed. Now, I'm just happy that God has allowed me to live in this period, to see what is unfolding. And I'm happy that he's allowed me to be in Memphis...We mean business now and we are determined to gain our rightful place in God's world. And that's all this whole thing is about. We aren't engaged in any negative protest and in any negative arguments with anybody. We are saying that we are determined to be men. We are determined to be people. We are saying, we are saying that we are God's children. And if we are God's children, we don't have to live like we are forced to live. Now, what does all of this mean in this great period of history? It means that we've got to stay together. We've got to stay together and maintain unity...Now let us maintain unity...The issue is injustice...We aren't going to let any mace stop us. We are masters in our non-violent movement in disarming police forces; they don't know what to do...Well, I don't know what will happen now; we've got some difficult days ahead. But it really doesn't matter with me now, because I've been to the mountaintop. And I don't mind. Like anybody, I would like to live a long life – longevity has its place. But I'm not concerned about that now. I just want to do God's will. And He's allowed me to go up to the mountain. And I've looked over, and I've seen the promised land. I may not get there with you. But I want you to know tonight, that we, as a people, will get to the promised land. So I'm happy tonight; I'm not worried about anything; I'm not fearing any man. Mine eyes have seen the glory of the coming of the Lord.'

# ROBERT FRANCIS KENNEDY
## 20 November 1925 – 6 June 1968

*'...it is perhaps well to ask what kind of a nation we are*
*and what direction we want to move in'*
4 April 1968

**Senator Kennedy was opposed to** the Vietnam War and in 1968 entered the campaign to win the Democratic nomination for the presidency. He was boarding a plane for a further campaign rally that night in Indianapolis, when he learned that Martin Luther King had been shot. Arriving in Indianapolis, he learned that King had died in hospital. Just before arriving at the rally the chief of police in Indianapolis told Kennedy that he could not provide adequate protection, and warned him that telling the audience that King was dead would be dangerous. The mainly African-American audience did not know of King's death. Standing on a podium mounted on flatbed truck, Kennedy spoke for only four minutes and 57 seconds. An effective speaker like his brother, Kennedy was thus the first to inform the audience of the death of Martin Luther King, causing some in the audience to shout and wail. Once the audience had calmed down, Kennedy acknowledged that many would be filled with anger, especially since the assassin was believed to be a white man, and that he had felt the same when his brother had been murdered. Riots broke out across America, but not in Indianapolis, which many attribute to the effect of this speech. Kennedy went on to win the Indiana and Nebraska Democratic primaries, and after the decisive California primary of 4 June, gave a victory speech just past midnight on 5 June at the Ambassador Hotel, Los Angeles. Shortly after, he was mortally wounded by Sirhan Sirhan, dying early in the morning of 6 June 1968, just two months after King's assassination.

'I have bad news for you, for all of our fellow citizens, and people who love peace all over the world, and that is that Martin Luther King was shot and killed tonight. Martin Luther King dedicated his life to love and to justice for his fellow human beings, and he died because of that effort. In this difficult day, in this difficult time for the United States, it is perhaps well to ask what kind of a nation we are and what direction we want to move in. For those of you who are black – considering the evidence there evidently is that there were white people who were responsible – you can be filled with bitterness, with hatred, and a desire for revenge. We can move in that direction as a country, in great polarization – black people amongst black, white people amongst white, filled with hatred toward one another. Or we can make an effort, as Martin Luther King did, to understand and to comprehend, and to replace that violence, that stain of bloodshed that has spread across our land, with an effort to understand with compassion and love. For those of you who are black and are tempted to be filled with hatred and distrust at the injustice of such an act, against all white people, I can only say that I feel in my own heart the same kind of feeling. I had a member of my family killed, but he was killed by a white man. But we have to make an effort in the United States, we have to make an effort to understand, to go beyond these rather difficult times. My favorite poet was Aeschylus. He wrote: "In our sleep, pain which cannot forget falls drop by drop upon the heart until, in our own despair, against our will, comes wisdom through the awful grace of God." What we need in the United States is not division; what we need in the United States is not hatred; what we need in the United States is not violence or lawlessness; but love and wisdom, and compassion toward one another, and a feeling of justice toward those who still suffer within our country, whether they be white or they be black.

So I shall ask you tonight to return home, to say a prayer for the family of Martin Luther King, that's true, but more importantly to say a prayer for our own country, which all of us love – a prayer for understanding and that compassion of which I spoke. We can do well in this country. We will have difficult times; we've had difficult times in the past; we will have difficult times in the future. It is not the end of violence; it is not the end of lawlessness; it is not the end of disorder. But the vast majority of white people and the vast majority of black people in this country want to live together, want to improve the quality of our life, and want justice for all human beings who abide in our land. Let us dedicate ourselves to what the Greeks wrote so many years ago: to tame the savageness of man and make gentle the life of this world. Let us dedicate ourselves to that, and say a prayer for our country and for our people.'

# DR SALVADOR ISABELINO ALLENDE
## 26 June 1908 – 11 September 1973

*'Long live Chile! Long live the people! Long live the workers!'*
11 September 1973

**This Marxist physician ran for the presidency** of Chile in 1952, 1958 and 1964 before his success in the 1970 election. The possibility of Allende winning the election was thought a disaster by the US government which wanted to protect US business interests and prevent any spread of communism through South America. In September 1970, President Nixon informed the CIA that an Allende government in Chile was not acceptable and authorized a budget to prevent Allende's Popular Unity party from coming to power, or to unseat him if he did so. Allende served as president from 4 November 1970 until a US-backed military coup d'état on 11 September 1973. Just before the capture of the Presidential Palace, with gunfire, air raids and explosions audible in the background, Allende gave this farewell speech to the people of Chile on live radio, speaking of himself in the past tense, and affirming his deep faith in Chile's future. He was killed, apparently in an act of suicide, and succeeded by the commander-in-chief of the Chilean army General Augusto Pinochet, who ran a military dictatorship based upon murder and torture for the next 16 years

'My friends, Surely this will be the last chance for me to address you. The Air Force has bombed the radio masts of Radio Magallanes. My words do not express bitterness but disappointment. May they morally punish those who have betrayed their oath: soldiers of Chile, titular commanders in chief, Admiral Merino, who has designated himself Commander of the Navy, and Mr Mendoza, the despicable general who only yesterday pledged his faith and loyalty to the Government, and who also has appointed himself Chief of the Carabineros *[paramilitary police]*. Given these facts, the only thing left for me is to say to workers: I am not going to resign! At a moment of historic transition, I will pay for my loyalty to the people with my life. And I say to them that I am certain that the seeds which we have planted in the good conscience of thousands and thousands of Chileans will not lie dry and withered forever. They have force at their disposal and will be able to dominate us, but social processes can be arrested by neither crime nor force. History is ours, and people make history.

Workers of my country: I want to thank you for the loyalty that you always had, the confidence that you vested in a man who was only an interpreter of great longings for justice, who gave his word that he would respect the Constitution and the law and did just that. At this definitive moment, the last moment when I can address you, I wish you to learn the lesson: foreign capital, imperialism, together with reaction, created the climate in which the Armed Forces broke their tradition, the tradition taught by General Schneider and reaffirmed by Commander Araya, victims of the same social sector who today are hoping, with foreign assistance, to take back the power to continue defending their profits and their privileges. I address you, above all, the modest woman of our land, the campesina *[countrywomen]* who believed in us, the mother who knew our concern for children. I address professionals of Chile, patriotic professionals who continued working against the subversion that was supported by professional associations, classist associations that also defended the advantages of capitalist society. I address the youth, those who sang and bestowed on us their joy and their spirit of struggle. I address the man of Chile, the worker, the farmer, the intellectual, those who will be persecuted, because in our country fascism has already been abroad for many hours – in terrorist attacks, blowing up the bridges, cutting the railroad tracks, destroying the oil and gas pipelines, in the face of the silence of those who had the duty to act. They were committed. History will judge them. Surely Radio Magallanes will be silenced, and the calm metal instrument of my voice will no longer reach you. It does not matter. You will continue hearing it. I will always be next to you. At least my memory will be that of a man of dignity who was loyal to his country. The people must defend themselves, but they must not sacrifice themselves. The people must not let themselves be destroyed or riddled with bullets, but they cannot be humiliated either. Workers of my country, I have faith in Chile and its destiny. Other men will overcome this dark and bitter moment when treason seeks to prevail. Go forward knowing that, sooner rather than later, the great avenues will open again and free men will walk through them to build a better society. Long live Chile! Long live the people! Long live the workers! These are my last words, and I am certain that my sacrifice will not be in vain, I am certain that, at the very least, it will be a moral lesson that will punish felony, cowardice, and treason.'

# GERALD RUDOLPH FORD JR
## 14 July 1913 – 26 December 2006

### '...a war that is finished'
### 23 April 1975

**An opponent of the Vietnam War** and supporter of civil rights, Ford had been minority leader of the Republicans in the House of Representatives, and a target for Democratic President Lyndon B. Johnson's ire. During Richard Nixon's Republican presidency, Vice-President Spiro Agnew was disgraced because he had accepted bribes and he resigned, Ford taking his place from 1973–4. As a result of the Watergate Affair, President Nixon eventually also resigned and Ford became president from 1974–7. Nixon had promised funds to prop up South Vietnam in its losing war against North Vietnam, but Congress refused Ford's request for further funding. On 21 April 1975, President Thieu of South Vietnam resigned, publicly blaming lack of US support for the lost war. Two days later, as frantic attempts were being made to expatriate Americans and Vietnamese nationals from South Vietnam, and 100,000 North Vietnamese were advancing on Saigon, Ford made this speech. A week later South Vietnam fell.

'Today, America can regain the sense of pride that existed before Vietnam. But it cannot be achieved by refighting a war that is finished as far as America is concerned. As I see it, the time has come to look forward to an agenda for the future, to unify, to bind up the Nation's wounds, and to restore its health and its optimistic self-confidence...I recognize the need for technology that enriches life while preserving our natural environment. My goal is to stimulate productivity, but use technology to redeem, not to destroy our environment. I will strive for new cooperation rather than conflict in the peaceful exploration of our oceans and our space. My goal is to use resources for peaceful progress rather than war and destruction. Let America symbolize humanity's struggle to conquer nature and master technology. The time has now come for our Government to facilitate the individual's control over his or her future – and of the future of America. Your generation of Americans is uniquely endowed by history to give new meaning to the pride and spirit of America. The magnetism of an American society, confident of its own strength, will attract the good will and the esteem of all people wherever they might be in this globe in which we live. It will enhance our own perception of ourselves and our pride in being an American. We can, we – and I say it with emphasis – write a new agenda for our future.'

# MOTHER TERESA (AGNESE GONXHA BOJAXHIU)
## 26 August 1910 – 5 September 1997

### 'Smile at each other'
### 11 December 1979

**This Albanian Catholic nun** with Indian citizenship founded the Missionaries of Charity in Calcutta (Kolkata) in 1950, and until her death ministered to the poor and sick. This is the conclusion of her Nobel Prize acceptance speech. She was awarded the Peace Prize in 1979 for 'work undertaken in the struggle to overcome poverty and distress, which also constitutes a threat to peace.'

'...I never forget some time ago about 14 professors came from the United States from different universities. And they came to Calcutta to our house. Then we were talking about that they had been to the home for the dying. We have a home for the dying in Calcutta, where we have picked up more than 36,000 people only from the streets of Calcutta, and out of that big number more than 18,000 have died a beautiful death. They have just gone home to God; and they came to our house and we talked of love, of compassion, and then one of them asked me: Say, Mother, please tell us something that we will remember, and I said to them: Smile at each other, make time for each other in your family. Smile at each other. And then another one asked me: Are you married, and I said: Yes, and I find it sometimes very difficult to smile at Jesus because he can be very demanding sometimes. This is really something true, and there is where love comes – when it is demanding, and yet we can give it to Him with joy. Just as I have said today, I have said that if I don't go to Heaven for anything else I will be going to Heaven for all the publicity because it has purified me and sacrificed me and made me really ready to go to Heaven. I think that this is something, that we must live life beautifully, we have Jesus with us and He loves us. If we could only remember that God loves me, and I have an opportunity to love others as he loves me, not in big things, but in small things with great love, then Norway becomes a nest of love. And how beautiful it will be that from here a centre for peace has been given. That from here the joy of life of the unborn child comes out. If you become a burning light in the world of peace, then really the Nobel Peace Prize is a gift of the Norwegian people. God bless you!'

# ALEKSANDR ISAYEVICH SOLZHENITSYN
## 11 December 1918 – 3 August 2008

### *'What is the joy about?'*
8 June 1978

**This superb Russian novelist and historian** suffered in prison camps in the Soviet Union for years because of his criticisms of the Soviet authorities. He was awarded the Nobel Prize in Literature in 1970, and was expelled from the Soviet Union in 1974. This is his commencement address at Harvard University.

'Harvard's motto is "Veritas". Many of you have already found out and others will find out in the course of their lives that truth eludes us if we do not concentrate with total attention on its pursuit. And even while it eludes us, the illusion still lingers of knowing it and leads to many misunderstandings. Also, truth is seldom pleasant; it is almost invariably bitter. There is some bitterness in my speech today, too. But I want to stress that it comes not from an adversary but from a friend. I have spent all my life under a Communist regime, and I will tell you that a society without any objective legal scale is a terrible one indeed. But a society with no other scale but the legal one is not quite worthy of man either. Hastiness and superficiality are the psychic diseases of the 20th century, and more than anywhere else this disease is reflected in the press. A decline in courage may be the most striking feature that an outside observer notices in the West today. The Western world has lost its civic courage, both as a whole and separately, in each country, in each government, in each political party, and, of course, in the United Nations. Such a decline in courage is particularly noticeable among the ruling and intellectual elites, causing an impression of a loss of courage by the entire society. There are many courageous individuals, but they have no determining influence on public life...

Should someone ask me whether I would indicate the West such as it is today as a model to my country, frankly I would have to answer negatively. No, I could not recommend your society in its present state as an ideal for the transformation of ours. But the fight for our planet, physical and spiritual, a fight of cosmic proportions, is not a vague matter of the future; it has already started. The forces of Evil have begun their decisive offensive, you can feel their pressure, and yet your screens and publications are full of prescribed smiles and raised glasses. What is the joy about? On the way from the Renaissance to our days we have enriched our experience, but we have lost the concept of a Supreme Complete Entity which used to restrain our passions and our irresponsibility. We have placed too much hope in political and social reforms, only to find out that we were being deprived of our most precious possession: our spiritual life. In the East, it is destroyed by the dealings and machinations of the ruling party. In the West, commercial interests tend to suffocate it. This is the real crisis. The split in the world is less terrible than the similarity of the disease plaguing its main sections. If humanism were right in declaring that man is born to be happy, he would not be born to die. Since his body is doomed to die, his task on Earth evidently must be of a more spiritual nature. It cannot be unrestrained enjoyment of everyday life. It cannot be the search for the best ways to obtain material goods and then cheerfully get the most out of them. It has to be the fulfilment of a permanent, earnest duty so that one's life journey may become an experience of moral growth, so that one may leave life a better human being than one started it.

It is imperative to review the table of widespread human values. Its present incorrectness is astounding. It is not possible that assessment of the President's performance be reduced to the question of how much money one makes or of unlimited availability of gasoline. Only voluntary, inspired self-restraint can raise man above the world stream of materialism. Even if we are spared destruction by war, our lives will have to change if we want to save life from self-destruction. We cannot avoid revising the fundamental definitions of human life and human society. Is it true that man is above everything? Is there no Superior Spirit above him? Is it right that man's life and society's activities have to be determined by material expansion in the first place? Is it permissible to promote such expansion to the detriment of our spiritual integrity? If the world has not come to its end, it has approached a major turn in history, equal in importance to the turn from the Middle Ages to the Renaissance. It will exact from us a spiritual upsurge, we shall have to rise to a new height of vision, to a new level of life where our physical nature will not be cursed as in the Middle Ages, but, even more importantly, our spiritual being will not be trampled upon as in the Modern era. This ascension will be similar to climbing onto the next anthropologic stage. No one on Earth has any other way left but – upward.'

# HERBERT PAUL 'HERB' BROOKS JR
## 5 August 1937 – 11 August 2003

*'This is your time. Their time is done'*
22 February 1980

**Brooks played ice hockey for the USA** in the 1964 and 1968 Olympic Games, and from 1972 coached college, national, European professional and National Hockey League (NHL) teams. Later he became a TV analyst and motivational speaker, dying at the age of 56 in a car crash. As a coach, he innovated with a 'hybrid' style of mixing North American 'dump-and-chase' tactics with European keeping possession of the puck. His players were encouraged to be fast, powerful, extremely fit and creative through his inspirational ways of motivating them and moulding individuals into team players. Herb Brooks had coached Team USA at the 1979 World Championship, and then was named general manager and head coach for the 1980 Winter Olympics at Lake Placid, New York State. His amateur and college players astonished the hockey world by winning the Olympic gold medal in a triumph that has been heralded by the press as the *'Miracle on Ice'*. The 2005 Disney film *Miracle* chronicled this extraordinary accomplishment when the unfancied US squad defeated the mighty Soviet Union in the semi-finals, before beating Finland two days later for the gold medal. America's college-age amateurs defeated a Soviet team that been invincible for 20 years. In reality a professional team (before the Olympics was opened to professional sportspeople), the Soviet Union had won the gold medal in 1956, 1964, 1968, 1972 and 1976. Of his 20 players, nine had played for Brooks at the University of Minnesota. Brooks said of his players:

'They were really mentally tough and goal-oriented. They came from all different walks of life, many having competed against one another, but they came together and grew to be a real close team. I pushed this team really hard, I mean I really pushed them! But they had the ability to answer the bell. Our style of play was probably different than anything in North America. We adopted more of a hybrid style of play – a bit of the Canadian school and a little bit of the European school. The players took to it like ducks to water, and they really had a lot of fun playing it. We were a fast, creative team that played extremely disciplined without the puck. Throughout the Olympics, they had a great resiliency about them. I mean they came from behind six or seven times to win. They just kept on moving and working and digging. I think we were as good a conditioned team as there was in the world, outside maybe the Soviet Union. We got hot and lucky at the right times, and it was just an incredible experience for all of us.'

At the time of the event the world was still in the grip of the Cold War, with the USA boycotting the subsequent 1984 Moscow Olympics. On 9 February 1980, Secretary of State Cyrus Vance announced the boycott, and on the same day in an exhibition match the Soviet Olympic team thrashed the US Olympic team 10-3. Most of the best players in the NHL at this time were Canadian, rather than American, and it was assumed that later that month the Soviets would win by a similar score in the Olympic Games. On 22 February 1980 in the semi-finals, the US team scored with ten minutes to play to take a 4-3 lead against the Soviets and then held on, to incredible scenes. Brooks later explained '*You're looking for players whose name on the front of the sweater is more important than the one on the back. I look for these players to play hard, to play smart and to represent their country.*' Brooks headed to the locker room straight after the game, saying '*It was not my spot. I always say sort of flippantly, "I had to go to the bathroom." Or, "If I'd have went on the ice when this thing happened, someone would have speared me or something." It's a great feeling of accomplishment and pride. They had to do it; it was their moment.*' In 1980, *Sports Illustrated* headlined the game the '*Greatest Sports Moment of the Century*'.

Just before the game, Brooks had pulled a crumpled piece of paper from his pocket and read this to his players:

'Great moments are born from great opportunity. And that's what you have here, tonight, boys. That's what you've earned here tonight. One game. If we played 'em ten times, they might win nine. But not this game. Not tonight. Tonight, we skate with them. Tonight, we stay with them. And we shut them down because we can! Tonight, we are the greatest hockey team in the world. You were born to be hockey players. Every one of you. And you were meant to be here tonight. This is your time. Their time is done. It's over. I'm sick and tired of hearing about what a great hockey team the Soviets have. Screw 'em. This is your time. Now go out there and take it.'

# EDWARD MOORE KENNEDY
### 22 February 1932 – 25 August 2009

*'...the cause endures'*
12 August 1980

**The liberal senator from Massachusetts**, and brother of the assassinated John and Robert Kennedy, unsuccessfully opposed the incumbent President Jimmy Carter in 1980 in the fight for the Democratic nomination to run for the presidency. Carter's political fortunes were sagging due to inflation, high unemployment and political problems resulting from the taking of American hostages in Iran. In July 1980 the Republicans had chosen Ronald Reagan as their nominee. Reagan opposed many of the traditional liberal Democratic policies which traced their roots back to Franklin D. Roosevelt and the 'New Deal', policies which used the power of the federal government to implement social change. Conservatives argued that the programmes resulted in inefficient, expensive government bureaucracies. It was against this background that Kennedy delivered the finest speech of his career.

'Well, things worked out a little different from the way I thought, but let me tell you, I still love New York. My fellow Democrats and my fellow Americans, I have come here tonight not to argue as a candidate but to affirm a cause. I'm asking you – I am asking you to renew the commitment of the Democratic Party to economic justice. I am asking you to renew our commitment to a fair and lasting prosperity that can put America back to work. This is the cause that brought me into the campaign and that sustained me for nine months across 100,000 miles in 40 different states. We had our losses, but the pain of our defeats is far, far less than the pain of the people that I have met. We have learned that it is important to take issues seriously, but never to take ourselves too seriously. The serious issue before us tonight is the cause for which the Democratic Party has stood in its finest hours, the cause that keeps our Party young and makes it, in the second century of its age, the largest political party in this republic and the longest lasting political party on this planet. Our cause has been, since the days of Thomas Jefferson, the cause of the common man and the common woman...For me, a few hours ago, this campaign came to an end. For all those whose cares have been our concern, the work goes on, the cause endures, the hope still lives, and the dream shall never die.'

# CÉSAR ESTRADA CHÁVEZ
## 31 March 1927 – 23 April 1993

*'I had to try'*

9 November 1984

**César Chávez became the best known** Latino Civil Rights activist and founded the United Farm Workers (UFW) labour union in the United States. His public-relations approach to unionism and aggressive but non-violent tactics made the farm workers' struggle a moral cause that received nationwide support. President Obama regards Chávez as one of his heroes, and his election slogan of *'Yes, we can'* closely resembles that of Chávez – *'Si, se puede'* (Yes, it can be done). In this speech, Chávez addressed many issues including the provision of safe vehicles to transport farmworkers, the intimidation tactics used by growers to discourage unionization among farmworkers, child labour concerns, union survival, pesticides and environmental damage, his philosophy of non-violence, and the role of the boycott in pressuring growers to acknowledge workers' needs.

'All my life, I have been driven by one dream, one goal, one vision: To overthrow a farm labor system in this nation which treats farm workers as if they were not important human beings. Farm workers are not agricultural implements. They are not beasts of burden – to be used and discarded.

... My motivation comes from my personal life – from watching what my mother and father went through when I was growing up; from what we experienced as migrant farm workers in California. That dream, that vision, grew from my own experience with racism, with hope, with the desire to be treated fairly and to see my people treated as human beings and not as chattel. It grew from anger and rage – emotions I felt 40 years ago when people of my color were denied the right to see a movie or eat at a restaurant in many parts of California. It grew from the frustration and humiliation I felt as a boy who couldn't understand how the growers could abuse and exploit farm workers when there were so many of us and so few of them...I began to realize what other minority people had discovered: That the only answer – the only hope – was in organizing. More of us had to become citizens. We had to register to vote. And people like me had to develop the skills it would take to organize, to educate, to help empower the Chicano people...But deep in my heart, I knew I could never be happy unless I tried organizing the farm workers. I didn't know if I would succeed. But I had to try...'

# RONALD WILSON REAGAN
## 6 February 1911 – 5 June 2004

*'The future doesn't belong to the fainthearted; it belongs to the brave'*
28 January 1986

**In January 1986 millions of Americans**, many of them schoolchildren watching from their classroom desks, tuned in to see seven astronauts, including Christa McAuliffe, a 37-year-old schoolteacher and the first ever 'civilian astronaut', lift off in the Space Shuttle *Challenger*. Just 73 seconds later, the Shuttle was consumed in a fireball, and all seven crew members died. These were the first deaths of American astronauts during an actual spaceflight, and the nation was shocked by the tragedy. Just a few hours after the disaster, President Reagan appeared nationwide on radio and television, honouring these 'pioneers' and offering comfort and assurance to a distressed people. It is doubtful whether Reagan wrote any of this speech, but his calm and sincerity touched a chord with the American public. His utter confidence in the greatness of the United States and its future prospects always came across in his years of presidency. Reagan was a remarkably gifted public speaker.

'Ladies and Gentlemen, I'd planned to speak to you tonight to report on the state of the Union, but the events of earlier today have led me to change those plans. Today is a day for mourning and remembering. Nancy and I are pained to the core by the tragedy of the Shuttle *Challenger*. We know we share this pain with all of the people of our country. This is truly a national loss. Nineteen years ago, almost to the day, we lost three astronauts in a terrible accident on the ground. But, we've never lost an astronaut in flight; we've never had a tragedy like this. And perhaps we've forgotten the courage it took for the crew of the Shuttle; but they, the *Challenger* Seven, were aware of the dangers, but overcame them and did their jobs brilliantly. We mourn seven heroes: Michael Smith, Dick Scobee, Judith Resnik, Ronald McNair, Ellison Onizuka, Gregory Jarvis, and Christa McAuliffe. We mourn their loss as a nation together. For the families of the seven, we cannot bear, as you do, the full impact of this tragedy. But we feel the loss, and we're thinking about you so very much. Your loved ones were daring and brave, and they had that special grace, that special spirit that says, "Give me a challenge and I'll meet it with joy." They had a hunger to explore the universe and discover its truths. They wished to serve, and they did. They served all of us. We've grown used to wonders in this century. It's hard to dazzle us. But for 25 years the United States space program has been doing just that. We've grown used to the idea of space, and perhaps we forget that we've only just begun. We're still pioneers. They, the members of the *Challenger* crew, were pioneers.

And I want to say something to the schoolchildren of America who were watching the live coverage of the Shuttle's takeoff. I know it is hard to understand, but sometimes painful things like this happen. It's all part of the process of exploration and discovery. It's all part of taking a chance and expanding man's horizons. The future doesn't belong to the fainthearted; it belongs to the brave. The *Challenger* crew was pulling us into the future, and we'll continue to follow them. I've always had great faith in and respect for our space program, and what happened today does nothing to diminish it. We don't hide our space program. We don't keep secrets and cover things up. We do it all up front and in public. That's the way freedom is, and we wouldn't change it for a minute. We'll continue our quest in space. There will be more Shuttle flights and more Shuttle crews and, yes, more volunteers, more civilians, more teachers in space. Nothing ends here; our hopes and our journeys continue. I want to add that I wish I could talk to every man and woman who works for NASA or who worked on this mission and tell them: "Your dedication and professionalism have moved and impressed us for decades. And we know of your anguish. We share it." There's a coincidence today. On this day 390 years ago, the great explorer Sir Francis Drake died aboard ship off the coast of Panama. In his lifetime the great frontiers were the oceans, and a historian later said, "He lived by the sea, died on it, and was buried in it." Well, today we can say of the *Challenger* crew: Their dedication was, like Drake's, complete. The crew of the Space Shuttle *Challenger* honored us by the manner in which they lived their lives. We will never forget them, nor the last time we saw them, this morning, as they prepared for the journey and waved goodbye and "slipped the surly bonds of earth" to "touch the face of God." Thank you.'

# RONALD WILSON REAGAN
### 6 February 1911 – 5 June 2004

### *'Mr. Gorbachev, tear down this wall!'*
### 12 June 1987

**This speech of the 'Great Communicator'** is remembered, in the words of the German newspaper *Bild*, as a speech that *'changed the world'*. Reagan challenged Mikhail Gorbachev, the Soviet head of state, to liberalize the Soviet Union and to allow Eastern Europe its freedom. Agreements were drawn up by the two superpowers regarding the levels of conventional forces, nuclear weapons and policy in Eastern Europe. The Berlin Wall was eventually torn down in 1989, and just two years later the Soviet Union collapsed. In 1994, Reagan bravely disclosed in a letter to the American public that he had been diagnosed with Alzheimer's disease.

'...We come to Berlin, we American Presidents, because it's our duty to speak in this place of freedom. But I must confess, we're drawn here by other things as well; by the feeling of history in this city – more than 500 years older than our own nation;...Behind me stands a wall that encircles the free sectors of this city, part of a vast system of barriers that divides the entire continent of Europe. From the Baltic South, those barriers cut across Germany in a gash of barbed wire, concrete, dog runs, and guard towers. Farther south, there may be no visible, no obvious wall. But there remain armed guards and checkpoints all the same – still a restriction on the right to travel, still an instrument to impose upon ordinary men and women the will of a totalitarian state. Yet, it is here in Berlin where the wall emerges most clearly; here, cutting across your city, where the news photo and the television screen have imprinted this brutal division of a continent upon the mind of the world. Standing before the Brandenburg Gate, every man is a German separated from his fellow men...Every man is a Berliner, forced to look upon a scar...

President von Weizsäcker has said, "The German question is open as long as the Brandenburg Gate is closed." Well today – today I say: As long as this gate is closed, as long as this scar of a wall is permitted to stand, it is not the German question alone that remains open, but the question of freedom for all mankind. Yet, I do not come here to lament. For I find in Berlin a message of hope, even in the shadow of this wall, a message of triumph.

In this season of spring in 1945, the people of Berlin emerged from their air-raid shelters to find devastation. Thousands of miles away, the people of the United States reached out to help. And in 1947 Secretary of State – as you've been told – George Marshall announced the creation of what would become known as the Marshall Plan. Speaking precisely 40 years ago this month, he said: "Our policy is directed not against any country or doctrine, but against hunger, poverty, desperation, and chaos."

In the Reichstag a few moments ago, I saw a display commemorating this 40th anniversary of the Marshall Plan. I was struck by a sign – the sign on a burnt-out, gutted structure that was being rebuilt. I understand that Berliners of my own generation can remember seeing signs like it dotted throughout the western sectors of the city. The sign read simply: "The Marshall Plan is helping here to strengthen the free world." A strong, free world in the West – that dream became real. Japan rose from ruin to become an economic giant. Italy, France, Belgium – virtually every nation in Western Europe saw political and economic rebirth; the European Community was founded.

Where four decades ago there was rubble, today in West Berlin there is the greatest industrial output of any city in Germany: busy office blocks, fine homes and apartments, proud avenues, and the spreading lawns of parkland. Where a city's culture seemed to have been destroyed, today there are two great universities, orchestras and an opera, countless theaters, and museums. Where there was want, today there's abundance – food, clothing, automobiles – the wonderful goods of the Kudamm. From devastation, from utter ruin, you Berliners have, in freedom, rebuilt a city that once again ranks as one of the greatest on earth. Now the Soviets may have had other plans. But my friends, there were a few things the Soviets didn't count on: Berliner Herz, Berliner Humor, ja, und Berliner Schnauze *[Berliner heart, Berliner humor, yes, and Berliner Schnauze – the typical Berlin way of talking]*.

In the 1950s – In the 1950s Khrushchev predicted: "We will bury you." But in the West today, we see a free world that has achieved a level of prosperity and well-being unprecedented in all human history. In the Communist world, we see failure, technological backwardness, declining standards of health, even want of the most basic kind – too little food... General Secretary Gorbachev, if you seek peace, if you seek prosperity for the Soviet Union and Eastern Europe, if you seek liberalization: Come here to this gate. Mr. Gorbachev, open this gate. Mr. Gorbachev – Mr. Gorbachev, tear down this wall!...'

# VÁCLAV HAVEL
## 5 October 1936 –

## 'We live in a contaminated moral environment'
### 1 January 1990

**In 1989 Communist rule in Poland**, Czechoslovakia, Hungary, Romania and Bulgaria collapsed, and the year ended with the toppling of the Berlin Wall. Havel, a playwright, had been elected president of Czechoslovakia on 29 December 1989, after the fall of Communism, and this was his first speech to the nation, a New Year's Day broadcast. A persistent theme in his writings is that under Communism almost everybody lived a double life, saying one thing in public and another in private. He referred to this *'contaminated moral environment'* under the Communist regime, giving his countrymen the message that their *'country is not flourishing'* but now *'the government has returned to you'*.

'My dear fellow citizens – For 40 years you heard from my predecessors on this day different variations on the same theme: how our country was prospering, how many million tons of steel we produced, how happy we all were, how we trusted our government, and what bright perspectives were opening up in front of us. I assume you did not propose me for this office so that I, too, would lie to you. Our country is not prospering. The enormous creative and spiritual potential of our nations is not being used sensibly. Entire branches of industry are producing goods that are of no interest to anyone, while we still lack the things we need. A state which calls itself a workers' state belittles and exploits workers. Our obsolete economy is wasting the scant energy we have available. The worst thing is that we live in a contaminated moral environment. We fell morally ill because we became used to saying something different from what we thought. We learned not to believe in anything, to ignore one another, to care only about ourselves. Concepts such as love, friendship, compassion, humility or forgiveness lost their depth and dimension, and for many of us they represented only psychological oddities, or they resembled lost greetings from ancient times, a little ridiculous in the era of computers and spaceships.

The previous regime – armed with its arrogant and intolerant ideology – reduced man to a force of production, and nature to a tool of production. In this it attacked both their very substance and their mutual relationship. It reduced gifted and autonomous people, skilfully working in their own nation, to the nuts and bolts of some monstrously huge, noisy and stinking machine, whose real meaning was not clear to anyone. We had all become used to the totalitarian system and accepted it as an unalterable fact and thus helped to perpetuate it. In other words, we are all – though naturally to differing extents – responsible for the functioning of the totalitarian machinery. None of us is just its victim. We are all also its co-creators. Why do I say this? It would be very unreasonable to interpret the sad legacy of the last 40 years as something alien, which some distant relative bequeathed to us. On the contrary, we have to accept this legacy as a sin we committed against ourselves. If we accept it as such, we will understand that it is up to us all, and up to us alone to do something about it. We cannot blame the previous rulers for everything, not only because it would be untrue, but also because it would blunt the duty that each of us faces today: namely, the obligation to act independently, freely, reasonably and quickly. Let us not be mistaken: the best government in the world, the best parliament and the best president, cannot achieve much on their own. And it would be wrong to expect a general remedy from them alone. Freedom and democracy involve participation and therefore responsibility from us all...Those who rebelled against totalitarian rule, and those who just managed to remain themselves and think freely, were all persecuted. We should not forget any of those who paid for our present freedom in one way or another. Self-confidence is not pride. Quite the opposite: only a person or a nation that is self-confident, in the best sense of the word, is capable of listening to others, accepting them as equals, forgiving its enemies and regretting its own guilt.

Our country, if that is what we want, can now permanently radiate love, understanding, the power of the spirit and of ideas. It is precisely this glow that we can give as our specific contribution to international politics. Let us teach ourselves and others that politics should be an expression of a desire to contribute to the happiness of the community rather than of a need to cheat or rape the community...I dream of a republic independent, free, and democratic, of a republic economically prosperous and yet socially just; in short, of a humane republic that serves the individual and that therefore contains the hope that the individual will serve it in turn. Of a republic of well-rounded people, because without such people it is impossible to solve any of our problems – human, economic, ecological, social, or political. People, your government has returned to you!'

# ALEXANDER ARIS MYINT SAN AUNG
## 1973 –

*'The lessons of the past will not be forgotten, but it is our hope*
*for the future that we celebrate today'*
10 December 1991

**The 18-year old Alexander** and his 14-year-old brother Kim travelled to
Oslo, where Alexander gave this acceptance speech for the Nobel Peace Prize that
was awarded to his mother Aung San Suu Kyi. The daughter of the assassinated hero
of Burmese independence, Aung San Suu Kyi was placed under house arrest on 20
July 1989 by the illegal military regime in Myanmar (Burma), without charge or trial.
In May 1990, despite the detention of Suu Kyi, her NLD party won the election with
82 per cent of parliamentary seats. The generals refused to recognize the results and
imposed martial law. In October 1990 she was granted the Rafto Human Rights
Prize. In 1991 the European Parliament awarded Suu Kyi the Sakharov Human
Rights award. On 14 October 1991, the Norwegian Nobel Committee announced that
Suu Kyi was the winner of the 1991 Peace Prize. She rejected an offer to free her
if she would leave Myanmar and withdraw from politics. In 1992, she announced
that she would use the $1.3 million prize money to establish a health and education
trust for the Burmese people. Her periods in detention or house arrest imposed by
an illegal regime are 1989–95, 2000–02, 2003–10. On the evening of 13 November
2010, Aung San Suu Kyi was released from house arrest. The Nobel Peace Prize
laureate had been detained for 15 of the previous 21 years.

'Your Majesties, Your Excellencies, Ladies and Gentlemen, I stand before
you here today to accept on behalf of my mother, Aung San Suu Kyi, this
greatest of prizes, the Nobel Prize for Peace. Because circumstances do
not permit my mother to be here in person, I will do my best to convey
the sentiments I believe she would express. Firstly, I know that she would
begin by saying that she accepts the Nobel Prize for Peace not in her own
name but in the name of all the people of Burma. She would say that
this prize belongs not to her but to all those men, women and children
who, even as I speak, continue to sacrifice their wellbeing, their freedom
and their lives in pursuit of a democratic Burma. Theirs is the prize and
theirs will be the eventual victory in Burma's long struggle for peace,
freedom and democracy. Speaking as her son, however, I would add that
I personally believe that by her own dedication and personal sacrifice
she has come to be a worthy symbol through whom the plight of all the
people of Burma may be recognized. And no one must underestimate

that plight. The plight of those in the countryside and towns, living in poverty and destitution, those in prison, battered and tortured; the plight of the young people, the hope of Burma, dying of malaria in the jungles to which they have fled; that of the Buddhist monks, beaten and dishonoured. Nor should we forget the many senior and highly respected leaders besides my mother who are all incarcerated. It is on their behalf that I thank you, from my heart, for this supreme honour. The Burmese people can today hold their heads a little higher in the knowledge that in this far distant land their suffering has been heard and heeded.

...This regime has through almost 30 years of misrule reduced the once prosperous "Golden Land" of Burma to one of the world's most economically destitute nations. In their heart of hearts even those in power now in Rangoon must know that their eventual fate will be that of all totalitarian regimes who seek to impose their authority through fear, repression and hatred. When the present Burmese struggle for democracy erupted onto the streets in 1988, it was the first of what became an international tidal wave of such movements throughout Eastern Europe, Asia and Africa. Today, in 1991, Burma stands conspicuous in its continued suffering at the hands of a repressive, intransigent junta, the State Law and Order Restoration Council. However, the example of those nations which have successfully achieved democracy holds out an important message to the Burmese people; that, in the last resort, through the sheer economic unworkability of totalitarianism this present regime will be swept away. And today in the face of rising inflation, a mismanaged economy and near worthless Kyat, the Burmese government is undoubtedly reaping as it has sown...I know that if she were free today my mother would, in thanking you, also ask you to pray that the oppressors and the oppressed should throw down their weapons and join together to build a nation founded on humanity in the spirit of peace...It only remains for me to thank you all from the bottom of my heart. Let us hope and pray that from today the wounds start to heal and that in the years to come the 1991 Nobel Prize for Peace will be seen as a historic step towards the achievement of true peace in Burma. The lessons of the past will not be forgotten, but it is our hope for the future that we celebrate today.'

# ELIZABETH GLASER
## 11 November 1947 – 3 December 1994

*'I believe in America'*
14 July 1992

**Married to the TV and film actor** and director Paul Michael Glaser, she contracted AIDS after receiving an HIV-contaminated blood transfusion in 1981 while giving birth. She unknowingly passed the virus to her infant daughter, Ariel, through breastfeeding, and her next son Jake, born in 1984, contracted HIV from his mother in the womb. The virus went undetected in all three family members until they underwent HIV testing in 1985, after Ariel began suffering from a series of unexplained illnesses. She had developed advanced AIDS at a time when the medical community knew very little about the disease and there were no available treatment options. With their daughter's condition rapidly deteriorating, the Glasers fought to have her treated intravenously with the new drug AZT, but it was too late and Ariel died in 1988. Grief-stricken but determined to save her son, Jake, along with other HIV-positive children, Glaser co-founded the Elizabeth Glaser Pediatric AIDS Foundation in 1988. She raised public awareness about HIV infection in children and pushed for funding for the development of paediatric AIDS drugs as well as research into mother-to-child transmission of HIV. Elizabeth Glaser died from AIDS in 1994, but made this heart-wrenching speech at the 1992 Democratic Convention, criticizing the government's lack of initiative in tackling the AIDS crisis. Her foundation is a major force in funding the study of paediatric HIV issues and tackling juvenile AIDS. Jake is still alive, and speaks for AIDS-related causes, as does Paul Michael Glaser, who is honorary chairman of her foundation.

'...Twenty years ago I wanted to be at the Democratic Convention because it was a way to participate in my country. Today, I am here because it's a matter of life and death. Exactly – Exactly four years ago my daughter died of AIDS. She did not survive the Reagan Administration. I am here because my son and I may not survive four more years of leaders who say they care, but do nothing. I – I am in a race with the clock. This is not about being a Republican or an Independent or a Democrat. It's about the future – for each and every one of us. I started out just a mom – fighting for the life of her child. But along the way I learned how unfair America can be today, not just for people who have HIV, but for many, many people – poor people, gay people, people of color, children.

A strange spokesperson for such a group: a well-to-do white woman. But I have learned my lesson the hard way, and I know that America has lost her path and is at risk of losing her soul. America wake up: We are all in a struggle between life and death. I understand – I understand the sense of frustration and despair in our country, because I know firsthand about shouting for help and getting no answer. I went to Washington to tell Presidents Reagan and Bush that much, much more had to be done for AIDS research and care, and that children couldn't be forgotten. The first time, when nothing happened, I thought, "They just didn't hear me." The second time, when nothing happened, I thought, "Maybe I didn't shout loud enough." But now I realize they don't hear because they don't want to listen. When you cry for help and no one listens, you start to lose your hope. I began to lose faith in America. I felt my country was letting me down – and it was...

I believe in America, but not a leadership that talks about problems but is incapable of solving them...I believe in America, but an America where there is a light in every home. A thousand points of light just wasn't enough: My house has been dark for too long. Once every generation, history brings us to an important crossroads. Sometimes in life there is that moment when it's possible to make a change for the better. This is one of those moments. For me, this is not politics. This is a crisis of caring...My daughter lived seven years, and in her last year, when she couldn't walk or talk, her wisdom shone through. She taught me to love, when all I wanted to do was hate. She taught me to help others, when all I wanted to do was help myself. She taught me to be brave, when all I felt was fear. My daughter and I loved each other with simplicity. America, we can do the same. This was the country that offered hope. This was the place where dreams could come true, not just economic dreams, but dreams of freedom, justice, and equality. We all need to hope that our dreams can come true. I challenge you to make it happen, because all our lives, not just mine, depend on it. Thank you.'

# MARY FISHER
## 6 April 1948 –

*A whisper of AIDS*
19 August 1992

**Contracting HIV from her second husband**, the artist Mary Fisher (born Lizabeth Davis Frehling) became an impassioned advocated for AIDS prevention and education, making two notable speeches to the Republican Convention, in Houston in 1992 and in San Diego in 1996. She is founder of a non-profit organization to fund HIV/AIDS research and education, the Mary Fisher Clinical AIDS Research and Education (CARE) Fund. Since May 2006 she has been a global emissary for UNAIDS, the United Nations' programme to fight HIV/AIDS. Fisher decided to be open about her illness, and after the Detroit Free Press published her story in February 1992, she was invited to speak at the convention. In 1995, the *New York Times* stated that Fisher and Elizabeth Glaser had *'brought AIDS home to America'*. Fisher created a support group for families affected by AIDS and healthcare workers, the Family AIDS Network, and continued speaking as its representative, promoting education, prevention and acceptance of sufferers. This is an emotive and important speech which altered American attitudes towards HIV.

'Less than three months ago at platform hearings in Salt Lake City, I asked the Republican Party to lift the shroud of silence which has been draped over the issue of HIV and AIDS. I have come tonight to bring our silence to an end. I bear a message of challenge, not self-congratulation. I want your attention, not your applause. I would never have asked to be HIV positive, but I believe that in all things there is a purpose; and I stand before you and before the nation gladly. The reality of AIDS is brutally clear. Two hundred thousand Americans are dead or dying. A million more are infected. Worldwide, forty million, sixty million, or a hundred million infections will be counted in the coming few years. But despite science and research, White House meetings, and congressional hearings, despite good intentions and bold initiatives, campaign slogans, and hopeful promises, it is – despite it all – the epidemic which is winning tonight...To all within the sound of my voice, I appeal: Learn with me the lessons of history and of grace, so my children will not be afraid to say the word "AIDS" when I am gone. Then, their children and yours may not need to whisper it at all. God bless the children, and God bless us all. Good night.'

# NELSON ROLIHLAHLA MANDELA
## 18 July 1918 –

---

### 'Let there be justice for all'
10 May 1994

**Nelson Mandela was the first president** of South Africa to be elected in a fully representative democratic election, holding office from 1994 to 1999. Mandela had served 27 years in prison, but following his release on 11 February 1990, he supported reconciliation and negotiation with the white population, and helped lead the transition towards multi-racial democracy in South Africa. He has received over 250 awards, including a Nobel Prize, and in 2009 the United Nations General Assembly announced that his birthday, 18 July, is to be known as '*Nelson Mandela International Day*' marking his contribution to world freedom. Mandela's compassionate presence moves his audience when he speaks, as he combines nobility with humility, bravery with forgiving. This extract come from his inaugural address having been elected president.

'We have triumphed in the effort to implant hope in the breasts of the millions of our people...As a token of its commitment to the renewal of our country, the new Interim Government of National Unity will, as a matter of urgency, address the issue of amnesty for various categories of our people who are currently serving terms of imprisonment. We dedicate this day to all the heroes and heroines in this country and the rest of the world who sacrificed in many ways and surrendered their lives so that we could be free. Their dreams have become reality. Freedom is their reward. We are both humbled and elevated by the honour and privilege that you, the people of South Africa, have bestowed on us, as the first President of a united, democratic, non-racial and non-sexist South Africa, to lead our country out of the valley of darkness. We understand it still that there is no easy road to freedom. We know it well that none of us acting alone can achieve success. We must therefore act together as a united people, for national reconciliation, for nation building, for the birth of a new world. Let there be justice for all. Let there be peace for all. Let there be work, bread, water and salt for all. Let each know that for each the body, the mind and the soul have been freed to fulfil themselves. Never, never and never again shall it be that this beautiful land will again experience the oppression of one by another and suffer the indignity of being the skunk of the world. Let freedom reign. The sun shall never set on so glorious a human achievement! God bless Africa!'

# BENAZIR BHUTTO
## 21 June 1953 – 27 December 2007

*'Women became the victims of a culture of exclusion*
*and male dominance'*
4 September 1995

**A reluctant convert to politics**, Bhutto was the eldest child of the former prime minister of Pakistan Zulfikar Ali Bhutto. The prime minister was overthrown by General Zia ul-Haq, and Benazir Bhutto spent 18 months in and out of house arrest. During this time she constantly attempted to get General Zia to drop murder charges against her father. Bhutto was hanged in April 1979, and Benazir Bhutto was arrested repeatedly, and placed under house arrest. She spent most of her five years' imprisonment in solitary confinement. Her Pakistan Peoples Party (PPP) won local elections but General Zia's response was to cancel national elections. Benazir Bhutto was hospitalized because of ill health caused by her prison conditions, and on her release was again imprisoned until December 1981, when she was placed under house arrest for over two years. In 1985, her brother Shahnawaz, who had fled the country, was found dead in France. In 1988 she became prime minister, the first woman elected to run a Muslim state, after Zia died in an aircraft explosion. However, she was deposed in 1990 by the new president because of alleged corruption. In 1993 she was re-elected prime minister but was again removed in 1996 on similar charges, and left for exile in Dubai in 1998. In 1993, her remaining brother Murtaza had won elections from exile and became a provincial legislator, returning home soon afterwards, only to be shot dead under mysterious circumstances in 1996. She declined a government offer that her party should head the national government after the 2002 elections, in which the party received the largest number of votes.

Benazir Bhutto eventually returned to Pakistan in October 2007, after reaching an understanding with President Musharraf by which she was granted amnesty, and all corruption charges were withdrawn. Observers said the military regime saw her as a natural ally in its efforts to isolate religious forces and their surrogate militants. She was killed a few weeks later after departing a PPP rally in Rawalpindi, two weeks before the scheduled 2008 general election where she was the leading opposition candidate. President Musharraf officially denied participating in the assassination of Benazir Bhutto as well as failing to provide her with proper security, and al-Qaeda claimed responsibility for the attack, calling Bhutto *'the most precious American asset.'* In 2007 she had said *'I fully understand the men behind al-Qaeda. They have tried to assassinate me twice before. The Pakistan Peoples Party and I represent everything they fear the most – moderation, democracy, equality for women, information, and technology. We represent the future of a modern Pakistan, a future that has no place in it for ignorance, intolerance, and terrorism...Despite threats of death, I will not acquiesce to tyranny, but rather lead the fight against it.'* While prime minister of Pakistan, Bhutto had made this speech on the subject of male domination of women at the Beijing Platform of Action Conference.

'There is a moral crisis engulfing the world as we speak, a crisis of injustice and inaction, a crisis of silence and acquiescence...On this solemn occasion I stand before you not only as a Prime Minister but as a woman and a mother – A woman proud of her cultural and religious heritage, a woman sensitive to the obstacles to justice and full participation that still stand before women in almost every society on earth...When the human spirit was immersed in the darkness of the Middle Ages, Islam proclaimed equality between men and women. When women were viewed as inferior members of the human family, Islam gave them respect and dignity. When women were treated as chattels, the Prophet of Islam (Peace Be Upon Him) accepted them as equal partners. Islam codified the rights of women. The Koran elected their status to that of men. It guaranteed their civic, economic, and political rights. It recognized their participative role in nation building. Sadly, the Islamic tenets regarding women were soon discarded. In Islamic society, as in other parts of the world, their rights were denied. Women were maltreated, discriminated against, and subjected to violence and oppression, their dignity injured and their role denied...

Women became the victims of a culture of exclusion and male dominance. Today more women than men suffer from poverty, deprivation, and discrimination. Half a billion women are illiterate. Seventy per cent of the children who are denied elementary education are girls. The plight of women in the developing countries is unspeakable. Hunger, disease, and unremitting toil is their fate...I am determined to change the plight of women in my country. More than sixty million of our women are largely sidelined. It is a personal tragedy for them. It is a national catastrophe for my nation. I am determined to harness their potential to the gigantic task of nation building...I dream of a Pakistan in which women contribute to their full potential. I am conscious of the struggle that lies ahead. But, with your help, we shall persevere. Allah willing, we shall succeed.'

# CHARLES EDWARD MAURICE SPENCER, 9TH EARL SPENCER
## 20 May 1964 –

*'A standard bearer for the rights of the truly downtrodden'*
6 September 1997

Lady Diana Spencer married the 32-year-old Charles, Prince of Wales, on 29 July 1981, just after celebrating her 20th birthday. The marriage fell apart and they officially separated on 9 December 1992, divorcing on 28 August 1996. The unexpected death of Diana in a car crash in 1997 affected the nation deeply. Many people felt that her husband had treated her shabbily, and admired the way that she had forged a new career in helping the victims of AIDS and landmines. The royal family had barely noticed her passing, it seemed, and public resentment built to a point where the queen was virtually forced to make a tribute to her, in a live television broadcast only the day before Diana's funeral. In reaction to her death, people had left public offerings of flowers, candles, cards and personal messages near her home in Kensington Gardens. By 10 September, the pile of flowers was five feet deep. Earl Spencer's speech was absolutely sensational. It was broadcast to the massed crowds outside Westminster Abbey, who began applauding Spencer's attack on the royal family's treatment of Lady Diana. Spencer's voice started cracking towards the end, as emotion began to overcome him. The crescendo of approval from outside filtered into Westminster Abbey. In the congregation, Diana's eldest son Prince William and his brother Harry began clapping. Prince Charles tapped his thigh and then immediately stopped. Queen Elizabeth, Prince Philip and the Queen Mother did not move. The bitterness of Spencer's attack, the references to 'blood family', and to his sister's tearful despair shocked the queen, her husband and son, as they realized how much Diana was missed by the nation. Spencer used the power of words, gestures and symbols in an act of revenge for his sister's death. *The Guardian* called the speech more a *'battle cry'* than a eulogy, with the Spencers regarding themselves as far more representative of the English ruling classes than the parvenu Germans known by the adopted name of Windsor. Probably for the first time in the 20th century, the royal family temporarily lost its standing in British society as an emblem of the people, as it showed how insulated it was from public feeling and opinion.

'I stand before you today, the representative of a family in grief, in a country in mourning, before a world in shock. We are all united, not only in our desire to pay our respects to Diana, but rather in our need to do so, because such was her extraordinary appeal that the tens of millions of people taking part in this service all over the world via television and radio who never actually met her feel that they too lost someone close to them in the early hours of Sunday morning. It is a more remarkable tribute to Diana then I can ever hope to offer to her today. Diana was the very essence of compassion, of duty, of style, of beauty. All over the world she was the symbol of selfless humanity. A standard bearer for the rights of the truly downtrodden. A very British girl who transcended nationality. Someone with a natural nobility who was classless and who proved in the last year that she needed no royal title to continue to generate her particular brand of magic. Today is our chance to say "thank you" for the way you brightened our lives, even though God granted you but half a life. We will all feel cheated always that you were taken from us so young and yet we must learn to be grateful that you came at all. Only now you are gone do we truly appreciate what we are without, and we want you to know that life without you is very, very difficult. We have all despaired for our loss over the past week and only the strength of the message you gave us through your years of giving has afforded us the strength to move forward. There is a temptation to rush, to canonize your memory. There is no need to do so. You stand tall enough as a human being of unique qualities, and do not need to be seen as a saint. Indeed, to sanctify your memory would be to miss out on the very core of your being – your wonderfully mischievous sense of humour with a laugh that bent you double, your joy for life transmitted wherever you took your smile and the sparkle in those unforgettable eyes, your boundless energy which you could barely contain...Without your God-given sensitivity, we would be immersed in greater ignorance at the anguish of Aids and HIV sufferers, the plight of the homeless, the isolation of lepers, the random destruction of landmines....'

# ELIEZER 'ELIE' WIESEL
## 30 September 1928 –

*'Indifference, after all, is more dangerous than anger and hatred'*
12 April 1999

**In 1944 Wiesel and his Jewish family** were rounded up in a Romanian ghetto, and then deported with the Jewish community to the concentration camp at Auschwitz-Birkenau. Wiesel was separated from his mother and sister who are presumed to have died there. Wiesel and his father were sent to the attached work camp and he managed to remain with his father for over eight months as they were forced to work as slave labour. In January 1945, just a few weeks after the two were marched to Buchenwald, Wiesel's father died from exhaustion, dysentery and starvation. Wiesel, a writer and political activist, received the 1986 Nobel Peace Prize and the Presidential Medal of Freedom for his work in the cause of peace. He was also the founding chair of the United States Holocaust Memorial, and has written over 40 books including *Night*, an account of his Holocaust experiences, first published in 1960. When Wiesel was awarded the Nobel Prize, the Norwegian committee called him a *'messenger to mankind'*, noting that through his works Wiesel had delivered a powerful message *'of peace, atonement and human dignity'* to humanity. This is a harrowing speech – Wiesel cannot forget the indifference of politicians to his plight and is fighting so such events cannot happen again, although he points to the situation in Kosovo as yet another failure of world leaders to prevent ethnic cleansing. It was delivered in the White House in front of President Clinton as part of the Millennium Lecture series.

'Fifty-four years ago to the day, a young Jewish boy from a small town in the Carpathian Mountains woke up, not far from Goethe's beloved Weimar, in a place of eternal infamy called Buchenwald. He was finally free, but there was no joy in his heart. He thought there never would be again. Liberated a day earlier by American soldiers, he remembers their rage at what they saw. And even if he lives to be a very old man, he will always be grateful to them for that rage, and also for their compassion. Though he did not understand their language, their eyes told him what he needed to know – that they, too, would remember, and bear witness. And now, I stand before you, Mr President – Commander-in-Chief of the army that freed me, and tens of thousands of others – and I am filled with a profound and abiding gratitude to the American people...

In a way, to be indifferent to that suffering is what makes the human being inhuman. Indifference, after all, is more dangerous than anger and hatred. Anger can at times be creative. One writes a great poem, a great symphony, one does something special for the sake of humanity because one is angry at the injustice that one witnesses. But indifference is never creative. Even hatred at times may elicit a response. You fight it. You denounce it. You disarm it. Indifference elicits no response. Indifference is not a response. Indifference is not a beginning, it is an end. And, therefore, indifference is always the friend of the enemy, for it benefits the aggressor – never his victim, whose pain is magnified when he or she feels forgotten. The political prisoner in his cell, the hungry children, the homeless refugees – not to respond to their plight, not to relieve their solitude by offering them a spark of hope is to exile them from human memory. And in denying their humanity we betray our own. Indifference, then, is not only a sin, it is a punishment. And this is one of the most important lessons of this outgoing century's wide-ranging experiments in good and evil. In the place that I come from, society was composed of three simple categories: the killers, the victims, and the bystanders.

Does it mean that we have learned from the past? Does it mean that society has changed? Has the human being become less indifferent and more human? Have we really learned from our experiences? Are we less insensitive to the plight of victims of ethnic cleansing and other forms of injustices in places near and far? Is today's justified intervention in Kosovo, led by you, Mr President, a lasting warning that never again will the deportation, the terrorization of children and their parents be allowed anywhere in the world? Will it discourage other dictators in other lands to do the same? What about the children? Oh, we see them on television, we read about them in the papers, and we do so with a broken heart. Their fate is always the most tragic, inevitably. When adults wage war, children perish. We see their faces, their eyes. Do we hear their pleas? Do we feel their pain, their agony? Every minute one of them dies of disease, violence, famine. Some of them – so many of them – could be saved. And so, once again, I think of the young Jewish boy from the Carpathian Mountains. He has accompanied the old man I have become throughout these years of quest and struggle. And together we walk towards the new millennium, carried by profound fear and extraordinary hope.'

# ANITA RODDICK
## 23 October 1942–10 September 2007

*'Froth with terrifying power over people's lives'*
27 November 1999

**The human rights activist and environmental** campaigner was best known as the founder of The Body Shop, producing and retailing cosmetic products that pioneered ethical consumerism. The Body Shop was one of the first to prohibit the use of ingredients tested on animals, and also one of the first to promote fair trade with third world suppliers. Anita Roddick flew to Seattle to speak out against the role of the World Trade Organization and she witnessed the 'Battle of Seattle', where she was tear-gassed with other protesters in a sidestreet. This impassioned speech is a well-founded attack on the World Trade Organization from a tremendously successful international business person. In 2004, Roddick was diagnosed with liver cirrhosis due to long-standing hepatitis C, which she believed came from an infected blood transfusion in 1971. She died as a result of the infection in 2007. One wishes that male business leaders and politicians had a tiny percentage of the common sense, bravery and humanity of this female business pioneer and multinational CEO.

'We are in Seattle arguing for a world trade system that puts basic human rights and the environment at its core. We have the most powerful corporations of the world ranged against us. They own the media that informs us – or fails to inform us. And they probably own the politicians too. It's enough to make anybody feel a little edgy. So here's a question for the world trade negotiators. Who is the system you are lavishing so much attention on supposed to serve? We can ask the same question of the gleaming towers of Wall Street or the City of London – and the powerful men and women who tinker with the money system which drives world trade. Who is this system for? Let's look more closely. Every day, the gleaming towers of high finance oversee a global flow of two trillion dollars through their computer screens. And the terrifying thing is that only three per cent of that – that's, three hundredths – has anything to do with trade at all. Let alone free trade between equal communities. It has everything to do with money. The great global myth being that the current world trade system is for anything but money.
    The other 97 per cent of the two trillion is speculation. It is froth

– but froth with terrifying power over people's lives. Reducing powerless communities access to basic human rights can make money, but not for them. But then the system isn't designed for them. It isn't designed for you and me either. We all of us, rich and poor, have to live with the insecurity caused by an out of control global casino with a built-in bias towards instability. Because it is instability that makes money for the money-traders. "The great enemy of the truth is very often not the lie – deliberate, contrived and dishonest", said John F. Kennedy, – "but the myth – persistent, persuasive and unrealistic." Asking questions can puncture these powerful myths. I spend much of every year travelling around the world, talking to people in the front line of globalization: women, community farmers, children. I know how unrealistic these myths are. Not just in developing countries but right under our noses. Like the small farmers of the USA, 500 of which go out of business every week. Half a century ago there were a million black farmers in the US. Now there are 1800. Globalization means that the subsidies go to the big farms, while the small family farms – the heart of so many American communities – go to the wall. Or the dark, cramped factories where people work for a pittance for 12 hour days without a day off. "The workers are not allowed to talk to each other and they didn't allow us to go to the bathroom," says one Asian worker in that garment factory. Not in Seoul. Not in Sao Paulo. But in San Francisco. We have a world trading system that is blind to this kind of injustice. And as the powers of governments shrink this system is, in effect, our new unelected, uncontrollable world government. One that outlaws our attempts to make things better...We have to be political consumers, vigilante consumers. With the barrage of propaganda served up to us every day, we have to be. We must be wise enough so that – whatever they may decide at the trade talks – we know where to put our energy and our money. No matter what we're told or cajoled to do, we must work together to get the truth out in cooperation for the best, not competition for the cheapest. By putting our money where our heart is, refusing to buy the products which exploit, by forming powerful strategic alliances, we will mould the world into a kinder more loving shape. And we will do so no matter what you decide this week. Human progress is on our side.'

# POPE JOHN PAUL II (KAROL JÓSEF WOJTYLA)
## 18 May 1920 – 2 April 2005

*'In this place of memories, the mind and heart and soul feel an extreme need for silence'*
23 March 2000

**The Polish cardinal of Kraków** became pope on 16 October 1978, serving until his death almost 27 years later, and he was the first non-Italian pope since the 1520s. Fluent in at least 12 languages, he visited 129 countries, drawing immense crowds. He made rapprochements with the Anglican, Eastern Orthodox and especially the Judaic religions. During the Second World War he had hidden from a German round-up of civilians in Warsaw, and managed to save some Jews from the Holocaust. In 2000, the Pope visited Yad Vashem, the Israeli National Holocaust Memorial, where he made this moving speech.

'The words of the ancient Psalm, rise from our hearts: "I have become like a broken vessel. I hear the whispering of many – terror on every side – as they scheme together against me, as they plot to take my life. But I trust in you, O Lord: I say, 'you are my God.'" In this place of memories, the mind and heart and soul feel an extreme need for silence. Silence in which to remember. Silence in which to try to make some sense of the memories which come flooding back...My own personal memories are of all that happened when the Nazis occupied Poland during the war. I remember my Jewish friends and neighbours, some of whom perished, while others survived. I have come to Yad Vashem to pay homage to the millions of Jewish people who, stripped of everything, especially of human dignity, were murdered in the Holocaust. More than half a century has passed, but the memories remain. Here, as at Auschwitz and many other places in Europe, we are overcome by the echo of the heart-rending laments of so many. Men, women and children cry out to us from the depths of the horror that they knew. How can we fail to heed their cry? No one can forget or ignore what happened. No one can diminish its scale. We wish to remember. But we wish to remember for a purpose, namely to ensure that never again will evil prevail, as it did for the millions of innocent victims of Nazism. How could man have such utter contempt for man? Because he had reached the point of contempt for God. Only a godless ideology could plan and carry out the extermination of a whole people. The honour given to the "Just Gentiles" by the state of Israel at Yad Vashem for having acted heroically to save Jews, sometimes to the point of giving their own lives, is a recognition that not even in the darkest hour is every light extinguished. That is why the Psalms and the entire Bible, though well aware of the human capacity for evil, also proclaims that evil will not have the last word. Out of the depths of pain and sorrow, the believer's heart cries out: "I trust in you, O Lord: I say, you are my God."

Jews and Christians share an immense spiritual patrimony, flowing from God's self-revelation. Our religious teachings and our spiritual experience demand that we overcome evil with good. We remember, but not with any desire for vengeance or as an incentive to hatred. For us, to remember is to pray for peace and justice, and to commit ourselves to their cause. Only a world at peace, with justice for all, can avoid repeating the mistakes and terrible crimes of the past. As bishop of Rome and successor of the Apostle Peter, I assure the Jewish people that the Catholic Church, motivated by the Gospel law of truth and love, and by no political considerations, is deeply saddened by the hatred, acts of persecution and displays of anti-Semitism directed against the Jews by Christians at any time and in any place. The church rejects racism in any form as a denial of the image of the Creator inherent in every human being. In this place of solemn remembrance, I fervently pray that our sorrow for the tragedy which the Jewish people suffered in the 20th century will lead to a new relationship between Christians and Jews. Let us build a new future in which there will be no more anti-Jewish feeling among Christians or anti-Christian feeling among Jews, but rather the mutual respect required of those who adore the one Creator and Lord, and look to Abraham as our common father in faith. The world must heed the warning that comes to us from the victims of the Holocaust, and from the testimony of the survivors. Here at Yad Vashem the memory lives on, and burns itself onto our souls. It makes us cry out: "I hear the whispering of many – terror on every side – but I trust in you, O Lord: I say, 'You are my God'."

# GEORGE W. BUSH JR
## 6 July 1946 –

*'Americans are asking, "Who attacked our country?"'*
20 September 2001

**On Tuesday, 11 September 2001**, four large passenger jets were hijacked by terrorists and then deliberately crashed, killing nearly 3,000 people. Two fully fuelled jets, carrying 92 people and 65 people respectively had departed Boston for Los Angeles. Both were diverted by the hijackers to New York City where they were piloted into the twin towers of the World Trade Center. The film footage is chilling. The impact and fire caused both 110-storey towers to collapse, killing 2,752 persons, including hundreds of rescue workers. United Airlines Flight 93, which had departed Newark for San Francisco, and American Airlines Flight 77, which had departed Dulles (Virginia) for Los Angeles, were also hijacked. Flight 77, with 64 people on board, was diverted to Washington, D.C., then piloted into the Pentagon building, killing everyone on board and 125 military personnel inside the building. Flight 93, with 44 people on board, was also diverted towards Washington but crashed into a field in Pennsylvania after passengers attempted to overpower the terrorists on board. The president gave this much-awaited speech before a Joint Session of Congress, outlining America's reaction to the unprecedented attack against its people. Of course, Bush probably did not write a word of it, and a team of writers had probably polished it for days, but it hits the right note of trying to appease the American people while drawing in other countries to support the United States in the war against terror. This is a speech on a knife-edge. There are some clichés, certainly, but it is a logical, thoughtful, progressive, positive speech of the type that appeals to all sectors of the American nation and its allies.

'In the normal course of events, presidents come to this chamber to report on the state of the Union. Tonight, no such report is needed. It has already been delivered by the American people. We have seen it in the courage of passengers who rushed terrorists to save others on the ground. Passengers like an exceptional man named Todd Beamer. And would you please help me welcome his wife Lisa Beamer here tonight? We have seen the state of our Union in the endurance of rescuers working past exhaustion. We've seen the unfurling of flags, the lighting of candles, the giving of blood, the saying of prayers in English, Hebrew and Arabic. We have seen the decency of a loving and giving people who have made the grief of strangers their own. My fellow citizens, for the last nine days, the entire world has seen for itself the state of the Union, and it is strong. Tonight, we are a country awakened to danger and called to defend freedom. Our grief has turned to anger and anger to resolution. Whether we bring our enemies to justice or bring justice to our enemies, justice will be done. I thank the Congress for its leadership at such an important time.

...On September the 11th, enemies of freedom committed an act of war against our country. Americans have known wars, but for the past 136 years they have been wars on foreign soil, except for one Sunday in 1941. Americans have known the casualties of war, but not at the center of a great city on a peaceful morning. Americans have known surprise attacks, but never before on thousands of civilians. All of this was brought upon us in a single day, and night fell on a different world, a world where freedom itself is under attack. Americans have many questions tonight. Americans are asking, "Who attacked our country?"... The terrorists' directive commands them to kill Christians and Jews, to kill all Americans and make no distinctions among military and civilians, including women and children. This group and its leader, a person named Osama bin Laden, are linked to many other organizations in different countries, including the Egyptian Islamic Jihad, the Islamic Movement of Uzbekistan. There are thousands of these terrorists in more than 60 countries. They are recruited from their own nations and neighborhoods and brought to camps in places like Afghanistan, where they are trained in the tactics of terror. They are sent back to their homes or sent to hide in countries around the world to plot evil and destruction. I will not forget the wound to our country and those who inflicted it. I will not yield, I will not rest, I will not relent in waging this struggle for freedom and security for the American people. The course of this conflict is not known, yet its outcome is certain. Freedom and fear, justice and cruelty, have always been at war, and we know that God is not neutral between them. Fellow citizens, we'll meet violence with patient justice, assured of the rightness of our cause and confident of the victories to come. In all that lies before us, may God grant us wisdom, and may He watch over the United States of America. Thank you.'

# POPE BENEDICT XVI (JOSEPH ALOIS RATZINGER)
## 16 April 1927 –

### *'To speak in this place of horror'*
28 May 2006

**Born in Germany, Joseph Ratzinger** grew up in a nation dominated by the Nazi Party, and was obliged to join the Hitler Youth, like all German boys. He deserted the German army towards the end of the war and was briefly held as a prisoner-of-war by the Allies in 1945. He was ordained in 1951, taught at the University of Bonn from 1959 and in 1966 took a chair in dogmatic theology at the University of Tübingen. His experiences as an academic in the 1960s, with student unrest espousing Marxism, led him to the view that religion was being subordinated to a political ideology that he considered '*tyrannical, brutal and cruel*'. He later became a leading campaigner against liberation theology, the movement to involve the Church in social activism, which for him was too close to Marxism. In 1969 he moved to Regensburg University in his native Bavaria and rose to become its dean and vice-president, being named cardinal of Munich by Pope Paul VI in 1977. As Cardinal Ratzinger, he now spent 24 years as one of the senior figures in the Vatican, heading the Congregation for the Doctrine of the Faith – once known as the Holy Office of the Inquisition. This made him John Paul II's 'enforcer', the reason for his nickname 'God's rottweiler', and he is seen as being passionately dedicated to Catholic doctrine. In 2005, at the age of 78, Joseph Ratzinger was the oldest cardinal to become pope since Clement XII was elected in 1730. The academic and accomplished pianist was looking forward to retirement when Pope John Paul II died in 2005, and has said that he never wanted to be pope. He explained to the cardinals his choice of name, after Pope Benedict XV who worked to bring peace during the First World War: '*I too hope in this short reign to be a man of peace.*'

As Pope Benedict XVI, he took over during one of the fiercest storms the Catholic Church has faced in decades – the scandal of child sex abuse by priests. A flood of allegations, lawsuits and official reports into clerical abuse reached a peak in 2009 and 2010. The pope has met and issued an unprecedented apology to victims, promised action and made clear that bishops must report abuse cases to the local authorities. His naturally traditionalist views were intensified by his experiences during the liberal 1960s. He has a reputation as a theological conservative, taking uncompromising positions on homosexuality, women priests and contraception. But for his supporters, this is exactly why he is the man to lead the Church through such challenging times. The pope espouses Christian compassion – speaking out recently against Roma deportations in France, and against human rights abuses in China and elsewhere. He criticized the war in Iraq, and has called for more urgency in protecting the environment and fighting the 'scandal' of poverty. In Poland, he visited Oświecim, which the Nazis had called Auschwitz, and became the second pope to walk the grounds of Hitler's most notorious death camp.

'To speak in this place of horror, in this place where unprecedented mass crimes were committed against God and man, is almost impossible – and it is particularly difficult and troubling for a Christian, for a pope from Germany. In a place like this, words fail; in the end, there can only be a dread silence – a silence which is itself a heartfelt cry to God: Why, Lord, did you remain silent? How could you tolerate all this? In silence, then, we bow our heads before the endless line of those who suffered and were put to death here; yet our silence becomes in turn a plea for forgiveness and reconciliation, a plea to the living God never to let this happen again...Pope John Paul came here as a son of that people which, along with the Jewish people, suffered most in this place and, in general, throughout the war. "Six million Poles lost their lives during the Second World War: a fifth of the nation," he reminded us...Pope John Paul II came here as a son of the Polish people. I come here today as a son of the German people. For this very reason, I can and must echo his words: I could not fail to come here. I had to come. It is a duty before the truth and the just due of all who suffered here, a duty before God, for me to come here as the successor of Pope John Paul II and as a son of the German people – a son of that people over which a ring of criminals rose to power by false promises of future greatness and the recovery of the nation's honour, prominence and prosperity, but also through terror and intimidation, with the result that our people was used and abused as an instrument of their thirst for destruction and power. Yes, I could not fail to come here...'

# ROSS C. 'ROCKY' ANDERSON
## 9 September 1951 –

*'Give us the truth!'*
30 August 2006

**The lawyer and Democrat politician** is currently the president of High Road for Human Rights, a movement working to protect the human rights of people around the world, and he was mayor of Salt Lake City, Utah from 1999–2007. In 2005 he accepted an invitation from the Veterans of Foreign Wars Association to participate in a visit by President Bush on 22 August. However, Anderson then emailed local advocacy leaders calling for *'the biggest demonstration* [Utah] *has ever seen'* to protest against Bush's appearance at the Veterans' National Convention at the Salt Palace. Speaking to a rally at Pioneer Park, Salt Lake City, Anderson justified his protest, asserting that the *'nation was lied into a war'*. The following year he was involved in another anti-Bush rally, characterizing the war in Iraq as *'illegal and immoral'*. Throughout his speech, Anderson stated that a true patriot can question government actions while still supporting America's troops, asserting, *' Blind faith in bad leaders is not patriotism.'* This was courageous, as Utah gave George W. Bush 67 per cent of its vote in 2000 and a massive 72 per cent in 2004, even after Bush's acts of incompetence were public knowledge. President Bush visited Salt Lake City on 30–31 August 2006 to promote his policies in Iraq and the 'war on terror', at the same time as Anderson was holding his second protest rally.

'A patriot is a person who loves his or her country. Who among you loves your country so much that you have come here today to raise your voice out of deep concern for our nation – and for our world? And who among you loves your country so much that you insist that our nation's leaders tell us the truth? Let's hear it: "Give us the truth! Give us the truth! Give us the truth!" Let no one deny we are patriots. We love our country, we hold dear the values upon which our nation was founded, and we are distressed at what our President, his administration, and our Congress are doing to, and in the name of, our great nation. Blind faith in bad leaders is not patriotism...Therefore it is absolutely necessary that there should be full liberty to tell the truth about his acts, and this means that it is exactly necessary to blame him when he does wrong as to praise him when he does right. Any other attitude in an American citizen is both base and servile. To announce that there must be no criticism of the

President, or that we are to stand by the President, right or wrong, is not only unpatriotic and servile, but is morally treasonable to the American public. Nothing but the truth should be spoken about him or anyone else. But it is even more important to tell the truth, pleasant or unpleasant, about him than about anyone else. We are here today as truth-tellers. And we are here to demand: "Give us the truth! Give us the truth! Give us the truth!"...

What incredible ineptitude and callousness for our President to talk about a Crusade while lying to us to make a case for the invasion and occupation of a Muslim country! Our children and later generations will pay the price of the lies, the violence, the cruelty, the incompetence, and the inhumanity of the Bush administration and the lackey Congress that has so cowardly abrogated its responsibility and authority under our checks-and-balances system of government. We are here to say, "We will not stand for it any more. No more lies. No more pre-emptive, illegal war, based on false information. No more God-is-on-our-side religious nonsense to justify this immoral, illegal war. No more inhumanity." Let's raise our voices, and demand, "Give us the truth! Give us the truth! Give us the truth!"...This is a new day. We will not be silent. We will continue to raise our voices. We will bring others with us. We will grow and grow, regardless of political party – unified in our insistence upon the truth, upon peace-making, upon more humane treatment of our brothers and sisters around the world. We will be ever cognizant of our moral responsibility to speak up in the face of wrongdoing, and to work as we can for a better, safer, more just community, nation, and world. So we won't let down. We won't be quiet. We will continue to resist the lies, the deception, the outrages of the Bush administration. We will insist that peace be pursued, and that, as a nation, we help those in need. We must break the cycle of hatred, of intolerance, of exploitation. We must pursue peace as vigorously as the Bush administration has pursued war. It's up to all of us to do our part. Thank you everyone for lending your voices to this call for compassion, for peace, for greater humanity. Let us keep in mind the injunction of Dr Martin Luther King, Jr: "Our lives begin to end the day we become silent about things that matter."

# BARACK HUSSEIN OBAMA II
### 4 August 1961 –

## 'Yes We Can!'
Presidential election victory speech, Grant Park, Chicago, 5 November 2008

**Born in Hawaii, of a Kenyan father** and American mother, the 44th president of the United States is the first African-American to be elected to that office. A professor at Chicago Law School for 12 years until 2004, Obama was also State senator for Illinois from 1997–2004. A strong opponent of the Iraq War, Obama delivered the keynote address at the Democratic National Convention in 2004 and later that year was elected senator for Illinois. He resigned from the Senate to run for president, defeating Hillary Clinton for the Democratic nomination, and then John McCain, the Republican nominee. Obama focused on his campaign theme of change in front of an estimated 240,000 people in his home constituency of Chicago. There were resonances of speeches by John F. Kennedy and Martin Luther King, and an emotional reference to his grandmother who had died just two days previously. This is a wonderful speech, directed at every American, stressing the need for change in an economically uncertain climate.

'If there is anyone out there who still doubts that America is a place where all things are possible; who still wonders if the dream of our founders is alive in our time; who still questions the power of our democracy, tonight is your answer. It's the answer told by lines that stretched around schools and churches in numbers this nation has never seen; by people who waited three hours and four hours, many for the very first time in their lives, because they believed that this time must be different; that their voice could be that difference. It's the answer spoken by young and old, rich and poor, Democrat and Republican, black, white, Latino, Asian, Native American, gay, straight, disabled and not disabled – Americans who sent a message to the world that we have never been a collection of Red States and Blue States: we are, and always will be, the United States of America. It's the answer that led those who have been told for so long by so many to be cynical, and fearful, and doubtful of what we can achieve to put their hands on the arc of history and bend it once more toward the hope of a better day. It's been a long time coming, but tonight, because of what we did on this day, in this election, at this defining moment, change has come to America.

I was never the likeliest candidate for this office. We didn't start with much money or many endorsements...This is your victory. I know you didn't do this just to win an election and I know you didn't do it for me. You did it because you understand the enormity of the task that lies ahead. For even as we celebrate tonight, we know the challenges that tomorrow will bring are the greatest of our lifetime – two wars, a planet in peril, the worst financial crisis in a century. Even as we stand here tonight, we know there are brave Americans waking up in the deserts of Iraq and the mountains of Afghanistan to risk their lives for us. There are mothers and fathers who will lie awake after their children fall asleep and wonder how they'll make the mortgage, or pay their doctor's bills, or save enough for college. There is new energy to harness and new jobs to be created; new schools to build and threats to meet and alliances to repair. The road ahead will be long. Our climb will be steep. We may not get there in one year or even one term, but America – I have never been more hopeful than I am tonight that we will get there. I promise you – we as a people will get there...For that is the true genius of America – that America can change. Our union can be perfected. And what we have already achieved gives us hope for what we can and must achieve tomorrow.

...This is our moment. This is our time – to put our people back to work and open doors of opportunity for our kids; to restore prosperity and promote the cause of peace; to reclaim the American Dream and reaffirm that fundamental truth – that out of many, we are one; that while we breathe, we hope, and where we are met with cynicism, and doubt, and those who tell us that we can't, we will respond with that timeless creed that sums up the spirit of a people: Yes We Can. Thank you, God bless you, and may God bless the United States of America.'

# Index

**Frederick II, King** (1712–1786)
'...shortly we have either beaten the Enemy, or we
never see one another again' 72

# G

**Galen, Blessed Cardinal Clemens August, Graf
von** (1878–1946)
'...mentally ill people in Germany have been
deliberately killed and more will be killed in the
future' 264

**Gandhi, Mohandas Karamchand** (1869–1948)
'I believe that in the history of the world, there has
not been a more genuinely democratic struggle
for freedom than ours' 270
'Non-violence is the first article of my faith' 234

**Garibaldi, Giuseppe** (1807–1882)
'I offer hunger, thirst, forced marches, battles, and
death' 154
'This people is its own master' 169

**Garrison, William Lloyd** (1805–1879)
On the Death of John Brown 168

**Glaser, Elizabeth** (1947–1994)
'I believe in America' 338

**Goebbels, Paul Joseph** (1897–1945)
'Now, people rise up and let the storm break
loose!' 272

**Gladstone, William Ewart** (1809–1898)
'Remember the rights of the savage' 190

**Gnaeus Julius Agricola** (40–93 CE)
'Death with honour is preferable to life with
ignominy' 38

**Gouraud, Henri Joseph Eugène** (1867–1946)
'Kill them, kill them in abundance, until they have
had enough' 229

**Grattan, Henry** (1746–1820)
'It was the act of a coward, who raises his arm to
strike, but has not courage to give the blow' 118

# H

**Hamilton, Andrew** (c.1676–1741)
'The loss of liberty, to a generous mind, is worse
than death' 68

**Hannibal Barca** (247–183 or 182 BCE)
Address to his Soldiers before the Battle of
Ticinus 25
Encouraging his Soldiers to Cross the Alps 22

**Harrison, Benjamin** (1833–1910)
'I believe that patriotism has been blown into a
higher and holier flame in many hearts' 194

**Havel, Václav** (1936–)
'We live in a contaminated moral environment' 334

**Henry, Patrick** (1736–1799)
'Give me liberty or give me death!' 80

**Hitler, Adolf** (1889–1945)
'In September 1939 I assured you that neither force
of arms nor time would overcome Germany' 268
'My patience now is at an end!' 244
'Work and bread!' 238

**Hugo, Victor-Marie** (1802–1885)
'...if there is a culprit here, it is not my son, –
it is I!' 158

# I

**Ickes, Harold Leclair** (1874–1952)
What is an American? 258

**Ingersoll, Robert Green** (1833–1899)
'He is the gentlest memory of our world' 198

**Isocrates** (436–338 BCE )
Panegyricus – On the Union of Greece to Resist
Persia 12

# J

**Jefferson, Thomas** (1743–1826)
'I advance with obedience to the work' 120

Pym, John (1584–1643)
*The Cry of all England 60*

# R

Raleigh, Sir Walter (c.1552–1618)
*'I thank my God heartily that He hath brought me into the light to die' 56*

Red Eagle, Chief (1781–1824)
*'I fear no man, for I am a Creek warrior' 135*

Red Jacket (c.1758–1830)
*'We gave them corn and meat; they gave us poison in return' 126*

Reagan, Ronald Wilson
(1911–2004)
*'Mr. Gorbachev, tear down this wall!' 332*
*'The future doesn't belong to the fainthearted; it belongs to the brave' 330*

Robespierre, Maximilien François Marie Isidore de (1758–1794)
*'Death is the commencement of immortality!' 112*
*'Our blood flows for the cause of humanity' 111*
*'Terror is nothing else than swift, severe, indomitable justice' 110*

Roddick, Anita (1942–2007)
*'Froth with terrifying power over people's lives' 348*

Roosevelt, Franklin Delano (1882–1945)
*'A date which will live in infamy' 265*
*'Freedom means the supremacy of human rights everywhere' 256*
*'The only thing we have to fear is fear itself' 240*
*'We are now in this war' 266*

Roosevelt, Theodore (1858–1919)
*'No people on earth have more cause to be thankful than ours' 208*
*'...not the doctrine of ignoble ease, but the doctrine of the strenuous life' 203*

# S

Schweitzer, Albert (1875–1965)
*The Problem of Peace 290*

Scythian Ambassador (fl.329 BCE)
*'Do not imagine that those whom thou conquerest can love thee' 18*

Sheil, Richard Lalor (1791–1851)
*On the Disabilities of the Jews 150*
*On the Irish as 'aliens' 147*

Smith, Goldwin (1823–1910)
*The Secret beyond Science 182*

Socrates (469–399 BCE)
*In his own Defence 9*
*On being Condemned to Death 11*
*On being Declared Guilty 10*

Solzhenitsyn, Aleksander Isayevich
(1918–2008)
*'What is the joy about?' 324*

Spencer, Charles Edward Maurice (1964–)
*'A standard bearer for the rights of the truly downtrodden' 344*

Stalin, Joseph (1878–1953)
*'The war you are waging is a war of liberation, a just war' 262*

Stephens, Alexander Hamilton
(1812–1883)
*The Cornerstone Speech 172*

# T

Tecumseh, Chief (1768–1813)
*'In the name of the Indian chiefs and warriors' 132*
*'My forefathers were warriors' 129*

Teresa, Mother (1910–1997)
*'Smile at each other' 323*

Terrell, Mary Church (1863–1954)
*'...our people are sacrificed on the altar of prejudice in the capital of the United States'* 210

Tone, Theobald Wolf (1763–1798)
*'...it is no great effort, at this day, to add the sacrifice of my life'* 116

Truman, Harry S. (1884–1972)
*'Democracy alone can supply the vitalizing force to stir the peoples of the world into triumphant action'* 284

Truth, Sojourner (Isabella Baumfree) (1797–1883)
*'Ain't I a woman?'* 155

# V

Viviani, Jean Raphaël Adrien René (1863–1925)
*'We are without reproach'* 215

# W

Washington, Booker Taliaferro (1856–1915)
*'One-third of the population of the South is of the Negro race'* 199

Washington, George (1732–1799)
*'I retire from the great theater of Action'* 95
*Preventing the Revolt of his Officers* 92
*'The eyes of all our countrymen are now upon us'* 83

Webster, Daniel (1782–1852)
*'An American no longer?'* 156
*'It was sealed in blood'* 160
*Second reply to Hayne* 141

Wiesel, Eliezer 'Elie' (1928–)
*'Indifference, after all, is more dangerous than anger and hatred'* 346

Wilberforce, William (1759–1833)
*'How can we bear to think of such a scene as this?'* 100

Wilhelm II, Kaiser (1859–1941)
*'The hour is grave'* 232

Wilkes, John (1725–1797)
*'This I know: a successful resistance is a revolution, not a rebellion!'* 76

Willard, Frances Elizabeth Caroline (1839–1898)
*'...there is nothing new under the sun'* 195

William I, King (c.1028–1087)
*'If you will not contend for glory, you must fight for life'* 42

Wilson, Thomas Woodrow (1856–1924)
*'It is a war against all nations'* 220

Wolfe, General James (1727–1759)
*'The impossibility of a retreat makes no difference in the situation of men resolved to conquer or die'* 73

Wycliffe, John (c.1328–1384)
*'And thus speaketh holy writ and no man can disprove it'* 48

# Z

Zola, Émile François (1840–1902)
*'I swear that Dreyfus is innocent'* 202

Quercus Publishing Plc
21 Bloomsbury Square
London
WC1A 2NS

First published in 2011

A catalogue record of this book is available
from the British Library

UK and associated territories:
978 0 85738 620 5
North America and associated territories:
978-1-84866-134-9

Printed and bound in China

10 9 8 7 6 5 4 3 2 1

Text by Terry Breverton
Edited by Philip de Ste. Croix
Designed by Paul Turner and Sue Pressley,
   Stonecastle Graphics Ltd
Index by Philip de Ste. Croix

All the pictures in this book © Topfoto,
with the exception of the following,
which are in the public domain: pages 36,
84, 107, 130, 196, 204, 278, 352, 356.

For permission to reprint extracts from speeches
the publishers gratefully acknowledge the
following:
p278 Winston S. Churchill, 'From Stettin in the
Baltic to Trieste in the Adriatic, an iron curtain
has descended across the Continent'. Reprinted by
permission of Curtis Brown Ltd on behalf of the
Estate of Winston S. Churchill.
p286 William Faulkner, 'When will I be blown up?',
© The Nobel Foundation 1950. Reprinted by
permission of Nobel Media AB.
p288 Nelson Mandela, 'No easy walk to freedom';
p312 'An ideal for which I am prepared to die';
p341 'Let there be justice for all' Reprinted by
permission of the Nelson Mandela Foundation.
p290 Albert Schweitzer, 'The Problem of Peace',
© The Nobel Foundation 1954. Reprinted by
permission of Nobel Media AB.
p308 Martin Luther King, Jr., 'I have a dream',
copyright 1963 Dr Martin Luther King Jr; copyright
renewed 1991 Coretta Scott King. Reprinted by
arrangement with The Heirs to the Estate of Martin
Luther King Jr.,c/o Writers House as agent for the
proprietor New York, NY.
p311 Malcolm X, 'The ballot or the bullet' from
Malcolm X Speaks, copyright 1965 & 1989 by
Betty Shabazz and Pathfinder Press. Reprinted by
permission of the publisher.
p316 Martin Luther King, Jr., 'I've been to the
mountaintop', copyright 1968 Dr Martin Luther
King Jr; copyright renewed 1996 Coretta Scott
King. Reprinted by arrangement with The Heirs
to the Estate of Martin Luther King Jr., c/o Writers
House as agent for the proprietor New York, NY.
p322 Mother Teresa, 'Smile at each other', © The
Nobel Foundation 1979. Reprinted by permission
of Nobel Media AB.
p324 Aleksandr Solzhenitsyn, 'What is the joy
about?', Harvard University, 8 June 1978.
p326 'Herb' Brooks, Jr, 'This is your time. Their time
is done'. Reprinted by permission of Kelly Brooks
Paradise for the Herb Brooks Foundation.
p336 Alexander Aris Myint San Aung, 'The lessons
of the past will not be forgotten, but it is our hope for
the future that we celebrate today', © The Nobel
Foundation 1991. Reprinted by permission of Nobel
Media AB.
p340 Mary Fisher, 'A Whisper of AIDS'. Reprinted
by permission of Julie Spahn for The Mary Fisher
Clinical AIDS Research and Education (CARE)
Fund at the University of Alabama at Birmingham.
p348 Anita Roddick, 'Froth with terrifying power over
people's lives'. Reprinted by permission of Dame
Anita Roddick, www.anitaroddick.com.
Every effort has been made to establish copyright
and contact copyright holders prior to going to
press. However, the publishers will be glad to
rectify in future editions any inadvertent omissions
brought to their attention.